Children
and
Exercise XII

International Series on Sport Sciences
Volume 17

Series Editor
Chauncey A. Morehouse, PhD
The Pennsylvania State University
University Park, Pennsylvania, USA

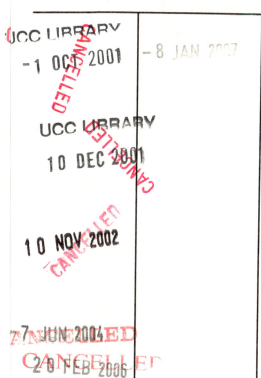

Children
and
Exercise XII

Edited by:

Joseph Rutenfranz, MD, PhD
Institute of Occupational Health
at the University Dortmund
Dortmund, Federal Republic of Germany

Rolf Mocellin, MD, PhD
University Children's Hospital
Cardiac Division
University of Freiburg
Freiburg, Federal Republic of Germany

Ferdinand Klimt, MD, PhD
Philipps University Marburg
Marburg, Federal Republic of Germany

Human Kinetics Publishers, Inc.
Champaign, Illinois

Library of Congress Cataloging-in-Publication Data

Children and exercise XII.

International series on sport sciences,
ISSN 0160-0559 ; v. 17)
Proceedings of a symposium held in Hardehausen,
FRG, Sept. 1985.
Includes bibliographies.
1. Pediatric sports medicine—Congresses.
2. Coronary heart disease in children—Prevention—
Congresses. 3. Children—Physiology—Congresses.
4. Physical fitness for children—Congresses.
I. Rutenfranz, Joseph, 1928-   . II. Mocellin,
Rolf. III. Klimt, Ferdinand. IV. Title: Children and
exercise 12. V. Series. [DNLM: 1. Child
Development—congresses. 2. Exertion—in infancy &
childhood—congresses. WE 103 C536 1985]
RC1218.C45C47   1986   618.92   86-10556
ISBN 0-87322-062-5

Proceedings of the XIIth International Congress on Pediatric Work Physiology
held in Hardehausen, Federal Republic of Germany, September 1985.

Developmental Editor: Gwen Steigelman, PhD
Production Director: Ernie Noa
Copy Editor: Jean Berry
Typesetter: Sandra Meier
Text Design: Julie Szamocki
Text Layout: Janet Little
Cover Layout: Julie Szamocki
Printed By: Braun Brumfield, Inc.

ISBN 0-87322-062-5
ISSN: 0160-0559
Copyright © 1986 by Human Kinetics Publishers, Inc.

Printed in the United States of America

10 9 8 7 6 5 4 3 2 1

Human Kinetics Publishers, Inc.
Box 5076, Champaign, IL 61820

Contents

Congress Organization

This volume represents the Proceedings of the XIIth International Congress on Pediatric Work Physiology, held in Hardehausen, West Germany, in September 1985.

Scientific and Organizing Committee
J. Rutenfranz
R. Mocellin
F. Klimt

Administrative Staff
M. Ahrens
H. Kylian
M. Widynski
D.M. DeVol
R. Flöring
F. Klimmer
K.-H. Schmidt

Sponsors

Deutsche Forschungsgemeinschaft (DFG)	Bonn
FISONS Arzneimittel	Köln
HELLIGE GmbH	Freiburg i.B.
BAYER AG	Leverkusen

The organizers wish to thank the sponsors who made the Symposium financially possible.

Our host, the staff of the Adults Agricultural College "Anton Heinen," Hardehausen (FRG), contributed very much to the excellent atmosphere of the Symposium.

Preface

Cardiovascular diseases are still one of the main medical problems of industrialized countries. In recent decades the most important risk factors or risk indicators have been identified in several epidemiological studies. It has become more and more evident that the various risk factors for cardiovascular diseases are not only a problem of elderly people but are clearly established during childhood. Because cardiovascular risk factors are partly genetically and partly behaviorally based, interventions should ideally begin during childhood and adolescence. As has been demonstrated during the previous Symposia of the *European Group for Pediatric Work Physiology*, this intervention must start during childhood to establish needed favorable lifestyle changes. In this context, it has been demonstrated that physical activity is of special importance.

Because optimal levels of health indicators are mainly combined with a sufficient level of daily physical activity, the topics of the present Symposium were centered around this concept for all subgroups of the child population, including school children, young workers, children with chronic disease, gifted children, and young athletes. Topics of the Symposium were, for example, age-related energy delivering processes, health indicators during childhood and adolescence, favorable levels of daily physical activity for health promotion, training of gifted children, young athletes and children with chronic diseases, motor learning, and maximal aerobic and anaerobic performances.

In the tradition of the group, the last session concentrated on an open question, the manipulation of gifted children and young athletes by dietary and hormonal treatments. The conclusions should be of great interest for the children themselves, for pediatricians, coaches, parents, and health or sports authorities. It was the unanimous opinion of the participants that any kind of hormonal or dietary manipulation of gifted children or young athletes must be banned by ethical codes and legal measures so that the benefits of training for children are maximized and do not result in detrimental effects during the later years of life.

Joseph Rutenfranz
Rolf Mocellin
Ferdinand Klimt

Pediatric Work Physiology XII

List of Participants

Prof. Dr. Asano, Katsumi
Department of Physiology
Institute of Health and Sport Sciences
University of Tsukuba
Tennodai 1-1-1, Sakura, Niihari
Ibaraki
Japan

Prof. Dr. Atomi, Yoriko
College of Arts and Sciences
University of Tokyo
3-8-1, Komaba, Meguro-ku
Tokyo 153
Japan

Drs. de Baar, Eric G.A.
Department of Physiology
State University of Utrecht
Vondellaan 24
NL-3521 GG Utrecht
The Netherlands

Dr. Bakken, Arne
Pediatric Department
University Hospital
Rikshospitalet
N-0027 Oslo 1
Norway

Prof. Dr. Bar-Or, Oded
McMaster University Canada
1200 Main Street West
Hamilton, Ontario
Canada

Dr. Bedu, Mario
University of Clermont Ferrand II
Campus Universitaire des Cezeaux
P.O.B. 66
F-63170 Aubière
France

Prof. Dr. Bell, Richard D.
College of Physical Education
University of Saskatchewan
Saskatoon, Saskatchewan
Canada

Dr. Bernink, Marjolijn
Department of Physiology
State University Utrecht
Vondellaan 24
NL-3521 GG Utrecht
The Netherlands

Prof. Dr. Beunen, Gaston
Institute of Physical Education
KU Leuven
Tervuurse Vest 101
B-3030 Heverlee
Belgium

Dr. Biersteker, Mariette W.A.
Department of Physiology
State University of Utrecht
Vondellaan 24
NL-3521 GG Utrecht
The Netherlands

Prof. Dr. Binkhorst, Robert A.
Department of Physiology
University of Nijmegen
Geert Grooteplein N 21A
NL-6525 EZ Nijmegen
The Netherlands

Dr. Blimkie, Cameron J.R.
Children's Exercise and Health Centre
McMaster University
Level 4, Box 2000, Station "A"
Hamilton, Ontario
Canada

Dr. Bratteby, Lars-Eric
Unit of Pediatric Physiology
University Hospital
S-751 85 Uppsala
Sweden

Dr. Brodie, David A.
University of Liverpool
P.O.B. 147
GB-Liverpool L69 3BX
U.K.

Dr. Bujnowski, Tadeusz
Institute of Pediatrics
Medical Academy Łódź
ul. Dzierżyńskiego 2/16
Pl-96 100 Skierniewice
Poland

Dr. Coudert, Jean
Laboratory of Physiology
Place Henri Dunant
F-Clermont-Ferrand
France

Prof. Dr. Davies, C.T.M.
Department of Physiology
Queens Medical Centre
GB-Nottingham NG7 2UH
U.K.

Dr. DeVol, Don M.
Institute of Occupational Health
  at the University of Dortmund
Ardeystr. 67
D-4600 Dortmund 1
West Germany

Dr. Dlin, Ronald A.
Wingate Institute
Wingate Post 42902
Netanya
Israel

Doz. Dr. Eriksson, Bengt O.
Department of Pediatrics
Division Cardiology
University of Göteborg
Ostra Sjukhuset
S-41685 Göteborg
Sweden

Dr. Falgairette, Guy
University of Clermont Ferrand II
Campus Universitaire des Cezeaux
P.O.B. 66
F-63170 Aubière
France

Prof. Dr. Feriencik, Kazimír
Department of Sport Medicine
  of the Institute of National Health
Gorkého 1
ČSSR-Bratislava
Czechoslovakia

Dr. Forsström, Jari
Uudenmaankatu 9 B 47
SF-Turku
Finland

Prof. Dr. Frenkl, Róbert
Department of Medicine
Hungarian University
  of Physical Education
Alkotás 44
H-1123 Budapest
Hungary

Prof. Dr. Gaisl, Georgine
Institut für Sportwissenschaften
Mozartgasse 14
A-8010 Graz
Austria

Prof. Dr. Gołębiowska, Maria
Institute of Pediatrics
Medical Academy Łódź
Al. Kościuszki 55 m.1
PL-90 514 Łódź
Poland

Mgr. Gołębiowski, Henryk
Institute of Pediatrics
Medical Academy Łódź
Al. Kościuszki 55 m.1
PL-90 514 Łódź
Poland

Prof. Dr. Hebbelinck, Marcel
Vrije Universiteit Brussel
Pleinlaan 2
B-1050 Brussel
Belgium

Drs. Ignatzy, Klaus
Johanniter Childrens Hospital
Arnold-Janssen-Str. 29
D-5205 St. Augustin
West Germany

Doz. Dr. Ilmarinen, Juhani
Institute of Occupational Health
Laajaniityntie 1
SF-01620 Vantaa
Finland

Drs. Jarmuszewski, Marc
Department of Physiology
State University of Utrecht
Vondellaan 24
NL-3521 GG Utrecht
The Netherlands

Prof. Dr. Kasch, Frederick W.
San Diego State University
4882 Edgeware Road
San Diego, CA 92116
USA

Prof. Dr. Kemper, Han C.G.
A.M.C. Medical Faculty
University of Amsterdam
Working Group of Exercise
  Physiology and Health
Meibergdreef 15
NL-1105 AZ Amsterdam
The Netherlands

Prof. Dr. Klausen, Klaus G.
August Krogh Institute
University of Copenhagen
Universitetsparken 13
DK-2100 Copenhagen
Denmark

Dr. Klimmer, Felix M.
Institute of Occupational Health
  at the University of Dortmund
Ardeystr. 67
D-4600 Dortmund 1
West Germany

Prof. Dr. Klimt, Ferdinand
Philipps University Marburg
Kugelgasse 10
D-3550 Marburg (Lahn)
West Germany

Prof. Dr. Koch, Günter
Institute of Physiology
Freie Universität Berlin
Arnimallee 22
D-1000 Berlin 33
West Germany

Dr. Kučera, Miroslav
Faculty of Pediatrics
Charles University Prague
V úvalu 84
ČSSR-15006 Praha 5
Czechoslovakia

Prof. Dr. Máček, Miloš
Faculty of Pediatrics
Charles University Prague
V úvalu 84
ČSSR-15006 Praha 5
Czechoslovakia

Dr. Máčková, Jiřina
Subkatedra TUL
Charles University Prague

Salmovska 5
ČSSR-120 00 Praha 2
Czechoslovakia

Dr. Matthews, Trevor
Consultant Pediatrician
Royal Lancaster Infirmary
Ashton Road
GB-Lancaster
U.K.

Dr. Matthys, Dirk
Pediatric Cardiologist
Akademisch Ziekenhuis
Kinderkliniek "C. Hooft"
De Pintelaan 185
B-9000 Gent
Belgium

Dr. Borgen Mellbye, Elisabeth
The Norwegian College
  of Physical Education and Sport
Huldreveien 31
N-0389 Oslo 3
Norway

Dr. Mészáros, János
Department of Medicine
Hungarian University
  of Physical Education
Alkotás 44
H-1123 Budapest
Hungary

Prof. Dr. Mocellin, Rolf
Cardiac Division
University Children's Hospital
University of Freiburg
Mathildenstrasse 1
D-7800 Freiburg
West Germany

Prof. Morehouse, C.A.
Co-Editor ISSS
Physical Education Sports Research
  Institute
The Pennsylvania State University
University Park, PA 16802
USA

Dr. Nygård, Clas-Håkan
Institute of Occupational Health
Laajaniityntie 1
SF-01620 Vantaa
Finland

Prof. Dr. Oseid, Svein
The Norwegian College
  of Physical Education and Sport

P.O.B. 40
Kringsjaa
N-0807 Oslo 8
Norway

Dr. Österback, Leo Leif
Research Institute for Sport and
  Physical Fitness
Rautpohjankatu 10
SF-40700 Jyväskylä
Finland

Dr. Oyen, Eva-Maria
Johanniter Childrens Hospital
Arnold-Janssen-Str. 29
D-5205 St. Augustin
West Germany

Dr. Pekkarinen, Heikki
University of Kuopio
Department of Physiology
P.O.B. 6
SF-70211 Kuopio
Finland

Dr. Peltenburg, Adelheid
Department of Physiology
State University Utrecht
Vondellaan 24
NL-3521 GG Utrecht
The Netherlands

Priv.-Doz. Dr. Piekarski, Claus
Institut für Arbeitswissenschaften
  der Ruhrkohle AG
Wengeplatz 1
D-4600 Dortmund 1
West Germany

Dr. van Praagh, Emmanuel
University of Clermont Ferrand II
Campus Universitaire des Cezeaux
P.O.B. 66
F-63170 Aubiere
France

Dr. Radvanský, Jiří
Faculty of Pediatrics
Charles University Prague
Vúvalu 84
ČSSR-15006 Praha 5
Czechoslovakia

Dr. Rasmussen, Birger
August Krogh Institute
University of Copenhagen
Universitetsparken 13
DK-2100 Copenhagen
Denmark

Dr. Reybrouck, Tony M.
University Hospital Pellenberg
Section Cardiovascular Rehabilitation
Weligerveld 1
B-3041 Pellenberg
Belgium

Prof. Dr. Ritzén, Martin
Karolinska Hospital
P.O.B. 60500
S-10401 Stockholm
Sweden

Prof. Dr. Dr. Rutenfranz, Joseph
Institute of Occupational Health
  at the University of Dortmund
Ardeystr. 67
D-4600 Dortmund 1
West Germany

Prof. Dr. Sargeant, Anthony J.
Working Group of Exercise
  Physiology and Health
University of Amsterdam
Academic Medical Centre (AMC)
Meibergdreef 15
NL-1105 AZ Amsterdam
The Netherlands

Doz. Dr. Saris, Wim H.M.
Department of Human Biology
University of Limburg
P.O.B. 616
NL-6200 MD Maastricht
The Netherlands

Dr. Schibye, Bente
Institute for Occupational Health
Department of Work Physiology
Baunegardsvej 73
DK-2900 Hellerup
Denmark

Drs. Schmidt, Klaus-Helmut
Institute of Occupational Health

at the University of Dortmund
Ardeystr. 67
D-4600 Dortmund 1
West Germany

Prof. Dr. Shephard, Roy J.
School of Physical and Health
  Education
University of Toronto
320 Huron Street
Toronto, Ontario M55 1A1
Canada

Dr. Sommer, Hans-Martin
Orthopädische Universitätsklinik
Schlierbacher Landstr. 200a
D-6900 Heidelberg 1
West Germany

Prof. Dr. Sopko, George
St. Louis University
Medical Center
Division of Cardiology
1325 S. Grand Blvd.
St. Louis, MO 63104
USA

Dr. Sowa, Karl
Institute of Occupational Health
  at the University of Dortmund
Ardeystr. 67
D-4600 Dortmund 1
West Germany

Drs. Spoelstra, Rob
Department of Physiology
State University of Utrecht
Vondellaan 24
NL-3521 GG Utrecht
The Netherlands

Dr. Stoboy, Annelore
Orthop. Klinik und Poliklinik
der Freien Universität Berlin
im Oskar-Helene-Heim
Clayallee 229
D-1000 Berlin 33
West Germany

Prof. Dr. Stoboy, Hans
Orthop. Klinik und Poliklinik
der Freien Universität Berlin

im Oskar-Helene-Heim
Clayallee 229
D-1000 Berlin 33
West Germany

Dr. Sunnegårdh, Jan
Department of Pediatrics
University Hospital
S-75014 Uppsala
Sweden

Dr. Suurnäkki, Timo
Department of Physiology
Institute of Occupational Health
Laajaniityntie 1
SF-01620 Vantaa
Finland

Dr. Szabó, Tamás
Központi Sportiskola
Istvánmezei 3
H-1146 Budapest
Hungary

Dr. Thierer, Reinhard
University of Paderborn
Fachbereich 2
Warburger Strasse 100
D-4790 Paderborn
West Germany

Dr. Vávra, Jan
Faculty of Pediatrics
Charles University Prague
V úvalu 84
ČSSR-15006 Praha 5
Czechoslovakia

Dr. Vos, Jan A.
Sportcentrum University of Nijmegen
Kwekerijweg 4
NL-6500 KL Nijmegen
The Netherlands

Prof. Dr. Vrijens, Jaques
Rijksuniversiteit Gent
Watersportlaan 2
B-9000 Gent
Belgium

Dr. Wanne, Olli
Cardiorespiratory Research Unit
The University of Turku

Kiinamyllynkatu 4-8
SF-20520 Turku 52
Finland

Dr. Wessel, Hans U.
Children's Memorial Hospital
2300 Children's Plaza
Chicago, IL 60614
USA

Dr. Weymans, Maria L.
Department of Physical Rehabilitation
University Hospital-Gasthuisberg
Herestraat
B-3000 Leuven
Belgium

Prof. Dr. Yoshizawa, Shigero
Faculty of Education
Nishi 3-4-23
Utsunomiya
Japan

Dr. Zonderland, Maria
Department of Physiology
State University of Utrecht
Vondellaan 24
NL-3521 GG Utrecht
The Netherlands

Part I
Introductory Papers

Aerobic and Anaerobic Energy Output in Children

Miloš Máček
Charles University, Prague, Czechoslovakia

The Pediatric Work Physiology Group has existed for about 18 years. One of the purposes of founding the organization was to initiate studies on work physiology in children in health and disease. Children are often compared with adults without understanding the differences in their abilities to react to different types of exercise. Moreover, the interpretation of the results of comparisons with adults is sometimes questionable.

One solution to these problems of comparison was to introduce relative workloads in the experiments with children and to express the results in relative values. Currently, however, it is not certain what types of exercise are suitable for children younger than 8 years of age. The incremental ergometry normally used is probably inadequate for the physiological and psychological status of children of this age. Many different comparisons between children and adults have been presented, but occasionally with questionable results when one or several parameters were compared. More significant were the studies that took into consideration the complexity of the cardiorespiratory system or metabolic patterns as a unit. Most practicing and nonpracticing pediatricians hold the view that the adaptation pattern of children is no better or worse than that of adults, but it is different.

Twenty years ago, only a few enthusiastic, isolated groups were interested in studies of the developmental physiology or work physiology in children. Now a number of institutes and research teams are occupied with problems of the trainability of children. The motives might involve training to win an Olympic gold medal or simply the growing knowledge that physical activity and sport are an inseparable part of a child's life in health and disease. One would hope that the latter is more often the motive.

In spite of a growing number of studies, many aspects of developmental physiology have not been investigated. Because of ethical limitations, data for children are scant, especially those of muscle metabolism. The general use of biopsies are an invasive technique that is limited in healthy children, and noninvasive methods have not yet been developed in this area.

The techniques of measurement of pulmonary ventilation, oxygen uptake, and circulation with easily obtainable results are well known and are used with children as routine methods. But the data for children up to 7 years of age are scant, even though this period comprises the first half of childhood. Indirect calorimetry and open systems seem to be of only limited value, because the cooperation of the child is reduced. This is unfortunate because many disorders that might appear later in life may begin during this period, such as obesity, some endocrine and neuromusculatory diseases, and ischemic heart disease.

MUSCLE METABOLISM

The power output at the cellular level is intensively studied in adults. Despite a lack of information for children, it is generally accepted that the principles of the adaptation pattern are similar to those of adults. One of the pioneer studies of muscle metabolism in children was that by Eriksson, Gollnick, and Saltin (1973). It was established that the rate-limiting enzyme for glycolysis phosofructokinase (PFK) has a lower activity in children, and this finding was suggested as an explanation for their lower anaerobic capacity. The breakdown of ATP and CP during exercise is probably at the same levels in children as in adults in relation to the oxygen deficit. But the values are higher if children are trained.

The studies of work efficiency in children have shown that work efficiency is virtually independent of body size, which implies that the cellular mechanism of energy utilization is already mature in early childhood (Cooper, Weiler-Ravell, Whipp, & Wasserman, 1984). Very few differences exist in pathways of oxidative phosphorylation in the systems of all living animals.

Fiber Distribution

Little information exists on fiber distribution in children and on its changes during training. Histochemical studies in different periods in the lives of animals and humans have shown (Colling-Saltin, 1980) that, at the end of the neonatal period, the level of the glycolytic potential is close to the level evaluated for the activity for PFK in muscles of adults. However, neither in children's nor in adults' muscles are the differences large enough to clearly delineate between different age groups. Similar findings in muscle metabolism were reported by Eriksson, Friberg, and Mellgren (1980) in patients with different types of congenital heart disease and in well-trained persons. Nevertheless, in addition to the genetic coding, the level of mechanical loading is a decisive factor for the differentiation and growth of young muscle, as was stated by Gutmann (1976).

Recent interesting findings by du Plessis et al. (1985) clarified this relationship. Adolescent boys have three times more transitional fibers than adults (13% versus 4%) and therefore a larger possibility exists for changes in muscle composition. Sufficient information on the influence and changes of training in children utilizing a single biochemical parameter is difficult to obtain. However, in recent years, a number of studies have been done that confirm the ability of children to sustain all kinds of exercise, including that of endurance (Berg, Keul, & Huber, 1980; Lehmann, Keul, & Korsten-Reck, 1981; Máček, Vávra, & Novosadová, 1976). But some of these comparisons are questionable if biochemical parameters between children and adults are compared and the changes of plasma volume are not taken into consideration. It has been established that plasma volume increases during exercise in children in contrast to the plasma decrease in adults (Máček et al., 1976). The changes in opposite directions amounted to about 10%. This finding was confirmed later by Senay, Rogers, and Jooste (1980) and others. For that reason, the comparisons without respect to the change of plasma volume are incorrect.

Catecholamine and Glycerol Levels

The changes in the production of catecholamines in the growing organism are not known exactly. Lehmann et al. (1981) did not find any differences in the catecholamine excretions during graded treadmill exercise at the same absolute exercise level. But when their data are recalculated for the same relative work loads, the values for the boys are lower. Lower values by about 25% were also found for maximal exercise. The close relationship between the increase of catecholamines and lactate has been shown, indicating a reduced maximal sympathetic activity.

The increase of blood glycerol reflects the intensity of lipolysis in adipose tissue. Results of Máček et al. (1976) are consistent with those obtained by Eriksson et al. (1973) in boys. No differences were found in boys as compared with adults by Carlson, Ekelund, and Orö (1963). In recent years, several new studies have been published dealing with the adaptation pattern of the cardiorespiratory system during exercise in children. However, the cardiorespiratory system cannot be considered as a unit without considering the changes in the metabolic rate. The oxygen transport system must be considered as a mediator in satisfying the needs of muscle metabolism.

Some interesting studies were done in Germany, 30 years ago, but the methods used were representative of the time, the statistical evaluations were lacking, and some morphological factors were overestimated. Nevertheless, the work of Helmreich, Bolt, and Wetzler (cited by Brock, 1954) introduced some new aspects in developmental physiology. They measured different variables of circulation in children and stated that the level of blood flow is higher in children than in adults, probably because of the relatively larger diameter of large vessels in relation to the heart size. These findings have not yet been reviewed by more sophisticated methods. Echocardiography could easily confirm or refute them. Few modern studies on peripheral circulation in children refer to these old measurements. Koch (1974) found that local flow in the working muscle is higher by 30% in children than in adults.

Lactic Acid (LA) Production

The critical question for pediatric exercise physiology is the lower increase of lactic acid (LA) in children during exercise. Attempts have been made to find the explanation and this so-called advantage or disadvantage has frequently been discussed. This question is inappropriate, however, because this statement implies a preference for the aerobic metabolism, which is not actually true.

Nevertheless, the usual finding of lower LA production in children has not been completely explained, though Cumming, Hartman, McCort, and McCullogh (1980) found higher levels than others of LA in children. If one accepts the new ideas of Brooks (1985) about the unity of the energy involved in the system, the lower LA production in children could be explained in another way. Brooks explains the increase in LA during exercise by the increase in metabolism. The constant part of the LA production as well as the nonlinear increase of LA is due to different mechanisms such as imbalance of the rate of its formation and disappearance from the blood in non-steady state conditions, probably due to reduced hepatic clearance. The other factor could be the increase of vasoconstriction mediated by the sympathetic nervous system with progressively increased load and reduced blood flow to the liver. This would diminish the ability of the liver to remove lactate from the blood and would allow greater production of lactate compared with its removal. As was found by Lehmann et al. (1981) the sympathetic activity in children is significantly lower than in adults at maximum exercise. One might hypothesize that the blood flow to the liver is consequently higher because of less vasoconstriction, and thus, the liver is able to remove the lactate from the blood at higher rates in children. Shorter half-time of oxygen increase in children (Máček & Vávra, 1980) reduces the oxygen deficit and the initial increase of LA but probably does not influence the lactate production during prolonged exercise.

ADAPTATION OF THE CARDIORESPIRATORY SYSTEM

The circulation studies suggest that the growth of each of the components of the cardiorespiratory response to exercise (e.g., muscles, heart, and lungs) is integrated so that temporal coupling among them is preserved at an optimal value, despite the overall change in body size (Cooper et al., 1984). Measurements of heart volume and internal cardiac dimensions (Blimkie, Cunningham, & Nichol, 1980) have indicated a decreasing ratio of heart size to body weight in children during growth. Therefore, the increase in stroke volume is slower in relation to the large increase in body size, for data gathered during the period of rapid growth. In these studies, the echocardiographic method was used. But when Eriksson et al. (1973) measured the stroke volume and expressed the obtained data on the basis of height cubed, the values for children and adults were similar. A pronounced increase in the stroke volume was noted after training in boys; it was higher than that in adults. This increase must be less related to the heart size and is more likely caused by the increased contractility or filling of the left ventricle.

It is generally accepted that a-vO$_2$ difference is higher in children in spite of lower Hb content. Cunningham, Paterson, Blimkie, and Donner (1984) using multiple regression reported that the increase of VO$_2$ was primarily caused by the changes in the stroke volume and later by the increase in the a-vO$_2$ difference. Still other factors could contribute to the perfection of the adaptation pattern of the cardiorespiratory system in children. For example, little is known about regional skeletal muscle blood flow in children during exercise; unknown is the content and function of myoglobin in children, and pulmonary oxygen debt, which could be used as an oxygen reserve in non-steady state situations in children.

CONCLUSION

In conclusion it might be stated that general principles of muscle metabolism and cardiorespiratory functions are identical in children and adults, subject to genetic control. When one considers the cardiorespiratory system as a mediator, it could be affected by various combinations of such variables as oxygen content in blood, stroke volume, and peripheral circulation. Eriksson's ideas (1972) are in much better agreement with various variables of metabolism and circulatory functions that occur after a training period, and they could be interpreted to indicate that a certain degree of fitness is necessary for functionally harmonious somatic development.

REFERENCES

Berg, A., Keul, J., & Huber, G. (1980). Biochemische Acutveränderungen bei Ausdauerbelastungen im Kindes- und Jugendalter. *Monatsschrift für Kinderheilkunde, 128*, 490-495.

Blimkie, C.J.R., Cunningham, D.A., & Nichol, P.M. (1980). Gas transport capacity and echocardiographically determined cardiac size in children. *Journal of Applied Physiology*, **49**, 994-999.

Brock, J. (Ed.). (1954). *Biologische Daten für den Kinderarzt* (2nd ed.) (2 vols.). Berlin: Springer-Verlag.

Brooks, G.A. (1985). Anaerobic threshold: Review of the concept and directions for future research. *Medicine and Science in Sports and Exercise*, **17**, 22-31.

Carlson, L.A., Ekelund, L.-G., & Orö, L. (1963). Studies in blood lipids during exercise. IV. *Journal of Laboratory and Clinical Medicine*, **61**, 724-729.

Colling-Saltin, A.-S. (1980). Skeletal muscle development in the human fetus and during childhood. In K. Berg & B.O. Eriksson (Eds.), *Children and exercise IX* (pp. 193-207). (International Series on Sport Sciences, Vol. 10). Baltimore: University Park Press.

Cooper, D.M., Weiler-Ravell, D., Whipp, B.J., & Wasserman, K. (1984). Aerobic parameters of exercise as a function of body size during growth in children. *Journal of Applied Physiology*, **56**, 628-634.

Cumming, G.R., Hartman, L., McCort, J., & McCullogh, S. (1980). High serum lactates do occur in young children after maximal work. *International Journal of Sports Medicine*, **1**, 66-69.

Cunningham, D.A., Paterson, D.H., Blimkie, C.J.R., & Donner, A.P. (1984). Development of cardiorespiratory function in circumpubertal boys: A longitudinal study. *Journal of Applied Physiology*, **56**, 302-307.

du Plessis, M.P., Smit, P.J., du Plessis, L.S.C., Geyer, H.J., Mathews, G., & Louw, H.N.J. (1985). The composition of muscle fibers in a group of adolescents. In R.A. Binkhorst, H.C.G. Kemper, & W.H.M. Saris (Eds.), *Children and exercise XI* (pp. 323-328). (International Series on Sport Sciences, Vol. 15). Champaign, IL: Human Kinetics.

Eriksson, B.O., Friberg, L.-G., & Mellgren, G. (1980). Muscle substrates, muscle enzyme activities, and muscle structure in infants with symptomatic ventricular septal defects. In K. Berg & B.O. Eriksson (Eds.), *Children and exercise IX* (pp. 239-250). (International Series on Sport Sciences, Vol. 10). Baltimore: University Park Press.

Eriksson, B.O., Gollnick, P.D., & Saltin, B. (1973). Muscle metabolism and enzyme activities after training in boys 11-13 years old. *Acta Physiologica Scandinavica*, **87**, 485-497.

Gutmann, E. (1976). Neurotrophic relations. *Annual Review of Physiology*, **38**, 177-216.

Koch, G. (1974). Muscle blood flow after ischemic work and during bicycle ergometer work in boys aged 12 years. *Acta Paediatrica Belgica*, **28** (Suppl.), 29-39.

Lehmann, M., Keul, J., & Korsten-Reck, U. (1981). Einfluß einer stufenweisen Laufbandergometrie bei Kindern und Erwachsenen auf die Plasmacatecholamine, die aerobe und anaerobe Kapazität. *European Journal of Applied Physiology*, **47**, 301-311.

Máček, M., & Vávra, J. (1980). The adjustment of oxygen uptake at the onset of exercise: A comparison between boys and young adults. *International Journal of Sports Medicine*, **1**, 70-72.

Máček, M., Vávra, J., & Novosadová, J. (1976). Prolonged exercise in prepubertal boys. I. Cardiovascular and metabolic adjustment. II. Changes in plasma volume and in some blood constituents. *European Journal of Applied Physiology*, **35**, 291-298; 299-303.

Senay, L.C. Jr., Rogers, G., & Jooste, P. (1980). Changes in blood plasma during progressive treadmill and cycle exercise. *Journal of Applied Physiology*, **49**, 59-65.

Nutritional Concerns for the Young Athlete

Wim H.M. Saris
Fred Brouns
University of Limburg, Maastricht, The Netherlands

Dietary manipulations are an important concern of many athletes, and it is not unrealistic to suppose that this is also true for the young growing athlete. Currently, youngsters are undertaking rigorous training programs at earlier stages in their lives than a few decades ago, and coaches look for any competitive edge to improve their performances. With respect to nutrition even the most informed have difficulty distinguishing myths from truths. On the other hand, adequate nutrition is of utmost importance for the growing body under severe physiological strain. Therefore, this article deals primarily with the nutritional concerns for the young athlete. Reviewing the literature one can conclude that little systematic evaluation is available.

NUTRITION AND GROWTH

One of the basic questions is, How detrimental are the intense training programs to the growth and development of children, without or in combination with adequate nutrition? It has been difficult to separate the effects of training from normal development in children. Differences in maturity and skill acquisition obscure the effects of training. With respect to growth, no information is available as yet about conditions of adequate nutrition in combination with intensive exercise. In a group of Olympic girl swimmers in Sweden no negative effects on growth were found (Eriksson et al., 1981); however, information about nutritional habits was not available. Malina (1984) concluded that the role of properly graded activity programs in influencing growth and maturation is not completely understood in well-nourished children.

In the literature, no longitudinal data are available about the effects of intense training programs in combination with a marginal or poor nutrition, which may be present in certain groups of young athletes. Studies in developing countries, under extremely adverse nutritional conditions, indicated that bone growth is inhibited and maturation is delayed (Himes,

1978). Bodily response apparently varies with the intensity and timing of the nutritional stress. Physical exercise may exaggerate the stress (Malina, 1984). Kato and Ishiko (1966) suggested that premature closure of the epiphyses of the lower extremities was caused by the combination of suboptimal nutrition and excessive loads carried on the shoulders. The stature of the children was reduced.

In the situation of malnutrition, the growing body adapts to these marginal living conditions. Food intake measurements in developing countries generally reveal that communities are existing on far lower levels of dietary energy than are recommended. Several possible explanations exist for the disparity between the recommendations based on well-nourished subjects and these observations. Besides methodological uncertainties, long-term adaptations can occur that increase the efficiency of energy utilization (James & Shetty, 1982). Excessive exercise may interact to interfere with skeletal growth under these suboptimal nutritional circumstances. The magnitude of this problem in the population of young gifted children is not known. There are indications that in some sport disciplines the risk of marginal nutritional support is higher. In general, this is related to body mass. In Table 1 the characteristics of these high-risk sport disciplines are summarized. Low weight can be achieved by chronic or acute dietary manipulations as can be observed, for instance, in gymnastics and weight-class sports, respectively.

Table 1   High Risk Sports Encouraging Marginal Nutrition

Criteria: Body composition	Sport discipline
Low weight, low stature	Gymnastics
Low weight, certain body image	Ballet dancing, figure skating, rhythmic gymnastics
Low weight	Weight-class sports (e.g., judo, wrestling, rowing)
Certain body image	Body building

CHRONIC DIETARY MANIPULATIONS FOR LOW WEIGHT

In gymnastics and ballet dancing chronic energy restrictions have received wide recognition and public attention. These include disturbances of maturation and growth, reproductive disorders, hematological function, and bone density and calcium loss. Recently, Lindboe and Slettebø (1984) reported on the death of an elite female gymnast caused by anorexia nervosa. The results of nutritional studies indicate that inadequate nutrition appears prevalent. Van Erp-Baart et al. (1985) concluded that, in a

for death tees

group of elite Dutch adolescent gymnasts, some girls had an energy imbalance for a long period of time.

From a study with ballet dancers Cohen, Potosnak, Frank, and Baker (1985) concluded that the normal diet did not fulfill the requirements for protein, carbohydrate, and some of the micronutrients. However, a normal vitamin status was found, probably because of a high intake of vitamin supplements. The available literature dealing with the nutritional habits of gymnasts and ballet dancers reveals continuous psychological pressure on the athlete to maintain a low body weight in order to obtain the ideal body image (Calabrese et al., 1983; Peterson, 1982; Cohen et al., 1985; Frisch, Wyshak, & Vincent, 1980). The long-term effects on growth and development of this type of chronic malnutrition are not known. It is far too easy to conclude that a tendency toward a lower stature in elite female gymnasts exists as a result of the apparent deficiency in nutrients and energy.

More information is available about related health problems such as athletic amenorrhea. Recently, Loucks and Horvath (1985) critically reviewed the proposed mechanisms for athletic amenorrhea. At present, the association with a restrictive diet is only speculative because data are limited. One cannot attribute differences in menstrual status to diet alone because, in most studies, groups also differed in both body composition and training. Interesting in this respect is the study of Stein, Schulter, and Diamond (1983). The protein synthesis rate (PSR) was measured in four groups of women: normally active women with normal food intake, normally active women with a slimming diet, competitive swimmers with an adequate diet, and ballet dancers with a reduced diet. The PSR rate was low in the low-intake groups, whereas menstrual irregularity occurred in the athletic groups.

The authors concluded that exercise stress and not energy deficiency was responsible for the menstrual abnormalities. Loucks and Horvath (1985) speculated that a hypothalamic dysfunction may be caused by an altered neurotransmitter synthesis due to an inadequate diet. They stressed the importance of longitudinal and cross-sectional studies in order to elucidate the problems of reversibility and other possible side effects such as osteoporosis.

SHORT-TERM WEIGHT CONTROL

The practice of starvation in order to achieve a rapid weight loss in the days before competition in weight-class sports (e.g., light-weight rowers, wrestlers, judo) is well known. Several methods are used, such as increased exercise instead of tapering off the training intensity, food restriction mostly combined with deprivation or total absence of fluid intake, or a combination of exercise and food restriction. Also, more drastic methods are frequently reported, including excessive sweat loss by using sweat suits, training in hot environments, or the use of diuretics. Potential risks exist for young athletes involved in these practices. In highly trained children, starvation leads to an excessive loss of lean body mass. Therefore, the net result is diminished body reserve for athletic events, which more than offsets any advantages of competing in a lower weight classification (Tipton & Tcheng, 1970; Houston, Marrin, Green, & Thomson, 1981).

Even more risky is the practice of dehydration. Children's thermoregulatory efficiency is lower than adults' (Bar-Or, 1980). Therefore, the young athlete is at a potentially greater risk of contracting heat-related illnesses. Less is known about the long-term effects, especially when these short-term weight reductions are repeated several times. Tipton mentioned weight-reduction frequencies of 25 to 30 times during one season in adolescent wrestlers (Round Table, 1981). He suggested further studies to evaluate the kidney function of former successful wrestlers 10 to 15 years after competition.

Weight reduction may lead to increased performance if the percentage of body fat is too high related to the optimal level for a specific sport. In this situation, weight reduction should occur during the preseason. Furthermore, new regulations should be enforced to prevent these nutritional malpractices in young athletes.

NUTRITIONAL CONCERNS OF THE ENDURANCE ATHLETE

With the increasing popularity of endurance exercise, especially long distance running, the list of possible negative side effects that may occur in young athletes is growing. Uncertainty about long-term implications has even led some people to question the value of running as an overall positive health measure (Rutenfranz, 1985). In addition to musculoskeletal overuse injuries, some potential risks exist based on nutritional and physiological considerations.

As mentioned earlier, the young athlete is more prone than adults to heat stress. Intense prolonged exercise may be detrimental to health and can lead to fatal heat stroke (American Academy of Pediatrics, 1983). Besides the slower acclimatization to exercise in the heat, children are less able to recognize thirst and therefore do not voluntarily replenish fluids lost during exercise (Bar-Or, Dotan, Inbar, Rothstein, & Zonder, 1980). Control of fluid intake is therefore of utmost importance for the child during long-term exercise, especially in a hot environment.

In addition to thermoregulatory problems, the risk exists of gastrointestinal complaints. Although it seems that these problems are quite common, only a few publications have focused attention on this topic. These publications are restricted to the adult athlete population. Sullivan (1981) and recently Keeffe, Lowe, and Goss (1984) reported that long distance runners frequently suffer from abdominal cramps (25%) or diarrhea (20%) during or after competition. Fogoros (1980) speculated that particularly the combination of diarrhea, dehydration, and intensive exercise may lead to severe problems during and after running. Although the pathophysiology of gastrointestinal disturbance during long distance running has not been studied, all evidence suggests that these health risks are even greater in the young athlete involved in endurance exercise.

Extensive literature emphasizes the importance of maintaining water, electrolyte, and energy (carbohydrate) balance in order to maintain optimal performance capacity and to reduce the risk of complete exhaustion (Blom, Vollestad, & Hermansen, 1984; Costill & Miller, 1980). In general, in endurance-type sports the energy need is increased while the time for meals is diminished because of the duration of the training sessions. Therefore, the athlete tends to nibble throughout the day. These in-between meals can be characterized by a high-carbohydrate content and a low-nutrient density (Saris, 1980). Especially in young children with a relatively low energy intake compared to adult athletes, as a result of this practice nutrient density can drop below the RDA. Therefore, extra attention has to be paid to the nutrient quality of in-between meals taken by young athletes in order to prevent possible nutrient deficiency.

Endurance training is also associated with a decrease in percentage of body fat. Weight loss during extensive training suggests that appetite regulation does not keep pace with the energy requirements. Recently Yates, Leehey, and Shisslak (1983) suggested a strong resemblance in physique and psychological behavior between anorexic patients and long distance runners. Although no data are available yet, weight loss can be considered as a possible risk in young athletes involved in endurance sports.

NUTRITIONAL MALPRACTICE

Durnin (1967) has noted that there is still no sphere of nutrition in which faddism and ignorance are more obvious than in athletics. Athletes attribute special characteristics to food items and supplements that seem to improve their performances, although an overwhelming amount of evidence indicates that, in well-nourished athletes, these special food items or supplements do not have any effect on performance. Based on theoretical considerations or supported by appropriate research, some useful applications of dietary principles to athletics and physical performance may in some areas have some beneficial effects (Williams, 1976).

An enormous number of athletes use nutrient supplements without any knowledge of why, how, and when to use them. This is also true for the young athlete. Parr, Porter, and Hodgson (1984) investigated the nutritional practices of 2,977 athletes in the United States, including high-school adolescents. The use of vitamin, mineral, and protein supplements was 44%, 13%, and 9%, respectively. High-school athletes did not differ from the adult population.

In addition to concluding that the scientific community has failed to provide the principles of good nutrition to those working closely with athletes, one can argue about the possible health risks of food fads and supplements. The harmful toxic effects of fat-soluble vitamins A, D, and K are well known. Less known are the possible harmful effects of excessive doses of water-soluble vitamins (Williams, 1976). For instance, large quantities of niacin can produce diabetes. Megadoses of vitamin C may cause gastric complaints and lower the blood concentration of vitamin B_{12}. The amount of protein that can be tolerated by the healthy organism has not been established. It has been hypothesized that protein overloading may, via pathways that are not entirely clear, result in proteinurea, focal glomerulosclerosis, and progressive decline in functioning nephrons (Soeters, 1985). This may lead to impaired kidney function.

REFERENCES

American Academy of Pediatrics (1983). Climatic heat stress and the exercising child. *The Physician and Sportsmedicine*, 11(8), 155-159.

Bar-Or, O. (1980). Climate and the exercising child—A review. *International Journal of Sports Medicine*, 1, 53-65.

Bar-Or, O., Dotan, R., Inbar, O., Rothstein, A., & Zonder, H. (1980). Voluntary hypohydration in 10- to 12-year-old boys. *Journal of Applied Physiology*, 48, 104-108.

Blom, P.C.S., Vollestad, N.K., & Hermansen, L. (1984). Diet and recovery process. *Medicine & Sport Science*, 17, 148-160.

Calabrese, L.H., Kirkendall, D.T., Floyd, M., Rapoport, S., Williams, G.W., Weiker, G.G., & Bergfeld, J.A. (1983). Menstrual abnormalities, nutritional patterns, and body composition in female classical ballet dancers. *The Physician and Sportsmedicine*, 11(2), 86-98.

Cohen, J.L., Potosnak, L., Frank, O., & Baker, H. (1985). A nutritional and hematologic assessment of elite ballet dancers. *The Physician and Sportsmedicine*, 13(5), 43-54.

Costill, D.L., & Miller, J.M. (1980). Nutrition for endurance sport: Carbohydrate and fluid balance. *International Journal of Sports Medicine*, 1, 2-14.

Durnin, J.V.G.A. (1967). The influence of nutrition. *Canadian Medical Association Journal*, 96, 715-720.

Eriksson, B.O., Enström, I., Karlberg, P., Lundin, A., Saltin, B., & Thoren, C. (1981, June). *Longitudinal study of the effect of swim-training on the cardiovascular system and on exercise capacity.* Paper presented at the Pediatric Work Physiology Meeting, Joutsa, Finland.

Fogoros, R.N. (1980). "Runner's trots." *Journal of the American Medical Association*, 243, 1743-1744.

Frisch, R.E., Wyshak, G., & Vincent, L. (1980). Delayed menarche and amenorrhea in ballet dancers. *New England Journal of Medicine*, 303, 17-19.

Himes, J.H. (1978). Bone growth and development in protein-calorie malnutrition. *World Review of Nutrition and Dietetics, 28,* 143-156.

Houston, M.E., Marrin, D.A., Green, H.J., & Thomson, J.A. (1981). The effect of rapid weight loss on physiological functions in wrestlers. *The Physician and Sportsmedicine, 9*(11), 73-78.

James, W.P.T., & Shetty, P.S. (1982). Metabolic adaptations and energy requirements in developing countries. *Human Nutrition: Clinical Nutrition, 36c,* 331-336.

Kato, S., & Ishiko, T. (1966). Obstructed growth of children's bones due to excessive labor in remote corners. In K. Kato (Ed.), *Proceedings of International Congress on Sport Sciences* (pp. 479-487). Tokyo: Japanese Union of Sport Sciences.

Keeffe, E.B., Lowe, D.K., & Goss, J.R. (1984). Gastrointestinal symptoms of marathon runners. *Western Journal of Medicine, 141,* 481-484.

Lindboe, C.F., & Slettebo, M. (1984). Are young female gymnasts malnourished? *European Journal of Applied Physiology, 52,* 457-462.

Loucks, A.B., & Horvath, S.M. (1985). Athletic amenorrhea: A review. *Medicine and Science in Sports and Exercise, 17,* 56-72.

Malina, R.M. (1984). Physical activity and motor development/performance in populations nutritionally at risk. In E. Pollitt (Ed.), *Energy-protein intake and activity* (pp. 59-83). New York: Alan R. Liss.

Parr, R.B., Porter, M.A., & Hodgson, S.C. (1984). Nutrition knowledge and practice of coaches, trainers, and athletes. *The Physician and Sportsmedicine, 12*(3), 127-138.

Peterson, M.S. (1982). Nutritional concerns for the dancer. *The Physician and Sportsmedicine, 10*(3), 137-143.

Round Table (1981). Weight reduction in wrestling. *The Physician and Sportsmedicine, 9*(9), 79-96.

Rutenfranz, J. (1985). Long-term effects of excessive training procedures on young athletes. In R.A. Binkhorst, H.C.G. Kemper, & W.H.M. Saris (Eds.), *Children and exercise XI* (pp. 354-357) (International Series on Sport Sciences, Vol. 15). Champaign, IL: Human Kinetics.

Saris, W.H.M. (1980). Topsport and sweetcakes (in Dutch). *Netherlands Journal of Nutrition, 41,* 399-402.

Soeters, P. (1985). Protein overloading. *Netherlands Journal of Nutrition, 46,* 354-358.

Stein, T.P., Schulter, M.D., & Diamond, C.E. (1983). Nutrition protein turnover and physical activity in young women. *American Journal of Clinical Nutrition, 38,* 223-228.

Sullivan, S.N. (1981). The gastrointestinal symptoms of running. *New England Journal of Medicine, 304,* 915.

Tipton, C.M., & Tcheng, T.K. (1970). Iowa wrestling study: Weight loss in high school students. *Journal of the American Medical Association, 214,* 1269-1274.

Van Erp-Baart, M.-A., Fredrix, L.W.H.M., Binkhorst, R.A., Lavaleye, T.C.L., Vergouwen, P.C.J., & Saris, W.H.M. (1985). Energy intake and energy expenditure in top female gymnasts. In R.A. Binkhorst, H.C.G. Kemper, & W.H.M. Saris (Eds.), *Children and exercise XI* (pp. 218-223) (International Series on Sport Sciences, Vol. 15). Champaign, IL: Human Kinetics.

Williams, M.H. (1976). *Nutrition aspects of human physical and athletic performance.* Springfield, IL: Thomas, 1976.

Yates, A., Leehey, K., & Shisslak, C.M. (1983). Running—An analogue of anorexia. *New England Journal of Medicine, 308,* 251-255.

Health Indicators and Risk Factors of Cardiovascular Diseases During Childhood and Adolescence

Richard D. Bell
University of Saskatchewan, Saskatoon, Canada
Miloš Máček
Charles University, Prague, Czechoslovakia
Joseph Rutenfranz
Institute of Occupational Health at the University of Dortmund, Dortmund, Federal Republic of Germany
Wim H.M. Saris
University of Limburg, Maastricht, The Netherlands

One of the inherent benefits of being associated with a group like the European Group of Pediatric Work Physiology is the opportunity for discussion on an informal level of ideas, methods, and results of questions of common interest and concern. Most investigators in the field of pediatric work physiology likely believe that many adult health-related concerns such as coronary heart disease and obesity begin early in childhood, and the early years thus offer the best possibility for positive intervention for many recognized risk factors. Unfortunately, however, there is not always agreement on what these specific health-related risk factors are and even less agreement on the critical dimensions of individual parameters.

The purpose of the following discussion is to suggest a checklist (see Table 1) of important health-related parameters and possible dimensions, where applicable, of these parameters in order to stimulate discussion so that a general consensus may ultimately be reached. The development of a health-related profile would greatly assist the many comparisons continually being made among younger age groups of various countries and would facilitate the identification of individuals who, at an early age, are already developing risk factors that might lead to complications in adult life. This discussion focuses attention on both inherent (genetic) and environmental (behavior-lifestyle) parameters that have been the subject of much previous research and discussion (Bar-Or, 1983; Montoye, 1975, 1985).

Table 1   Health and Risk Indicators for Cardiovascular Disease in Children

Variable	Health indicators	Risk factors
Genetically determined factors		
Blood pressure	Systolic 100 to 120 mmHg	Systolic > 140 mmHg
	Diastolic 75 to 85 mmHg	Diastolic > 90 mmHg
Glucose tolerance	Glycosuria −	Glycosuria +
Genetically and behaviorally determined factors		
Body composition	♂ < 15% fat	> 20% fat
	♀ < 20% fat	> 30% fat
Blood lipids	TC ≤ 4.9 mmol/l	> 5.9 mmol/l
	HDL ≥ 1.3 mmol/l	< 0.8 mmol/l
	HDL/TC ≥ 0.3	< 0.18
	LDL ≤ 1.8 [2.8] mmol/l	> 2.2 [3.8] mmol/l
	TG ≤ 0.9 mmol/l	> 1.7 mmol/l
Apolipoproteins	Apo-A ≥ 2.1 mmol/l	< 1.4 mmol/l
	Apo-B ≤ 0.8 mmol/l	> 1.3 mmol/l
	Apo-A/Apo-B ≥ 3.0	< 1.5
Aerobic power	TBM ♂ > 40 ml $min^{-1}kg^{-1}$	< 35 ml $min^{-1}kg^{-1}$
	TBM ♀ > 35 ml $min^{-1}kg^{-1}$	< 30 ml $min^{-1}kg^{-1}$
	LBM ♂ > 55 ml $min^{-1}kg^{-1}$	< 50 ml $min^{-1}kg^{-1}$
	LBM ♀ > 50 ml $min^{-1}kg^{-1}$	< 45 ml $min^{-1}kg^{-1}$
Determined by lifestyle		
Smoking habits	No smoking	Regular smoking before 12 years of age; > 10 cigarettes/day during adolescence
Physical activity	Sport scores > 300	Sport scores < 200

BLOOD PRESSURE

Among other factors, elevated blood pressure levels are generally recognized as an abnormal stress reaction or as a sign of hyperkinetic circulation, both of which are major risk indicators associated with the development of coronary heart disease. Children are also susceptible to elevated levels of stress whether the source is at home, school, or the playing field. Because childhood blood pressure levels seem to be a good index of adult blood pressure behavior, detecting possible abnormalities at an early age is important. Assuming that the proper techniques and equipment have been utilized, blood pressure measurements should be an integral part of any pediatric health assessment program. Unfortunately, however, the definition of elevated blood pressure levels remains somewhat vague, with many separate threshold levels being proposed over the years. One commonly accepted definition, suggested by the World Health Organization, defines high blood pressure as a level that is equal to or exceeds the mean value for the age group plus two standard deviations.

Even though normal levels of blood pressure vary greatly in children, elevated blood pressure varies much less and tracks much more consistently. A value of 140/90 mmHg in children over 12 years of age represents the 95th percentile, and the risk of developing CHD increases proportionally as blood pressure levels increase above this (Kirschsieper & Rutenfranz, 1966; Rose & Blackburn, 1968; WHO, 1977). It is proposed then that "normal" systolic blood pressure levels range from 100 to 120 mmHg and diastolic blood pressure levels from 75 to 85 mmHg. Excessive systolic blood pressure levels would be above 140 mmHg with diastolic values greater than 90 mmHg (Berenson, Voors, Webber, & Frerichs, 1978).

GLUCOSE TOLERANCE

As a screening device for the possible presence of childhood diabetes, the presence or absence of glycosuria should be ascertained under the proper dietary conditions. A functional method for diabetic screening is still lacking and for this reason tests like a glucose tolerance test might be employed in suspect cases (Montoye, Block, Keller, & Willis, 1977).

BODY COMPOSITION

Obesity in childhood is of increasing concern to many investigators because it is a recognized risk factor in the development of coronary heart disease as well as other health-related conditions like hypertension. Prior to puberty a relative constancy in body fat values exists, with values ranging between 15% and 20% for both boys and girls. After puberty, however, percentage of body fat decreases to 10% to 12% for boys but increases to 20% to 25% for girls. Suggested values for normal percentage of body fat are less than 15% for boys and less than 25% for girls. Excessive values for boys might be those greater than 20% and for girls greater than 30% body fat (Haschke, 1983; Pařízková, 1977).

BLOOD LIPIDS

Optimal levels for specific blood lipids and lipoproteins are considered important and are still the subject of numerous current investigations because cardiovascular diseases remain a serious health problem in most industrialized societies. A major existing problem is the lack of general agreement on which blood lipids and/or lipoproteins are the most important in terms of identifying potential health-risk situations. Early investigations emphasized the total serum cholesterol (TC) and serum triglyceride (TG) concentrations, whereas more current studies seem to focus attention on such parameters as total serum cholesterol, low density serum lipoprotein (LDL), and high density serum lipoprotein (HDL). The use of specific apolipoprotein profiles as health-risk indicators is also suggested by recent investigations although minimal data are available on children (American Health Foundation, 1979).

The variance of these factors appears to be proportionally the same in different populations even though the mean values are different. Theoretically desirable as it might be to have everyone centered around some low "ideal" value, in practice it seems that the only way to lower the average to an acceptable level is to shift the whole distribution to a lower level. Individual differences ultimately determine who, within a population, will develop a specific disease and who will remain healthy. The need is to shift the average of the underlying factors toward the more favorable or normal values. This problem is particularly important in children not only because atherosclerosis begins early in life but also because behavioral patterns including eating and smoking habits, physical activity, and sports participation are commonly established at this time (WHO, 1982).

Total Cholesterol

The total cholesterol concentration is lower in developing countries, intermediate in the Mediterranean area, and higher in the more developed countries of Northern Europe and North America. The values of TC are also age and sex dependent and increase with age, especially in boys. Generally accepted is that values higher than 5.9 mmol/l are at risk, whereas values between 5.2 and 5.9 mmol/l should be considered suspect and further investigation would be advisable (American Health Foundation, 1979). A value smaller than 4.9 mmol/l is proposed as a health-indicator level.

HDL-Cholesterol

The protective effect of a high HDL-concentration is recognized and is strongly but inversely correlated to individual risk of developing coronary heart disease in adults. As a result, its concentration in children should also be closely followed as it helps to elucidate the interaction between genetic and environmental factors. A value lower than 0.8 mmol/l could be considered at risk, whereas values lower than 1.1 mmol/l should be considered as suspect (American Health Foundation, 1979). A value greater than 1.3 mmol/l is proposed as a health-indicator level.

HDL-C/Total Cholesterol Ratio

The ratio HDL/TC has been suggested as an important determinant for the risk of developing coronary heart disease. This ratio should not be lower than 0.18, and values lower than 0.25 should be considered as suspect (Linder & DuRant, 1982; Montoye, 1985). A ratio greater than 0.3 is proposed as a health indicator.

LDL

High levels of LDL are generally thought to be associated with an increased risk of developing coronary heart disease. In direct measurements, values higher than 2.2 mmol/l could be considered at risk, whereas calculated values higher than 3.8 mmol/l have a similar connotation (Masopust et al., 1985). A value smaller than 1.8 [2.8] mmol/l is proposed as a health-indicator level.

Triglycerides

Generally speaking, no significant changes with age in TG have been observed in girls but in boys a slight increase during puberty has been noticed. At risk values for TG might be 1.7 mmol/l or higher, whereas values greater than 1.4 mmol/l should be considered as suspect (Montoye, 1985). A value smaller than 0.9 mmol/l is proposed as a health-indicator level.

APOLIPOPROTEINS

In contrast to data on cholesterol and triglyceride concentrations, sufficient information is lacking on the apolipoprotein profile (with specific emphasis on Apo-A, Apo-B, and the Apo-A/Apo-B ratio) in children and its changes during puberty. The ratio Apo-A/Apo-B appears to be negatively but significantly correlated with both TC and LDL/TC and has been mentioned recently as a potential risk factor. Values for Apo-A lower than 1.4 mmol/l could be considered as a risk indicator. Apo-B, on the other hand, is inversely correlated with both Apo-A and HDL/TC, and an elevated level is considered as a risk indicator. Values higher than 1.3 mmol/l could be considered at risk. A decreased ratio of Apo-A/Apo-B below 1.5 expresses a higher risk, especially in boys. Values for Apo-A greater than 2.1 mmol/l and lower than 0.8 mmol/l for Apo-B might be regarded as health indicators. These reference values for the apolipoproteins, however, are based on a single recent study (Máček et al., 1985) and further research is necessary (Zonderland, 1985).

AEROBIC POWER

Maximal oxygen uptake ($\dot{V}O_2$max) indicates the ability of the cardio-respiratory system to deliver oxygen to the working muscles. $\dot{V}O_2$max increases progressively during the prepubertal years with slightly lower values for girls. Following puberty, however, $\dot{V}O_2$max tends to level off or even decrease in girls, whereas boys demonstrate a further increase followed by a leveling off after the age of 18 years. The level of aerobic power in children is affected by different factors. In younger children the genetic factors are probably more important, whereas behavioral factors such as the intensity of physical training become important later on. In most children over 12 years of age, high levels of aerobic power are directly related to the amount of physical activity even though specific causative mechanisms are difficult to identify. For this reason it is difficult to specify actual trends of aerobic power that would be considered as risk values. High levels of aerobic power as a result of high levels of physical activity are associated with more favorable levels of body weight, reduced adiposity, and increased HDL-C concentrations. Sedentary lifestyles are usually associated with lower aerobic power values, although a causal relationship cannot be established in all cases because some of the individuals classified as sedentary may be inactive due to other health problems.

It may be possible, however, to express a lower limit of aerobic power that, in the absence of other health-related problems, may represent a risk. Generally this level is 35 ml kg^{-1} min^{-1} for boys and 30 ml kg^{-1} min^{-1} for girls. Levels that might be used as health indicators are greater than 40 ml kg^{-1} min^{-1} for boys and greater than 35 ml kg^{-1} min^{-1} for girls. Because the relationship between aerobic power and lean body mass is relatively constant during childhood and adolescence, this parameter is likely to be more useful in defining specific health-related categories. For this reason, values based on lean body mass lower than 50 ml kg^{-1} min^{-1} for boys and 45 ml kg^{-1} min^{-1} for girls have been proposed as risk factor indicators, and values higher than 55 ml kg^{-1} min^{-1} for boys and 50 ml kg^{-1} min^{-1} for girls might be used as health indicators (Kemper et al., 1983; Thorén, Seliger, Máček, Vávra, & Rutenfranz, 1973).

SMOKING HABITS

Although the role of smoking in the pathogenesis of atherosclerosis has not been clearly established, all health authorities agree that high levels of smoking constitute a significant health-risk factor, especially in the development of coronary heart disease. Smoking habits vary widely from one country to another for a variety of socioeconomic reasons but recent trends seem to show a continuously increasing prevalence and intensity of smoking among adolescents, especially young females, in spite of the educational efforts of schools and health-related authorities. Recent evidence shows that the percentage of smokers in German, Norwegian, and Czechoslovakian children aged 12 to 16 years ranged from 0% to 56%. An ideal consumption value might well be 0 cigarettes per day, but more than 10 per day seems to be a definite health risk (Máček et al., 1985; WHO, 1977), especially if regular smoking starts before the age of 12 years.

PHYSICAL ACTIVITY

The establishment of a physically active lifestyle may be important for children in order to develop adequate adult cardiorespiratory capacities as well as proper attitudes toward the potential benefits of regular physical activity. However, a major difficulty in assessing physical activity patterns in various countries is the lack of existing standardized and accepted methods of evaluation. In recent years various studies have proposed that physical activity levels could be measured by means of questionnaires. From these studies, risk factors and health indicators can then be postulated (Lange Andersen, Masironi, Rutenfranz, & Seliger, 1978; Saris, 1985). For example, sport scores over 300 (over 500 is highly trained) would be considered healthy, whereas scores below 200 would indicate an unsatisfactory level of regular physical activity and, likely, a limited cardiorespiratory capacity (Lange Andersen et al., 1984).

CONCLUDING REMARKS

It is hoped that this discussion has emphasized the importance of identifying not only the various risk factor levels cited but, perhaps even more importantly, levels that can be used as health indicators for children.

REFERENCES

American Health Foundation (1979). Conference on the health effects of blood lipids: Optimal distributions for populations. Workshop report: Epidemiological Section. *Preventive Medicine, 8,* 612-678.

Bar-Or, O. (1983). *Pediatric sports medicine for the practitioner.* New York: Springer.

Berenson, G.S., Voors, A.W., Webber, L.S., & Frerichs, R.R. (1978). Blood pressure in children and its interpretation. *Pediatrics, 61,* 333-335.

Haschke, F. (1983). Body composition of adolescent males. I. Total body water in normal adolescent males. II. Body composition of the male reference adolescent. *Acta Paediatrica Scandinavica, 307* (Suppl.).

Kemper, H.C.G., Dekker, H.J.P., Ootjers, M.G., Post, B., Snel, J., Splinter, P.G., Storm-van Essen, L., & Verschuur, R. (1983). Growth and health of teenagers in the Netherlands: Survey of multidisciplinary longitudinal studies and comparison to recent results of a Dutch study. *International Journal of Sports Medicine, 4*, 202-214.

Kirschsieper, H.M., & Rutenfranz, J. (1966). Bestimmung des arteriellen Blutdruckes. In H. Opitz & F. Schmid (Eds.), *Handbuch der Kinderheilkunde*. Bd. II/1. Pädiatrische Diagnostik (pp. 213-225). Berlin, New York: Springer.

Lange Andersen, K., Ilmarinen, J., Rutenfranz, J., Ottmann, W., Berndt, I., Kylian, H., & Ruppel, M. (1984). Leisure time sport activities and maximal aerobic power during late adolescence. *European Journal of Applied Physiology, 52*, 431-436.

Lange Andersen, K., Masironi, R., Rutenfranz, J., & Seliger, V. (1978). *Habitual physical activity and health*. (WHO Regional Publications, European Series, No. 6). Copenhagen: World Health Organization.

Linder, C.W., & DuRant, R.H. (1982). Exercise, serum lipids, and cardiovascular disease—Risk factors in children. *Pediatric Clinics of North America, 29*, 1341-1354.

Máček, M., Rutenfranz, J., Lange Andersen, K., Masopust, J., Vávra, J., Klimmer, F., Kylian, H., Danek, K., Máčková, J., Flöring, R., & Ottmann, W. (1985). Favourable levels of cardiovascular health and risk indicators during childhood and adolescence. *European Journal of Pediatrics, 144*, 360-367.

Masopust, J., Máček, M., Rutenfranz, J., Vávra, J., Radvanský, J., & Máčková, J. (1985). Stanovení referenčního rozmezí lipidových parametrú dětské školní populaci. *Biochemia Clinica Bohemoslovaca, 14*, 15-26.

Montoye, H.J. (1975). *Physical activity and health: An epidemiological study of an entire community*. Engelwood Cliffs, NJ: Prentice-Hall.

Montoye, H.J. (1985). Risk indicators for cardiovascular disease in relation to physical activity in youth. In R.A. Binkhorst, H.C.G. Kemper, & W.H.M. Saris (Eds.), *Children and exercise XI* (pp. 3-25). Champaign, IL: Human Kinetics.

Montoye, H.J., Block, W., Keller, J.B., & Willis, P.W. (1977). Glucose tolerance and physical fitness: An epidemiologic study in an entire community. *European Journal of Applied Physiology, 37*, 237-242.

National Heart, Lung, and Blood Institute. (1977). Report of the task force on blood pressure control in children. *Pediatrics, 59* (Suppl. 5), 797-820.

Pařizková, J. (1977). *Body fat and physical fitness*. The Hague: Nijhoff.

Rose, G.A., & Blackburn, H. (1968). *Cardiovascular survey methods*. (WHO, Monograph Series, No. 56). Geneva: World Health Organization.

Saris, W.H.M. (1985). The assessment and evaluation of daily physical activity in children. A review. *Acta Paediatrica Scandinavica, 318* (Suppl.), 37-48.

Thorén, C., Seliger, V., Mácek, M., Vávra, J., & Rutenfranz, J. (1973). The influence of training on physical fitness in healthy children and children with chronic diseases. In F. Linneweh (Ed.), *Current aspects of perinatology and physiology of children* (pp. 83-112). Berlin, New York: Springer.

World Health Organization (1977, October). *WHO/ISFC meeting on precursors of atherosclerosis in children.* Geneva: World Health Organization.

World Health Organization, Expert Committee (1982). *Prevention of coronary heart disease.* (Technical Report Series, No. 678). Geneva: World Health Organization.

Zonderland, M.L. (1985). *Lipid and apolipoprotein profiles in premenarcheal athletes. The relation with training, nutrition and biological maturation.* Utrecht: Rijksuniversiteit, Proefschrift.

Part II
Age-Related
Metabolic Processes

The Anaerobic-to-Aerobic Power Ratio in Adolescent Boys and Girls

Cameron J.R. Blimkie
McMaster University, Hamilton, Ontario, Canada
Paul Roche
M.M. Robinson High School, Burlington, Ontario, Canada
Oded Bar-Or
McMaster University and Chedoke-McMaster Hospitals, Hamilton, Ontario, Canada

Relatively few studies have been made on the development of maximal anaerobic power in children or adolescents (Davies, Barnes, & Godfrey, 1972; di Prampero & Cerretelli, 1969; Inbar & Bar-Or, in press; Kurowski, 1977). By comparison, numerous investigators have studied the development of peak mechanical aerobic power in children and adolescents (Blimkie, 1982; Lange Andersen, Seliger, Rutenfranz, & Mocellin, 1974; Lange Andersen, Seliger, Rutenfranz, & Skrobak-Kaczynski, 1976; Rutenfranz et al., 1981; Seliger & Bartunek, 1976; Wirth et al., 1978).

These studies provide valuable information about the independent development of the aerobic and anaerobic energy systems. However, to the authors' knowledge, with the exception of a report by di Prampero and Mognoni (1981), no other studies have described the development of these systems in relation to each other, within the same individual, during either childhood or adolescence. A simple metabolic index such as the anaerobic-to-aerobic power ratio might prove useful in assessing either the degree or nature of physiological dysfunction in various pediatric diseases. It may also help assess the potential for specialized performance by young athletes in predominantly endurance or power-sports events requiring arm or leg involvement, or both.

The purposes of this article are therefore (a) to introduce the concept of the anaerobic-to-aerobic power ratio, (b) to describe the development of this ratio in healthy children and adolescents, and (c) to discuss its usefulness in pediatric health and disease.

POWER RATIO DERIVATION

The power ratio, defined as the ratio between peak mechanical anaerobic power and peak mechanical aerobic power, can be derived separately for the arms and legs.

Peak Anaerobic Power

Because of its applicability to either arm or leg ergometry, the Wingate Anaerobic Test (WAnT) described by Bar-Or (1981) was the method chosen for the measurement of anaerobic power. Resistance was predetermined, based on body mass (Dotan & Bar-Or, 1983) and peak power was calculated as the highest mechanical power output over either a 3-s period (Blimkie & Bar-Or, in preparation) or a 5-s period (Bar-Or, 1981), during a 30-s supramaximal exercise bout.

Peak Aerobic Power

Peak aerobic power may be derived from various protocols that lend themselves to arm and leg ergometry and that elicit maximal exercise performance. The choice of protocol may be dictated by the health status of subjects. The authors have most commonly utilized the McMaster Progressive Cycle Test (Bar-Or, 1983) for both clinical and research purposes. In this test, initial resistance and increments for both arm cranking and leg cycling are based on body height, so that total exercise time ranges between 8 and 12 min. Subjects are requested to pedal at 50 rev • min^{-1}, the pace being set by a visual electronic Ergostat Universal Synchronizer; actual pedaling frequency is measured electromagnetically. Work load is increased every 2 min and peak aerobic power is calculated as the prorated power during the final exercise stage.

RATIO CHANGES DURING GROWTH

Prepubertal Development

No reports have been published of the within-individual development of both anaerobic and aerobic power among prepubertal children. However, calculations based on the independent assessment of aerobic power (Cumming, 1977) and anaerobic power (Bar-Or, 1983) suggest that the power ratio should increase continuously from early childhood (8 years) until puberty, in both boys and girls (see Table 1). The increase in the

Table 1   Peak Anaerobic Power, Peak Aerobic Power, and the Peak Power Ratio During Prepubertal Years

Age (yr)	PPAn (W · kg⁻¹)	PPAer (W · kg⁻¹)	PP ratio
Girls			
8	5.90	3.15	1.87
9	6.90	3.10	2.22
10	7.85	3.07	2.56
11	8.40	3.00	2.80
12	8.35	2.95	2.83
13	8.30	2.90	2.86
14	9.00	2.80	3.21
Boys			
8	6.75	3.55	1.90
9	7.40	3.75	1.97
10	8.00	3.90	2.05
11	9.00	3.75	2.40
12	9.25	3.55	2.60
13	9.60	3.40	2.82
14	9.90	3.50	2.83

Note. PPAn = peak anaerobic power; PPAer = peak aerobic power; PP ratio = peak power ratio, calculated using aerobic data from Cumming (1977) and anaerobic data from Bar-Or (1983). Values are approximated means.

ratio is due, in girls, to a continuous growth in anaerobic power (per kg body mass), with a slight decrease in aerobic power during this period of development. In boys, the ratio increases during this period because of a continuous growth in anaerobic power, with little or no change in aerobic power (see Table 1).

Pubertal and Postpubertal Development

The ratio concept was recently investigated in relatively small samples of healthy adolescent boys and girls as part of a larger study of the development of anaerobic power during adolescence. The results are presented here as preliminary observations. A total of 24 boys and 27 girls between 14 and 18 years of age performed both an anaerobic (Wingate Anaerobic Test) and aerobic (McMaster Progressive Cycle Test) cycle test with legs to determine peak power. Physical and performance characteristics are presented in Table 2 and Figure 1.

Results from this study show that the power ratio gradually levels off for both sexes during adolescence (see Figure 2). These results are based

Table 2   Physical and Performance Characteristics of Subjects

n	Age (yr)	Height (cm)	Weight (kg)	PPAn (W)	PPAer (W)
Girls					
7	14.5	165.4	53.8	437.5	147.6
	±0.3	±6.0	±11.4	±66.8	±20.8
8	15.5	164.8	55.6	524.7	186.8
	±0.3	±7.7	±8.3	±94.8	±36.5
4	16.4	166.6	59.5	617.3	197.9
	±0.3	±9.3	±9.0	±131.2	±31.4
3	17.6	162.2	54.6	565.2	131.2
	±0.2	±6.3	±2.0	±28.1	±18.2
5	18.8	162.2	55.0	542.0	164.5
	±0.7	±7.3	±9.0	±152.9	±30.8
Boys					
6	14.5	162.2	54.7	579.3	211.0
	±0.3	±9.5	±10.2	±129.3	±50.8
5	15.6	174.4	60.6	679.0	236.9
	±0.3	±9.1	±8.6	±102.8	±18.2
5	16.5	180.6	68.2	774.9	306.7
	±0.3	±5.6	±6.1	±90.8	±51.9
4	17.7	175.4	77.3	784.8	256.2
	±0.1	±5.5	±27.4	±93.5	±31.4
4	18.7	178.3	71.7	898.9	285.6
	±0.8	±6.4	±6.8	±185.8	±41.2

Note.   PPAn = anaerobic peak power; PPAer = aerobic peak power. Values are means ± *SD*.

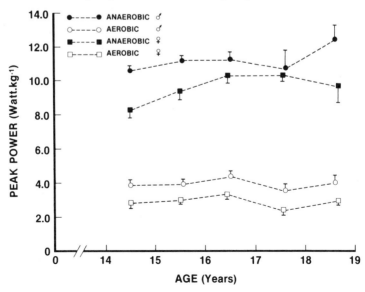

Figure 1   Development of peak anaerobic and aerobic leg power in adolescent boys and girls. Means ± SEM.

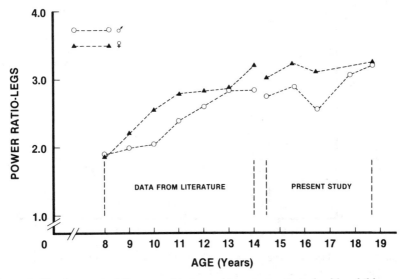

Figure 2 Development of the anaerobic-to-aerobic power ratio in healthy children and adolescents. Means ± SEM. Ratios for prepubertal children were calculated using data from Cumming (1977) for aerobic and Bar-Or (1983) for anaerobic.

on small samples and remain to be confirmed; however, the ratio does appear to attain a plateau, beginning around the onset of adolescence, and remains stable until early adulthood. This pattern in both sexes seems to be due to rather stable values for both anaerobic and aerobic power corrected for body weight across ages (see Figure 1).

APPLICATION

Factors other than growth and maturation, such as disease and athletic training, may also affect the development of this ratio. As shown in Figure 3, children with neuromuscular disease have a substantially lower power ratio than healthy controls of the same age. Additionally, as might be expected from a theoretical point of view, athletes who specialize in power and strength events demonstrate higher power ratios (e.g., 4.4, power lifters; 3.5, gymnasts) than those who specialize in mixed events (3.2, wrestlers) or mostly endurance events (2.8, ultramarathoners), at least for adult males (Skinner, personal communication, 1985). See Figure 3 for these values. Whether other pediatric diseases or athletic training during childhood and adolescence have any impact on the development of this power ratio remains to be investigated.

Although the concept of a power ratio seems valid and potentially useful from a practical perspective, the authors contend that more normative data (including observations on younger children, children with various pediatric diseases, and young athletic populations) for anaerobic

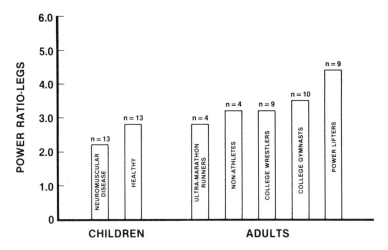

Figure 3 Anaerobic-to-aerobic power ratio in healthy, patient, and athletic male populations. Adult data are from Skinner (personal communication, 1985).

performances of both arms and legs and for aerobic performance during arm cranking are required before the developmental aspects and the diagnostic utility of this ratio concept are clearly established.

Acknowledgments

The authors thank Michael Browne, Dianne Moroz, Sherry Reed, Stephan Terhljan, and John Hay for their technical assistance in the data collection. Special thanks are given to the Halton County School Board, and to the principal, teachers, and students for their cooperation and assistance.

This study was supported in part by a grant from the Conn Smythe Research Foundation for Crippled Children, Canada, and the Postdoctoral Fellowship Program of the Medical Research Council of Canada.

REFERENCES

Bar-Or, O. (1981). Le test anaérobie de Wingate. Caractéristiques et applications. *Symbioses*, **13**, 157-172.

Bar-Or, O. (1983). *Pediatric sports medicine for the practitioner: From physiologic principles to clinical applications*. New York: Springer-Verlag.

Blimkie, C.J.R. (1982). Gas transport capacity and cardiorespiratory function in 9 to 15 year old boys during exercise, in relation to growth, maturation, heart size and regular physical activity. Unpublished doctoral dissertation. University of Western Ontario, London, Ontario.

Blimkie, C.J.R., & Bar-Or, O. *Development of anaerobic power during adolescence. Influence of lean tissue.* Manuscript in preparation.

Cumming, G.R. (1977). Exercise studies in clinical pediatric cardiology. In H. Lavallée & R.J. Shephard (Eds.), *Frontiers of activity and child health. Proceedings of the Seventh International Symposium of Paediatric Work Physiology* (pp. 17-45). Québec, Canada: Éditions du Pélican.

Davies, C.T.M., Barnes, C., & Godfrey, S. (1972). Body composition and maximal exercise performance in children. *Human Biology, 44,* 195-214.

di Prampero, P.E., & Cerretelli, P. (1969). Maximal muscular power (aerobic and anaerobic) in African natives. *Ergonomics, 12,* 51-59.

di Prampero, P.E., & Mognoni, P. (1981). Maximal anaerobic power in man. *Medicine sport, 13,* 38-44.

Dotan, R., & Bar-Or, O. (1983). Load optimization for the Wingate Anaerobic Test. *European Journal of Applied Physiology, 51,* 409-417.

Inbar, O., & Bar-Or, O. (in press). Anaerobic characteristics in male children and adolescents. *Medicine and Science in Sports and Exercise.*

Kurowski, T.T. (1977). *Anaerobic power of children from ages 9 through 15 years.* Unpublished master's thesis. Florida State University, Tallahassee, FL.

Lange Andersen, K., Seliger, V., Rutenfranz, J., & Mocellin, R. (1974). Physical performance capacity of children in Norway. 1. Population parameters in a rural inland community with regard to maximal aerobic power. *European Journal of Applied Physiology, 33,* 177-195.

Lange Andersen, K., Seliger, V., Rutenfranz, J., & Skrobak-Kaczynski, J. (1976). Physical performance capacity of children in Norway. 4. The rate of growth in maximal aerobic power and the influence of improved physical education of children in a rural community—Population parameters in a rural community. *European Journal of Applied Physiology, 35,* 49-58.

Rutenfranz, J., Lange Andersen, K., Seliger, V., Klimmer, F., Berndt, I., & Ruppel, M. (1981). Maximum aerobic power and body composition during the puberty growth period: Similarities and differences between children of two European countries. *European Journal of Pediatrics, 136,* 123-133.

Seliger, V., & Bartunek, Z. (1976). *Mean values of various indices of physical fitness in the investigation of Czechoslovak population aged 12-55 years.* Prague: Charles University.

Wirth, A., Träger, E., Scheele, K., Mayer, D., Diehm, K., Reischle, K., & Weicker, H. (1978). Cardiopulmonary adjustment and metabolic response to maximal and submaximal physical exercise of boys and girls at different stages of maturity. *European Journal of Applied Physiology, 39,* 229-240.

Optimal Velocity of Muscle Contraction for Short-Term (Anaerobic) Power Output in Children and Adults

Anthony J. Sargeant
Academic Medical Centre, Amsterdam, The Netherlands
Patricia Dolan
Polytechnic of Central London, London, England

Investigations of short-term (anaerobic) power output in children have consistently indicated lower values than in adult groups. This difference is reduced but not eliminated when standardization is made for body or active-muscle size (Bar-Or, 1983; Davies & Young, 1984; di Prampero & Cerretelli, 1969; Sargeant, Dolan, & Thorne, 1985). It was hypothesized that one of the reasons for these observed differences might be that measurements of power output may not be made at the optimal velocity for maximum power output because of systematic differences between the groups. Therefore, power output was determined over a wide range of contraction velocities in order to ascertain the optimal velocity for true maximum power as indicated by the force-velocity relationship (Sargeant, Hoinville, & Young, 1981).

METHODS

A total of 24 adult males, 16 adult females, and 25 male children (mean age, 13.7 years) were studied. Short-term (anaerobic) power was assessed using an isokinetic cycle ergometer. The data reported here are maximum peak force (PF_{max}) and maximum peak power (PP_{max}). Measurements were made at three or more crank velocities designed to span the optimal velocity for maximum power production. All measurements are given as the mean of the right and left legs. For further discussion of these techniques readers are referred to Sargeant et al. (1981). Upper leg muscle (plus bone) volumes were estimated by anthropometry (Sargeant & Davies, 1977).

RESULTS

Measurement of maximum peak force over a range of crank velocities indicated that an inverse linear relationship existed between force and velocity in all three groups. These relationships are given by:

Male adults: $y = 253 - 1.076X$ $(r = -0.85, p < .001)$
Female adults: $y = 254 - 1.05X$ $(r = -0.73, p < .001)$
Male children: $y = 220 - 0.95X$ $(r = -0.40, p < .001)$

Where y was the maximum peak force standardized for upper leg muscle (plus bone) volume (N • $liter_{ULV}^{-1}$) and X was the crank velocity (rev • min^{-1}). There was no significant difference between the male and female adults but the slope of the regression for both these groups differed significantly from the group of children ($p < .05$).

When the maximum peak power was calculated, this demonstrated a parabolic relationship with crank velocity, where the apex of the parabola indicated the optimum velocity (V_{opt}) for maximum power output (see Figure 1). Mean V_{opt} was not significantly different among the groups. The mean for all subjects combined was 118 ± 17 rev • min^{-1} (see Table 1). Calculating maximum peak power at the optimum velocity for each

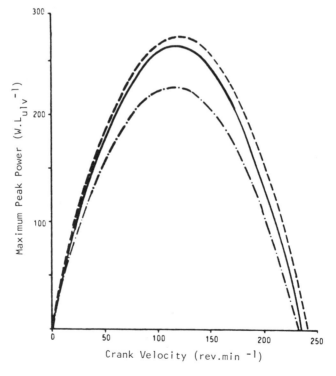

Figure 1 The relationship between the calculated maximum peak power and crank velocity for adult males (---) adult females (—), and children (•—•—).

Table 1 Optimum Velocity (V$_{opt}$) and Maximal Peak Power (PP$_{max}$) Calculated at Optimum Velocity in the Three Groups of Subjects Studied

Variable		V$_{opt}$ (rev • min^{-1})	PP$_{max}$ (W)	PP$_{max}$ (W • 1 ULV^{-1})
Male adults	M	114.3	1239	269
(n = 24)	SD	±14.7	±227	±36
Female adults	M	119.5	820	274
(n = 16)	SD	±19.9	±156	±63
Male children	M	120.0	795	224
(n = 25)	SD	±17.4	±152	±37

Note. PP$_{max}$ is given in absolute terms (W) and standardized for upper leg muscle plus bone volume (W • liter$_{ULV}^{-1}$). Values are expressed as the mean ± SD.

individual indicated that in absolute terms the male children were, on average, 36% less powerful than the adult males but only 3% less powerful than the adult females. However, when standardized for the size of the active muscle mass significant differences between the male and female adult group disappeared, but the power output of the male children was ~ 17% less than either adult group (p < .02; see Table 1).

DISCUSSION

These results confirm the previous observations of a significant difference in short-term (anaerobic) power output between adults and children even when corrected for body or muscle size. These differences cannot be accounted for by any systematic error resulting from measurements made at inappropriate contraction velocities, because the maximum peak power was calculated at the identified optimum velocity in the present study.

It seems possible that the differences might be explained by the ratio of muscle length to *true* cross-sectional area (i.e., when account is taken of the pennate and oblique orientation of the fibers in the leg extensor muscles). Thus, when longitudinal growth stops the muscle fibers may continue to increase the fiber cross-sectional area, changing the angle of pennation and effective force production. Neither leg muscle volume nor simple horizontal cross-sectional area of the thigh muscles would adequately reflect such differences between the age groups in *true* cross-sectional area of the active muscle and the associated changes in mechanical advantage.

REFERENCES

Bar-Or, O. (1983). *Pediatric sports medicine for the practitioner: From physiologic principles to clinical applications.* New York: Springer Verlag.

Davies, C.T.M., & Young, K. (1984). Effects of external loading on short term power output in children and young male adults. *European Journal of Applied Physiology,* **52**, 351-354.

di Prampero, P.E., & Cerretelli, P. (1969). Maximum muscular power (aerobic and anaerobic) in African natives. *Ergonomics,* **12**, 51-59.

Sargeant, A.J., & Davies, C.T.M. (1977). Limb volume composition and maximum aerobic power output in relation to habitual preference in young male subjects. *Annals of Human Biology,* **4**, 49-55.

Sargeant, A.J., Dolan, P., & Thorne, A. (1985). Isokinetic measurement of maximum leg force and anaerobic power output in children. In J. Ilmarinen & I. Välimäki (Eds.), *Children and Sport* (pp. 93-98). Berlin: Springer Verlag.

Sargeant, A.J., Hoinville, E., & Young, A. (1981). Maximum leg force and power output during short-term dynamic exercise. *Journal of Applied Physiology: Respiratory, Environmental, Exercise Physiology,* **51**(5), 1175-1182.

Pharmacogenetic and Pharmacokinetic Factors in the Drug Metabolism of Adolescent and Child Athletes

Róbert Frenkl
Gábor Szöts
János Mészáros
Hungarian University of Physical Education, Budapest, Hungary
Tamás Szabó
Központi Sportiskola, Budapest, Hungary

The microsomal enzyme system of the liver has an important role in the biotransformation of substances that are foreign to the body, a category to which drugs also belong. In previous investigations (Frenkl, Györe, Mészáros, & Szeberényi, 1980; Frenkl, Györe, & Szeberényi, 1980), this system was found to respond to physical exercise by enzyme induction. Thus, exercise produces the same effect as drug-triggered enzyme induction, but this action is endogenous. Boel, Andersen, Rasmussen, Hansen, and Dessing (1984) corroborated these observations. They found the rate of drug metabolization was related to the aerobic power of the subjects.

Attention has been drawn to the factor of age by another observation of a significantly faster excretion of canrenone following Verospiron[R] administration in 20-year-old subjects in comparison with a group whose mean age was 42 years. On the other hand, canrenone excretion was significantly faster in a group of 20-year-old athletes than in a nonathletic group of the same age (see Figure 1). Canrenone is a metabolite of Verospiron[R] (aldactone). The elimination of antipyrine, a recognized indicator of microsomal enzyme activity, was also found to proceed faster in the physically well trained, both in human studies and in animal experiments (Frenkl, Györe, Mészáros, & Szeberényi, 1980; Frenkl, Györe, & Szeberényi, 1980).

This paper reports on some studies concerned with whether the phenomenon termed "the exercise-trained liver" develops in childhood and adolescence as a result of physical exercise. The factor of aging has

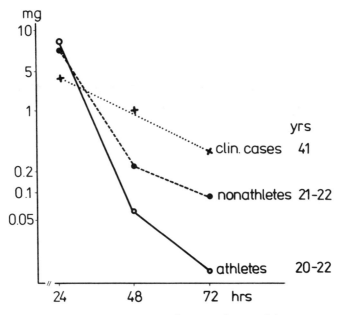

Figure 1 Urinary canrenone excretion as a function of age and fitness.

been studied in connection with pharmacokinetics almost exclusively in the elderly (Crooks, O'Malley, & Stevenson, 1976; Vestal, 1979), and so this line of study also was interesting because of its implications for younger age groups. Yet, the effects of exercise appeared more important, because the literature dealing with the factor of age in these processes indicates that other, external factors (such as smoking, alcohol ingestion, and habits of food intake) have a greater effect on drug kinetics than does aging alone.

Another relevant aspect is the role of pharmacogenetic factors (Szórády, Kozocsa, & Sánta, 1981) in athletic youths 11 to 14 years of age, namely, the distribution of the acetylator phenotypes and the correlation between pharmacogenetic and pharmacokinetic activity. The pituitary-adrenocortical response to an all-out exercise in child and adolescent athletes engaged in diverse sports will also be discussed.

MATERIAL AND METHODS

The subjects consisted of child, adolescent, and junior athletes in different events and nonathletic youths ranging in age from 11 to 18 years. Serum antipyrine concentration was estimated by the method of Brodie, Axelrod, Soberman, and Levy (1949). Acetylator phenotypes were assessed by a modified technique of Bratton and Marshall (1939). Serum levels of cortisol were estimated fluorometrically. Differences between means were analyzed statistically by student t-tests.

RESULTS

First, antipyrine elimination rate was studied before and after a course of strength training of secondary-school children 16 years of age who previously had only taken part in physical-education lessons at school. Without any change in the rate of elimination, the 1.5-hr exercise repeated four times weekly for seven weeks brought about an altered metabolization of antipyrine, in particular, in regard to its initial concentration in the blood (see Figure 2).

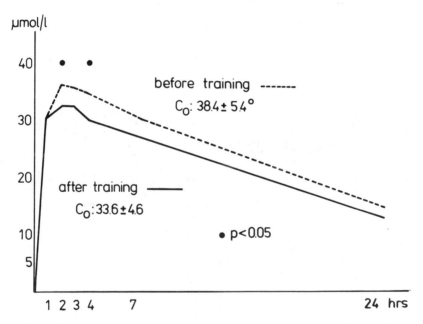

Figure 2   The effect of 7 weeks of strength training on the antipyrine metabolism of 15- to 16-year-old boys.

Acetylator activity was studied in athletes participating in diverse events (aged 11 to 14 years). There were 45% who qualified as slow acetylators (see Figure 3). By taking 10 each of the phenotypes, acetylator activity was repeatedly assessed in two groups of 11-year-old table-tennis players before and after an intense training session. When compared to the resting values, no change in acetylator activity could be observed as a result of the acute exercise in either group (see Figure 4). Antipyrine elimination was then compared in 10 of each of the slow and fast acetylators.

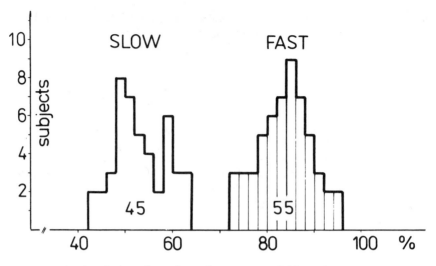

Figure 3 The distribution of acetylator phenotypes in children of 11 to 14 years.

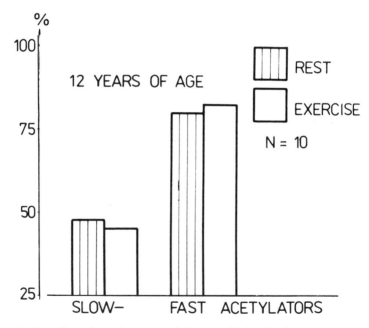

Figure 4 The effect of exercise on acetylation in table-tennis players.

The elimination curves differed at several points. A significant difference was observed in the compartment of distribution (see Figure 5).

The role of steroid hormones is an interesting point in the regulation of microsomal processes. The response to an all-out exercise of the adrenal

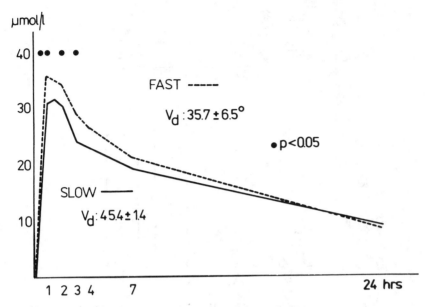

Figure 5 Serum antipyrine levels in slow and fast acetylators.

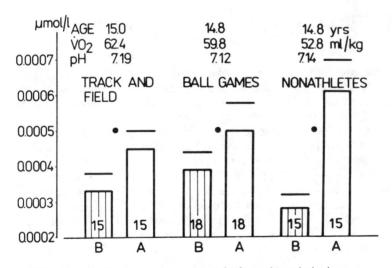

Figure 6 The effect of all-out exercise on serum hydrocortisone in juniors.

cortex was studied in young subjects engaged in diverse sports events as well as in nonathletes. Track and field athletes and soccer players gave a significant but less accentuated response than the nonathletic subjects. The same laboratory exercise failed to induce a rise in the cortisol level of child swimmers; instead, a statistically significant drop was noted in those whose initial level had been high (see Figures 6 and 7).

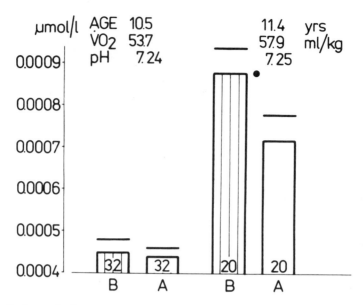

Figure 7   Serum hydrocortisone in swimmers grouped according to level of preexercise serum hormone.

DISCUSSION

Some components of drug metabolism were studied in young subjects, both athletic and nonathletic. The hereditary factor in drug metabolism was not influenced by sports activity, and it was also free from the effects of sport-specific selection, because the distribution of acetylator phenotypes was comparable to the incidence of the phenotypes observed previously in a population of nonathletic children by Szórády et al. (1981). Acetylator activity assessed before and after an acute bout of exercise did not produce any change either. Nevertheless, the possibility that drug metabolism of the slow and fast acetylators may differ in some other phase of biotransformation cannot be ruled out by the comparison of the pharmacogenetic and pharmacokinetic relationships of the present subjects; therefore, this line of study seems worth continuing.

Seven weeks of strength training effectively modified the drug metabolism of previously nonathletic youngsters of 16 years of age. This observation appears important for several reasons. First, it demonstrates that strength training is effective in this respect. It should be noted that most of the previous observations referred to the effects of endurance events. Second, this was the first evidence in young subjects of an exercise effect on drug absorption and liver-function change. Third, it was found that a longer period of strength training or an exercise modality different from strength training developed lasting effects, because the characteristic signs of faster drug metabolism failed to develop during a strength training of the short duration.

Conforming to previous observations (Frenkl, Csalay, & Csákváry, 1969), the pituitary-adrenocortical response of athletic youth to exercise was less marked than the nonathletes' response, a finding similar to that seen in adults and interpreted also in this case as a sign of adaptation. The steroidemia found in the initial phase of the training regimen may contribute to the development of any subsequent metabolic adaptation.

The results obtained in child swimmers indicate that an acute bout of ergometric exercise does not necessarily lead to an increase in cortisol level. Instead, when the base level of concentration was higher, it decreased; that is, it became "normal." This has been considered as confirming the notion that in human subjects, presumably in children and adolescents as well, the main factor in the adjustment of circulating corticoids is the metabolic manifestation of emotional activity.

SUMMARY

The relationships between physical fitness and drug metabolism, including the hereditary and acquired components of metabolization, were studied in young subjects. The 45:55 rate of incidence of the slow and fast acetylators among the athletes did not differ from that of the nonathletic subjects. Acetylator phenotype assessment used to study the subjects' pharmacogenetic status was uninfluenced by an acute bout of physical exercise because postexercise data corresponded to those obtained at rest. However, the slow and the fast acetylators were found to differ in their pharmacokinetic behavior when antipyrine was used as a tracer. This point needs further research.

Seven weeks of strength training may modify the decomposition of antipyrine in school children of 16 years of age, but was insufficient to induce the faster rate of metabolization so specific to physically fit individuals. Serum cortisol rose significantly after all-out exercise, but the extent of this rise was smaller in the junior track and field athletes and ball players than in the nonathletic subjects. The same exercise failed to bring about a rise in the circulating corticoids of child swimmers. In a subgroup of swimmers in which the preexercise level was high, the response to the customary exercise was a significant drop in the steroid concentration. In view of previous experience, corticoid regulation also seems to be controlled by emotional factors in young subjects.

REFERENCES

Boel, J., Andersen, L.B., Rasmussen, B., Hansen, S.H., & Dessing, M. (1984). Hepatic drug metabolism and physical fitness. *Clinical Pharmacological Therapy, 36*, 121-126.

Bratton, A.C., & Marshall, E.K. (1939). A new coupling component for sulfanilamide determination. *Journal of Biological Chemistry*, **128**, 537-550.

Brodie, B.B., Axelrod, H., Soberman, R., & Levy, B.B. (1949). The estimation of antipyrine in biological materials. *Journal of Biological Chemistry*, **179**, 25-29.

Crooks, J., O'Malley, K., & Stevenson, I.H. (1976). Pharmacokinetics in the elderly. *Clinical Pharmacokinetics*, **1**, 280-296.

Frenkl, R., Csalay, L., & Csákváry, G. (1969). A study of stress reaction elicited by muscular exertion in trained and untrained man and rats. *Acta Physiologica Academiae Scientiarium Hungaricae*, **36**, 365-370.

Frenkl, R., Györe, Á., Mészáros, J., & Szeberényi, Sz. (1980). A study of the enzyme inducing effect of physical exercise in man: The "trained liver." *Journal of Sports Medicine*, **20**, 371-376.

Frenkl, R., Györe, Á., & Szeberényi, Sz. (1980). The effect of muscular exercise on the microsomal enzyme system of the rat liver. *European Journal of Applied Physiology*, **44**, 135-140.

Szórády, I., Kozocsa, G., and Sánta, A. (1981). Potesetta alkalmazása a gyermekgyógyászatban: Therapiás és pharmacogeneticai vizsgálatok [Pediatric usage of Potesetta[R]: Therapeutic and pharmacogenetic studies, in Hungarian]. *Gyermekgyógyászat*, **32**, 75-85.

Vestal, R.E. (1979). Aging and pharmacokinetics: Impact of altered physiology in the elderly. In A. Cherkin (Ed.), *Physiology and cell biology of aging* (Aging, Vol. 8) (pp. 185-201). New York: Raven Press.

Part III
Anaerobic Threshold

Lactate Threshold and $\dot{V}O_2$max of Trained and Untrained Boys Relative to Muscle Mass and Composition

Yoriko Atomi
Tetsuo Fukunaga
Yoriko Yamamoto
Hideo Hatta
University of Tokyo, Tokyo, Japan

It is well known that lower blood lactate concentration is found during exercise in prepubertal children than in untrained adults (Åstrand, 1952; Ericksson, Gollnick, & Saltin, 1973; Máček, Vávra, & Novosadová, 1976). In 1984, Atomi, Fukunaga, Hatta, Yamamoto, and Kuroda reported that the lactate threshold (LT), the work rate at which blood lactate accumulation begins during running, decreased 10% with age from 9 to 11 years. Shown was the important role of leg muscle composition in determining the LT and its change with age; that is, the ratio of the cross-sectional area of the gastrocnemius muscle was significantly and negatively related to the LT in both relative and absolute terms. Plantar flexion is primarily an action of both the gastrocnemius muscle and soleus muscle in humans. It has been reported that the soleus muscle contains predominantly slow-twitch fibers (Gollnick, Sjödin, Karlsson, Jansson, & Saltin, 1974) and that the muscle's respiratory capacity or the proportion of slow-twitch fibers may be an important determinant of the LT in bicycle exercise (Ivy, Withers, Van Handel, Elger, & Costill, 1980).

On the other hand, it has been reported that adult endurance athletes have both higher $\dot{V}O_2$max and LT. Several researchers have previously indicated that young athletic children of prepubertal ages have the same high $\dot{V}O_2$max as adult athletes. However, there have been no reports of the comparison of LT in nonathletic and athletic boys. It has been hypothesized that the primary determinant of $\dot{V}O_2$max is cardiovascular capacity, whereas that of LT is a peripheral one involving the quantitative and qualitative characteristics of working muscles (Ivy et al., 1980). Therefore, this study compares the LT between nonathletic and athletic boys of prepubertal ages and the relationship between the LT and muscle composition of both groups.

METHODS

A total of 24 boys aged 11 to 12 years participated in this study. Eleven had trained 3 hours a day, 6 days a week for more than 3 years; 13 were untrained. Informed consent was obtained in accordance with established protocol for human subjects.

Measurement of LT and $\dot{V}O_2$max

The lactate threshold test was performed by level running on a treadmill. The initial speed of 80 to 110 m • min^{-1} was increased by 10 m • min^{-1} every 3 min with 1 min rest. The determination of LT was performed using the method described by Ivy et al. (1980). It was assumed that LT occurred just before the onset of blood lactate accumulation. The LT was assessed in both absolute ($\dot{V}O_2$, ml • kg^{-1}min^{-1}) and relative (% $\dot{V}O_2$max) terms. One or two weeks later, $\dot{V}O_2$max was determined by another treadmill test of increasing speed. Oxygen uptake was measured by an automatic gas analyzer (Anima Co., Japan) calibrated by a Scholander microgas analyzer. Blood samples were obtained by means of venous puncture performed on an earlobe at rest in the LT test, immediately and 3 min after $\dot{V}O_2$max tests. The concentration of lactic acid of immediately deproteinized samples was measured by an enzymatic method.

Estimation of the Capacity of Maximal Lactate Production

The peak lactate concentration was measured immediately and 3 min after 200-m running events on a track.

Measurement of Muscle Composition

Muscle cross-sectional areas of the leg and thigh were measured by an ultrasonic method (SS-120, Echo-Vision, Aloka, Japan). The measured sites of the thigh and leg were the midpoint of the femur and the distal seven tenths of the tibia, respectively. These were the areas of almost maximal girth. The ratio (G/PF) of the area of the gastrocnemius muscle (G) to the total plantar flexor area (PF) was calculated in order to assess the development of the soleus muscle.

RESULTS

No significant differences were found between the mean data of chronological and skeletal age, body height, or body weight of trained and untrained groups (see Table 1). Mean $\dot{V}O_2$max of trained boys was significantly higher than that of untrained boys (see Table 2). Mean LT of trained boys was significantly higher than that of untrained boys in both relative values (78.9 ± 3.4 versus 63.7 ± 1.7% $\dot{V}O_2$max) and absolute values (45.5 ± 2.4 versus 33.2 ± 4.1 ml • kg^{-1}min^{-1}), respectively. The individual $\dot{V}O_2$-lactate curves in both groups are shown in Figures 1(a) and 1(b). The blood lactate concentration in untrained boys increased at a lower $\dot{V}O_2$ than in trained boys.

G/PF ratio was significantly negatively related to the LT in both relative and absolute terms in each group. No significant correlations were found between the LT and both thigh and leg muscle cross-sectional areas. $\dot{V}O_2$max in ml • kg^{-1} • min^{-1} was not significantly correlated to leg muscle composition but was significantly related to leg and thigh muscle area in the untrained group ($p < .05$) (see Figure 2). The plots for trained boys seemed to be located in the same relation as for untrained boys. Mean values of blood lactate concentration at LT and peak lactate concentration in trained boys after 200-m running events were not significantly

Table 1 Physical Characteristics of the Subjects

Characteristic	Untrained boys (n = 13)	Trained boys (n = 11)
Chronological age (yr)	11.8 ± 0.1	11.7 ± 0.1
Skeletal age (yr)	11.4 ± 0.1	11.3 ± 0.1
Body height (cm)	145.5 ± 1.7	143.2 ± 1.0
Body weight (kg)	36.2 ± 1.4	35.9 ± 0.9
Lean body mass (kg)	28.9 ± 0.9	29.2 ± 0.8

Note. The values are mean ± *SE*.

Table 2 Mean Data of $\dot{V}O_2$max, LT, and Leg and Thigh Muscle Composition

	Untrained boys	Trained boys
$\dot{V}O_2$max (l • min^{-1})	1.89 ± 0.05	2.07 ± 0.03
(ml • kg^{-1} • min^{-1})	51.2 ± 1.1	58.0 ± 1.0
LT (ml • kg^{-1} • min^{-1})	33.2 ± 4.1	45.5 ± 2.4
(% $\dot{V}O_2$max)	63.7 ± 1.7	78.6 ± 3.4
Leg muscle area (cm^2)	45.6 ± 0.3	48.2 ± 2.1
Total plantar flexor area (cm^2)	34.9 ± 2.6	36.4 ± 1.7
Gastrocnemius muscle area (cm^2)	15.4 ± 1.2	16.0 ± 0.7
Gastrocnemius/total plantar flexor area (%)	44.0 ± 0.7	44.1 ± 0.7
Thigh-muscle area (cm^2)	74.8 ± 2.5	95.1 ± 2.9
Leg-extensor area (cm^2)	45.0 ± 1.0	55.6 ± 1.7

Note. The values are mean ± *SE*. $\dot{V}O_2$max = maximal oxygen uptake; LT = lactate threshold.

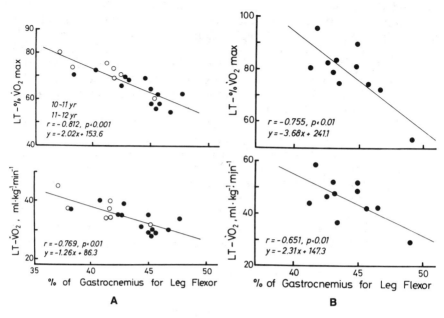

Figure 1 The comparisons of the relationships between gastrocnemius muscle ratio for plantar flexor area and lactate threshold in untrained boys (a) and trained boys (b).

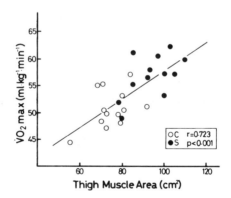

Figure 2 The relationship between thigh muscle area and maximal oxygen uptake. Correlation coefficient and regression line were calculated using the data on untrained boys.

different from untrained boys (2.0 ± 0.1 versus 1.9 ± 0.1; 13.4 ± 0.5 versus 11.6 ± 0.7 mM, respectively).

DISCUSSION

The lactate threshold and $\dot{V}O_2$max of trained boys in both relative and absolute terms were higher than untrained boys in the present study. The differences in the LT in both relative terms (23%) and absolute terms (37%) were very evident, compared with the difference in $\dot{V}O_2$max (12%). Because the physiological maturity of both groups was similar, according to the data for skeletal age, it can be said that the higher LT might be the result of the habitual training activity 2 to 3 hours a day, 6 days a week over 2 to 3 years, although the genetic factor should not be ignored. Last year, it was reported that a decrease in the LT was observed from 9/10 years to 11/12 years of age in nonathletic children, in accordance with the increase in G/PF (Atomi et al., 1984). It seems that LT of highly trained boys does not decrease with age; on the contrary, the LT tended to increase with training in the same developmental ages, based on the large difference of LT compared with the difference in $\dot{V}O_2$max.

Because the mean values of G/PF, muscle composition of plantar flexors, were not significantly different between trained and untrained groups, this factor did not seem to contribute to the difference of the level of the LT of both groups; that is, the higher the ratio of G/PF, the lower the LT level. It would be interesting to know the factor that determines the ratio, G/PF. It does not seem to be due to environmental factors but to genetic or environmental factors in infancy.

The individual curves of $\dot{V}O_2$-lactate concentration in both groups were very different. Trained boys could exercise and maintain lower lactate levels at higher $\dot{V}O_2$ levels. But the capacity to produce lactate seemed to be the same in both groups, because peak lactate concentration after a 200-m run was not significantly different between the two groups. Therefore, the specificity of the $\dot{V}O_2$-lactate curve of trained boys seemed to be dependent on the capacity to remove or oxidize lactate during exercise, in a similar manner to that shown in rats by Donovan and Brooks (1983).

In the present study, the qualitative characteristics of the leg muscle were significantly related to the LT during running, while the quantitative characteristics of the thigh muscle were significantly related to $\dot{V}O_2$max during running. The large difference in the LT during running between trained and untrained boys seemed to be due to habitual vigorous activity of soccer training.

CONCLUSION

Trained boys aged 11 to 12 show higher LT during running, rather than higher $\dot{V}O_2$max, compared with untrained boys. It is hypothesized that the higher $\dot{V}O_2$max in trained boys is partly due to the greater development of thigh muscle mass, but the LT by running in trained boys might be dependent on qualitative characteristics (probably higher oxidative capacity) of plantar flexors. Leg muscle composition might be somewhat related to the LT during running in both groups.

REFERENCES

Åstrand, P.-O. (1952). *Experimental studies of physical working capacity in relation to sex and age*. Copenhagen: Munksgaard.

Atomi, Y., Fukunaga, T., Hatta, H., Yamamoto, Y., & Kuroda, Y. (1984). *Lactate threshold and its change with growth, related to leg muscle composition in prepubertal children*. Paper presented at the meeting of the International Congress of Child and Sports.

Donovan, C.M., & Brooks, G.A. (1983). Endurance training affects lactate clearance, not lactate production. *American Journal of Physiology, 244*, E83-E92.

Eriksson, B.O., Gollnick, P.D., & Saltin, B. (1973). Muscle metabolism and enzyme activities after training in boys 11-13 years old. *Acta Physiologica Scandinavica, 87*, 485-497.

Gollnick, P.D., Sjödin, B., Karlsson, J., Jansson, E., & Saltin, B. (1974). Human soleus muscle: A comparison of fiber composition and enzyme activities with other leg muscles. *Pflügers Archiv, 348*, 247-255.

Ivy, J.L., Withers, R.T., Van Handel, P.J., Elger, D.H., & Costill, D.L. (1980). Muscle respiratory capacity and fiber type as determinants of the lactate threshold. *Journal of Applied Physiology, 48*, 523-527.

Máček, M., Vávra, J., & Novosadová, J. (1976). Prolonged exercise in prepubertal boys. 1. Cardiovascular and metabolic adjustment. *European Journal of Applied Physiology, 35*, 291-298.

Training Prescriptions for 9- to 17-Year-Old Figure Skaters Based on Lactate Assessment in the Laboratory and on the Ice

Georgine Gaisl
Institute of Sport Sciences, University Graz, Graz, Austria
Gerhard Wiesspeiner
Institute of Biomedical Engineering, Technical University, Graz, Austria

Since 1974, the authors have been involved with training optimization, at the beginning with the help of laboratory investigations (Gaisl, 1979, 1984; Gaisl, König, Pessenhofer, & Schwaberger, 1980; Gaisl, Pessenhofer, Schwaberger, König, 1981) and later with the help of field investigations (Franz & Gaisl, 1983; Gaisl, König, & Wiesspeiner, 1985, in press). The main interest was in optimization of training for endurance sports. In the spring of 1984, trainers for the Austrian National Team and Junior Team in figure skating sought assistance in the training optimization of 11 team members. As a cooperative effort, training and test schemes were developed and dates set for the necessary laboratory and field investigations.

PURPOSE OF THE STUDY

At the beginning of the first preparation period and four months afterward, spiroergometric laboratory investigations objictified the level of *basic endurance* (general condition) and its evaluation was checked. At the beginning of the second preparation period and again seven weeks later, field investigations objictified and checked the level of *specific endurance*. A third investigation on ice sought to improve the performance of *free skating*.

METHODS

A total of 11 figure skaters, 9 to 17 years old, members of the Austrian National Team and Junior Team, participated in the laboratory investigations. Table 1 shows their physical characteristics. Because of illness,

Table 1   The Physical Characteristics of Subjects (N = 11)

Variables	M	SD
Age (yr)	12.6	2.5
Height (cm)	154.2	11.6
Weight (kg)	43.6	12.2

accident, school schedules, and other problems, not every athlete participated in all field investigations.

Investigation in the Laboratory

During load, oxygen consumption was measured by Oxyscreen (Jaeger) and heart rate was recorded (Hellige). With 5% upgrade, the initial speed of 6 km/h (1.66 m/s) of a treadmill was increased in increments of 2 km/h (0.55 m/s) for 3-min intervals until each subject's maximum was attained. Before and at the end of each load phase and after 3 min of recovery, a sample of blood was taken from the hyperemized earlobe for lactate determination (Roche 640 Lactate-Analyzer). Lactate concentration was measured immediately. Running speed, heart frequency, oxygen consumption, and percentage of maximal oxygen consumption at the anaerobic threshold, 4 mmol/l (Keul, Kindermann, & Simon, 1978; Mader et al., 1976) were analyzed on an Epson QX-10 Computer. From the results, certain recommendations were formulated for the improvement of general condition.

Field Investigation

Shown in Figure 1 is the graphic representation of the test course for the determination of specific endurance. After a warm-up skate of 6 min, the skating test was repeated three times. The duration of each run was measured. Before, during the whole run, and during the first 10 min of recovery, heart rate was recorded by telemetry or with portable ECG monitors. Before and after warm-up, after each run, and at the 3rd, 6th, and 10th min of recovery, lactate was measured (see Figure 2).

After the first field test, it was recognized that the test course was too short. Therefore, the course was elongated by 100 m for the second field test (see Figure 1). Five weeks after the second test, a third test was conducted with the purpose of simulating competition. Repetition of free skating served to increase the stress. After warm-up, free skating was

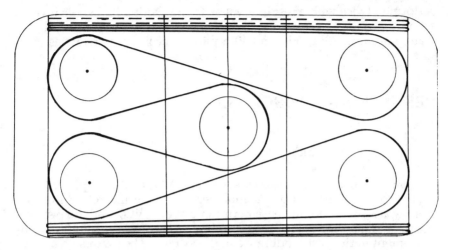

Figure 1 Graphic presentation of test course.

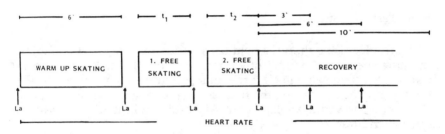

Figure 2 Time diagram of the first and second field investigation. t_n = individual run time; L_A = lactate investigation.

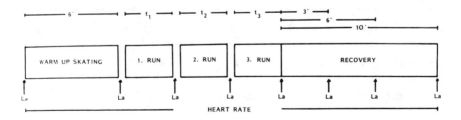

Figure 3 Time diagram of the third field investigation. t_n = individual run time; L_A = lactate investigation.

performed twice with a rest interval of 1 min. During the whole investigation, heart rate was recorded. Before and after warm-up, after each free skate, and at the 3rd, 6th, and 10th min of recovery, lactate was measured (see Figure 3).

RESULTS AND DISCUSSION

Laboratory Investigation

As shown in Table 2, maximal speed and $\dot{V}O_2$max/kg improved during the course of the first preparation period. At the anaerobic threshold there was a significant increase in running speed, $\dot{V}O_2$, and the percentage of $\dot{V}O_2$max (see Table 3). This indicated there was a significant improvement in the basic endurance of the skaters. The skaters paid more attention to conditioning than before because it was possible to evaluate the individual's conditioning by quantifying physical condition with the laboratory test.

Field Tests T_1 and T_2

The results of the first two field tests on ice are compared in Table 4. Running speed was significantly improved from the first to the second test. Each lactate value in all three runs and in the recovery period was significantly higher during the first test (T_1) than in the second test (T_2). Heart rate showed a similar trend. All results indicated an increase in specific endurance.

Table 2   Change of Maximal Values (N = 11)

Variable	May M and SD	September M and SD	%[a]	F
Max. speed (km/h)	11.75 1.20	12.50 1.32	6.2	ns[b]
Max. heart rate (beats/min⁻¹)	193.1 7.9	197.9 7.2	2.4	ns
$\dot{V}O_2$max (ml/min⁻¹/kg⁻¹)	43.6 3.7	46.0 3.0	2.5	ns

[a]% = percentage change.
[b]ns = not significant.

Table 3 Change of Values at the Anaerobic Threshold ($N = 11$)

Variable	May M and SD	September M and SD	%[a]	F[b]
Speed (km/h)	8.83 0.90	10.51 1.23	17.4	< 0.05
Heart rate (beats/min^{-1})	179.2 11.0	188.4 11.3	5.0	< 0.2
$\dot{V}O_2$ (ml/min^{-1}/kg^{-1})	35.0 3.9	41.0 4.0	15.7	< 0.05
Percentage of $\dot{V}O_2$max (%)	79.52 4.8	89.21 6.6	11.5	< 0.05

[a]% = percentage change.
[b]Level of significance (t-test).

Table 4 Comparison of First (T_1) and Second (T_2) Field Tests ($N = 7$)

Test item		Speed (m/s) T_1	T_2	Heart rate (beats/min^{-1}) T_1	T_2	Lactate (mmol/l) T_1	T_2
1st run	M	3.98	4.64	193.3	192.1	7.24	6.17
	SD	0.16	0.31	17.9	8.3	2.05	0.95
2nd run	M	3.90	4.61	198.2	195.1	7.90	6.74
	SD	0.26	0.29	9.7	10.5	2.96	1.30
3rd run	M	3.85	4.43	203.2	197.4	7.36	6.64
	SD	0.23	0.44	10.4	11.5	1.90	1.65
3 min recovery	M			124.8	124.9	8.48	5.67
	SD			12.9	18.4	3.33	1.60
6 min recovery	M			119.0	110.6	7.07	4.84
	SD			16.0	13.3	3.70	1.65
10 min recovery	M			115.4	113.0	5.75	3.70
	SD			12.1	12.4	3.34	1.10

The Third Field Test

This test was carried out only once (because of scheduling problems) and was used for optimization of free skating. As can be seen in Table 5, heart rate was nearly the same after the first and second runs. In con-

Table 5 Mean Heart Rates and Lactate Concentrations While Free Skating (N = 7)

Variable	Heart rate (beats/min^{-1})		Lactate (mmol/l)	
	M	SD	M	SD
At rest	105.8	19.1	1.02	0.29
6 min warm-up skating	174.3	18.3	3.03	1.24
1st free skating	197.4	8.4	6.57	3.34
2nd free skating	197.7	7.3	7.94	3.66
3 min recovery	115.4	14.1	7.01	3.80
6 min recovery	109.6	15.1	6.29	3.68
10 min recovery	104.4	15.0	5.18	3.27

trast, the lactate values increased (as expected). Mean lactate concentration of 7.94 mmol/l was higher at the end of the second run than the maximum values measured in the laboratory. This demonstrated the importance of sport-specific load (Föhrenbach, Mader, & Hollmann, 1981; Keul, Dickhut, Berg, Lehmann, & Huber, 1981; Liesen, Ludemann, Schmengler, Föhrenbach, & Mader, 1985).

CONCLUSIONS

Through standardization of methods by quantitative measurements of performance capacity variables, lactate, and heart rate, the following results were obtained: an objective evaluation of training effect, an increase in motivation, and improvement in general and specific endurance.

Acknowledgments

This study was supported by Grant No. 4619 from the Austrian Research Council (Fonds zur Förderung der wissenschaftlichen Forschung). The authors wish to thank team trainers Mrs. E. Kögl and H. Cuno for their excellent cooperation.

REFERENCES

Föhrenbach, R., Mader, A., & Hollmann, W. (1981). Umfang und Intensität im Dauerlauftraining von Mittelstreckenläuferinnen des DLV und Maßnahmen zur individuellen Trainingsund Wettkampfoptimierung. *Leistungssport,* **11,** 458-472.

Franz, W., & Gaisl, G. (1983). Die Bestimmung des aerob-anaeroben Übergangs bei den Skilangläufern in der Vorbereitungsperiode im Feldtest. *Leistungssport, 13*, 38-40.

Gaisl, G. (1979). Der aerob-anaerobe Übergang und seine Bedeutung für die Trainingspraxis. *Leistungssport, 9*, 235-243.

Gaisl, G. (1984). Die Bedeutung der Bestimmung der aeroben und anaeroben Schwelle für die Trainingsoptimierung im Skilanglauf. *Leibesübung-Leibeserziehung, 38*, 67-70.

Gaisl, G., König, H., Pessenhofer, H., & Schwaberger, G. (1980). Die Trainingsoptimierung im Mittelund Langstreckenlauf mit Hilfe der Bestimmung des aerob-anaeroben Schwellenbereiches. *Deutsche Zeitschrift für Sportmedizin, 31*, 131-140.

Gaisl, G., König, H., & Wiesspeiner, G. (1985). Schätzung der Laktatwerte bei erfahrenen und unerfahrenen Mittelund Langstreckenläufern. *Leistungssport, 15*, 13-14.

Gaisl, G., König, H., & Wiesspeiner, G. (in press). Feldlaktatuntersuchungen bei den Mittelund Langstreckenläufern in der Vorbereitungsperiode. *Deutsche Zeitschrift für Sportmedizin.*

Gaisl, G., Pessenhofer, H., Schwaberger, G., & König, H. (1981). Use of aerobic and anaerobic threshold for optimizing the training of fitness for daily activities for aging and convalescents. *Hermes, 15*, 419-525.

Keul, J., Kindermann, W., & Simon, G. (1978). Die aerobe und anaerobe Kapazität als Grundlage für die Leistungsdiagnostik. *Leistungssport, 8*, 22-32.

Keul, J., Dickhut, H.H., Berg, A., Lehmann, M., & Huber, G. (1981). Allgemeine und sportartspezifische Leistungsdiagnostik im Hochleistungssport. *Leistungssport, 11*, 382-398.

Liesen, H., Ludemann, E., Schmengler, D., Föhrenbach, R., & Mader, A. (1985). Trainingssteuerung im Hochleistungssport: einige Aspekte und Beispiele. *Deutsche Zeitschrift für Sportmedizin, 36*, 8-18.

Mader, A., Liesen, H., Heck, H., Philippi, H., Rost, R., Schürch, P., & Hollmann, W. (1976). Zur Beurteilung der sportartspezifischen Ausdauerleistungsfähigkeit im Labor. *Sportarzt und Sportmedizin, 27*, 80-88; 109-112.

Anaerobic Strain in Children During a Cross-Country Skiing Competition

Timo Suurnäkki
Center for Industrial Safety, Helsinki, Finland
Juhani Ilmarinen
Clas-Håkan Nygård
Institute of Occupational Health, Helsinki, Finland
Paavo V. Komi
University of Jyväskylä, Jyväskylä, Finland
Jan Karlsson
Karolinska Hospital, Stockholm, Sweden

Cross-country skiing is popular among children during wintertime in Nordic countries, and in Finland young elite skiers participate in skiing competitions and training sessions almost daily. This study was carried out at the National Junior Ski Competition held annually at Joutsa, where approximately 300 girls and boys divided into age groups of 8, 10, 12, and 14 years participate. Most of the children approach the competition very seriously. According to the few earlier reports carried out under field conditions (Christensen and Höberg, 1950; Ilmarinen, Nygård, Komi, & Karlsson, 1984), this kind of event places maximum physiological stress and strain on the children. The physiological strain on a child's organism during maximum competition is not well known. There is some evidence that cardiovascular strain is almost at its maximum during skiing competitions (Ilmarinen, Nygård, Komi, & Karlsson, 1981, 1984).

This report includes data from one part of a larger research project concerning the physiological strain of skiing on children. The main object of this study was to determine the anaerobic strain in 8- to 14-year-old skiers under field conditions.

METHOD

A total of 40 girls and 39 boys from among the children participating in the ski competition in 1982 were selected for this study (Table 1). Questionnaire-based data concerning the amount of training during that

Table 1 Average Skiing Distance, Skiing Time, and Amount of Training (N = 79; 39 Boys, 40 Girls)

Age group (yr)	N	Distance (km)	Time (min)	M	Min	Max	km/day
⩽ 8 boys	8	1.5	7-10	99	20	210	1.5
⩽ 8 girls	8	1.5	6-10	122	20	344	2.0
9 to 10 boys	12	2.0	7-9	168	50	350	3.0
9 to 10 girls	12	2.0	7-8	157	13	370	2.5
11 to 12 boys	10	3.0	11-14	312	219	500	5.0
11 to 12 girls	12	3.0	12-15	238	105	360	4.0
13 to 14 boys	9	5.0	17-21	671	230	1210	10.0
13 to 14 girls	8	3.0	11-14	251	74	545	4.0

(Winter training (km) spans M, Min, Max, km/day columns)

season and details of the appropriate competition are shown in Table 1. The average skiing speed was calculated from the distance covered and the total skiing time for the competition. The level of anaerobic strain during a competition was estimated according to the concentration of blood lactate (LA, mmol • l^{-1}). Capillary blood was sampled from the fingertip immediately (1 to 3 min) after the race. The samples were analyzed by the FIA (Flow Injection Analysis) method (Karlsson et al., 1983; Rydevik, Nord, & Ingman, 1982).

Data were available from a previous study, carried out in 1981, on 13 of the children, 8 girls and 5 boys, whose ages ranged from 8 to 14 years (mean age 11.5 years in 1982). During the intervening year, 9 of 13 subjects had changed to a higher competitive age group, which entailed a longer skiing distance. The data were analyzed to assess the effects of one year's biological maturity on children's anaerobic strain when skiing and also to compare strain in children and adult elite skiers in competition.

RESULTS

Anaerobic Strain

Concentrations of blood lactate (LA) were remarkably high immediately after the race (see Figure 1). For girls the LA-concentration was 11.2 mmol • l^{-1} (variation 7.8-14.2 mmol • l^{-1}) and significantly higher than that of boys, 10.1 mmol • l^{-1} (4.6 to 12.7). In fact, in each age group the levels of LA were higher in girls than in boys, the differences being significant in the youngest and oldest age groups. Among girls, the LA was lowest in the 8-year-old group and highest in 14-year-olds. Among boys, the lowest level of LA was in the 8-year-old group and highest in 10-year-olds. Individual differences in LA levels were large in all age groups.

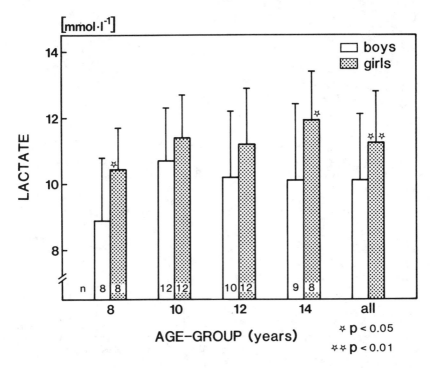

Figure 1 Blood lactate (*M, SD*) of boys and girls in each age group and overall after the ski competition, statistical tests calculated by sex for each age group, and in total.

Skiing Speed and LA

Comparison of mean skiing speed and LA indicated [see Figures 2(a) to 2(d)] that speed was not unambiguously connected with the rise of LA level, as there were large variations among the age groups and sexes. Among 8- and 12-year-old boys the LA level was higher at higher speeds ($r = 0.79$ and 0.67). No differences were found between 10-year-old boys and girls and LA levels did not increase with speed in these age groups. The means and standard deviations of skiing speed for each age group and sex are given in Table 2.

Training, Speed, and LA

The amount of training was positively correlated with speed in the skiing competition among both boys ($r = 0.46$, $p < .01$) and girls ($r = 0.36$, $p < .05$) [see Figures 3(a) and 3(b)]. However, the individual variation in mean speed was remarkable when the subjects had skied for less than 300 km during training. The speed of "untrained" girls varied from 3.0 to 4.5 m • s^{-1} and correspondingly in boys from 2.5 to 4.5 m • s^{-1}. There

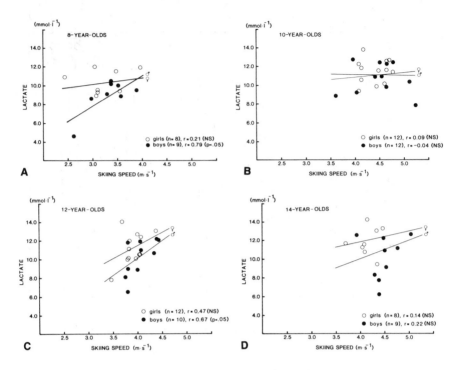

Figures 2(a) to 2(d)   Blood lactate in relation to mean skiing speed in each age group, individual plotting and regression lines ($y = ax + b$).

Table 2   Mean Skiing Speed (m · s⁻¹) During Competition Among Girls and Boys in Age Groups

				Age group (yr)		
		≤ 8	9 to 10	11 to 12	13 to 14	All
Girls	M	3.2	4.4	3.9	4.2	4.0
	SD	0.5	0.3	0.2	0.2	0.4
	n	8	12	12	8	40
Boys	M	3.4	4.5	4.0	4.5	4.2
	SD	0.4	0.5	0.3	0.3	0.6
	n	8	12	10	9	39
All	M	3.3	4.5	4.0	4.3	4.1
	SD	0.4	0.4	0.2	0.3	0.6
	N	16	24	22	17	79

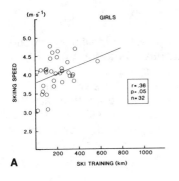
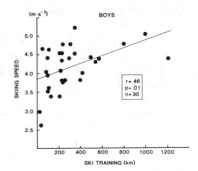

A   B

Figures 3(a) and 3(b) Mean skiing speed for girls and boys in relation to the amount of ski training during the winter preceding the study.

was no correlation between the amount of training and LA levels overall, but within age groups there was a positive correlation between these factors ($r = 0.53$, $p < .01$) in 10-year-old girls.

Follow-Up

Mean skiing time was a little longer in 1981 among boys than girls, and the one-year follow-up examination of 13 children indicated that the difference increased during the year (see Table 3). However, mean skiing speed was the same for both sexes. The speed increased by 0.3 m • s^{-1}, although most of the children had moved up to age groups with longer skiing routes. LA increased from 6.0 to 9.9 mmol • l^{-1} and the change was more marked among girls than among boys. The subjects' positions in the final

Table 3 Skiing Time, Speed, and Anaerobic Strain of Girls and Boys in 1981 and 1982

		Skiing time (min)		Skiing speed (m • s^{-1})		Lactate mmol • l^{-1})		Final position of group in the results	
		1981	1982	1981	1982	1981	1982	1981	1982
Girls	M	9.6	10.2	3.8	4.1	5.8	10.7	20	16
($n = 8$)	SD	2.8	3.0	0.6	0.6	1.9	0.9	15	9
Boys	M	10.4	13.5	3.8	4.1	6.3	8.7	27	30
($n = 5$)	SD	2.4	5.3	0.6	0.4	1.7	1.6	16	11
All	M	9.9	11.5	3.8	4.1	6.0	9.9	23	22
($N = 13$)	SD	2.5	4.2	0.6	0.5	1.8	1.5	15	12

results were worse among the boys studied than among the girls, especially in 1982.

The skiing speed among children compared to adult elite skiers (6 male and 6 female elite skiers at Joutsa in 1982, unpublished data) was 1.8 m • s^{-1} less for the boys (M = 4.1 versus 5.9 m • s^{-1}) and 1.3 m • s^{-1} less for the girls (M = 4.1 versus 5.4 m • s^{-1}). However, there were implications of higher levels of anaerobic strain among children than adults. LA-concentration among children compared to adult elite skiers (27 male and 25 female elite skiers at Lahti in 1981 [Komi, personal communication]) was 1.2 mmol • l^{-1} higher for the boys (M = 8.7 versus 7.5 mmol • l^{-1}) and 1.7 mmol • l^{-1} higher for the girls (M = 10.7 versus 9.0 mmol • l^{-1}).

DISCUSSION

Full aerobic capacity ($\dot{V}O_2$max, ml • kg^{-1} • min^{-1}) develops quite early, and in 6- to 8-year-old children it almost equals that of adults (Bar-Or, 1984; Flandrois, Grandmontagne, Mayet, Favier, & Frutosso, 1982; Saris, 1982; Saris, Noordeloos, Ringnalda, van 't Hof, & Binkhorst, 1985). In contrast, children's anaerobic capacity develops slowly, reaching the levels of adults at the ages of 13 to 16 years. This level is achieved somewhat earlier in girls than in boys (Bar-Or, 1984; Flandrois et al., 1982). It is estimated that the slower development of anaerobic capacity is caused perhaps by the biochemical incompetence of the child's organism to either produce or manipulate the end products of metabolism (e.g., lactate) efficiently enough (Eriksson, Karlsson, & Saltin, 1971; Wirth et al., 1978). According to earlier studies, the maximal LA concentration in children reported has been either at the level of 6 to 8 mmol • l^{-1} (de Knecht & Binkhorst, 1980; Eriksson & Koch, 1973; Flandrois et al., 1982; Keul, 1982; Koch, 1980) or almost the same as in adults, more than 10 mmol • l^{-1} (Cumming & Hnatiuk, 1980). Different studies have also reported large individual variations in the level of anaerobic strain.

The results of this study supported earlier observations (Ilmarinen et al., 1981, 1984) that the level of anaerobic strain in children is almost at its peak during skiing. Indeed the LA concentrations found in this study were even higher (46% among girls, 35% among boys) than those found earlier. Moreover, the higher levels of anaerobic strain among boys than among girls found in 1981 were not found at the follow-up in 1982. Methodological factors were identical and, therefore, do not account for these variations, nor do weather conditions. The mean skiing speed was a little higher among the youngest groups (0.4-1.1 m • s^{-1}) in 1982 and among the oldest in 1981.

Comparison of the results in different years according to the skiing speed is not appropriate, because the skiing distance changed in some cases due to the changes in the age groups, and also the individual physiological work capacity changes with age. Thus, it is not likely that skiing speed had an essential influence on those differences. This type of field study very commonly encounters difficulties in standardizing all possible confounding factors.

Motivation is one of the central factors in maximal physical efforts, and it can even have a marked effect on subjects' success in a laboratory test (Cumming & Hnatiuk, 1980). Therefore, in children's skiing competition, motivation will have a strong effect on the final results, quite apart from physiological capacity. It has been suggested by Hermansen (1971) that strong motivation may produce higher LA values in competition than in laboratory tests.

Why were there higher LA values among girls than among boys in all age groups? The concentration of blood LA is associated with the duration of physical load so that the highest values will be reached during the first few minutes (Hermansen, 1971). This factor can only explain the differences in the oldest group (14 years old), where the skiing course was shorter for girls than for boys. The earlier physical maturation of girls may also involve some metabolic dissimilarities to boys, for example, in the amount of muscle mass, enzyme reactions, or LA kinetics (Eriksson, Gollnick, & Saltin, 1973). In these subjects, the individual biological age could also explain at least some of the differences between the sexes.

According to the present and earlier results (Ilmarinen et al., 1981, 1984) both anaerobic and aerobic strain will be almost at a peak in children during skiing competition. Modern work physiologists do not believe that this kind of maximum strain constitutes a health risk in very fit children. According to Keul (1982) the metabolic and hormonal regulation system is less effective during short-term load (under 2 min) in children than in adults. Because children cannot raise their glycolysis significantly with training, LA training (anaerobic training) is neither sensible nor acceptable for children entering skiing competition.

On the contrary, children may have better oxidative capacity than adults to endure physical load. So, in accordance with Keul (1982), the various types of aerobic sports or activities with duration of more than 5 min are recommended for children. There still remains the question of the physiological and psychological readiness of children for continuous loads in competition.

More research should be done on the suitability of intensive and unbalanced sports training for immature children. A longitudinal study taking 8-year-old "competitive skiers" and controls (which also covers other types of sport) through the growth spurt could be planned to include continuous measurements of both biological development and health status, and also analyses of work physiology during competition and training under field conditions.

REFERENCES

Bar-Or, O. (1984). The growth and development of children's physiologic and perceptional responses to exercise. In J. Ilmarinen & I.

Välimäki (Eds.), *Children and sport. Paediatric work physiology* (pp. 3-17). Berlin, New York: Springer-Verlag.

Christensen, E.H., & Högberg, P. (1950). Physiology of skiing. *Arbeitsphysiologie*, **14**, 292-303.

Cumming, G.R., & Hnatiuk, A. (1980). Establishment of normal values for exercise capacity in a hospital clinic. In K. Berg & B.O. Eriksson (Eds.), *Children and exercise IX* (pp. 79-91) (International Series on Sport Sciences, Vol. 10). Baltimore: University Park Press.

de Knecht, S., & Binkhorst, R.A. (1980). Physical characteristics of children with congenital heart disease: Body characteristics and physical working capacity. In K. Berg & B.O. Eriksson (Eds.), *Children and exercise IX* (pp. 333-346) (International Series on Sport Sciences, Vol. 10). Baltimore: University Park Press.

Eriksson, B.O., Gollnick, P.D., & Saltin, B. (1973). Muscle metabolism and enzyme activities after training in boys 11-13 years old. *Acta Physiologica Scandinavica*, **87**, 485-497.

Eriksson, B.O., Karlsson, J., & Saltin, B. (1971). Muscle metabolites during exercise in pubertal boys. *Acta Paediatrica Scandinavica* (Suppl. 217), 154-157.

Eriksson, B.O., & Koch, G. (1973). Effect of physical training on hemodynamic response during submaximal and maximal exercise in 11- to 13-year-old boys. *Acta Physiologica Scandinavica*, **87**, 27-39.

Flandrois, R., Grandmontagne, M., Mayet, M.-H., Favier, R., & Frutosso, J. (1982). La consommation maximale d'oxygene chez le jeune français, sa variation avec l'age, le sexe et l'entrainement. *Journal de Physiologie* (Paris), **78**, 186-194.

Hermansen, L. (1971). Lactate production during exercise. In B. Pernow & B. Saltin (Eds.), *Muscle metabolism during exercise* (pp. 401-407) (Advances in Experimental Medicine and Biology, Vol. 11). New York: Plenum Press.

Ilmarinen, J., Nygård, C.-H., Komi, P.V., & Karlsson, J. (1981). Lasten kuormittuminen kilpahiidossa. [Effect of ski-competition on heart rate and blood lactate among boys and girls of age 8-12 years, in Finnish]. *Liikunta ja tiede*, **18**, 146-150.

Ilmarinen, J., Nygård, C.-H., Komi, P.V., & Karlsson, J. (1984). Heart rate and blood lactate level of 8- to 12-year-old boys and girls during cross-country ski-competitions. In J. Ilmarinen & I. Välimäki (Eds.), *Children and sport. Paediatric work physiology* (pp. 189-195). Berlin, New York: Springer-Verlag.

Karlsson, J., Jacobs, I., Sjödin, B., Tesch, P., Kaiser, P., Sahl, O., & Karlberg, B. (1983). Semi-automatic blood lactate assay: Experiences from an exercise laboratory. *International Journal of Sports Medicine*, **4**, 52-55.

Keul, J. (1982). Zur Belastbarkeit des kindlichen Organismus aus biochemischer Sicht. In H. Howald & E. Hahn (Eds.), *Kinder im Leistungssport. 19th Magglinger Symposium* (pp. 31-49). Basel: Birkhäuser Verlag.

Koch, G. (1980). Aerobic power, lung dimensions, ventilatory capacity, and muscle blood flow in 12- to 16-year-old boys with high physical activity. In K. Berg & B.O. Eriksson (Eds.), *Children and exercise IX* (pp. 99-108) (International Series on Sport Sciences, Vol. 10). Baltimore: University Park Press.

Rydevik, U., Nord, L., & Ingman, F. (1982). Automatic lactate determination by flow injection analysis. *International Journal of Sports Medicine,* **3**, 47-49.

Saris, W.H.M. (1982). *Aerobic power and daily physical activity in children with special reference to methods and cardio-vascular risk indicators.* Nijmegen: Katholieke Universiteit, Proefschrift.

Saris, W.H.M., Noordeloos, A.M., Ringnalda, B.E.M., van 't Hof, M.A., & Binkhorst, R.A. (1985). Reference values for aerobic power of healthy 4- to 18-year-old Dutch children: Preliminary results. In R.A. Binkhorst, H.C.G. Kemper, & W.H.M. Saris (Eds.), *Children and exercise XI* (pp. 151-160) (International Series on Sport Sciences, Vol. 15). Champaign, IL: Human Kinetics Publishers.

Wirth, A., Träger, E., Scheele, K., Mayer, D., Diehm, K., Reischle, K., & Weicker, H. (1978). Cardiopulmonary adjustment and metabolic response to maximal and submaximal physical exercise of boys and girls at different stages of maturity. *European Journal of Applied Physiology,* **39**, 229-240.

Aerobic Power and Endurance Running in Young Children

Shigehiro Yoshizawa

T. Ishizaki

H. Honda

Utsunomiya University, Utsunomiya, Japan

— environmental reasons for ↓ in activity

The more urbanized the population, the less their daily physical activity has been in Japan as well as in other countries. Parallel to this phenomenon, morbidity due to cardiovascular diseases now ranks first among causes of death, and the second and third mortality rates are due to cerebral and cardiovascular strokes, respectively. Therefore, from the standpoint of preventive medicine, the following studies were performed to develop objective, rational, and persuasive procedures for endurance running that maintain or improve the essential development of aerobic capacity for young children.

STUDY 1—METHODS AND RESULTS

The performances in an endurance run were found to be more highly correlated to aerobic power ($\dot{V}O_2max$ in terms of body weight) among rural adolescents than urban ones. This was partly due to the difference in the amount and/or intensity of daily physical activities (Yoshizawa, 1971). Accordingly, $\dot{V}O_2max$ and the 5-min endurance run of rural children and adolescents could have been more objectively measured and were, therefore, determined by means of a track run. Expired air was collected in Douglas bags and analyzed for O_2 and CO_2 by the Scholander technique. Heart rates were recorded by telemetric procedures (Yoshizawa, Ishizaki, & Honda, 1983).

It was found, as shown in Table 1, that even in young children, males were significantly superior to females not only in $\dot{V}O_2max$ related to body weight but also in the 5-min endurance run performance (Yoshizawa et al., 1983). The fact that the relative values of $\dot{V}O_2max$ (ml/kg/min) of young children (aged 5 or 6 years) were fairly comparable to those of adolescents (aged 17 or 18 years) suggests that even young children, if running distances and the durations are not long, are able to perform endurance runs.

Table 1   Aerobic Power and 5-Minute Endurance Run Performance of Boys and Girls

Age (yr)	N		Body weight (kg)		$\dot{V}O_2$max (ml/kg/min)		Heart rate (beats/min)		Respiratory exchange ratio		5-min run	
	M	F	M	F	M	F	M	F	M	F	M	F
4	13	24	16.71 (1.70)	17.91 (1.76)	47.5 (4.9)	45.1 (4.6)	199.7 (6.2)	204.1 (9.1)	1.17 (0.07)	1.18 (0.07)	799 (52)	779 (44)
5	38	33	18.29 (2.07)	18.35 (2.05)	50.5[b] (4.5)	44.9 (4.4)	202.7 (7.3)	205.7 (7.9)	1.11 (0.09)	1.12 (0.08)	861[b] (53)	763 (56)
6	35	24	21.07 (2.65)	19.64 (1.82)	49.3[b] (2.7)	45.6 (4.3)	203.9 (6.9)	204.4 (7.5)	1.04 (0.06)	1.04 (0.06)	934[b] (56)	824 (71)
7	33	22	23.39 (3.09)	22.14 (2.26)	49.9[b] (2.9)	46.6 (3.9)	200.5 (6.3)	205.2[a] (7.8)	1.02 (0.04)	1.03 (0.04)	983[b] (63)	889 (82)
8	35	23	26.16 (3.33)	25.22 (3.02)	52.0[b] (3.5)	47.7 (4.6)	203.4 (7.8)	206.3 (8.3)	1.04 (0.04)	1.06 (0.06)	1026[b] (59)	915 (73)
9	22	17	28.40 (3.98)	27.76 (3.52)	52.9[b] (3.1)	48.9 (3.8)	199.6 (6.2)	199.1 (6.7)	1.07 (0.03)	1.11 (0.05)	1040[b] (65)	944 (89)
10	23	13	28.99 (3.08)	31.50[a] (3.96)	53.4[b] (4.5)	49.5 (6.2)	195.2 (4.9)	197.3 (8.1)	1.09 (0.09)	1.08 (0.09)	1085[b] (52)	983 (48)
11	26	20	32.25 (3.08)	35.25 (3.96)	51.7[b] (4.5)	46.0 (4.5)	191.8 (5.4)	197.5[b] (7.9)	1.10 (0.09)	1.13 (0.10)	1131[b] (60)	1017 (63)
12	34	26	35.87 (6.26)	37.65 (6.38)	52.5[b] (4.7)	47.7 (4.6)	194.5 (7.1)	195.2 (6.7)	1.13 (0.10)	1.09 (0.11)	1199[b] (71)	1094 (78)
13	17	22	37.11 (7.30)	40.76 (5.83)	55.6[b] (7.2)	48.4 (5.4)	193.6 (4.2)	193.8 (4.9)	1.06 (0.05)	1.07 (0.05)	1241[b] (76)	1138 (79)
14	21	19	46.62	46.51	55.2[b]	44.0	194.0	194.4	1.11	1.13	1302[b]	1123

(Cont.)

Table 1 (Cont.)

Age (yr)	N		Body weight (kg)		$\dot{V}O_2$max (ml/kg/min)		Heart rate (beats/min)		Respiratory exchange ratio		5-min run	
	M	F	M	F	M	F	M	F	M	F	M	F
15	19	19	51.59 (9.65)	48.59 (5.84)	58.4[b] (5.1)	44.7 (4.4)	191.9 (4.9)	188.9 (4.2)	1.07 (0.08)	1.10 (0.11)	1343[b] (103)	1089 (66)
16	23	17	54.65[a] (6.84)	49.18 (5.00)	54.9[b] (4.0)	43.6 (7.3)	190.0 (8.4)	191.1 (12.3)	1.05 (0.08)	1.10 (0.09)	1327[b] (127)	1064 (89)
17	22	23	56.98[b] (6.16)	51.58 (4.32)	54.0[b] (5.4)	43.1 (5.3)	193.2 (7.2)	194.6 (8.5)	1.04 (0.09)	1.10 (0.09)	1320[b] (78)	1060 (90)
18	7	9	57.35 (5.38)	51.74 (4.39)	52.4[b] (8.0)	40.1 (7.9)	190.0 (9.5)	188.7 (9.1)	1.11 (0.07)	1.08 (0.09)	1340[b] (114)	1024 (58)

Note. Values are means (and SD).

[a]$p < .05$; [b]$p < .001$.

STUDY 2—METHODS AND RESULTS

In order to determine the circulorespiratory responses of young children in the 5-min run, 5 male and 5 female subjects, whose physical characteristics are given in Table 2, ran on the track with verbal instructions and motivations for 5 min (Yoshizawa, 1983). Mean values of covered distances, as shown in Table 3, were very similar to the corresponding values given in Table 1. The mean values of $\dot{V}O_2$max (ml/kg/min) and heart rate in the 5th min, as shown in Table 4, are also comparable to the corresponding values in Table 1. The subjects, therefore, were able to run with a near maximal effort, but they could not keep the constant running pace for the full 5 min.

No sex differences were found in covered distances for 5 min, but mean values of $\dot{V}O_2$ (ml/kg/min) in each minute during the run were lower for females. So it is possible that the females ran under more anaerobic and exhausting conditions and necessarily exhibited higher respiratory exchange ratios, although there were no statistical differences between the

Table 2 Physical Characteristics (Means and SD) of Subjects

N	Sex	Age (yr; mo)	Height (cm)	Weight (kg)
5	M	4; 11 (0; 04)	105.9 (3.9)	17.68 (2.20)
5	F	5; 01 (0; 01)	108.1 (5.6)	18.24 (2.33)

Table 3 Covered Distances in Each Minute and Total Minutes in 5-Min Endurance Run

		1st min	2nd min	Time 3rd min	4th min	5th min	Total
Means	M	169.8	152.6	151.2	154.2	163.2	795.2
(SD)		(18.3)	(12.0)	(10.2)	(9.3)	(9.8)	(50.3)
	F	176.8	155.6	148.2	149.6	155.6	785.4
		(9.6)	(6.1)	(5.9)	(10.3)	(4.1)	(31.1)
Max.	M	194	170	165	166	177	872
	F	190	163	155	160	162	824
Min.	M	143	140	141	141	153	742
	F	164	149	142	135	151	754

Table 4 Circulorespiratory Changes in Boys and Girls During the Run and Recovery

Variables	$\dot{V}O_2$ (l/min)		$\dot{V}O_2$ (ml/kg/min)		Heart rate (beats/min)		O^2pulse (ml/beat)		Respiratory exchange ratio	
	M	F	M	F	M	F	M	F	M	F
At rest	0.163 (0.034)	0.154 (0.017)	9.2 (1.5)	8.5 (0.7)	103.3 (12.7)	104.2 (7.1)	1.6 (0.3)	1.5 (0.2)	0.824 (0.112)	0.792 (0.038)
Run										
1st min	0.677 (0.092)	0.616 (0.120)	38.5 (3.8)	33.8 (6.1)	174.3 (11.4)	171.0 (6.9)	3.9 (0.4)	3.6 (0.6)	0.826 (0.059)	0.931 (0.076)
2nd min	0.862 (0.091)	0.827 (0.129)	50.1[a] (2.9)	45.2 (1.8)	186.6 (14.7)	194.0 (5.7)	4.6 (0.3)	4.3 (0.7)	0.960 (0.076)	1.057 (0.068)
3rd min	0.859 (0.137)	0.837 (0.102)	48.5 (4.3)	46.0 (2.2)	192.6 (10.5)	196.4 (5.8)	4.5 (0.6)	4.3 (0.6)	0.931 (0.040)	1.021 (0.068)
4th min	0.865 (0.103)	0.854 (0.095)	49.3 (2.3)	47.0 (3.3)	195.2 (8.3)	197.4 (7.0)	4.5 (0.5)	4.3 (0.6)	0.910 (0.062)	1.015 (0.046)
5th min	0.923 (0.133)	0.853 (0.088)	52.2[a] (3.9)	46.9 (2.4)	198.8 (8.8)	200.2 (5.6)	4.6 (0.6)	4.3 (0.5)	0.895 (0.054)	0.999 (0.017)

(Cont.)

Table 4 (Cont.)

Variables	$\dot{V}O_2$ (l/min)		$\dot{V}O_2$ (ml/kg/min)		Heart rate (beats/min)		O_2-pulse (ml/beat)		Respiratory exchange ratio	
	M	F	M	F	M	F	M	F	M	F
Recovery										
1 min	0.512	0.585	29.0	32.1	166.0	174.0	3.1	3.4	0.940	1.068
	(0.089)	(0.130)	(3.2)	(3.2)	(11.5)	(11.5)	(0.5)	(1.0)	(0.087)	(0.076)
2 min	0.217	0.255	12.1	13.9	126.8	137.8	1.7	1.9	0.971	1.102
	(0.053)	(0.045)	(1.8)	(1.4)	(10.5)	(7.2)	(0.4)	(0.3)	(0.079)	(0.133)
3 min	0.172	0.187	9.7	10.3	117.4	124.2	1.5	1.5	0.860	1.002
	(0.021)	(0.018)	(0.8)	(0.8)	(10.1)	(6.5)	(0.2)	(0.2)	(0.048)	(0.044)
4 min	0.165	0.169	9.3	9.3	118.0	122.2	1.4	1.4	0.811	0.865
	(0.018)	(0.021)	(0.3)	(1.0)	(10.0)	(7.8)	(0.2)	(0.1)	(0.045)	(0.030)
5 min	0.159	0.160	9.0	8.8	117.8	121.8	1.4	1.3	0.799	0.828
	(0.028)	(0.009)	(0.7)	(0.9)	(11.1)	(8.3)	(0.2)	(0.1)	(0.028)	(0.026)
6 min	0.158	0.156	8.9	8.7	115.2	119.2	1.4	1.3	0.758	0.772
	(0.031)	(0.012)	(0.8)	(1.2)	(11.4)	(9.6)	(0.3)	(0.1)	(0.026)	(0.014)

Note. Values are means (and *SD*).
$^{a}p < .05$.

boys and the girls. Such performances probably required slower recovery after the endurance run for the females. Recovery of $\dot{V}O_2$ and heart rate were significantly higher for young children than for adolescents (Yoshizawa, 1983). This was partly due to the smaller ratios of rest values to maximal ones and partly due to more aerobic performances in the endurance run.

STUDY 3—METHODS AND RESULTS

The same subjects ran on a flat treadmill at various velocities, so that more accurate circulorespiratory responses could be measured and optimal and safe running velocities could be utilized (Yoshizawa, Honda, Urushibara, & Nakamura, 1981). The running velocities in the 5-min endurance run gradually decreased at about the 3rd min; therefore the duration time of the run was set at 3 min. The velocities were increased from test to test up to the velocity at which not all the subjects could continue to run for 3 min. The running velocities were, therefore, 120, 140, 160, 180, and 200 m/min for males and 100, 120, 140, 160, and 180 m/min for females.

As shown in Figures 1 and 2, at the same velocities and time, males ran with lower heart rates than the girls, except at 100 m/min. But no

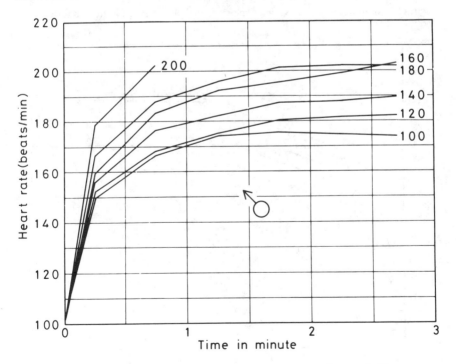

Figure 1 Boys' heart rates at various velocities (m/min) during flat treadmill run.

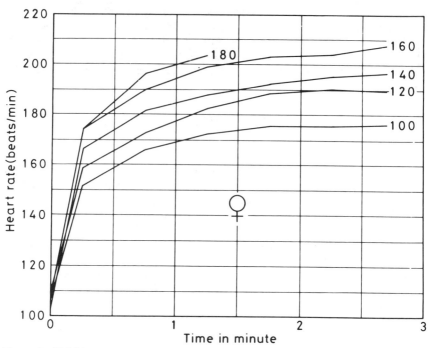

Figure 2   Girls' heart rates at various velocities (m/min) during flat treadmill run.

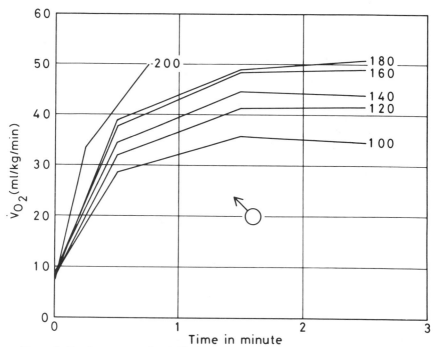

Figure 3   Boys' oxygen uptakes (ml/kg/min) at various velocities (m/min) during flat treadmill run.

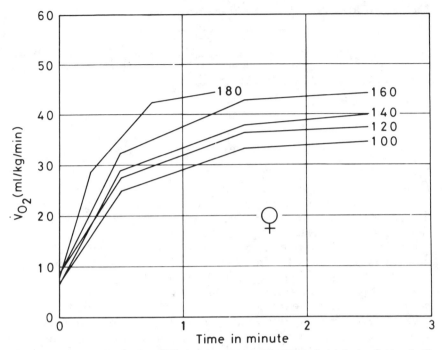

Figure 4   Girls' oxygen uptakes (ml/kg/min) at various velocities (m/min) during flat treadmill run.

statistically significant differences were found between boys and girls. However, sex differences did exist in oxygen uptake. The $\dot{V}O_2$ (ml/kg/min) for females was significantly lower at 120 and 140 m/min, respectively (see Figures 3 and 4), and so they were forced to run in the more anaerobic conditions, as previously indicated. These lower $\dot{V}O_2$ (ml/kg/min) were mostly due to their lower circulorespiratory capacities, which were clearly shown by the $\dot{V}O_2$ (l/min)-heart rate relationships. As the mean values of respiratory exchange ratios in the 3rd and last minute did not exceed unity at 140 m/min (Yoshizawa et al., 1983), optimal and safe velocities in the 3-min endurance run should take sex differences into consideration, the recommended velocities being 140 m/min for male and 120 m/min for female young children. In addition, it was found that the intensity of work was sufficient so that $\dot{V}O_2$max was achieved in 1 min in young children.

STUDY 4—METHODS AND RESULTS

In order that not only increased speed but also increased recovery for heart rate and $\dot{V}O_2$ could be determined in the endurance run, 4 male and 4 female young children, whose physical characteristics are shown in Table 5, also ran on the flat treadmill longer than in the previous experiment. In addition, they sat quietly for 17 min after the cessation of

Table 5 Physical Characteristics (Means and SD) of Subjects

N	Sex	Age (yr; mo)	Height (cm)	Weight (kg)
4	M	4; 09 (0; 04)	106.3 (4.7)	17.46 (2.23)
4	F	4; 08 (0; 05)	107.8 (4.3)	17.38 (1.63)

running (Yoshizawa, Honda, & Urushibara, 1984). Exhaustion time for each child was predicted by using the velocity-duration curve that was determined in advance. Mean values of heart rate and $\dot{V}O_2$ in the last 30 s are given in Table 6.

The increased heart rates in the first 30 s were significantly higher than those of $\dot{V}O_2$ (see Table 7). This was probably partly due to the nervous control by the impulses from the leg muscles. On the other hand, percentage of recovery of $\dot{V}O_2$ in the first 30 s was almost twice that of the percentage of heart rate recovery over the same time period. It had also been observed that the differences in recovery rates between heart rate and $\dot{V}O_2$ were larger for young children than for adolescents (Yoshizawa, 1983). Accordingly, it was confirmed again that, in a comparatively short duration of exhaustive endurance running, young children were able to run in more aerobic conditions. It is noteworthy that, in spite of larger differences of $\dot{V}O_2$ between the rest and the final 30 s during the run in males, the increased rates of $\dot{V}O_2$ in the early periods of running were higher for males than for females in the common and same velocities of 140 and 160 m/min.

Shown in Table 8 are heart rates and $\dot{V}O_2$ of the total subjects ($n = 9$ for each sex) who participated in the experiments of Phases III and IV.

Table 6 Mean (and SD) Values of Heart Rate and Oxygen Uptake at Rest and in the Last 30 S

Sex	Velocities (m/min)	Heart rate (beats/min)		$\dot{V}O_2$ (l/min)	
		At rest	For the last 30 s	At rest	For the last 30 s
M	140	105.7 (6.5)	196.5 (14.8)	0.124 (0.008)	0.716 (0.124)
	160	102.5 (6.5)	196.5 (9.1)	0.128 (0.024)	0.764 (0.112)
	180	96.2 (5.2)	198.2 (10.2)	0.124 (0.020)	0.813 (0.099)
	200	96.5 (5.9)	199.5 (11.1)	0.129 (0.028)	0.837 (0.148)
F	120	114.0 (14.0)	191.5 (9.1)	0.137 (0.013)	0.608 (0.044)
	140	115.5 (12.3)	194.0 (12.0)	0.138 (0.015)	0.689 (0.059)
	160	116.0 (14.5)	200.0 (10.5)	0.140 (0.014)	0.738 (0.019)
	180	115.2 (11.3)	199.0 (7.3)	0.146 (0.020)	0.761 (0.028)

Table 7 Mean Values of Increase and Recovery Rate (%) of Heart Rate and Oxygen Uptake During and After a Flat Treadmill Run at Different Velocities, Statistical Differences Between Heart Rate and Oxygen Uptakes as Indicated

Sex	Velocities (m/min)	Increase Rates (%) During Run									
		0'00" to 0'30"	0'30" to 1'00"	1'00" to 1'30"	1'30" to 2'00"	2'00" to 2'30"	2'30" to 3'00"	3'00" to 3'30"	3'30" to 4'00"	4'00" to 4'30"	4'30" to 5'00"
						Heart rate					
M	140	56.0	82.5	91.5	100.0	94.8	98.3	99.0	96.2	98.0	100.0
	160	59.5[d]	77.4	86.6	92.9	92.8	96.0	98.0	97.8	100.2[b]	—
	180	59.2[c]	84.6	89.8	94.3	95.1[a]	93.8[b]	95.4[c]	97.2[c]	—	—
	200	65.0[a]	88.6	93.6[b]	96.2[c]	—	—	—	—	—	100.0
F	120	52.9	70.5	81.9	84.5	87.1	89.1	90.9	94.3	95.3	100.0
	140	58.2[c]	77.8	85.3	94.9	96.4	97.5	101.3	100.7[a]	—	—
	160	49.0	76.5	89.0	95.4	98.1	92.9[c]	98.2[c]	—	—	—
	180	54.7[d]	83.0	91.5	101.9[b]	—	—	—	—	—	—
						$\dot{V}O_2$					
M	140	53.3	88.6	99.6	104.7	104.2	103.6	101.7	103.1	98.8	100.0
	160	47.2	84.7	92.5	100.0	99.6	102.9	101.4	102.2	103.1[b]	—
	180	42.5	79.9	92.9	95.7	102.4[a]	104.1[b]	100.7[c]	101.5[c]	—	—
	200	49.2	88.1	93.9[b]	95.2[c]	—	—	—	—	—	—
F	120	39.2	81.5	97.4	93.3	96.7	102.4	101.2	104.6	97.3	100.0
	140	43.5	82.4	91.8	98.0	99.5	98.9	101.5	101.2[a]	—	—
	160	39.8	76.0	92.4	92.5	93.4	92.8[c]	100.9[c]	—	—	—
	180	38.9	83.2	96.0	99.0[b]	—	—	—	—	—	—

(Cont.)

Table 7 (Cont.)

Sex	Velocities (m/min)	Recovery rates (%) after run						
		0'00" to 0'30"	0'30" to 1'30"	1'30" to 3'00"	3'00" to 5'00"	5'00" to 8'00"	8'00" to 12'00"	12'00" to 17'00"
		Heart rate						
M	140	14.6	68.3	86.2	94.2	92.3	96.9	97.8
	160	16.8	63.8	85.9	90.1	93.4	93.1	93.1
	180	14.2	60.4	81.4	85.9	88.8	88.9	89.5
	200	7.8	51.6	81.2	89.8	91.3	92.0	95.5
F	120	27.7	64.6	77.4	87.8	93.3	95.5	—
	140	14.5	61.9	80.4	85.3	86.7	84.3	95.3
	160	11.2	64.3	81.2	91.7	90.0	93.3	93.9
	180	14.4	50.6	74.6	86.9	89.0	90.0	92.2
		$\dot{V}O_2$						
M	140	31.1[e]	78.8[e]	92.4[e]	95.8	97.8	100.3	100.5
	160	32.1[e]	80.7[d]	93.0	96.2	99.0	99.5	100.2
	180	31.4[e]	80.5[e]	90.3[d]	95.6[d]	95.5	101.0	102.6
	200	25.0[e]	74.5[e]	89.6[e]	94.5	97.9	99.3	99.5
F	120	39.7	78.8[d]	93.9[d]	96.6	97.8	99.5	—
	140	29.7[d]	78.4[e]	94.2	97.7	99.2[d]	100.1	100.9
	160	30.2[d]	77.7[d]	92.9	96.7	97.8	100.6	101.0
	180	30.2[d]	74.5[d]	90.5[e]	96.1[d]	98.3[d]	99.3[d]	99.8

[a], [b], and [c] The respective number of 3, 2, and 1 subjects who could run until the corresponding time.
[d] $p < 0.05$; [e] $p < 0.01$.

Table 8 Differences (Means and SD) in Heart Rate and Oxygen Uptake Between Both Sexes With the Same Velocities in a Flat Treadmill Run (n = 9 for each sex)

Velocities (m/min)	Sex	At rest	Heart rate (beats/min)					
			0'00" to 0'30"	0'30" to 1'00"	1'00" to 1'30"	1'30" to 2'00"	2'00" to 2'30"
140	M	104.5 (9.6)	157.4 (9.4)	179.8 (8.9)	185.1 (7.6)	191.3 (9.9)	189.5 (7.0)
	F	108.1 (11.2)	160.4 (8.4)	179.3 (8.1)	185.5 (9.1)	191.3 (9.3)	193.4 (9.4)
160	M	100.9 (5.4)	158.2 (8.0)	179.5 (7.9)	188.4 (8.2)	192.9 (7.8)	194.7 (9.1)
	F	111.2[a] (11.4)	166.0 (13.7)	185.8 (12.0)	195.6 (10.2)	199.8 (8.7)	201.3 (8.5)

Velocities (m/min)	Sex	At rest	$\dot{V}O_2$ (ml/kg/min)		
			0'00" to 1'00"	1'00" to 2'00"	2'00" to 3'00"
140	M	8.1 (1.2)	33.0[b] (1.2)	43.3[b] (4.8)	43.0[b] (3.1)
	F	7.1 (1.1)	28.5 (1.3)	38.0 (2.2)	39.7 (2.2)
160	M	8.2 (1.1)	34.9[a] (4.7)	45.7[a] (4.4)	46.8[a] (2.9)
	F	8.2 (1.0)	30.5 (3.1)	41.9 (3.1)	43.2 (2.9)

[a]$p < .05$; [b]$p < .01$.

The heart rates for females were almost equal to or higher than those for males, but $\dot{V}O_2$ (ml/kg/min) were significantly higher for males than females. Such sex differences necessarily provide evidence that the young males were qualitatively superior to the young females in their circulo-respiratory systems for endurance performance.

REFERENCES

Yoshizawa, S. (1971). Ecological study of aerobic work capacity in urban and rural adolescents. *Japanese Journal of Physical Fitness, 20,* 125-133.

Yoshizawa, S., Honda, H., Urushibara, M., & Nakamura, N. (1981). The studies on aerobic work capacities of preparatory school children (III). *Japanese Journal of Physical Fitness, 30,* 73-85.

Yoshizawa, S., Ishizaki, T., & Honda, H. (1983). The studies on the development of aerobic work capacity of Japanese rural children and adolescents aged from 4 to 18 years. *Japanese Journal of Physical Education, 28,* 199-214.

Yoshizawa, S. (1983). An experimental study on the teaching method of general endurance for young children. Bulletin of the Faculty of Education, Utsunomiya University, Sect. 1, 29, 127-141.

Yoshizawa, S., Honda, H., & Urushibara, M. (1984). The studies on aerobic work capacity of preparatory school children (IV). *Japanese Journal of Physical Fitness, 33,* 173-183.

Part IV
Physical Activity, Training, and Cardiovascular Risk Indicators

Evaluation of the Physical Activity of School Children During a Physical-Education Lesson

Klaus Klausen
Birger Rasmussen
Bente Schibye
University of Copenhagen, Copenhagen, Denmark

Physical-education teachers have been concerned about the progressive reduction in the number of physical-education lessons in Danish public schools over the past three decades. The effect of increasing the number of lessons from two to five per week was studied over a 3-year period by following two experimental classes (five lessons, or 225 min, per week) from the start of the fourth and sixth grades to the end of the sixth and eighth grades, respectively. For comparison two control classes (two lessons, or 90 min, per week) of the same grades were followed over the same period. The main objective of increasing the number of lessons per week was to evaluate the overall pedagogical, psychological, sociological, and physiological effects on the children. No deliberate attempts were made to increase the physical activity during each physical-education lesson. In order to evaluate the physiological training effect of the lesson, a preliminary investigation of the heart rate (HR) level during a lesson was conducted on each child in all four classes after the first year (Callesen, Klausen, Larsen, & Rasmussen, 1983). The present investigation dealt with the results from a final evaluation of the activity level of each child at the end of the 3-year period using, in principle, the same methods as during the investigation after the 1st year.

METHODS

The HR was recorded continuously during the physical-education lesson using the MEMOLOG system (Novo Diagnostic Systems, Novo Alle, DK-2880 Bagsvard, Denmark). The ECG signals were picked up by means of electrodes placed on the chest and stored in the MEMOLOG, which was set to sample the HR over 30-s periods. The heart rate could be followed continuously on a display, if desired, and the children were restricted very little during exercise by the HR recording. After the lesson the HR samples were transferred from the memory in the MEMOLOG into a computer (PDP-11) for later treatment. The HR samples were also transferred to an analog recorder, which provided a continuous printout of the HR in beats/min every 30 s of the lesson. In this way changes could be followed and identified with the different types of activities that were registered simultaneously with the HR sampling (see Figures 1 and 2).

A time study was conducted simultaneously with the HR recordings. The number of minutes during a physical-education lesson that the children were not being taught was noted, that is, the wasted minutes from a physiological point of view. The HR samples were taken during the lesson only when actual teaching was occurring (i.e., teaching lesson). Also noted was the amount of time the children were inactive (reclining, sitting, or standing). Part of the inactive time was devoted to receiving instructions from the teacher. On a day when the subject was not involved in school physical education, the maximal aerobic power ($\dot{V}O_2$max) of each child was determined indirectly from measurements of HR after 6-min submaximal exercise on a Monark bicycle ergometer (Klausen, Rasmussen, Glensgaard, & Jensen, 1985).

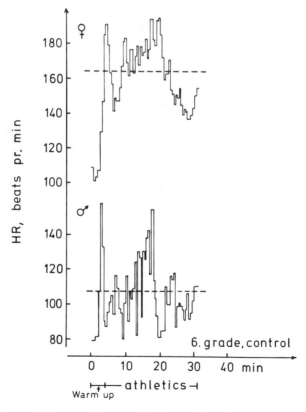

Figure 1 Printout of HRs sampled every 30 s in one girl and one boy during a physical-education lesson (45 min) with athletics. Note the difference in average HR (dotted line).

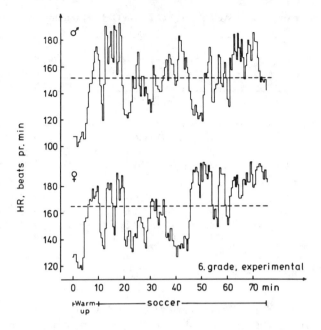

Figure 2 Printout of HRs sampled every 30 s in one girl and one boy during a double physical-education lesson (90 min) with soccer. Note the high average HR (dotted line) in both children.

RESULTS

In Table 1 the mean values (± 1 *SE*) are given for age, height, and weight for girls and boys in the four classes. By comparison with data from Tanner, Whitehouse, & Takaishi (1966), the mean heights of the girls and boys were slightly above the 75th percentile, and the mean weights were a little below the 75th percentile, indicating that the present children were somewhat taller and heavier than in the investigation of Tanner and his colleagues. On the other hand, the height-weight relationship was identical with data from a previous Danish investigation (Asmussen, Heebøll-Nielsen, & Molbech, 1959). At the same age, however, the present children are 3 to 5 cm taller than the children investigated in 1959. The average $\dot{V}O_2$max (ml/min/kg body weight) of girls and boys is also given in Table 1. These values are rather high compared with other investigations (Saris, Noordeloos, Ringnalda, van 't Hof, & Binkhorst, 1985), indicating that the aerobic fitness of the children in both the experimental and in the control classes was rather high.

In Figure 1, the HR recordings from two children attending the same physical-education lesson are shown. Note that, although similarities exist between the two curves, one child had an average HR of 164, whereas the other had a HR of only 107. In Figure 2, two HR recordings from a

Table 1   Mean Age, Height, Weight, and $\dot{V}O_2$max of Girls (F) and Boys (M) in Four Classes

Groups			Age (yr)	Height (cm)	Weight (kg)	$\dot{V}O_2$max (ml/min/kg)
6th Grade						
Experimental	F	(n = 11)	12.1 ± 0.04	154.9 ± 2.89	44.6 ± 3.40	50.2 ± 1.36
	M	(n = 7)	12.3 ± 0.13	156.2 ± 2.60	43.8 ± 2.08	54.4 ± 3.36
Control	F	(n = 7)	12.1 ± 0.06	158.1 ± 2.52	45.3 ± 2.62	51.4 ± 3.51
	M	(n = 11)	12.1 ± 0.08	156.0 ± 2.37	42.5 ± 2.25	61.8 ± 1.14
8th Grade						
Experimental	F	(n = 10)	14.0 ± 0.12	165.7 ± 1.97	53.3 ± 3.24	50.0 ± 2.63
	M	(n = 7)	14.5 ± 0.10	171.6 ± 3.77	56.6 ± 4.02	53.8 ± 3.80
Control	F	(n = 8)	14.6 ± 0.10	167.5 ± 1.49	54.4 ± 2.14	45.9 ± 1.58
	M	(n = 10)	14.6 ± 0.08	170.4 ± 3.24	55.6 ± 3.76	54.1 ± 4.14

Note.   All values are means ± *SE*.

double lesson (90-min lesson) are presented. Of special note is that the average HR for the girl as well as the boy was very high, which shows that integration of the two sexes in a physical-education lesson may be equally beneficial for girls and boys even if they are playing a traditional "boys' game" such as soccer.

In order to evaluate the training effect of the lesson, the average HR of each child was calculated. The means of these averages are shown in Table 2 for girls, boys, and girls plus boys in each class. No significant differences in mean HR could be observed either between the girls and the boys or between classes. However, the mean HR during the teaching lesson in the two sixth grades was about 10 beats/min higher than in the two eighth-grade classes. The HR tended to be higher during the warm-up period than during the rest of the lesson in the eighth grades, whereas the opposite was the case in the sixth grades.

The percentage distribution of all 30 s HR counts for each class separately is shown in Figures 3 and 4. The HR distribution is given for the teaching lesson, the warm-up period, and the teaching lesson minus the warm-up period. Mean HRs are indicated by dotted lines. The hatched and the double-hatched areas denote the HRs above 150 and 170, respectively. As can be seen, these areas are of the same magnitude in the experimental and in the control classes both in the sixth grades and in the eighth grades. However, these areas are much more pronounced in the figures from the sixth grade (see Figure 3) than in the figures from the eighth grade (see Figure 4). This further strengthens the impression that the intensity of exercise during a physical-education lesson all in all is higher in the sixth grades than in the eighth grades.

Shown in Figure 5 is the average percentage distribution of the active and passive periods during a physical-education lesson in the four classes. Also shown is the amount of time spent at a high activity level, that is,

Table 2   Mean HRs of Girls (F) and Boys (M), and F + M in Four Classes During Teaching Lesson, During Warm-Up, and During a Teaching Lesson Minus the Warm-Up Period

Groups			Mean HR (beats/min)		
			Teaching lesson	Warm-up	Teaching lesson minus warm-up
6th Grade					
Experimental	F	(n = 11)	134 ± 4.5	128 ± 3.4	135 ± 4.8
	M	(n = 7)	138 ± 7.8	130 ± 6.2	139 ± 8.0
	F + M		135 ± 4.0	129 ± 3.1	136 ± 4.2
Control	F	(n = 7)	140 ± 6.6	130 ± 7.7	142 ± 6.8
	M	(n = 11)	136 ± 5.6	136 ± 4.9	137 ± 6.6
	F + M		138 ± 4.2	134 ± 4.2	139 ± 4.7
8th Grade					
Experimental	F	(n = 10)	128 ± 3.8	135 ± 4.4	127 ± 4.3
	M	(n = 7)	129 ± 2.5	139 ± 4.5	127 ± 3.3
	F + M		128 ± 2.4	137 ± 3.1	127 ± 2.8
Control	F	(n = 8)	131 ± 3.4	133 ± 5.5	130 ± 3.3
	M	(n = 10)	126 ± 4.3	123 ± 4.6	127 ± 4.4
	F + M		128 ± 2.8	127 ± 3.6	128 ± 2.8

Note. All values are means ± *SE*.

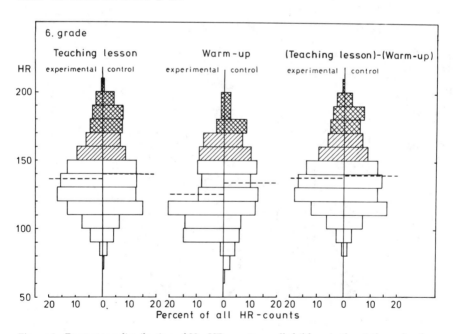

Figure 3   Percentage distribution of 30 s HR counts on all children in the sixth grades during the teaching lesson, the warm-up period, and the teaching lesson minus the warm-up period. Means are shown as dotted lines, and HRs above 150 and 170 are shown as single- and double-hatched areas, respectively.

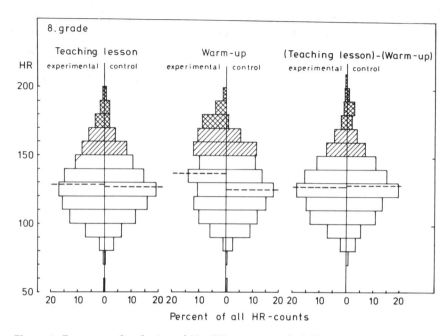

Figure 4 Percentage distribution of 30 s HR counts on all children in the eighth grade. For further explanation, see Figure 3.

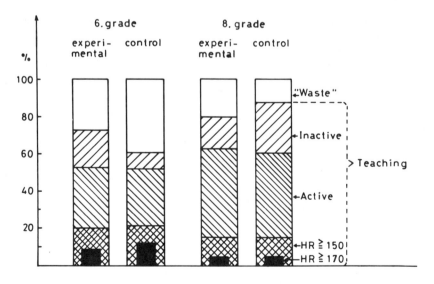

Figure 5 Average percentage distribution of active and inactive time during the physical-education lessons in the two experimental and the two control classes. "Waste" denotes time at the beginning and/or the end of the physical education lesson when the children are on their own (without teacher). In the "active" column are shown how much time (percentage of the total lesson) was spent with HR above 150 and 170, respectively.

with HRs over 150 and 170 beats/min, respectively. It appears that the eighth grades had less "waste" time than the sixth grades. This means, first of all, that the eighth-grade children spent less time in the locker room than the sixth grades. On the other hand, the eighth grades had more inactive time and less time with high level of activity than the sixth grades. Especially the time spent with a HR above 170 was very short in the eighth grades.

DISCUSSION

The HR or the ΔHR (HR during exercise minus HR at rest) is generally accepted to reflect the relative load on aerobic metabolic power and the circulatory system. However, the relation between HR and aerobic metabolic rate ($\dot{V}O_2$ l/min) depends to some extent on the muscle mass involved in the exercise. Thus, at a given submaximal $\dot{V}O_2$ the HR during arm exercise may be from 10 to 50 beats/min higher than during leg exercise. This difference increases as the $\dot{V}O_2$ increases (Asmussen & Hemmingsen, 1958; Clausen, Klausen, Rasmussen, & Trap-Jensen, 1973). Also the type of exercise will influence the relationship between HR and $\dot{V}O_2$; for instance, during an identical time period in which the same amount of work is performed, the mean HR during intermittent exercise will be higher than during continuous exercise (e.g., Åstrand, Åstrand, Christensen, & Hedman, 1960). The activities in the physical-education lesson in the four classes varied during the investigation period from gymnastics and athletics to basketball, volleyball, and soccer. Hence, both the variation of the HR and the mean HR during a lesson will be influenced by these factors. Because large muscle groups are activated in all physical-education activities, it seems justified to assume that HR reflects the children's relative work load during a lesson and thus may be used to evaluate the training effect on the circulatory system.

The average HR in Table 2 and the percentage distribution of the HR given in Figures 3 and 4 both show that the sixth graders on an average exercised at a higher relative work load than the eighth-grade classes. The difference between sixth and eighth grades was most pronounced in the teaching-lesson minus the warm-up period. This may indicate that the small children are more engaged in the activities offered to them in the physical-education lesson. However, a further analysis of the two sixth grades revealed that the relatively high average HRs in the two classes were due to soccer. In both classes the activity in the lessons alternated between soccer and athletics. The mean HR of all children tested during soccer was significantly higher ($p \leqslant .005$) than the mean HR of the children tested during athletics. In fact, the mean HR during athletics resembled the mean HR in the two eighth grades, who had volleyball, basketball, and gymnastics with apparatus. This was probably due mainly to two factors: (a) the ball games took place in relatively small gymnasiums, which limited the number of children who could play at the same time, and (b) the organization of athletics and gymnastics in groups with different activities implied that the actual performance time of each child was greatly reduced.

It is difficult to comment upon the possible training effect of physical-education lessons, because the work intensity (HR), which will improve aerobic power, depends principally upon physical fitness. The higher the fitness, the higher the work intensity needed to improve it. However, it seems that the activity level in the lessons was not the explanation for the relatively high fitness levels of the children, because no positive correlation could be found between the children's aerobic power (ml/min/kg) and the average HR during the lessons. In fact, a significant, negative correlation ($p \leqslant .05$) was found between the two variables for the boys in both the sixth and the eighth grades. The relatively high aerobic power of all the children in both the experimental and the control classes may therefore have been due to a high level of physical activity during leisure time rather than to the physical-education lessons offered to them at school. Thus, a questionnaire revealed that the children in the sixth and eighth grades on the average participated in various organized sports activities for 5 and 8 hours per week, respectively.

Because the physical fitness of the experimental and the control classes was virtually the same, it may therefore be concluded that most of the activities in the physical-education lessons did not provide an activity level that was sufficient to improve the fitness of the children in the experimental classes, even with an increase of the number of lessons per week from two to five. However, it must be pointed out that the main purpose of the present experiment has not been to increase the work intensity during the physical-education lessons, but rather to motivate the children for regular exercise when they leave school.

Acknowledgment

This investigation was supported by grants from The Danish Sports Research Council.

REFERENCES

Asmussen, E., Heebøll-Nielsen, K., & Molbech, S. (1959). Description of muscle tests and standard values of muscle strength in children. *Communications*, no. 5 (Suppl.). Hellerup, Denmark: The Testing and Observation Institute of the Danish National Association for Infantile Paralysis.

Asmussen, E., & Hemmingsen, I. (1958). Determination of maximum working capacity of different ages in work with the legs or with the arms. *Scandinavian Journal of Clinical and Laboratory Investigation*, **10**, 68-71.

Åstrand, I., Åstrand, P.-O., Christensen, E.H., & Hedman, R. (1960). Intermittent muscular work. *Acta Physiologica Scandinavica, 48*, 448-453.

Callesen, M., Klausen, K., Larsen, K., & Rasmussen, B. (1983). Evaluation of the activity level of school children during a physical education lesson. In R. Telema et al. (Eds.), *Research in school physical education* (pp. 210-216) (Reports of physical culture and health, no. 38). Jyväskylä, Finland.

Clausen, J.P., Klausen, K., Rasmussen, B., & Trap-Jensen, J. (1973). Central and peripheral circulatory changes after training of the arms or legs. *American Journal of Physiology, 225*, 675-682.

Klausen, K., Rasmussen, B., Glensgaard, L.K., & Jensen, O.V. (1985). Work efficiency of children during submaximal bicycle exercise. In R.A. Binkhorst, H.C.G. Kemper, & W.H.M. Saris (Eds.), *Children and exercise XI* (pp. 210-217) (International Series on Sport Sciences, Vol. 15). Champaign, IL: Human Kinetics.

Saris, W.H.M., Noordeloos, A.M., Ringnalda, B.E.M., van 't Hof, M.A., & Binkhorst, R.A. (1985). Reference values for aerobic power of healthy 4- to 18-year-old Dutch children: Preliminary results. In R.A. Binkhorst, H.C.G. Kemper, & W.H.M. Saris (Eds.), *Children and exercise XI* (pp. 151-160) (International Series on Sport Sciences, Vol. 15). Champaign, IL: Human Kinetics.

Tanner, J.M., Whitehouse, R.E., & Takaishi, M. (1966). Standards from birth, to maturity, for height, weight, height velocity, and weight velocity: British children, 1965. *Archives of Disease in Childhood, 41*, 454-476.

Behavioral Intentions and Activity of Children

Roy J. Shephard
University of Toronto, Toronto, Canada
Gaston Godin
Laval University, Quebec City, Canada

Previous studies of attitudes toward exercise have been hampered by failure to use an appropriate theoretical model. A model that has had some success in the explanation of other types of human behavior is that developed by Fishbein (1967). The applicability of this model to the question of physical activity was considered by examining the responses of a substantial population of adolescents in relation to their reported current activity, their previous interest in sports, the attitudes of their parents, and their socioeconomic status.

METHODS

The subjects were 698 students of both sexes, aged 12 to 14 years, attending Grades 7 to 9 at two junior high schools in the Toronto area. Both of the schools had required physical education programs for students of this age. Questionnaires were completed by all of the students and, where possible, data were also collected from their parents.

Specific questions concerning attitudes, normative beliefs, and behavioral intentions toward exercise were posed within the general framework of the Fishbein model. This model postulates that behavioral intention (BI) is proportional to the weighted sum of attitudes toward performance of a specified activity (Aact), and the subjective norm developed from the perceived beliefs of significant others (SN):

$$BI = W_1 (Aact) + W_2 (SN)$$

Aact in turn is based upon the summation of various beliefs about performing a specified activity, multiplied by the corresponding subjective evaluation of these outcomes:

$$\text{Aact} = \sum_{1}^{n} b_i \cdot e_i$$

Likewise, the subjective norm is the summed product of the perceived normative beliefs of significant others, multiplied by the motivation to comply with these beliefs:

$$\text{SN} = \sum_{1}^{n} NB_i \cdot MC_i$$

All students filled out previously validated questionnaires during a regular physical- and health-education class. In addition, 198 students were able to return questionnaires completed by both of their parents. The questions used in both the student and the adult instruments were developed as suggested by Ajzen and Fishbein (1980). The intentional component was assessed on a likely/unlikely scale by answering the question "At the present time I intend to do active sports or vigorous physical activities a few times a week during my leisure time."

The Aact measure summed responses from semantic differential scales with such end points as good/bad and exciting/boring. The behavioral beliefs examined the extent of agreement with such propositions as "I think that doing active sports or vigorous physical activities a few times a week during my leisure time would help me fill free time." The corresponding E item evaluated "helping you fill free time" on a good/bad scale. The subjective norm was tested by rating agreement with the proposition "I think that doing active sports or vigorous physical activities a few times per week, during my leisure time, is something that people who are most important to me believe I should do." Motivation to comply, in turn, was assessed by propositions such as "I would like to do active sports or vigorous activities the way my (significant others) think I should."

Physical-activity habits were assessed using a questionnaire developed by Godin (1983). An activity score was calculated for each individual, based on the weekly frequency of participation at each of three intensity levels corresponding to 9, 5, and 3 METS. In the case of the parents, behavior was expressed in the form of a discriminant coefficient. Students indicated their free-time physical activity between the ages of 6 and 11 years, whereas their parents also indicated free-time activity during adolescence (12 to 17 years). Students were finally asked to rate the current free-time activity of their mothers and fathers.

Socioeconomic status was assessed from the years of schooling, the nature of the final diploma or degree, and the reported occupation, using the classification of Blishen (1968).

RESULTS

The regression of intention to exercise on a combination of the Fishbein variables Aact and SN yielded an R^2 of 0.337 in the children and 0.423 in all subjects. Attitude carried a significant beta weight (see Table 1). Subjective norm added a small but still statistically significant beta weight; however, because of the number of combinations of variables to be examined, it was arbitrarily decided to delete this item, together with other items achieving a beta weight of less than 0.15.

After consideration of all possible variables, including two- and three-way interactions, the main items in the children remained attitude (with a beta weight of 0.531 ($p < .001$) and the two-way interaction between current physical activity habits and prior experience of physical activity (beta weight 0.200, $p < .001$). The implication of the interaction was that current exercise patterns explained more of the variation of intentions to exercise in children who had been active at an earlier age. The cumulative R^2 was 0.337 after inclusion of these two variables, and 0.381 ($F = 43.5$, $p < .01$) after inclusion of all external variables. The potential ceiling of R^2 after attenuation for the unreliability of measures was 0.451 for the two-element and 0.777 for the multiple-element model. Thus, the implication was that the extended models gave a better prediction of intentions to exercise than did the basic Fishbein model in this sample of adolescent children and their parents.

Table 1 Squared Multiple Correlations and Beta Weights for the Basic Fishbein Model and an Extended Model

Model	All children (N = 630) R^2	Children and parents (N = 192) R^2
Fishbein model	0.337** Aact = 0.582** SN = 0.140[a]	0.423** Aact = 0.582** SN = 0.152*
Fishbein model + all external variables	0.381** Aact = 0.531** Habit × prior experience = 0.200**	0.452** Aact = 0.559** Habit × prior experience = 0.234**

[a]Deleted from analysis, beta weight under 0.150.
*$p < .05$; **$p < .001$.

Multivariate analysis (MANOVA) of the subcomponents B and E provided details of the cognitive structure of exercise beliefs in the students (see Tables 2, 3, and 4). Low and high intenders differed significantly

Table 2 Scores for Exercise Beliefs and Evaluation of Associated Consequences Classified by Exercise Intentions[a]

Exercise belief	Degree of belief[b]		Evaluation of consequences[c]	
	Low intenders N = 132	High intenders N = 551	Low intenders N = 132	High intenders N = 551
Being healthy	1.04	1.56**	1.49	1.77**
Looking better	1.05	1.42**	1.36	1.68**
Being tired	0.72	0.99*	−0.11	0.66**
Feeling better	0.95	1.42**	1.45	1.71**
Filling free time	0.44	1.02**	0.70	1.26**
Being fun	0.41	1.33**	1.33	1.69**
Being physically fit	1.31	1.72**	1.28	1.78**

[a]Possible scores range from +2 to −2.
[b]Hotelling value ($F = 26.3$, df 7 and 675; $p < .001$).
[c]Hotelling value ($F = 24.4$, df 7 and 675; $p < .001$).
*$p < .01$; **$p < .001$.

Table 3 Scores for Exercise Beliefs and Evaluation of Associated Consequences Classified by Gender[a]

Exercise belief	Degree of belief[b]		Evaluation of consequences[c]	
	Boys N = 354	Girls N = 333	Boys N = 356	Girls N = 330
Being healthy	1.51	1.40*	1.70	1.75
Looking better	1.29	1.41*	1.51	1.73***
Being tired	1.03	0.83**	0.64	0.35***
Feeling better	1.36	1.29	1.67	1.65
Filling free time	0.95	0.86	1.17	1.12
Being fun	1.27	1.03***	1.69	1.55**
Being physically fit	1.63	1.64**	1.70	1.66

[a]Possible scores range from +2 to −2.
[b]Hotelling value ($F = 5.10$, df 7 and 679; $p < .001$).
[c]Hotelling value ($F = 8.19$, df 7 and 678; $p < .001$).
*$p < .05$; **$p < .01$; ***$p < .001$.

Table 4 Scores for Exercise Beliefs and Evaluation of Associated Consequences Among Children of Different School Grades[a]

Exercise belief	Degree of belief[b]			Evaluation of Consequences[c]		
	Grade 7 N = 222	Grade 8 N = 221	Grade 9 N = 245	Grade 7 N = 222	Grade 8 N = 224	Grade 9 N = 240
Being healthy	1.43	1.49	1.45	1.67	1.74	1.76
Looking better	1.33	1.38	1.34	1.55	1.63	1.67
Being tired	0.97	0.95	0.89	0.68**	0.39	0.45
Feeling better	1.33	1.35	1.30	1.64	1.66	1.69
Filling free time	1.00	0.91	0.81	1.18	1.15	1.12
Being fun	1.33***	1.10	1.03	1.61	1.65	1.63
Being physically fit	1.67	1.69	1.56*	1.67	1.74	1.65

[a]Possible scores range from +2 to −2.
[b]Hotelling value ($F = 2.05$, df 14 and 1356; $p < .05$).
[c]Hotelling value ($F = 1.77$, df 14 and 1352; $p < .05$).
*$p < .05$; **$p < .01$; ***$p < .001$.

with respect to each of the exercise beliefs and an evaluation of the associated outcomes. Gender differences were seen with respect to "looking better" (girls > boys), "being healthy," "being tired," and "having fun" (boys > girls). Students from Grade 7 evaluated "being tired" more positively than older students and also had a stronger belief that exercise was "fun"; students in Grade 9 had a lesser belief that exercise would help them to be physically fit.

Data from the subsample of children whose parents also completed questionnaires were comparable to figures obtained from the larger sample. The strength of the student's intention to exercise was positively correlated with the mother's intention to exercise ($p < .05$), the father's current physical activity ($p < .05$), and the family's socioeconomic status ($p < .05$).

DISCUSSION

If the behavior of these students had corresponded precisely with the Fishbein model, the only determinants of exercise intentions would have been attitude and subjective norm. In keeping with other critics of the basic model (Bentler & Speckart, 1979; Brinberg, 1979; Chassin et al., 1981; Saltzer, 1981; Stutzman & Green, 1982), an added contribution resulted from a number of other variables. It seems fair to point out that the Fishbein model was devised initially in the context of marketing—choosing a particular brand of toothpaste, a particular variety of synagogue, or a

specific political candidate. However, physical activity is a more fundamental human behavior; thus it may be influenced by an inherent drive
from hypothalamic activity centers or by conditioned responses accumu-
lated over a lifetime.

This research indicated that, with a greater prior experience of physical activity, the influence of current physical activity also becomes
stronger. These findings support the observations of Engstrom (1979),
Harris (1970), Sofranko and Nolan (1972), and Yoesting and Burkhead
(1973), all of whom stressed the importance of early physical activity to
adult leisure behavior. In theoretical terms, the preferred model of exercise behavior seems to be that of Triandis (1971), which considers past
experience in addition to attitudes and subjective norms.

CONCLUSIONS

Exercise behavior cannot be explained entirely by the marketing model
of Fishbein and associates. Account must be taken not only of attitudes
and subjective norms but also of external variables, particularly the individual's prior experience of exercise. During adolescence, prior experience of physical activity and parental attitudes toward exercise have a
significant influence upon intentions to exercise. These data support
attempts at the early socialization of children into physical activity. The
results further demonstrate that students with a high intention to exercise have strong positive beliefs about the value of physical activity.
Finally, despite recent progress in female emancipation, "looking better"
remains a prime motivator for girls, and account must be taken of such
gender differences when promoting an increase in physical activity.

REFERENCES

Ajzen, I., & Fishbein, M. (1980). *Understanding attitudes and predicting
social behaviour*. Englewood Cliffs, NJ: Prentice-Hall.

Bentler, P.M., & Speckart, G. (1979). Models of attitude-behavior relations. *Psychological Review*, **86**, 452-464.

Blishen, B.R. (1968). A socio-economic index for occupations in Canada.
In B.R. Blishen, F.E. Jones, K.D. Naegele, & J. Porter (Eds.), *Canadian
society, sociological perspectives* (pp. 741-753). Toronto: MacMillan.

Brinberg, D. (1979). An examination of the determinants of intention and
behavior: A comparison of two models. *Journal of Applied Social Psychology*, **9**, 560-575.

Chassin, L., Corty, E., Presson, C.C., Olshavsky, R.W., Besenberg, M., & Sherman, S.J. (1981). Predicting adolescents' intentions to smoke cigarettes. *Journal of Health and Social Behaviour*, **22**, 445-455.

Engström, L.-M. (1979). Physical activity during leisure time, a strategy for research. *Scandinavian Journal of Sports Sciences*, **1**, 32-39.

Fishbein, M. (1967). Attitudes and prediction of behaviour. In M. Fishbein (Ed.), *Readings in attitude theory and measurement* (pp. 477-492). New York: Wiley.

Godin, G. (1983). *Psychosocial factors influencing intentions to exercise of young students*. Unpublished doctoral thesis, University of Toronto, Toronto.

Harris, D.V. (1970). Physical activity history and attitudes of middle-aged men. *Medicine and Science in Sports*, **2**, 203-208.

Saltzer, E.B. (1981). Cognitive moderators of the relationship between behavioral intentions and behavior. *Journal of Personality and Social Psychology*, **41**, 260-271.

Sofranko, A.J., & Nolan, M.F. (1972). Early life experiences and adult sports participation. *Journal of Leisure Research*, **4**, 6-18.

Stutzman, T.M., & Green, S.B. (1982). Factors affecting energy consumption: Two field tests of the Fishbein-Ajzen model. *Journal of Social Psychology*, **117**, 183-201.

Triandis, H.C. (1971). *Attitude and attitude change*. New York: Wiley.

Yoesting, D.R., & Burkhead, D.L. (1973). Significance of childhood recreation experience on adult leisure behaviour: An explanatory analysis. *Journal of Leisure Research*, **5**, 25-36.

A Method for Assessing the Movement Activity of Normal Children and Children With Cardiovascular Diseases

Miroslav Kučera
Charles University, Prague, Czechoslovakia

Movement activity is a fundamental requisite of every primate (Eaton, 1983). It depends directly on several basic factors: heredity, the stage and trend of evolution, and on the conditions under which the individual is living. The assessment of the quality and quantity of movement is a prerequisite of any investigation of the evolution of an individual within the ontogenetic period (dez Chaplais & Macfarlane, 1984). In the hierarchy of these values, however, it is necessary to consider the priority of locomotion (Busby & Broughton, 1983), which is an important constituent of evolution-dynamics control.

Based on these principles, the investigation of the movement activity of children and its qualitative and quantitative evaluation has been introduced as a routine practice. These investigations are based on the results of the analysis of spontaneous movement activity (Kučera, 1985) as a tentative expression of the actual individual need for movement. The norms for these measurements apply to healthy children (see Figure 1). Childhood is characterized by a high need for activity, and this need is attenuated by secondary factors (Kupke, 1983; Rodano, 1985). The distribution of the population by the need for movement (see Figure 2) is affected, in the first place, by genetic conditions, but there are also other factors that must be taken into account.

Illness that affects movement manifestations (Butler, Engelbrecht, Major, Tait, Stallard, & Patrick, 1984) is among these secondary factors (Chiarenza, Papakostopoulos, Giordana, & Guareschi-Cazzullo, 1983), and the nature of these manifestations enables us to judge the characteristic or even the seriousness of the disease, and vice versa (Gillberg, 1985). These are the assumptions considered in introducing the screening method with regard to some psychiatric disorders (Kučera & Brunclíková, 1985), as well as for children under care for cardiovascular diseases.

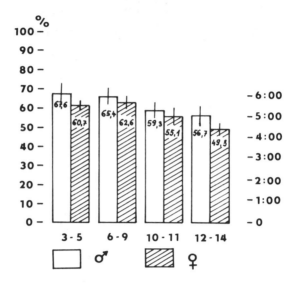

Figure 1 Spontaneous daily activity in children (aged 3 to 5, 6 to 9, 10 to 11, and 12 to 14) during 9 hr (in % and hours).

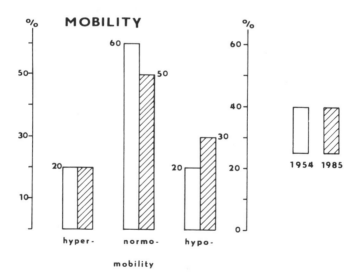

Figure 2 Distribution of the population (aged 4 years) by the need for movement.

METHOD

The examinations were carried out in the hospital gymnasium, where a total of 15 gymnastic apparatus and other equipment of various kinds was available. The examiners were located within viewing distance of the gymnasium area, but not inside it. The children, accompanied by their parents, were brought to the gymnasium and left there for at least 30 min to become accustomed to the environment. The examiners did not induce the children to move or influence them in any way. After two of these exposures, the actual evaluation began.

Hospitalized children underwent the preparatory stages of becoming familiar with the environment on the day before the evaluation, outpatient children immediately upon arriving at the clinic. The parents were first acquainted with the principle of the evaluation; the child was then fitted with the electrode and transmitter. It was advantageous to place the latter in the pocket of a vest or shorts. The transmitter and receiver system was then connected to the recorder, and the child was instructed "to do what you want." The parents were left close to the child and in some cases asked to play with him or her. In addition to the pulse rate (recorded twice every minute for a period of 10 s during the evaluation), the time of active movement was measured using a stopwatch or a video recorder (Rodano, 1985), and the activities and apparatus and other equipment used were recorded.

These observations were carried out for a period of 10 min during the morning. If the child fails to cooperate and refuses any activity whatsoever, the method cannot be used. In this particular evaluation, 2 boys had to be rejected completely and 12 boys and 14 girls were examined without recording the pulse rate, because they refused to have the electrodes applied.

This method was used to examine a total of 234 children born in 1980 (i.e., aged 4 years). These children were registered in district medical centers because of heart findings. The stages and types of the diseases varied considerably, and this particular evaluation was a part of a routine checkup. That is why the group included children with serious conditions as well as individuals affected minimally. The subjects were residents of the same geographical region. They were randomly selected with the aid of a computer system.

RESULTS

The values obtained were processed and the subjects divided into four groups on the basis of an index analysis. The first index reflected the activity and the time measurement as well as apparatus and equipment used (see Table 1), the second index the maximum, average, and minimum pulse rate (see Table 2). The classification system used in the analysis was derived from the data relating to healthy children.

Table 1 Activity Analysis for 4-Year-Old Boys and Girls

Group	HR_{ave}	HR_{max}	HR_{min}	Percentage increase of pulse rate[a]	Time of activity (min)	Types of activity	Types of apparatus
Boys							
I	< 150	< 170	< 130	< 145	< 50	< 3	< 3
II	< 160	< 190	< 145	< 155	< 70	< 6	< 5
III	> 161	> 191	> 146	> 156	> 71	> 7	> 6
Girls							
I	< 150	< 170	< 130	< 145	< 50	< 3	< 3
II	< 160	< 190	< 145	< 155	< 70	< 6	< 5
III	> 161	> 191	> 146	> 156	> 71	> 7	> 6

[a]Percentage increase of heart rate relative to heart rate at rest.

Table 2 Index Calculation

Activity index I_1	Pulse-rate index I_2
Low < 4	Low < 5
Medium 5 to 7	Medium 6 to 9
High > 8	High > 10

On being assigned the appropriate indexes, the subjects were divided into four groups:

1. Low I_1 and low I_2
2. High I_1 and low I_2
3. High I_1 and high I_2
4. Low I_1 and high I_2.

The number of subjects in each group according to the classification indexes I to IV were 24, 115, 58, and 3, respectively. Because only the high and low categories were used in the classification, an auxiliary index (I) was used to determine the medium group. This is the sum of the activity and pulse rate indexes, that is, $I = I_1 + I_2$. With classifications of I as up to 12, II as up to 15, and III as 16 and over, children with medium values could be assigned to one of these basic groups, mostly to Group II. Tables 3 and 4 show the heights, weights, and diagnoses of all examined children, and Tables 5, 6, and 7 show the values by individual groups

Table 3   Anthropometric Data for Children 4 Years Old

Group		Height (cm)				Weight (kg)		
	n	S	M	SD	n	S	M	SD
I	28	2842	101.5	5.7	27	433	16.03	2.37
II	111	11256.5	101.41	4.99	93	1477.7	15.88	2.38
III	54	5433	100.61	4.32	55	891	16.2	2.20
IV	3	304	101.33	3.51	3	47.5	15.83	7.63

Table 4   Diagnosis (%) for Children 4 Years Old

	Group I (n = 24)	Group II (n = 115)	Group III (n = 36)	Group IV (n = 3)
VSD	33.3	39.8	44.4	100.0
PS	20.8	6.4	11.1	
AS	12.5	10.8	8.3	
ASD	12.5	26.8	19.4	
CHD	4.1	0.9	8.3	
PAP	4.1	0	0	
TGA	4.1	3.7	0	
FOA	4.1	3.7	0	
PDA	0	3.7	0	
CA	0	1.8	0	
MGA	0	0	2.7	
DORV	0	0	2.7	

Note. VSD = ventricle septal defect; PS = pulmonary stenosis; AS = aortic stenosis; ASD = atrial septal defect; CHD = congenital heart disease; PAP = partial anomal pulmonary veins return; TGA = transposition of great arteries; MGA = malrotation of great arteries; FOA = foramen ovale appertum; DORV = double outflow tract.

Table 5   Kinds of Activity (*M* and *SD*) for 4 Groups of Children

Group	N	Active movement (%)	Kinds of activity	Apparatus used
I	24	53.68	4.37	3.07
		26.9	2.02	1.56
II	115	78.8	7.8	5.92
		11.8	1.96	1.52
III	58	81.0	8.73	6.46
		10.5	2.4	1.53
IV	3	87.13	2.33	2.0
		9.18	0.57	0

Table 6 Heart Rate per Minute (*M* and *SD*) for 4 Groups of Children

Group	N	M and SD	Maximal	Minimal	% increase M to the rest values
I	24	137.27	154.96	117.11	131.30
		11.62	11.50	9.8	11.22
II	115	148.7	167.5	128.7	133.2
		8.6	10.0	11.9	22.2
III	58	164.4	188.9	139.5	145.1
		5.7	10.7	12.9	11.2
IV	3	168.6	196.0	134.0	160.3
		9.35	3.46	9.16	14.7

Table 7 Values of Indexes (*M* and *SD*) for 4 Groups of Children

Group	N	I_1	I_2	I
I	24	4.96	4.37	9.22
		1.53	0.77	1.47
II	115	8.09	5.5	13.58
		1.05	1.37	2.03
III	58	8.51	9.29	17.89
		0.75	1.10	1.26
IV	3	9.33	5.00	14.6
		0.57	0	0.57

according to the above classification. Figure 3 illustrates the pulse rates of the individual groups. Figure 4 gives the total active time, number of activities, and apparatus and equipment used, Figure 5 the values for the separate indexes by group.

DISCUSSION

The investigation made use of the interrelation between spontaneous movement activity, the stage of evolution of the organism, and its health condition. Based on the analysis of movement manifestations, the children were divided into four groups with a view to the quality and quantity of movement activity. The first and fourth groups were children whose activity had been secondarily affected by disease, on the one hand, and by the manner of the movement regimen on the other. This is reflected, on the one hand, in the small selection of movement activities and consequently in the small response of the pulse rate and, on the other, in

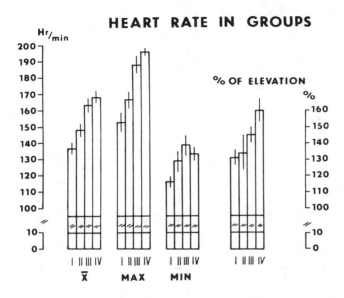

Figure 3   Pulse rate in testing groups.

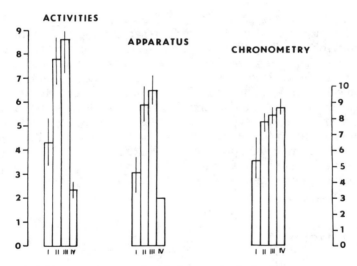

Figure 4   Activities, apparatus used, and chronometry in the 4 groups.

the large reaction of the circulation. Therefore, although the first group may not be cardiovascularly afflicted, their condition may be significantly affected by physical training. Also, the number of children assigned to the groups corresponds to this. The first group thus indicates that their cardiovascular apparatus is not being fully exploited. The fourth indicates, on the contrary, that it is working under maximum load. The appropriate clinical diagnoses and functional tests confirm this. The second group,

INDEX

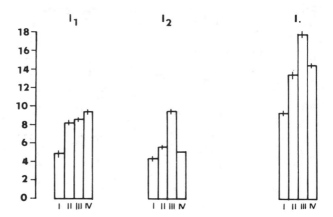

Figure 5   Values of indexes in the 4 groups.

with a large amount of activity but small pulse-rate response, is similar to the first but has a substantially larger reserve in the number of movement patterns. The third group corresponds to the norm for healthy children. The movement analysis in the gymnasium is advantageous because, for most children, it is not connected with the stressful environment of the medical room (Schmitt, 1984). The method of secret observation has a similar effect. All of the data must be recorded at the same time and analyzed comprehensively. Considering just one quantity might distort the examination considerably. The comparison of children with a cardiological diagnosis with a group of healthy children (Kučera & Brunclíková, 1985) indicates that the children of the first and fourth groups correspond to hypomobile population, the second to normomobile, and the third to hypermobile.

CONCLUSION

The analysis of spontaneous movement activity with an accurate expression of its quality and quantity in an environment suitable to the patient is an auxiliary method of determining the degree of affliction of a child at an early age. The movement manifestations depend directly not only on the stage of evolution and growth but also on the manner of education and the health condition.

REFERENCES

Busby, K.A., & Broughton, R.J. (1983). Waking ultradian rhythms of performance and motility in hyperkinetic and normal children. *Journal of Abnormal Child Psychology*, **11**, 431-442.

Butler, P., Engelbrecht, M., Major, R.E., Tait, J.H., Stallard, J., & Patrick, J. (1984). Physiological index of walking for normal children and its use as an indicator of physical handicapped. *Developmental Medicine and Child Neurology*, **26**, 607-612.

Chiarenza, G.A., Papakostopoulos, D., Giordana, F., & Guareschi-Cazzullo, A. (1983). Movement-related brain macropotentials during skilled performances: A developmental study. *Electroencephalography & Clinical Neurophysiology*, **56**, 373-383.

dez Chaplais, J., & Macfarlane, J.A. (1984). Review of 414 late walkers. *Archives of Diseases in Childhood*, **59**, 512-516.

Eaton, W.O. (1983). Measuring activity level with actometers: reliability, validity, and arm length. *Child Development*, **54**, 720-726.

Gillberg, C.I. (1985). Children with minor neurodevelopmental disorders. *Developmental Medicine and Child Neurology*, **27**, 3-16.

Kučera, M. (1985). Spontaneous physical activity in preschool children. In R.A. Binkhorst, H.C.G. Kemper, & W.H.M. Saris (Eds.), *Children and exercise XI* (pp. 175-182) (International Series on Sport Sciences, Vol. 15). Champaign, IL: Human Kinetics.

Kučera, M., & Brunclíková, J. (1985). Spontaneous physical activity in differential diagnosis of hyperkinetic syndrome in children. In *IVth European Congress of Sports Medicine* (Abstract) (p. 119). Prague: J.E. Purkyně Soc.

Kupke, I.R. (1983). Risikoindikatoren der Atherogenese im frühen Kindesalter. Untersuchungen von Kindern in Düsseldorfer Kindergärten. *Monatsschrift für Kinderheilkunde*, **131**, 502-508.

Rodano, R. (1985). Expectation of muscular force in training exercises. *Hungarian Review of Sports Medicine*, **26**, 3-14.

Schmitt, B.D.M. (1984). Preschoolers who refuse to be examined. *American Journal of Diseases of Children*, **138**, 443-446.

Changes in Physical Activity of Children Aged 6 to 12 Years

Wim H.M. Saris
University of Limburg, Maastricht, The Netherlands
Johannes W.H. Elvers
Martin A. van 't Hof
Robert A. Binkhorst
University of Nijmegen, Nijmegen, The Netherlands

Epidemiological studies of physical activity in childhood may provide insight in the etiology of problems related to inactivity as well as the possibilities of their prevention. The hypothesis has been proposed that physical activity in childhood determines the level of activity in later life. Therefore, information about daily physical-activity patterns in children is needed. Perhaps even more important are data about the natural history of activity patterns during childhood. What are the factors that dictate a change in lifestyle, including more sedentary habits? The present study was part of a health-education project (Saris, Binkhorst, Cramwinckel, Hegger, & König, 1982a) and was designed to describe the longitudinal development of daily physical activity in children 6 to 12 years of age. In 406 subjects at least four consecutive biannual measurements were made.

METHODS

From a controlled study concerning the effects of a health-education program, all 217 boys and 189 girls participating in the study for the entire 6 years, starting at the age of 6, were selected for data analyses. Because the results of the evaluation after 6 years of health education showed no differences between the experimental and the control groups for any of the variables, no distinction between groups was made in this analysis.

The data were collected every 2 years in the same month during the spring at the ages of 6, 8, 10, and 12 years. Body weight, height, and thickness of four skinfolds (biceps, triceps, subscapular, and suprailiac) were measured. Percentage of body fat was calculated using the Durnin and Womersley tables (1974). Aerobic power was measured with a continuous stepwise increased submaximal treadmill test (Saris, de Koning, Elvers, de Boo, & Binkhorst, 1984). Oxygen consumption was measured during the 2nd min of the workload. Simultaneous ECG was recorded from which heart rate was calculated. Expired air volume was measured by means of a dry gasmeter and the gas analysis was made with an O_2-paramagnetic analyzer and the CO_2 with an infrared analyzer.

Physical activity was measured in two different ways. First, from a questionnaire, completed by the teacher, the physical-activity score (PA score, %) was calculated (Saris, Binkhorst, Cramwinckel, van Waesberghe, & van der Veen-Hezemans, 1980). Second, total energy expenditure (TEE) was calculated from the 24-hr heart rate during a normal school day and the individual regression equation between heart rate (HR) and oxygen uptake. It was possible to calculate the energy spent above 50% of the aerobic power (EE > 50) as an indicator of more intense activities from the calculated maximal aerobic power, the individual regression equation, and the 24-hr heart rate profiles (Saris, 1982b).

The energy intake (EI) was recorded with the 24-hr recall technique. Specially trained dieticians visited the families at home. In most cases the parents gave information about what was eaten the day before. At the age of 12, the children were also actively involved in the interviews. The food consumption data were converted into energy intake using the computerized Dutch nutrient databank.

The data analysis involved two approaches. First, to evaluate the usefulness of the different variables in order to assess the stability of a child's rank over time (often referred to as "tracking"), the interperiod-correlation matrix was calculated. In general, such a matrix shows the magnitude of the measurement error that generally hinders an accurate prediction of the tracking of a variable. Second, in an attempt to assess some factors that may be of importance to the level of physical activity, the fractions of those subjects in the upper and lower strata (25%) of the EE > 50 distribution at the age of 12 years were calculated and compared to both extreme quartiles over the previous 6 years.

RESULTS

Average values for boys and girls of the anthropometric, aerobic-power, and physical-activity indices at the initial survey and the follow-up examinations are given in Table 1. There was a small increase in skinfold thickness with increasing age. Aerobic power per kilogram was more or less stable over the years, although there was a tendency for lower values at the age of 12 years, especially in girls. Mean HR values over 24 hr decreased steadily over the years, whereas the TEE increased by about 200 kcal every two years. This was not reflected by an increase of the EE > 50, which means that the relative contribution of the most intense activities to the daily TEE decreased. This observation was in agreement

Table 1 Anthropometric, Aerobic Power, Physical Activity Indices, and Energy Intake (Mean ± SD) for Various Examinations of the Same Group of Children

Variable	6 yr Boys	Girls	p	8 yr Boys	Girls	p	10 yr Boys	Girls	p	12 yr Boys	Girls	p
Body composition												
Weight (kg)	21.5± 3	21.3± 3		27.2 ± 4	26.3± 5	*	33.8± 6	33.5± 6		41.1± 8	42.9± 8	*
Height (cm)	118 ± 5	118 ± 5		131 ± 6	130 ± 6		142 ± 6	142 ± 7		154 ± 8	156 ± 7	*
Sum 4 skinfolds (mm)	22 ± 5	25 ± 6	***	22 ± 7	26 ± 8	***	24 ± 12	30 ± 11	***	26 ± 14	32 ± 12	***
Aerobic power												
$\dot{V}O_2max \cdot kg^{-1}$ ($ml \cdot kg^{-1} \cdot min^{-1}$)	55.4± 10	50.4± 9	***	57.0± 7	51.3± 8	***	58.8± 10	52.3± 9	***	55.3± 10	46.4± 8	***
Physical activity												
Mean HR day^{-1}	96.7± 7	98.4± 7	*	91.1± 8	92.9± 7	*	87.3± 8	89.5± 7	*	84.6± 7	87.7± 8	**
TEE (kcal·day^{-1})	1770 ±257	1618 ±241	***	2018 ±279	1832 ±263	***	2556 ±390	2017 ±366	***	2413 ±409	2320 ±390	**
EE > 50 (kcal·day^{-1})	335 ±208	256 ±245	*	309 ±235	239 ±209	*	364 ±234	211 ±232	**	259 ±184	218 ±174	*
PA score (%)	64 ± 18	57 ± 15	***	60 ± 10	51 ± 11	***	60 ± 12	50 ± 11	***	58 ± 10	47 ± 9	***
Nutrition												
EI (kcal·day^{-1})	1776 ±441	1621 ±401	***	1991 ±486	1814 ±468	***	2016 ±461	1771 ±468	***	2338 ±606	2140 ±600	***

Note. Boys n = 217; girls n = 189; p = probability of student.
*p < .05; **p < .01; ***p < .0001.

with the PA score. Energy intake had an increase with age comparable with TEE. However, at the age of 10 the expected EI was not present. Possible explanations for these lower values were given in an earlier publication (Saris, 1982b).

In general, girls had significantly lower values for aerobic power, physical activity indices, and EI and significantly higher values for skinfold thicknesses and mean 24-hr HR. These sex differences were consistent over the years. Table 2 presents the interperiod correlation matrix of some important variables, in order to assess the magnitude of the measurement error and the intraindividual variability. Although no objective criteria exist for the evaluation of the variables, it was suggested by Bloom (1964) that a minimum level of consistency is represented by a correlation of .50 or higher over a period of 1 year or more. According to this criterion, body composition can be classified as a stable trait. Aerobic power also just satisfies this criterion. However, the indices of daily physical activity can be considered as unstable traits.

Van 't Hof (1985) suggested that with a correlation lower than .70 to .80 (using a fictitious zero-time-lag point) the error of measurement is rela-

Table 2   The Interperiod Correlation Matrix (r) for the Body Composition, Aerobic Power, and Physical Activity Measurements

Periods	Weight			Sum of skinfolds		
2 years	0.95	0.96	0.93	0.80	0.88	0.86
	(6 vs 8)	(8 vs 10)	(10 vs 12)			
4 years	0.84	0.87		0.71	0.71	
	(6 vs 10)	(8 vs 12)				
6 years	0.78			0.60		
	(6 vs 12)					
	Aerobic power			PA score		
2 years	0.49	0.50	0.58	0.40	0.44	0.46
4 years	0.49	0.55		0.38	0.47	
6 years	0.56			0.35		
	TEE			EI		
2 years	0.40	0.42	0.39	0.25	0.31	0.23
4 years	0.37	0.30		0.22	0.28	
6 years	0.35			0.20		
	EE > 50					
2 years	0.14	0.15	0.11			
4 years	0.15	0.18				
6 years	0.13					

Note. The age comparisons in parentheses under the weight matrix apply to all other matrices.

tively high; therefore, tracking over the years is not possible. Especially for the physical activity indices this was the case. Therefore, data analyses to assess the stability of a child's rank in the distribution over time are difficult with the traditional statistical techniques. Liu, Stamler, Dyer, McKeever, and McKeever (1978) suggested another approach in order to reduce the impact of a large intraindividual variation. Grouping of data on the basis of intervals of the variable reduces the level of intraindividual variation within the specific groups. Examination of the extreme groups on the basis of the mean results may reveal some relationships between variables over the years.

In Tables 3 and 4 such an approach was chosen for EE > 50. Boys and girls were ranked according to a low (1st < 25th percentile) or high (4th > 75th percentile) level of EE > 50 at the age of 12 years. The mean results of the same quartile groups at the times of the previous measurements are given in the tables. For the sake of a clearer overview, only mean results are given. A similar pattern was found for the differences between the extreme EE > 50 groups for boys and girls. Differences in EE > 50 levels at the age of 12 years were tracked backward over 4 years. No differences were found in other physical-activity variables over the years. Of interest was the relationship to aerobic power. The groups of boys and girls with a high EE > 50 had a significantly lower aerobic power. This difference was consistent over the years. Furthermore, no differences were found in body composition indices in any of the measurements in the two extreme EE > 50 groups.

DISCUSSION

A follow-up study of physical activity indices and some other important factors that may influence the activity level was completed in order to find out whether the origin of inactivity can be traced in childhood and whether future inactive adolescents or adults can be identified early in life.

Repeated measurements of a variable such as EE > 50 with a large intraindividual variation and measurement error pose analytical problems. The predictive values of all the physical activity indices including EI were relatively low, as can be seen from the interperiod correlation matrix. This lack of consistency was inherent in the measurement over only 1 day. Theoretically, repeated measurements contribute to a reduction of intraindividual variation. However, from a practical point of view, most authors are skeptical about the small improvement of the predictive value related to the invested efforts (Beaton et al., 1979; Hofman, 1983).

Mostly the estimates of variables such as those in this study are rather imprecise compared to measurements of weight and height. Therefore, it was not surprising that a number of studies have failed to show relationships between physical activity and other variables such as EI (Montoye, 1985). It should also be apparent that to conclude that no relationship

Table 3 Mean Anthropometric, Aerobic Power, and Physical Activity Indices for Boys in Relation to EE > 50 Levels at the Age of 12 Years

Variable	Quartiles											
	6 yr			8 yr			10 yr			12 yr		
	1st[a]	4th[b]	p[c]	1st	4th	p	1st	4th	p	1st	4th	p
Body composition												
Weight (kg)	21.4	21.6	*	27.4	27.4		33.9	33.7		41.5	41.2	
Length (cm)	118	118		132	131		142	141		155	154	
Sum 4 skinfolds (mm)	21	22		22	21		24	22		25	24	
Aerobic power												
$\dot{V}O_2$max · kg^{-1} (ml · kg^{-1}min^{-1})	59	56	*	58	56	*	59	56	**	57	54	**
Physical activity												
TEE (kcal · day^{-1})	1676	1777		1972	2056		2196	2265		2308	2664	*
EE > 50 (kcal · day^{-1})	367	335		219	360	***	319	440	**	138	706	***
PA score (%)	64	63		60	60		59	60		57	59	
Nutrition												
EI (kcal · day^{-1})	1825	1754		1868	1935		1987	2097		2312	2360	

[a]Lowest 25% group; [b]highest 25% group; [c]Wilcoxon's signed rank test.
*$p < .05$; **$p < .01$; ***$p < .001$.

Table 4   Mean Anthropometric, Aerobic Power, and Physical Activity Indices for Girls in Relation to EE > 50 Levels at the Age of 12 Years

Variable	6 yr			8 yr			10 yr			12 yr		
	1st[a]	4th[b]	p[c]	1st	4th	p	1st	4th	p	1st	4th	p
Body composition												
Weight (kg)	21.3	21.3		26.5	26.3		33.4	33.6		42.8	42.9	
Length (cm)	118	118		130	130		141	142		155	156	
Sum 4 skinfolds (mm)	25	26		26	26		28	30		31	31	
Aerobic power												
$\dot{V}O_2max \cdot kg^{-1}$ ($ml \cdot kg^{-1}min^{-1}$)	52	48	**	53	50	**	53	52	*	49	46	**
Physical activity												
TEE ($kcal \cdot day^{-1}$)	1646	1609		1824	1830		2027	2012		2169	2567	
EE > 50 ($kcal \cdot day^{-1}$)	298	321	**	150	273	**	198	322	**	29	624	***
PA score (%)	59	60		48	50		48	50		47	48	
Nutrition												
EI ($kcal \cdot day^{-1}$)	1618	1633		1901	1856		1683	1771		1967	2116	

Quartiles

[a]Lowest 25% group; [b]highest 25% group; [c]Wilcoxon's signed rank test.
*$p < .05$; **$p < .01$; ***$p < .001$.

exists within the population in such studies would be erroneous (Frank, Berenson, & Webber, 1978). Selection of a homogeneous group is an approach that can reduce the impact of the large intraindividual variation when only 1-day observations are available.

Using a ranking procedure (see Tables 3 and 4), there are two interesting findings to be considered in more detail. For both groups of boys and girls, EE > 50 was significantly inversely related to aerobic power. Second, there was no relationship to body fatness.

In a review of risk indicators for cardiovascular disease in relation to physical activity, Montoye (1985) concluded that of the well-known indicators body fatness is the most prominent one related to physical activity. Fat children are less active than lean children. In this study, physical activity was defined as the energy expenditure spent above a relative level (50%) of the individual aerobic power. The literature has established that the percentage of body fat is inversely related to physical fitness. Because no relation was found in this study, it is suggested that EE > 50 is a measure of physical activity independent from percentage of body fat. This may also explain the finding that EE > 50 is inversely related to aerobic power. If the physical fitness of a child is low, the heart rate for a given work load is higher than for a physically fit child. Therefore, the relative contribution of EE > 50 to the TEE is higher in children with a low aerobic power. However, the TEE does not differ essentially between groups of children with a high or low aerobic power, as was shown by Saris (1982b).

If this observation of higher EE > 50 for children with a low aerobic power is confirmed, our ideas about physical activity in relation to fitness of children must be changed. Relative to their capacity, unfit children seem to be even more active than fit children.

In support of the usefulness of the TEE and EE > 50 indices as indicators of physical activity, the findings in Table 1 are of interest. Boys and girls differed in the levels of aerobic power, and in this situation TEE and EE > 50 also differed significantly. Boys had a higher TEE and EE > 50. These findings were confirmed by the results from the PA score and EI over the years. Weight and especially lean body mass may play an important role in this situation. Boys had a higher lean body mass over the years.

The absolute amount of energy spent at over 50% of the aerobic power was constant over the years. Because TEE increased with age, one can conclude that the contribution of EE > 50 to the TEE decreased over the years. On the other hand, the period of time that the child had an activity level higher than 50% of the individual aerobic power was in general the same over the years because EE > 50 and aerobic power per kilogram did not change. In this situation the observations of the teachers were interesting. They gave a lower score for daily physical activity over the years for boys and girls. Relative to the TEE this finding was in agreement with the EE > 50 index. Also, the differences between boys and girls were the same for the PA score and EE > 50.

The sex difference and observational changes in physical activity were in agreement with findings in the literature for older age groups (Ilmarinen

& Rutenfranz, 1980; Verschuur & Kemper, 1985). However, the finding that the absolute level of EE > 50 as an index of intense activities was constant over the years has not been reported up to this time.

Acknowledgment

This study was supported by a grant of the Dutch preventive foundation.

REFERENCES

Beaton, G.H., Milner, J., Corey, P., McGuire, V., Cousins, M., Stewart, E., de Ramos, M., Hewitt, D., Grambsch, P.V., Kassim, N., & Little, J.A. (1979). Sources of variance in 24-hour dietary recall data: Implications for nutrition study design and interpretation. *American Journal of Clinical Nutrition, 32*, 2546-2559.

Bloom, B.S. (1964). *Stability and change in human characteristics.* New York: Wiley.

Durnin, J.V.G.A., & Womersley, J. (1974). Body fat assessed from total body density and its estimation from skinfold thickness. *British Journal of Nutrition, 37*, 77-86.

Frank, G.C., Berenson, G.S., & Webber, L.S. (1978). Dietary studies and the relationship of diet to cardiovascular disease risk factor variables in 10-year-old children—The Bogaluso Heart Study. *American Journal of Clinical Nutrition, 31*, 328-340.

Hofman, A. (1983). *Blood pressure in childhood.* Epidemiological probes into the etiology of high blood pressure. Unpublished doctoral dissertation, Erasmus University, Rotterdam.

Ilmarinen, J., & Rutenfranz, J. (1980). Longitudinal studies of the changes in habitual physical activity of school children and working adolescents. In K. Berg & B.O. Eriksson (Eds.), *Children and Exercise IX* (pp. 149-159) (International Series on Sport Sciences, Vol. 10). Baltimore: University Park Press.

Liu, K., Stamler, J., Dyer, A., McKeever, J., & McKeever, P. (1978). Statistical methods to assess and minimize the role of intra-individual variability in obscuring the relationship between dietary lipids and serum cholesterol. *Journal of Chronic Diseases, 31*, 399-418.

Montoye, H.J. (1985). Risk indicators for cardiovascular disease in relation to physical activity in youth. In R.A. Binkhorst, H.C.G. Kemper, & W.H.M. Saris (Eds.), *Children and exercise XI* (pp. 3-25) (International Series on Sport Sciences, Vol. 15). Champaign, IL: Human Kinetics.

Saris, W.H.M., Binkhorst, R.A., Cramwinckel, A.B., Hegger, W.G., & König, K.G. (1982a). The development of a health education program for schoolchildren. *Tijdschrift voor Sociale Geneeskunde*, **60**, 680-684.

Saris, W.H.M., Binkhorst, R.A., Cramwinckel, A.B., van Waesberghe, F., & van der Veen-Hezemans, A.M. (1980). The relationship between working performance, daily physical activity, fatness, blood lipids, and nutrition in schoolchildren. In K. Berg & B.O. Eriksson (Eds.), *Children and exercise IX* (pp. 166-174) (International Series on Sport Sciences, Vol. 10). Baltimore: University Park Press.

Saris, W.H.M., de Koning, F., Elvers, J.W.H., de Boo, T., & Binkhorst, R.A. (1984). Estimation of W_{170} and maximal oxygen consumption in young children by different treadmill tests. In J. Ilmarinen & I. Välimäki (Eds.), *Children and sport. Paediatric work physiology* (pp. 86-92). Berlin, New York: Springer-Verlag.

Saris, W.H.M., Noordeloos, A.M., Cramwinckel, A.B., Boeyen, I., Elvers, J.W.H., v. Veen, M., König, K.G., & Binkhorst, R.A. (1982b). Aerobic power, daily physical activity and some cardio-vascular disease risk indicators in children ages 6-10 years. In W.H.M. Saris (Ed.), *Aerobic power and daily physical activity in children with special reference to methods and cardio-vascular risk indicators* (pp. 153-176). Thesis. Meppel, The Netherlands: Krips Repro.

van 't Hof, M.A. (1985). The organization of developmental studies. In R.A. Binkhorst, H.C.G. Kemper, & W.H.M. Saris (Eds.), *Children and exercise XI* (pp. 224-232) (International Series on Sport Sciences, Vol. 15). Champaign, IL: Human Kinetics.

Verschuur, R., & Kemper, H.C.G. (1985). Habitual physical activity in Dutch teenagers measured by heart rate. In R.A. Binkhorst, H.C.G. Kemper, & W.H.M. Saris (Eds.), *Children and exercise XI* (pp. 194-202) (International Series on Sport Sciences, Vol. 15). Champaign, IL: Human Kinetics.

Daily Physical Activity and Some Health Indicators in Young Workers

Juhani Ilmarinen
Institute of Occupational Health, Helsinki, Finland
Joseph Rutenfranz
Hannegret Kylian
Christian Hussels
Felix M. Klimmer
Peter Knauth
Institute of Occupational Health,
Dortmund, Federal Republic of Germany

On leaving school or technical college, most young people in Europe go directly into full-time employment. This change in daily routine and the new, unfamiliar demands of professional work can have several effects on both lifestyle and health. In an earlier study (Ilmarinen & Rutenfranz, 1980), it was shown that a dramatic decrease in daily physical activity occurred when most people changed from school to work. The aim of this study was to find out the possible effects of changes in daily physical activity on health among young workers.

METHODS

A total of 37 male apprentices, whose mean age was 18.5 years, participated in the study. Their work was, for example, as fitters, toolmakers, turners, and technicians involved in coordinated motor and sensory functions. The characteristics of the subjects are given in Table 1. Heart rate (HR) recordings with a portable Howel Corder cassette recorder (Rutenfranz et al., 1977) were carried out during both work and leisure time. Activities during HR recordings were written in a diary (Edholm, 1966). Blood pressure was measured sitting at rest, and total cholesterol was analyzed by a standardized method using venous blood samples.

A subgroup of 19 apprentices participated in submaximal bicycle exercise tests. The tests were carried out with three stepwise-increasing work

Table 1 Characteristics of Male Apprentices

	Age (yr)	Height (cm)	Weight (kg)	Fat (%)	VC (l)
M	18.54	178.15	70.07	17.89	4.33
SD	0.99	7.30	10.82	6.63	0.81
n	37	37	37	37	37

Note. Apprentices were precision mechanics (n = 8); maintenance engineers (n = 3); fitters (machine, n = 2); toolmakers (n = 2); turners (n = 4); technicians (communication engineering, n = 10); electricians (telecommunications engineering, n = 8).

loads, each load lasting 6 min without any rest between loads. The highest load corresponded to 85% of the estimated maximal HR of the subjects (Lange Andersen, Shephard, Denolin, Varnauskas, & Masironi, 1971). The VO_2max was calculated according to the relationship between HR and work load (Lindemann, Rutenfranz, Mocellin, & Sbresny, 1973). The body fat and lean body mass (LBM) were calculated from the triceps and subscapular skinfolds (Parízková, 1974).

Daily physical activities, including journeys to and from work, indoor and outdoor pursuits, and sport activities of the 19 apprentices were assessed by retrospective recalls, using a standardized questionnaire. The subjects were asked about their engagement in different activities during the previous year. The activity scores were calculated by summarizing the product of hours/years and MET (multiple of resting metabolic rate). This procedure is described in more detail by Ilmarinen and Rutenfranz (1980). Smoking habits (cigarettes/day) were ascertained before the exercise test.

RESULTS

The cumulative distribution of minutes in different HR classes showed that the apprentices were somewhat more active during their leisure time than at work (see Figure 1). However, the difference was small, with HR being higher than 100 beats/min^{-1} for 12% of leisure time (47 min daily per person) and 8% of the work time (42 min daily per person). Heart rates higher than 120 beats/min^{-1} were found only during leisure time. The number of minutes spent at different activity levels indicated that during work an average of 8 min was spent at MET levels higher than 5 times the basal metabolic rate. During leisure time, an average of 42 min was spent at intensities higher than 5 METs and about 12 min at intensities higher than 8 METs (see Figure 2).

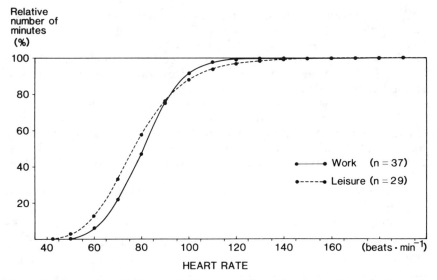

Figure 1 Cumulative distribution of minutes in different heart rate classes during work and during leisure time of 37 male apprentices. The curve of work time is based on a total of 20,194 minutes and the curve of leisure time on 14,641 minutes, respectively.

DAILY PHYSICAL ACTIVITY

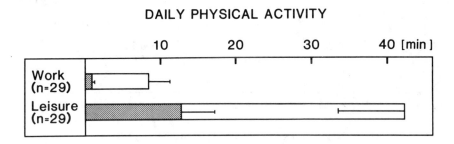

Figure 2 Average (± *SE*) number of minutes during work and leisure time in different levels of physical activity of 29 apprentices. The clear area □ represents the total time spent in activities with intensities higher than 5 METs. The shaded area ▨ represents the total time spent in activities with intensities higher than 8 METs.

The subgroup of 19 apprentices was divided into two groups according to their scores for leisure-time physical activity. Individual scores lower and higher than the mean (1,393) of the subgroup were used as the criterion. The group with "low" leisure-time physical activity had highly significantly ($p < .001$) lower scores ($M = 955 \pm 260$) than the group with "high" leisure-time physical activity ($M = 2,145 \pm 792$). Systolic and diastolic blood pressure were largely on the same level in both groups. The total cholesterol seemed to be somewhat lower in groups with "high" than with "low" physical activity, and the same tendency was found in body fat. The differences between the groups, however, were not statistically significant (see Table 2). In smoking habits (cigarettes/day), about two thirds were nonsmokers in both groups.

Because the daily physical activity score was a total of all kinds of sport activities, the significance of different sports on health indicators was studied in more detail. Therefore, the subjects were divided in two groups, nonaerobic and aerobic, according to the type of sport they played. The absolute and relative maximal oxygen consumption was significantly higher in the aerobic sport group than in the nonaerobic group (see Table 3). Systolic and diastolic blood pressure seemed to be somewhat higher in the aerobic sport group than in the nonaerobic group, but the differ-

Table 2   Total Cholesterol and Body Fat in Relation to the Total Scores of Leisure-Time Physical Activity

Leisure-time physical activity group[a]		Total cholesterol (mg %)	Fat (%)
Low	M	196.6	17.6
	SD	39.4	7.6
	n	12	12
High	M	179.6	15.9
	SD	31.1	3.0
	n	7	7
All	M	190.3	17.0
	SD	36.6	6.2
	n	19	19

[a]Mean scores—low = 955 ± 260; high = 2,145 ± 792 ($p < .001$).

Table 3   Maximal Oxygen Consumption and Type of Sport

Type of sport		$\dot{V}O_2max$ ($l \cdot min^{-1}$)	($ml \cdot kg^{-1} \cdot min^{-1}$)	($ml \cdot LBM^{-1} \cdot min^{-1}$)
Nonaerobic	M	2.66	39.5	49.0
	SD	0.52	7.2	9.7
	n	11	11	11
Aerobic[a]	M	3.39*	49.3**	57.5*
	SD	0.76	6.3	7.6
	n	8	8	8

[a]Criteria for inclusion under aerobic-sport activities (type of sport): football, running over 400 m, cycling, rowing, swimming, skiing, canoeing, jogging; member of a sports club and participating in competitive aerobic sport.
*$p < .05$; **$p < .01$.

ences were not significant. Total cholesterol tended to be lower in the aerobic than in the nonaerobic group (see Table 4). The mean body fat of 14.2 ± 2.1% in the aerobic group was significantly lower ($p < .05$) than the corresponding value of 19.0 ± 7.5% of the nonaerobic group. The mean vital capacity was higher ($p < .05$) in the aerobic group (4.6 ± 0.8) than in the nonaerobic group (3.9 ± 0.7).

The number of minutes/day in activity classes over 5 METs during work was an average 13.8 min in the aerobic and 5.5 min in the nonaerobic group ($p < .05$). Only a few minutes in activity over 8 METs were noted in both groups (see Table 5). No significant differences were found between the groups in the number of minutes over 5 METs during leisure time.

To study the importance of the $\dot{V}O_2$max on other health indicators, the subgroup of 19 apprentices was divided into two groups according to the

Table 4 Blood Pressure and Total Cholesterol of Apprentices According to Type of Sport

Type of sport		Systolic (mmHg)	Diastolic (mmHg)	Cholesterol (mg %)
Nonaerobic	M	117.1	71.4	201.6
	SD	7.6	7.1	41.4
	n	11	11	11
Aerobic	M	120.6	74.4	174.8*
	SD	6.2	4.2	23.0
	n	8	8	8

*$p = .058$.

Table 5 Mean Number of Minutes/Day in Activities Higher Than 5 and 8 METs[a] During Work According to Type of Sport

Sport activity		Min spent in activities higher than 5 METs	Min spent in activities higher than 8 METs
Nonaerobic	M	5.5	0.9
	SD	3.0	0.6
	n	11	11
Aerobic	M	13.8*	2.0
	SD	3.8	1.0
	n	8	8

[a]Based on HR recordings; activities classified according to Edholm (1966).
*$p < .05$; Mann-Whitney test.

mean $\dot{V}O_2$max in ml $\cdot$ kg^{-1} $\cdot$ min^{-1}. The higher 50% of the apprentices had mean $\dot{V}O_2$max of 49.9 $\pm$ 5.1 ml $\cdot$ kg^{-1} $\cdot$ min^{-1}, which was significantly higher ($p < .001$) than the value of 36.6 $\pm$ 4.6 of the lower 50% of the youths. The results of systolic and diastolic blood pressure did not differ significantly between these two groups, although the values of the greater $\dot{V}O_2$max group were slightly higher (SBP 120.0 $\pm$ 5.8 mmHg, DBP 74.5 $\pm$ 4.4 mmHg) than the corresponding values of the smaller $\dot{V}O_2$max group (SBP 117.0 $\pm$ 8.4 mmHg, DPB 70.6 $\pm$ 7.3 mmHg). The total cholesterol was significantly lower in the higher $\dot{V}O_2$max group than in the lower $\dot{V}O_2$max group. The same tendency was found in the percentage of body fat (see Table 6). The smoking habits seemed also to be different.

Table 6 Total Cholesterol and Body Fat Related to the $\dot{V}O_2$max (ml $\cdot$ kg^{-1} $\cdot$min^{-1})

$\dot{V}O_2$max (ml $\cdot$ kg^{-1} $\cdot$ min^{-1})		Total cholesterol (mg %)	Fat (%)
Lower[a] 50	M	205.1*	19.1
	SD	44.0	7.2
	n	9	9
Higher[b] 50	M	177.0	15.1
	SD	23.3	4.8
	n	10	10

[a]Mean $\dot{V}O_2$max of lower 50% (36.6 $\pm$ 4.6 ml $\cdot$ kg^{-1} $\cdot$ min^{-1}).
[b]Mean $\dot{V}O_2$max of higher 50% (49.9 $\pm$ 5.1 ml $\cdot$ kg^{-1} $\cdot$ min^{-1}) ($p < .001$).
*$p < .05$.

The greater $\dot{V}O_2$max group contained 1 smoker and 9 nonsmokers, whereas the smaller $\dot{V}O_2$max group included 5 smokers and 4 nonsmokers.

The daily physical activity of the two groups differed both during work and leisure time. The group with greater $\dot{V}O_2$max had in leisure time an average of about 35 min/day at the level of 5 METs or more and about 7 min/day at the level of 8 METs or more. The corresponding values of the group with smaller $\dot{V}O_2$max were 18 min (> 5 METs) and 2 min (> 8 METs). During work, the first group had an average of about 11 min and the latter group about 6 min in the level of 5 METs (see Figure 3).

DISCUSSION

The results showed that the apprentices who were more active in their leisure time, who practiced aerobic sport, and who had higher $\dot{V}O_2$max than the average had superior health indicators, such as lower total cholesterol, lower percentage of body fat, and were less likely to smoke.

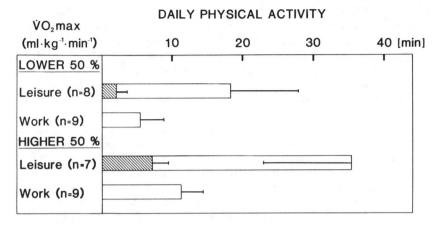

Figure 3 Average ($\pm$ *SE*) number of minutes during leisure time and work of apprentices, who have been divided in two groups according to the $\dot{V}O_2$max ml • kg^{-1} • min^{-1} (lower 50%, higher 50%). For a detailed explanation, see Figure 2.

The most effective predictor of good health was the $\dot{V}O_2$max. It is apparent that the scores for leisure-time physical activity do not differentiate among many miscellaneous activities, and the effects on health indicators are therefore difficult to ascertain by questionnaire. A better way seems to be the careful analysis of aerobic sport activities, although it was not possible to know if the aerobic activities had been carried out with the necessary intensity.

The $\dot{V}O_2$max, however, is an objective output of aerobic activities, and it seems to be therefore relevant to study the health effects of physical activities among young adults (mean age 18.5 ± 0.99 years), who have finished the growth period. Among children, the risk indicators of coronary heart disease and $\dot{V}O_2$max were not consistently related, according to Verschuur, Kemper, and Besseling (1984) and Montoye (1985), because the differences among the subjects in physical activity, health indicators, and $\dot{V}O_2$max were rather small. The present group of apprentices included both physically passive and active subjects and the $\dot{V}O_2$max varied remarkably. At the age of 19 to 24 years, the physical activity habits seemed to be similar to those of the general population (Oja, Vuori, & Urponen, 1984), which suggested that the apprentices had already established their lifestyles in regard to habitual physical activity.

The health status of the apprentices seemed to be better than that of adults whose work also involved coordinated motor and sensory functions. In a group of 37 adults, aged on the average 42.5 years, the systolic and diastolic blood pressure and total cholesterol were significantly higher than those of the present subjects, aged 18.5 years. The mean $\dot{V}O_2$max of adults, as an absolute figure and related to body weight and lean body mass, was also significantly lower than that of the apprentices (Ilmarinen, 1978).

Even though the present subjects had generally better health status than adults in the same jobs, the data on the less-active and less-fit group of apprentices at the age of about 18.5 years were indicative of future health problems, if their lifestyles remain unchanged. Earlier studies have shown that sport activities decrease with increasing age among children (Ilmarinen & Rutenfranz, 1980; Lange Andersen et al., 1984). The $\dot{V}O_2$max values of these apprentices at age 18.5 years seemed to be somewhat lower than the values found at age 17 to 18 years. It appeared that the transition to a working status decreased the sports activities of the youths and this change was already reflected in the maximal aerobic power.

The heart rate recordings indicated that even the most active apprentices spent only a few minutes per day in activities over 8 METs. It was apparent that the activities over 5 METs, which lasted about 36 min in the fit and 18 min in the unfit group, can explain the differences between the groups. This means that about 30 min of aerobic activities daily, including some minutes of activity higher than 8 METs, can be recommended for young workers to maintain good health.

REFERENCES

Edholm, O.G. (1966). The assessment of habitual activity. In K. Evang & K. Lange Andersen (Eds.), *Physical activity in health and disease* (pp. 187-197). Oslo: Universitetsforlaget.

Ilmarinen, J. (1978). *Beziehungen zwischen beruflicher und sportlicher körperlicher Aktivität und kardiopulmonaler Leistungsfähigkeit.* Untersuchungen bei Männern mittleren Alters unter besonderer Berücksichtigung prophylaktischer Aspekte der koronaren Durchblutungsstörungen. Unpublished doctoral dissertation, Deutsche Sporthochschule, Köln.

Ilmarinen, J., & Rutenfranz, J. (1980). Longitudinal studies of the changes in habitual physical activity of schoolchildren and working adolescents. In K. Berg & B.O. Eriksson (Eds.), *Children and exercise IX* (pp. 149-159) (International Series on Sport Sciences, Vol. 10). Baltimore: University Park Press.

Lange Andersen, K., Ilmarinen, J., Rutenfranz, J., Ottmann, W., Berndt, I., Kylian, H., & Ruppel, M. (1984). Leisure time sport activities and maximal aerobic power during late adolescence. *European Journal of Applied Physiology, 52*, 431-436.

Lange Andersen, K., Shephard, R.J., Denolin, H., Varnauskas, E., & Masironi, R. (1971). *Fundamentals of exercise testing.* Geneva: World Health Organization.

Lindemann, H., Rutenfranz, J., Mocellin, R., & Sbresny, W. (1973). Methodische Untersuchung zur indirekten Bestimmung der maximalen O_2-Aufnahme. *European Journal of Applied Physiology, 32*, 25-53.

Montoye, H.J. (1985). Risk indicators for cardiovascular disease in relation to physical activity in youth. In R.A. Binkhorst, H.C.G. Kemper, & W.H.M. Saris (Eds.), *Children and exercise XI* (pp. 3-25). Champaign, IL: Human Kinetics.

Oja, P., Vuori, I., & Urponen, H. (1984). Physical activity and use of health services in early adulthood. In J. Ilmarinen & I. Välimäki (Eds.), *Children and sport. Paediatric work physiology* (pp. 262-271). Berlin, New York: Springer-Verlag.

Parízková, J. (1974). Body composition, nutrition and exercise. *Medicina dello Sport*, **27**, 2-33.

Rutenfranz, J., Seliger, V., Andersen, K.L., Ilmarinen, J., Flöring, R., Rutenfranz, M., & Klimmer, F. (1977). Erfahrungen mit einem transportablen Gerät zur kontinuierlichen Registrierung der Herzfrequenz für Zeiten bis zu 24 Stunden. *European Journal of Applied Physiology*, **36**, 171-185.

Verschuur, R., Kemper, H.C.G., & Besseling, C.W.M. (1984). Habitual physical activity and health in 13- and 14-year-old teenagers. In J. Ilmarinen & I. Välimäki (Eds.), *Children and sport. Paediatric work physiology* (pp. 255-261). Berlin, New York: Springer-Verlag.

Influence of Physical Activity on Heart Rate Variability During Pulse-Conducted Exercise Tests in 7-Year-Old School Children

Jari Forsström
Kari Antila
Marja-Liisa Mäntymaa
Leena Pihlakoski
Ilkka Välimäki
University of Turku, Turku, Finland

An exercise test on a bicycle is a useful method for measuring the circulatory adaptation to physical stress. In the pulse-conducted triangular test, the work load can be controlled either manually or automatically with an automatic control unit. In this test, the load on the ergometer is adjusted so that an optimally linear increase in the heart rate (HR) for each subject tested is achieved. The HR acceleration usually used for children is 8 beats/min² (Petäjoki, Arstila, & Välimäki, 1974).

The HR variability (HRV) is the irregularity of the HR caused by the autonomic nervous control of the heart (Sato, Hasegawa, & Hotta, 1980). It can easily be quantified by statistical indices of variation (Tarlo, Välimäki, & Rautaharju, 1971; Antila, 1979). In the pulse-conducted exercise test, these indices computed for the entire duration of the test do not give much relevant information about the dynamic HR control because the HR is continuously increased and the cardiovascular system is constantly adjusting to new demands. To quantify the HRV during exercise, Antila (1979) used a gliding-window technique, where the change in the HRV indices were dynamically displayed during the test. The HRV indices showed an exponential decrease with working time in adults (Antila, 1979).

Computation of the power spectrum for the HR can be used to display several simultaneous oscillatory components of the HRV. Hyndman, Kitney, and Sayers (1971) have shown that blood pressure and HR fluctuate spontaneously. These superimposed periodic rhythms were seen as three separate spectral peaks in the power spectrum of the HRV. The activity at the lowest frequency band of less than 0.1 Hz is associated with the vasomotor thermoregulation, the peak around 0.1 Hz is caused by

141

blood pressure control mechanisms, and the higher frequency bands correspond to respiration.

The purpose of this study was to find out whether any differences in the HR control exist between physically trained and physically inactive children as early as the age of seven years.

METHODS

A total of 35 seven-year-old children from two parallel classes in an urban school were studied. The children were divided into a physically active, a normal, and an inactive group by interviewing the children, their classmates, and teachers (Välimäki, Hursti, Pihlakoski, & Viikari, 1980). All 12 children of the active group were also active members of sports clubs. The inactive and normal groups included 10 and 13 children, respectively. The children in the inactive group appeared to have hobbies other than those involving physical activity.

Exercise Testing

The pulse-conducted bicycle exercise test technique introduced by Arstila (1972) was used. The exercise test was performed using an electronically braked bicycle ergometer (Siemens-Elema 380, Siemens, Solna, Sweden). The work load of the ergometer was automatically adjusted to obtain a linear increase in the HR with an acceleration of 8 beats/min² (Arstila, 1972; Petäjoki et al., 1974). The test was continued for as long as the subject was able to continue pedaling at a regular rate of 60 rev/min; therefore the test was considered to represent a maximal test.

Signal Acquisition and Processing

During the exercise test, the ECG was continuously recorded from a bipolar chest lead onto magnetic tape by a four-channel FM tape recorder (Epsylon Labcorder MR-800 T-251, Epsylon Industries Ltd., North Feltham, Middlesex, England). The recordings were visually examined by a storage monitor (Advance Oscilloscope 2200^R, Advance Electronics Ltd., Roebuck Rd., Hainaults, Essex, England). The tape record was then replayed at eight times the real-time speed. The R waves in the ECG were identified by a special analog QRS detector built in the authors' laboratory. The ECG was band-pass filtered at 8-25 Hz and a trigger pulse was generated at each R wave. The triggering threshold level was manually adjusted and the correct triggering was visually verified by an oscilloscope (Advance Oscilloscope 2200^R, Advance Electronics Ltd.). The intervals were measured by an interval counter (accuracy ± 1 ms) and stored in digital form on the disk memory of a laboratory computer (Nova 3, Data General Corporation, Southboro, MA, USA).

The linear HR trend was removed from the exercise record by subtracting from the R-R intervals the linear regression between the HR and time. A gliding-window technique was applied to quantify the HRV (Lindqvist, Oja, Hellman, & Välimäki, 1983). A window of 50 successive R-R intervals was moved through the record by steps of one R-R interval. At each window, the HR variability indices for the interval were computed. The overall HR variation was measured as RMSM (the root mean square of the differences from the mean interval) and the short-term or beat-to-beat HR variation as RMSSD (the root mean square for successive interval differences). The respective coefficients of variation, CV (the percentage of RMSM of the mean R-R interval) and CVS (the percentage of RMSSD of the mean R-R interval) were calculated as indices of the relative HRV (Tarlo et al., 1971; Antila, 1979).

The HRV signal derived by the use of the gliding-window technique was further studied by computing an exponential approximation of the HRV versus time. The exponential curve fit of the form

$$HRV = Beta \times e^{Time \times Gamma}$$

where Time is working time (min) and HRV is the HRV index used, was computed for each case. Also the half life of the HRV, $t_{1/2}$, was calculated from this equation.

For a further analysis, the interval vector was low-pass filtered and equispaced by using a $\sin(x)/x$ digital filter with a sampling frequency of 2.2 Hz and a cutoff frequency of 1.0 Hz. Each record of the filtered signal was corrected for linear trend. The resulting equi-spaced time series was fast Fourièr transformed and the power spectrum of the signal was computed.

Analysis

All the mean values are presented as the mean ± standard error of the mean. The comparisons of the mean values were made using the student t-test. The half lives and spectral bands were compared using the nonparametric Wilcoxon test.

RESULTS

The HRs of the three groups at the beginning of the test did not differ significantly. The regressions between HR and time were linear for all the subjects. The slope was 8/min² indicating that the automatic control unit did work as expected. The maximal HR in the exercise test was equal in the three groups. The mean was 185.7 ± 3.6 for the inactive, 188.1

± 2.4 for the normal, and 187.4 ± 3.8 for the active subject group. The total work/body weight estimated by the automated pulse-conducted exercise test was greatest for the active and smallest for the inactive group (Välimäki, Hursti, Pihlakoski, Wanne, Halkola, & Viikari, 1980). The difference was statistically significant ($p = .002$) between the inactive and active groups and between the normal and inactive groups ($p = .01$). The difference between the normal and active groups did not reach statistical significance ($p > .05$).

A typical plot of the instantaneous HR with the RMSM computed with the gliding-window technique is shown in Figure 1. There were no significant differences in the beta or gamma values or the half lives for any HRV index used between the groups. Thus it appears that the basic exponential decay in the HRV was similar in all groups studied.

The HRV indices after the trend correction were calculated for the first 3 min and for the time 3 to 6 min during the exercise test. In each case, the indices were smaller during the latter period. The ratio HRV index during the former period to the respective HRV index during the latter period was also calculated. This ratio was almost significantly greater in the active group for the RMSM ($p = .04$) and for the CV ($p = .04$) than in the inactive group. There were no statistically significant differences for the RMSSD And the CVS (see Table 1).

The periodic HR variation was quantified by a spectral analysis. The HRV was quantified in the very low frequency component range (0.0 Hz to 0.025 Hz), in the low frequency component range (0.025 Hz to 0.075

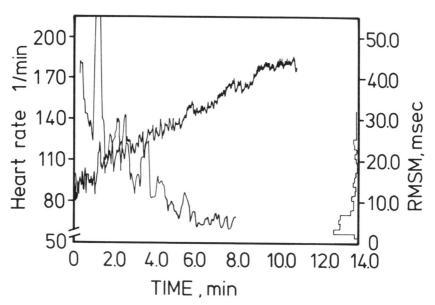

Figure 1 A typical plot of the instantaneous HR and the RMSM in the pulse-conducted exercise test.

Table 1   Indices of HR variation for the three groups

Index	Inactive (n = 10)	Normal (n = 13)	Active (n = 12)
HRV for 0 to 3 min			
RMSM	44.39 ± 3.99	48.79 ± 3.28	47.71 ± 3.08
CV	8.85 ± 0.62	9.65 ± 0.46	9.71 ± 0.34
RMSSD	14.16 ± 2.06	13.11 ± 1.76	12.97 ± 2.06
CVS	2.78 ± 0.33	2.56 ± 0.28	2.53 ± 0.34
HRV for 3 to 6 min			
RMSM	22.98 ± 1.32	23.63 ± 1.15	21.10 ± 1.86
CV	5.65 ± 0.22	5.77 ± 0.20	5.19 ± 0.33
RMSSD	5.17 ± 0.46	5.08 ± 0.55	4.84 ± 0.80
CVS	1.27 ± 0.10	1.23 ± 0.12	1.18 ± 0.17
HRV (0 to 3)/HRV (3 to 6)			
RMSM	1.93 ± 0.13*	2.06 ± 0.09*	2.33 ± 0.09*
CV	1.58 ± 0.10*	1.68 ± 0.07*	1.92 ± 0.08*
RMSSD	2.70 ± 0.23	2.68 ± 0.26	2.76 ± 0.36
CVS	2.19 ± 0.18	2.18 ± 0.21	2.26 ± 0.29

Note. HR variation is for first 3 min and for the next 3 min during the exercise test and for the ratio HRV index during the former period to respective HRV index during the latter period. Values are mean ± *SEM*.
*$p \leqslant .05$.

Hz), in the intermediate frequency component range (0.075 Hz to 0.125 Hz), and in the high frequency component range (0.125 Hz to 0.175 Hz). The absolute power and the relative (percent) power in the respective frequencies are shown in Figure 2. In the intermediate frequency component range (0.075 Hz to 0.125 Hz) the variation was highest in the inactive group. The difference was statistically significant between the active and the inactive groups both for the absolute values ($p = 0.5$) and for the relative values ($p = .03$). In the high frequency component range (0.125 Hz to 0.175 Hz) the differences between the three groups were not statistically significant. In the very low frequency component range the HRV was greatest in the active group. This difference in relative values was statistically significant both compared to the inactive group ($p = .03$) and compared to the normal group ($p = .03$).

DISCUSSION

In the pulse-conducted exercise test, the children did not exhibit any remarkable differences in HRV. The decrease in the long-term HRV was greater in the active than in the inactive group. In the spectral analysis, this long-term HRV was seen in the very low frequency spectral band

Table 2   The Absolute and Relative (% From the Whole Power) Values ($M \pm SD$) in the Four Spectral Bands for the Three Groups

	Inactive (n = 10)	Normal (n = 13)	Active (n = 12)
0.000 to 0.025 Hz	368.0 ± 51.1	315.4 ± 58.7*	552.0 ± 85.7*
%	35.88 ± 5.65*	36.56 ± 5.88*	56.72 ± 6.55*
0.025 to 0.075 Hz	354.7 ± 65.7	350.4 ± 72.8	251.4 ± 112.2
%	29.71 ± 5.20	33.67 ± 5.39*	19.18 ± 4.32*
0.075 to 0.125 Hz	147.0 ± 25.2*	96.0 ± 13.4	80.7 ± 19.8*
%	12.16 ± 1.75*	9.85 ± 1.04	7.32 ± 1.23*
0.125 to 0.175 Hz	53.5 ± 10.4	38.9 ± 6.1	32.5 ± 6.2
%	4.30 ± 0.72	3.92 ± 0.47	3.15 ± 0.52

*$p \leqslant .05$.

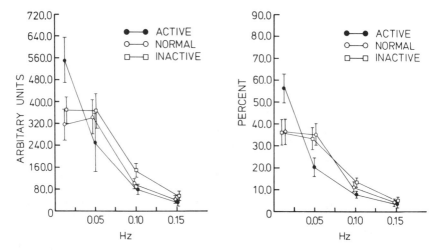

Figure 2   Absolute and relative values in the four spectral bands for the three groups.

(0.0 Hz to 0.025 Hz). This slow oscillation, which decreased rapidly during the test, originated from the complex interaction between the cardiovascular regulatory mechanisms and the automatic control of the ergometer work load. At lower heart rates in the beginning of the test, the HR was very unstable, and a linear increase was therefore almost impossible to achieve. At higher heart rates, the control of the heart rate is much more efficient and accurate and the increase in the HR was very close to linear.

The active children had the largest HRV in the very low frequency spectral band. The relative decrease in the long-term variation was also most prominent in the active children. These results may be explained by the observation that a better state of fitness coincides with a greater cardiac stroke volume (SV), which may give the child more flexibility to regulate the cardiac output during exercise (Eriksson & Koch, 1973). Thus, children with a greater SV can increase their cardiac output more efficiently by also regulating the SV. In consequence the dependence between the HR and cardiac output is less limited; that is, the dynamic range of the HR control is larger. If the inactive children regulate their cardiac outputs earlier mainly by changing their HRs, linear increases in the HRs are also easier to achieve. Unfortunately, data on the stroke volumes of these children were not documented. On the other hand, it has been found that no differences in SV can be detected between 8-year-old children with different physical activity levels (Hamilton & Andrew, 1976).

In the spectral analysis, the inactive group showed a larger variation in the spectral band 0.075 Hz to 0.125 Hz during the first minutes of the exercise. This band is related to the oscillations in blood pressure regulation. This difference could be explained also by the hypothesis that the regulation of the blood pressure in the inactive is more dependent on the heart rate than in the active group and thus the regulatory oscillations can be more clearly seen in the inactive than in the active children.

The analysis of the heart rate during a pulse-conducted exercise test is problematic because the oscillations detected are due to the complex interaction between the cardiovascular regulatory mechanisms and the control of the work load. On the other hand, if the test is performed accurately and similarly in each child, the oscillations detected in the HR are worth analyzing. Also, the slow oscillations contain information about the hemodynamic regulation during an exercise test.

CONCLUSION

It is concluded that there are limited intergroup differences in the heart rate control during exercise among children with different levels of physical activity.

REFERENCES

Antila, K. (1979). Quantitative characterization of HR during exercise. *Scandinavian Journal of Clinical and Laboratory Investigation, 39* (Suppl. 153), 1-68.

Arstila, M. (1972). Pulse-conducted triangular exercise-ECG test. *Acta Medica Scandinavica* (Suppl. 529).

Eriksson, B.O., & Koch, G. (1973). Effect of physical training on hemodynamic response during submaximal and maximal exercise in 11- to 13-year-old boys. *Acta Physiologica Scandinavica, 87,* 27-39.

Hamilton, P., & Andrew, G.M. (1976). Influence of growth and athletic training on heart and lung functions. *European Journal of Applied Physiology*, **36**, 27-38.

Hyndman, B.W., Kitney, R.I., & Sayers, B. McA. (1971). Spontaneous rhythms in physiological control systems. *Nature*, **233**, 339-341.

Lindqvist, A., Oja, R., Hellman, O., & Välimäki, I. (1983). Impact of thermal vasomotor control on the HR variability of newborn infants. *Early Human Development*, **8**, 37-47.

Petäjoki, M.-L., Arstila, M., & Välimäki, I. (1974). Pulse-conducted exercise test in children. *Acta Paediatrica Belgica*, **28** (Suppl.), 40-47.

Sato, I., Hasegawa, Y., & Hotta, K. (1980). Autonomic nervous control of the heart in exercising man. *Pflügers Archiv*, **384**, 1-7.

Tarlo, P.A., Välimäki, I., & Rautaharju, P.M. (1971). Quantitative computer analysis of cardiac and respiratory activity in newborn infants. *Journal of Applied Physiology*, **31**, 70-75.

Välimäki, I., Hursti, M.-L., Pihlakoski, L., & Viikari, J. (1980). Exercise performance and serum lipids in relation to physical activity in school children. *International Journal of Sports Medicine*, **1**, 132-136.

Välimäki, I., Hursti, M.-L., Pihlakoski, L., Wanne, O., Halkola, L., & Viikari, J. (1980). Relation of serum lipids to ergometric performance in school children. In Physical training in health promotion and medical care (Abstract). *Publications of the University of Kuopio*, **1**, 83.

Influence of Habitual Levels of Physical Activity on the Cardiorespiratory Endurance Capacity of Children

Maria L. Weymans
Tony M. Reybrouck
Hugo J. Stijns
Jacqueline Knops
University of Leuven, Leuven, Belgium

In adults, an increased level of physical activity leads to a higher physical performance capacity (Fagard, 1985). It has been questioned, however, whether in children below the age of puberty an increased level of physical activity or a physical-training program induces changes in the oxygen transport system (Shephard, 1978). Therefore, the purpose of the present study was to investigate whether cardiorespiratory performance capacity in children is influenced by the daily level of physical activity and whether this relationship is the same at all ages.

METHODS

The subjects were 257 healthy children (140 boys and 117 girls) from schools in the region of Leuven (Belgium). Age varied from 5.7 to 18.5 years (median 11.5) for boys and 6.0 to 16.5 years (median 11.5) for girls. Body weight ranged from 18.5 to 80.0 kg (median 35.9) for boys and 16.9 to 68.0 kg (median 36.5) for girls. Body height varied from 114 to 190 cm (median 146.5) for boys and 111.5 to 176.2 (median 149.1) for girls. When plotted on a standard reference grid for height and weight (Stuart & Meredith, 1946), 136 of the 140 boys and 114 of 117 girls were situated between the 3rd and the 97th percentile for weight and height, respectively.

All children performed a graded exercise test on the occasion of a routine medical examination. A written informed consent was obtained from the parents. Exercise tests were performed on a treadmill. The speed was set at 4.8 km/h for children younger than 6 years and 5.6 km/h for children aged 6 years or more. The inclination of the belt was increased stepwise by 2% every minute, until exhaustion (Chandramouli, Ehmke, & Lauer, 1975).

Oxygen uptake ($\dot{V}O_2$) and carbon dioxide output ($\dot{V}CO_2$) were determined by the open circuit method. The children breathed through a low resistance two-way valve with small dead space. Expired gas was collected every minute in Douglas bags. The volume of expired air was measured by a dry gas meter, and the concentrations of O_2 and CO_2 were analyzed by electronic gas analyzers. Both gas analyzers were calibrated with test gas, previously analyzed by the Scholander technique. $\dot{V}O_2$ and $\dot{V}CO_2$ were reduced to STPD and $\dot{V}_E$ was converted to BTPS. Heart rate (HR) was measured by an electrocardiograph from a bipolar lead. Cardiorespiratory performance of the children was assessed by measuring the ventilatory threshold (VT). The VT was determined as the highest exercise intensity at which the $\dot{V}_E$ ceases to increase linearly with increasing $\dot{V}O_2$. Above this threshold an exponential increase is observed for $\dot{V}_E$. This onset of hyperventilation was further checked through reference to the exercise intensity at which

- the $\dot{V}CO_2$ began to increase nonlinearly,
- a systematic increase of the ventilatory equivalent for O_2 ($\dot{V}_E/\dot{V}O_2$) occurred, without a concomitant increase in the ventilatory equivalent for CO_2 ($\dot{V}_E/\dot{V}CO_2$) (Caiozzo et al., 1982; Reybrouck, Ghesquiere, Cattaert, Fagard, & Amery, 1983),
- a progressive increase of the fractional concentration of O_2 in the mixed expired air (F_EO_2) occurred, and
- an excess rise of the respiratory gas exchange ratio was found (Caiozzo et al., 1982; Reybrouck et al., 1983).

VT was expressed in $mlO_2 \cdot min^{-1} \cdot kg^{-1}$.

The habitual level of physical activity (HLPA) in the children was assessed by a standardized questionnaire. Information was obtained on the number of hours of sport participation at school and during leisure time, recreational exercises, other leisure-time activities, and how the children moved to and from the school. The number of hours of physical activity were cumulated as a score. When repeated within a time lapse of 1 month the scores obtained with this questionnaire were highly reproducible ($r = 0.99, p < .001$). Also, no significant differences were found among the scores obtained by four observers ($F = 0.13; p > .05$) in a group of children aged 10 to 12 years. The children were subdivided into two activity groups; children with a score below 5 formed the less active group and those with a score of 5 or above formed the more active group.

ANALYSIS

To study the main effects of sex, age, and HLPA on the VT, a general-linear model three-way analysis of variance was performed. The influence of sex and age on the HLPA was analyzed by a two-way analysis of variance. The children were also subdivided into age groups of 2 years and, as the number of children was not equal in all age classes, least square means were used to detect significant sex and age differences for HLPA between these classes (SAS, 1982). The VT of the two activity groups was fitted by a polynomial using a regression procedure.

RESULTS

The results of an analysis of variance on the effects of sex and age on HLPA and the interaction of these variables are reported in Table 1. HLPA was significantly influenced by sex and age, but the interaction of these two variables revealed no significant effect. For the boys, the mean HLPA was significantly higher (4.95 ± 2.37) than for the girls (4.08 ± 1.67) ($p < .0001$). Because the effect of sex on HLPA was statistically significant, the effect of age was separately analyzed for boys and girls. In both sexes, age significantly influenced HLPA.

Table 1   Influence of Sex, Age, and Habitual Level of Physical Activity (HLPA) on the Ventilatory Threshold (VT), and Sex and Age on the HLPA

Source	VT (F values)	HLPA (F values)
Total group		
Sex	65.48***	12.81***
Age	8.34***	4.19***
HLPA	0.84	
Sex × age	1.57	1.31
Sex × HLPA	3.27**	
Age × HLPA	2.07**	
Sex × age × HLPA	1.11	
Boys		
Age	4.36****	4.54***
HLPA	2.53*	
Age × HLPA	1.90*	
Girls		
Age	7.17***	5.03****
HLPA	0.94	
Age × HLPA	1.25	

*$p < .05$; **$p < .01$; ***$p < .001$; ****$p < .0001$.

The mean values for the HLPA, expressed by a score in boys and girls, subdivided in age groups of 2 years, are presented in Figure 1. In boys, HLPA increased with advancing age and a significant difference was found between the younger (5 to 6 years and 7 to 8 years) and the older age groups. Also the HLPA of 11- to 12-year-old boys was significantly

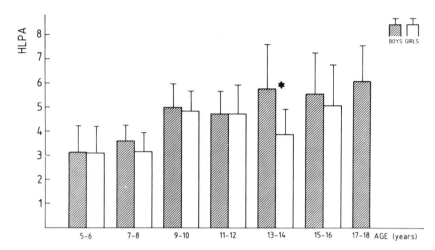

Figure 1 Habitual level of physical activity in boys and girls for different age groups. The data represent the mean and standard deviation of the mean. ★ = $p < .005$: refers to a statistical difference between boys and girls.

lower than that of 17- to 18-year-old boys. In girls, also, the younger children (5 to 6 years and 7 to 8 years) showed a lower degree of HLPA than the older ones, except for the age group of 13 to 14 years, which showed no statistical difference. Indeed, the girls of the latter age group showed a remarkably low degree of physical activity, which was significantly lower than that of the oldest ones (15 to 16 years). The sex difference for HLPA increased with advancing age and was only significant for the age class of 13 to 14 years ($p < .005$).

Because VT was significantly influenced by sex, the influence of age and HLPA on this variable was separately analyzed for both sexes. In boys, VT was significantly influenced by age and HLPA. Also, a significant interaction was found between age and HLPA. In girls, a significant effect of age on VT was found but no significant influence of HLPA on VT could be detected. No significant interaction was found between age and HLPA on this variable. In boys, when VT of the two activity groups was related to age, no difference for VT between these groups could be detected in the age span of 12 to 16 years (Figure 2). However, before and after this age period, the most active boys reached the highest VT and the less active ones the lowest. Similarly, when VT was related to body weight the same results were found. A significant difference between the two activity groups for VT was only found below and above the range of 40 to 58 kg of body weight, at which the most active boys reached the highest value for VT and the less active ones the lowest.

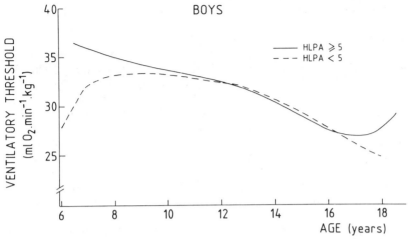

Figure 2 Influence of habitual level of physical activity on the ventilatory threshold ($mlO_2 \cdot min^{-1} \cdot kg^{-1}$). (—): activity score ≥ 5; (- - -): activity score < 5.

DISCUSSION

A standardized questionnaire has been shown to be very useful in obtaining information about the habitual level of physical activity in children (Lange Andersen et al., 1984). Although many authors accept that estimation of physical activity by questionnaire and interview are poor, the information obtained is nevertheless useful and possibly the best available tool. With advancing age, boys became more active in this study, whereas the HLPA of girls increased only until they reached puberty. This corresponds with the evolution during growth of the attitude toward sport participation of boys and girls.

The findings in this study that girls are less active than boys, especially when they become more mature, is in agreement with the study of Lange Andersen et al. (1984). Besides the hormonal influence, a lower habitual level of physical activity can be expected to be responsible for the decreased cardiorespiratory endurance capacity with increasing age in girls compared to boys (Lange Andersen, Seliger, Rutenfranz, & Mocellin, 1974).

Traditionally, the maximal oxygen uptake has been accepted as an objective criterion of cardiorespiratory endurance capacity (Shephard et al., 1968). However, there are some conflicting opinions about the influence of physical activity on $\dot{V}O_2max$ in children. Some authors have reported no significant difference between the $\dot{V}O_2$max of trained and untrained children before puberty (Kobayashi et al., 1978; Mirwald, Bailey, Cameron, & Rasmussen, 1981; Mocellin & Wasmund, 1972).

As children are already very active, training must be very intensive to produce a significant increase of $\dot{V}O_2$max (Stewart & Gutin, 1976). Indeed, some authors have reported a significant increase of $\dot{V}O_2$max after training in prepubertal boys (Ekblom, 1969; Eriksson & Koch, 1973). On the other hand, Weber, Kartodihardjo, & Klissouras (1976) found a significantly higher $\dot{V}O_2$max for trained twins compared with untrained ones before and after puberty. However, during puberty they did not observe a difference in $\dot{V}O_2$max. Recent investigations, however, have shown the ventilatory threshold to be a better indicator of maximal endurance capacity than $\dot{V}O_2$max (Reybrouck et al., 1983). Therefore, in the present study this measure is used to assess the cardiorespiratory endurance capacity.

In adults, VT is significantly influenced by the level of physical activity. Trained athletes reach metabolic acidosis at a higher exercise intensity than do sedentary subjects (Wasserman & Whipp, 1975). In training experiments, Davis, Frank, Whipp, and Wasserman (1979) showed a 15% increase in VT after 9 weeks of conditioning.

In this study, only for the boys was a significant influence of the degree of physical activity on the ventilatory threshold observed. Because in girls the HLPA was rather low, no discriminatory effect of HLPA on VT was found. However, before and after the age span of 12 to 16 years, the more active boys showed a higher VT than the less active ones. This is in agreement with the studies of Weber et al. (1976) and Blimkie, Cunningham, and Nichol (1980), who found the same results for the influence of training on maximal oxygen uptake in boys. In boys, the age span of 12 to 16 years corresponds to a range in body weight of 40 to 57 kg, deduced from a standard reference grid (Stuart & Meredith, 1946) and can be expected to represent the period at which puberty occurs (Tanner, 1962).

It can be postulated that during puberty the influence of HLPA on VT may be overruled by the influence of other more dominant factors. During the growth spurt, the hormonal activity reaches its maximum and may neutralize the influence of other factors such as physical training.

CONCLUSION

It is concluded that more active boys show a higher cardiorespiratory endurance capacity than do the less active ones, except during puberty, when the influence of other factors may be more dominant. Because in girls the HLPA was lower, a discriminatory effect of HLPA on VT was not shown.

REFERENCES

Blimkie, C.J.R., Cunningham, D.A., & Nichol, P.M. (1980). Gas transport capacity and echocardiographically determined cardiac size in children. *Journal of Applied Physiology*, **49**, 994-999.

Caiozzo, V.J., Davis, J.A., Ellis, J.F., Azus, J.L., Vandagriff, R., Prietto, C.A., & McMaster, W.C. (1982). A comparison of gas exchange indices used to detect the anaerobic threshold. *Journal of Applied Physiology*, **53**, 1184-1189.

Chandramouli, B., Ehmke, D.A., & Lauer, R.M. (1975). Exercise-induced electrocardiographic changes in children with congenital aortic stenosis. *Journal of Pediatrics*, **87**, 725-730.

Davis, J.A., Frank, M.H., Whipp, B.J., & Wasserman, K. (1979). Anaerobic threshold alterations caused by endurance training in middle-aged men. *Journal of Applied Physiology*, **46**, 1039-1046.

Ekblom, B. (1969). Effect of physical training in adolescent boys. *Journal of Applied Physiology*, **27**, 350-355.

Eriksson, B.O., & Koch, G. (1973). Effect of physical training on hemodynamic response during submaximal and maximal exercise in 11- to 13-year-old boys. *Acta Physiologica Scandinavica*, **87**, 27-39.

Fagard, R. (1985). Habitual physical activity, training and blood pressure in normo- and hypertension. *International Journal of Sports Medicine*, **6**, 57-67.

Kobayashi, K., Kitamura, K., Miura, M., Sodeyama, H., Murase, Y., Miyashita, M., & Matsui, H. (1978). Aerobic power as related to body growth and training in Japanese boys: A longitudinal study. *Journal of Applied Physiology*, **44**, 666-672.

Lange Andersen, K., Seliger, V., Rutenfranz, J., & Mocellin, R. (1974). Physical performance capacity of children in Norway. 1. Population parameters in a rural inland community with regard to maximal aerobic power. *European Journal of Applied Physiology*, **33**, 177-195.

Lange Andersen, K., Ilmarinen, J., Rutenfranz, J., Ottmann, W., Berndt, I., Kylian, H., & Ruppel, M. (1984). Leisure time sport activities and maximal aerobic power during late adolescence. *European Journal of Applied Physiology*, **52**, 431-436.

Mirwald, R.L., Bailey, D.A., Cameron, N., & Rasmussen, R.L. (1981). Longitudinal comparison of aerobic power in active and inactive boys aged 7.0 to 17.0 years. *Annals of Human Biology*, **8**, 405-414.

Mocellin, R., & Wasmund, U. (1972). Investigations on the influence of a running-training program of the cardiovascular and motor performance capacity in 53 boys and girls of a second and third primary school class. In O. Bar-Or (Ed.), *Pediatric work physiology. Proceedings of the 4th international symposium* (pp. 279-285). Natanya: The Wingate Institute for Physical Education and Sport.

Reybrouck, T., Ghesquiere, J., Cattaert, A., Fagard, R., & Amery, A. (1983). Ventilatory thresholds during short- and long-term exercise. *Journal of Applied Physiology*, **55**, 1694-1700.

SAS Institute, Inc. (1982). *SAS users guide: Statistics*. NC: Cary.

Shephard, R.J., Allen, C., Benade, A.J.S., Davies, C.T.M., di Prampero, P.E., Hedman, R., Merriman, J.E., Myhre, K., & Simmons, R. (1968). The maximum oxygen intake: An international reference standard of cardiorespiratory fitness. *Bulletin of the World Health Organization*, **38**, 757-764.

Shephard, R.J. (1978). *Human physiological work capacity* (International biological programme, Vol. 15). Cambridge: Cambridge University Press.

Stewart, K., & Gutin, B. (1976). Effects of physical training on cardiorespiratory fitness in children. *Research Quarterly*, **47**, 110-120.

Stuart, H.C., & Meredith, H.V. (1946). Use of body measurements in the school health program. *American Journal of Public Health*, **36**, 1365-1386.

Tanner, J.M. (1962). *Growth at adolescence* (2nd ed.). Oxford, U.K.: Blackwell Scientific.

Wasserman, K., & Whipp, B.J. (1975). Exercise physiology in health and disease. *American Review of Respiratory Disease*, **112**, 219-249.

Weber, G., Kartodihardjo, W., & Klissouras, V. (1976). Growth and physical training with reference to heredity. *Journal of Applied Physiology*, **40**, 211-215.

Physical Work Capacity and Strain in Children Aged 8 to 12 Years During a Skiing Competition

Juhani Ilmarinen
Clas-Håkan Nygård
Institute of Occupational Health, Helsinki, Finland
Timo Suurnäkki
Center for Industrial Safety, Helsinki, Finland
Paavo V. Komi
University of Jyväskylä, Jyväskylä, Finland
Ilkka Välimäki
Olli Wanne
University of Turku, Turku, Finland

In an earlier study, Ilmarinen, Nygård, Komi, and Karlsson (1984) showed that a children's ski race involves not only aerobic stress but also great anaerobic stress. Judging from heart rate and lactate values, the children studied were using close to a maximal effort. Lactate values were almost as high as those measured in adult skiers after a ski race. Tiainen and Telama (1984) found that children spent very little time training and preparing themselves for a skiing competition. The combination of severe strain and meager training raises questions about the effects of physical work capacity (PWC) and strain in children. The aim of this study was to measure PWC in children participating in a ski race and to evaluate the relationship of PWC to aerobic and anaerobic strain and also to skiing performance.

MATERIALS AND METHODS

A total of 18 randomly chosen children (12 boys and 6 girls) who were all competing in the National Junior Skiing Competition at Joutsa in Finland participated in the study. The children's ages ranged from 8 to 12 years, mean 9.5 years (see Table 1). Anthropometric data for the subjects, including weight, height, body mass index, percentage of fat, and lean body mass (LBM) are summarized for 15 children in Table 1.

Table 1 Age and Anthropometrics of Children Participating in a Ski Race

		Age (yr)	Weight (kg)	Height (cm)	BMI (kg $\cdot$ m^{-2})	Fat (%)	LBM (kg)
Boys	M	9.8	37.2	140.5	18.6	15.3	31.2
	SD	1.7	10.0	12.3	2.3	4.7	6.7
	n	9	9	9	9	9	9
Girls	M	9.1	31.6	137.5	16.8*	12.3	27.5
	SD	1.3	3.1	7.9	0.5	1.0	3.3
	n	6	6	6	6	6	6
All	M	9.5	35.0	139.3	17.9	14.1	29.7
	SD	1.5	8.3	10.5	2.0	3.9	5.7
	n	15	15	15	15	15	15

*$p < .05$.

The boys had greater body mass than the girls ($p < .05$) as well as a higher percentage of fat and lean body mass, although the differences were not statistically significant. To estimate physical work capacity (PWC) an automatic pulse-conducted bicycle ergometer test (Arstila, 1972) was used with a heart rate increment of 8 beats/min^{-1} (Välimäki, Petäjoki, Arstila, Viherä & Wendelin, 1978). Cardiopulmonary capacity was estimated from the work (in Watts) the subjects performed at a heart rate of 170 beats/min^{-1} (PWC$_{170}$), which has a good correlation with $\dot{V}O_2$max for children (Franz, Wiewel, & Mellerowicz, 1984).

Cardiovascular strain during the competition was measured by continuous heart rate recordings with a portable Howel Corder cassette recorder (Rutenfranz et al., 1977). The heart rate recordings were carried out on 12 boys, 4 in each age group. For the estimation of metabolic strain during the competition, the blood lactate level (LA) was measured. Samples were taken from the fingertip 2 to 3 min after the competition. The samples were analyzed immediately by the flow injection analysis method (Karlsson et al., 1983).

The mean skiing speed (m $\cdot$ s^{-1}) was calculated from the skiing time and the length of the course. The physical work capacity was expressed in Watts in absolute numbers (PWC$_{170}$), in relation to body weight (PWC$_{170}$/BW) and in relation to lean body mass (PWC$_{170}$/LBM). The maximum heart rate (HR max) was the highest heart rate obtained either from the ergometer test or from the skiing competition. Student t-test for two independent samples was used to test the differences between the data for boys and girls.

RESULTS

The boys had a higher absolute physical work capacity than the girls, but the difference was not statistically significant (see Table 2). However, as functions of body weight and lean body mass, the capacity of boys and girls were at the same level. The maximum heart rate was on average about 196 beats/min^{-1}, and differences between the boys and girls were not statistically significant.

Table 2 Physical-Work Capacity (Absolute and Related to the Body Weight) and Maximum Heart Rate of Children Participating in a Ski Race

		PWC$_{170}$ (W)	PWC$_{170}$/BW (W · kg^{-1})	PWC/LBM (W · kg^{-1})	HR max (beats/min^{-1}
Boys	M	118.5	3.2	3.7	198.7
	SD	37.2	0.6	0.6	12.0
	n	10	9	9	12
Girls	M	104.2	3.2	3.9	191.2
	SD	28.7	0.4	0.7	7.1
	n	6	6	6	6
All	M	113.1	3.2	3.8	196.2
	SD	34.0	0.5	0.6	11.0
	n	16	15	15	18

The cardiovascular strain for the 12 boys during the competition was about 186 beats/min^{-1}, which corresponded to 93.5% of the maximum heart rate (see Table 3). The highest heart rate during the ski race ranged individually from 181 to 217 beats/min^{-1}. For 7 of the 9 children, the maximum heart rate was higher in the ski race than in the ergometer test.

The average lactate level was 6.4 mmol · l^{-1} just after the competition (see Table 4). The mean speed during the competition was 3.9 m · s^{-1}.

Table 3 The Cardiovascular Strain on the Boys During a Ski Race (n = 12)

	HR (beats/min^{-1})	HR max (beats/min^{-1})	HR max (%)
M	185.5	197.4	93.5
SD	9.2	11.8	3.0

Table 4   The Metabolic Strain and the Mean Speed of the Boys (n = 12) and Girls (n = 6) During a Ski Race

		Lactate (mmol · l⁻¹)	Speed (m · s⁻¹)
Boys	M	6.5	4.0
	SD	1.8	0.8
Girls	M	6.1	3.8
	SD	1.8	0.4
All	M	6.4	3.9
	SD	1.8	0.7

The girls had lower lactate values than the boys but also somewhat lower mean speed during the competition, but the differences were not statistically significant.

Physical work capacity had a negative correlation (r = -0.44) to the relative cardiorespiratory strain (HR as a percentage of HR max) during the ski race (see Figure 1). The correlation for physical work capacity related to lean body mass with the relative strain was r = -0.21 and for physical work capacity related to body weight there was no correlation (r = -0.01). The PWC$_{170}$ had a negative correlation (r = -0.60) to the mean heart rate during the ski race (see Figure 2). For PWC$_{170}$/LBM and

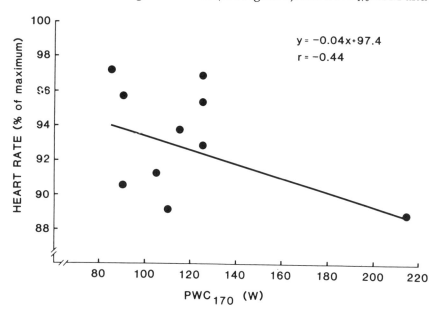

Figure 1   Mean heart rate during the ski competition as a percentage of maximum for the boys (n = 10) in relation to absolute physical work capacity (PWC$_{170}$).

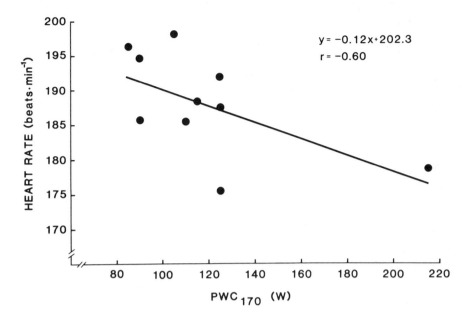

$$y = -0.12x + 202.3$$
$$r = -0.60$$

Figure 2 Mean heart rate (beats/min^{-1}) of the boys (n = 10) during the ski competition in relation to absolute physical work capacity (PWC$_{170}$).

PWC$_{170}$/BW the correlations were lower, r = -0.47 and -0.26, respectively. PWC$_{170}$/LBM had a slight negative correlation (r = 0.16) to the lactate level measured immediately after the ski race (see Figure 3). The PWC$_{170}$ had a slight positive correlation (r = 0.28) to the mean speed during the ski race (see Figure 4). The PWC$_{170}$/BW had no correlation (r = 0.04) to the final position of the children in the ski race (see Figure 5).

DISCUSSION

The children studied were about average weight and height for Finnish children of their age (Dahlström et al., 1984). The boys had a higher percentage of body fat than the girls and a higher body mass index, which indicated that the boys had a larger muscle mass. This influenced the absolute physical work capacity (PWC$_{170}$), which was somewhat higher for the boys than for the girls. The differences, however, were not statistically significant.

The children in this study had a higher PWC$_{170}$ (mean = 113 W) than 11- to 12-year-old Czechoslovakian children (mean = 69 W) (Seliger & Bartúněk, 1976) and 11-year-old Austrian children (mean = 83 W) (Gaisl & Buchberger, 1980). It was also higher than that of the children investigated by Mocellin (1985), who were about 10 years old and whose mean PWC$_{170}$ was 63 W. The PWC$_{170}$ had a negative correlation to heart rate

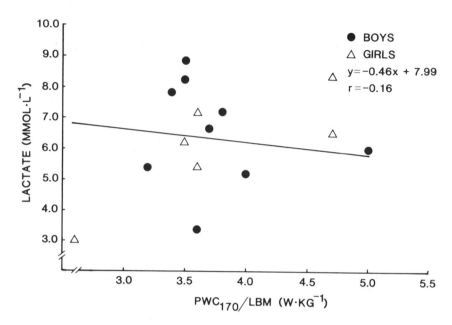

Figure 3   Blood lactate level (mmol • l⁻¹) after the ski competition in relation to the physical work capacity expressed in watts per kilogram of lean body mass (PWC_{170}/LBM) for the boys (n = 9) and the girls (n = 6).

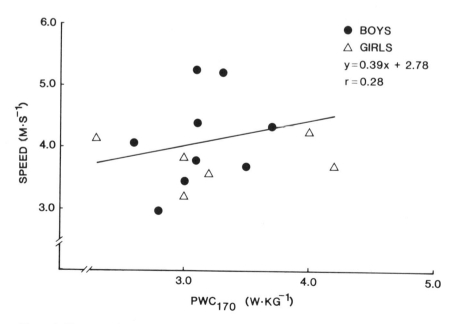

Figure 4   The mean skiing speed (m • s⁻¹) in relation to the physical work capacity expressed in watts per kilogram of body weight (PWC_{170}/BW) for the boys (n = 9) and the girls (n = 6).

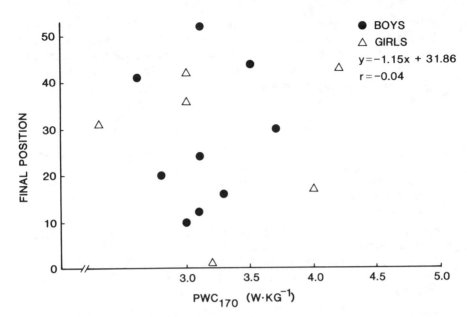

Figure 5 The final position in the ski race in relation to the physical work capacity expressed in watts per kilogram body weight (PWC_{170}/BW) for the boys ($n = 9$) and the girls ($n = 6$).

response of the children during the ski race. This indicated that a good physical work capacity decreases the cardiorespiratory strain in such races. However, when the body weight (PWC_{170}/BW) is considered, the correlation was not as good. This was due to the fact that the body weight and the work capacity increase simultaneously in children with age (Matsui et al., 1972). The body mass index (kg • m^{-2}) had a negative correlation to the cardiorespiratory strain, which means that the heavier and taller children had less strain in the ski race than the smaller children, presumably because of their superior physical work capacity.

The correlation between physical work capacity and blood lactate level was low ($r = -0.16$), which could be explained by the fact that PWC_{170} measures aerobic capacity, although a ski race is also a highly anaerobic event for children. A study with a larger sample of children participating in a similar ski race in Joutsa showed still higher LAs than this study (Suurnäkki, Ilmarinen, Nygård, Komi, & Karlsson, 1984).

The physical work capacity of the children in this study had no correlation with their final position in the ski race. This might be explained partly by the fact that PWC_{170} measured with an ergometer is a test of aerobic capacity but a ski race also requires anaerobic capacity and skiing skills.

REFERENCES

Arstila, M. (1972). Pulse-conducted triangular exercise-ECG test. A feedback system regulating work during exercise. *Acta Medica Scandinavica*, **529** (Suppl.).

Dahlström, S., Viikari, J., Åkerblom, H., Lähde, P.-L., Pesonen, E., Pietikäinen, M., Suoninen, P., & Louhivuori, K. (1984). Height, weight, and age at menarche of Finnish children and young adults. Results from a multicenter study 1980. *Duodecim*, **100**, 838-848.

Franz, I.-W., Wiewel, D., & Mellerowicz, H. (1984). Comparative measurements of $\dot{V}O_2$max and PWC_{170} in school children. In H. Löllgen & H. Mellerowicz (Eds.), *Progress in ergometry. Quality control and test criteria* (pp. 247-250). Berlin, New York: Springer-Verlag.

Gaisl, G., & Buchberger, J. (1980). Determination of the aerobic and anaerobic thresholds of 10- to 11-year-old boys using blood-gas analysis. In K. Berg & B.O. Eriksson (Eds.), *Children and exercise IX* (pp. 93-98) (International Series on Sport Sciences, Vol. 10). Baltimore: University Park Press.

Ilmarinen, J., Nygård, C.-H., Komi, P.V., & Karlsson, J. (1984). Heart rate and blood lactate level of 8- to 12-year-old boys and girls during cross-country ski competitions. In J. Ilmarinen & I. Välimäki (Eds.), *Children and sport. Paediatric work physiology* (pp. 189-195). Berlin, New York: Springer-Verlag.

Karlsson, J., Jacobs, I., Sjödin, B., Tesch, P., Kaiser, P., Sahl, O., & Karlberg, B. (1983). Semi-automatic blood lactate assay: Experiences from an exercise laboratory. *International Journal of Sports Medicine*, **4**, 52-55.

Matsui, H., Miyashita, M., Miura, M., Kobayashi, K., Hoshikawa, T., & Kamei, S. (1972). Maximum oxygen intake and its relationship to body weight in Japanese adolescents. *Medicine and Science in Sports*, **4**, 29-32.

Mocellin, R. (1985). Children with cardiac disease and exercise. In R.A. Binkhorst, H.C.G. Kemper, & W.H.M. Saris (Eds.), *Children and exercise XI* (pp. 26-41) (International Series on Sport Sciences, Vol. 15). Champaign, IL: Human Kinetics.

Rutenfranz, J., Seliger, V., Andersen, K.L., Ilmarinen, J., Flöring, R., Rutenfranz, M., & Klimmer, F. (1977). Erfahrungen mit einem transportablen Gerät zur kontinuierlichen Registrierung der Herzfrequenz für Zeiten bis zu 24 Stunden. *European Journal of Applied Physiology*, **36**, 171-185.

Seliger, V., & Bartúněk, Z. (1976). *Mean values of various indices of physical fitness in the investigation of Czechoslovak population aged 12-55 years.* Prague: Charles University.

Suurnäkki, T., Ilmarinen, J., Nygård, C.-H., Komi, P.V., & Karlsson, J. (1984). Lasten anaerobinen kuormittuminen kilpahiidossa (Anaerobic strain in children in a skiing competition, in Finnish). *Liikunta ja tiede*, **21**, 259-266.

Tiainen, J., & Telama, R. (1984). Children and parents in skiing competitions. In J. Ilmarinen & I. Välimäki (Eds.), *Children and sport. Paediatric work physiology* (pp. 196-200). Berlin, New York: Springer-Verlag.

Välimäki, I., Petäjoki, M.-L., Arstila, M., Viherä, P., & Wendelin, H. (1978). Automatically controlled ergometer for pulse-conducted exercise test. In J. Borms & M. Hebbelinck (Eds.), *Pediatric work physiology* (pp. 47-51) (Medicine and sport, Vol. 11). Basel: Karger.

HDL$_2$-Cholesterol of Children (10 to 12 Years of Age) Related to $\dot{V}O_2$max, Body Fat, and Sex

Yoriko Atomi
Yoshio Kuroda
Toshio Asami
Takashi Kawahara
University of Tokyo, Tokyo, Japan

Recently several population studies have demonstrated a significant inverse relationship between serum high density lipoprotein cholesterol (HDL-Chol) levels and prevalence of coronary heart disease (Castelli et al., 1977; Miller & Miller, 1975; Rhoads, Culbrandsen, & Kagan, 1976) in adults. Human serum total HDL can be divided into two major components, HDL$_2$ and HDL$_3$, which have generally been defined in terms of the density intervals in their ultracentrifugal isolation. The major differences in serum total HDL as well as in serum HDL-Chol levels, within a normal population such as the Modesto sample, arise predominantly from differences in serum levels of the HDL$_2$ component (Anderson, Nichols, Pan, & Lindgren, 1978). The percent total HDL associated with the HDL$_2$ component increased greatly in female HDL, whereas that of the HDL$_3$ component increased in male HDL (Anderson et al., 1978).

Of particular interest is the positive effect of exercise on HDL-Chol because increased levels of the lipid component have been associated with a reduction in risk to atherosclerosis in adults (Gordon, Castelli, Hjortland, Kannel, & Dawber, 1977; Miller, 1978). Some studies investigated the relationship between serum lipids and lipoprotein and physical activity in children, but the results do not necessarily agree. No study was found to show subclasses of HDL$_2$ and HDL$_3$ related to physical activity in children. Therefore, the aim of the present study was to investigate HDL$_2$-Chol and other serum lipids of preadolescent children (10 to 12 years of age), related to physical activity levels, aerobic power, body fat, and sex.

MATERIALS AND METHODS

The subjects were 21 trained boys, 21 untrained boys, and 10 untrained girls between the ages of 10 and 12 years, residing in Tokyo. Trained boys had been participating in a soccer club for more than 3 years. They trained 3 hrs a day, 6 days a week, throughout the year. $\dot{V}O_2$max was measured by treadmill running. Body fat was measured by underwater weighing. Residual volume was measured by means of the oxygen dilution method according to Rahn, Fenn, and Otis (1949). Blood samples were drawn from the medial cubital vein following 12 to 14 hours of fasting and 36 to 40 hrs after any intense exercise. Skeletal ages were evaluated by radiographs of the left hand using the TW_2 method.

HDL and HDL_3 fractions were measured by ultracentrifugation. The concentrations of serum total HDL-cholesterol and HDL_2-cholesterol were determined enzymatically (cholesterol oxidase, cholesterol esterase, Kyowa Hakko KK., Japan). The concentration of serum HDL_2-cholesterol was calculated from total HDL-cholesterol minus HDL_3-cholesterol. The concentrations of triglyceride and cholesterol were measured by an automatic analyzer (Hitachi Co. Ltd., Japan). Oxygen uptake and carbon dioxide were measured by an automatic gas analyzer (Anima, R-1500PS).

RESULTS

No significant difference was found for skeletal age, body weight, and body height among the 3 groups (see Table 1). Body fat of the girls was significantly higher than those of the 2 groups of boys. Mean $\dot{V}O_2$max per body weight of the three groups was significantly different from each other, that is, 54.0 ± 1.0, 48.9 ± 1.0, and 45.0 ± 2.5 ml • $kg^{-1}min^{-1}$, respectively. Serum triglyceride of girls was significantly higher than that of the trained boys (see Table 2). Total cholesterol of the trained boys was significantly higher than that of the other 2 groups. HDL-Chol and HDL_2-Chol of the trained boys were higher than those of the untrained boys but not the girls. No difference was found in the ratio of HDL-Chol and total cholesterol among the 3 groups.

Table 1 Physical Characteristics (Mean ± SE) of the Subjects

Variable	Soccer n = 21	Control n = 21	Female n = 10
Chronological age (yr)	12.0 ± 0.1	12.0 ± 0.1	11.3 ± 0.2
Skeletal age (yr)	11.8 ± 0.3	11.7 ± 0.3	11.1 ± 0.4
Height (cm)	145.1 ± 1.3	143.4 ± 1.4	141.3 ± 2.5
Weight (kg)	37.6 ± 1.4	35.9 ± 1.3	35.0 ± 2.3
% fat (%)	17.8 ± 1.1	18.9 ± 1.1	$24.2 \pm 1.8^*$
$\dot{V}O_2$max/wt (ml/kg • min)	$54.0 \pm 1.0^*$	48.9 ± 1.0	$45.0 \pm 2.5^*$

$^*p < .05.$

Table 2 Serum Lipoprotein and Lipids (Mean ± SE) of the Subjects

Variable	Soccer $n = 21$	Control $n = 21$	Female $n = 10$
TG (mg/dl)	70.4 ± 3.7	73.6 ± 6.3	86.6 ± 8.3†
T-Chol (mg/dl)	177.2 ± 5.4*	173.7 ± 6.7	174.0 ± 8.2†
HDL-Chol (mg/dl)	74.9 ± 3.4*	65.8 ± 2.5	72.2 ± 3.9
HDL₂-Chol (mg/dl)	51.9 ± 3.1*	42.6 ± 2.4	49.1 ± 4.0
HDL₃-Chol (mg/dl)	23.0 ± 0.7	23.2 ± 0.6	23.1 ± 0.9
HDL-C/T-Chol	0.42 ± 0.02	0.39 ± 0.02	0.40 ± 0.02
HDL₂/HDL₃	2.33 ± 0.20*	1.80 ± 0.17	2.17 ± 0.20

*$p < .05$ for S-C; †$p < .05$ for F-S.

Correlation coefficients among serum lipids, body fat, and V̇O₂max are shown in Table 3. Total cholesterol showed a significant relationship to HDL-Chol and the two HDL subfractions among them. The correlation coefficient between total cholesterol and HDL₃-Chol was the highest. HDL-Chol showed markedly higher correlations of HDL₂-Chol ($p < .001$). HDL₂-Chol was significantly related to V̇O₂max in males ($p < .05$) (see Figure 1a). On the other hand, HDL₃-Chol was not significantly related to total cholesterol, triglyceride concentration, and body fat in males ($p < .05$) (see Figure 1b). The distribution of HDL₃-Chol of females was somewhat different from that of males.

Table 3 Significant Levels of Correlation Coefficients

Variable	HDL	% HDL	HDL₂	HDL₃	HDL₂/₃	TG	% fat	V̇O₂max/wt
T-Chol	**					***	*	
		_*	*	***				
		(*)		(*)				
HDL-Chol	***	***	*	***			*	*
		(***)		(**)				
% HDL			***		***	_***		
HDL₂					***			*
					(***)			
HDL₃						*	**	
HDL₂/₃								*
TG								
% fat								_***
								(*)

Note. ( ) for female children; − for negative correlation.
*$p < .05$; **$p < .01$; ***$p < .001$.

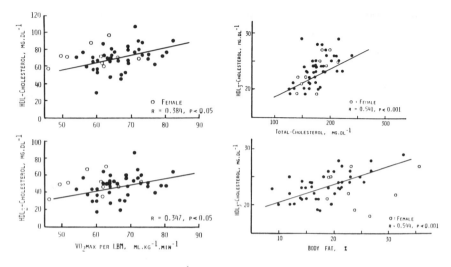

Figure 1   (a) The relation between V̇O₂max (per LBM) and HDL-Cholesterol and HDL₂-Cholesterol in children; (b) the distribution of HDL₃-Cholesterol, related to total cholesterol and body fat in children.

DISCUSSION

The values of total cholesterol in the present subjects agreed with the data of Dutch girls (Zonderland et al., 1984), American swimmers (Smith, Sparrow, Heusner, Van Huss, & Conn, 1985), and Japanese children (Okuni, Hayashi, Kiryu, & Yamauchi, 1980) of the same ages, but was relatively higher than data for American children reported by Linder, DuRant, and Mahoney (1983) and Thorland and Gilliam (1981). One of the reasons for the high values of total cholesterol in Japanese children might be the nutritional tendencies of Japanese children in recent years, which have become increasingly similar to European and American children.

High values of HDL₂-Chol were reported for the athletes as compared with control adults (Kraus et al., 1977; Wood & Haskell, 1979), whereas no information is available about the relationship between physical activity and HDL subfractions in children and adolescents. In the present study, HDL-Chol and HDL₂-Chol concentrations of trained children were higher than those of untrained boys. These differences were probably not induced by the differences in physical characteristics and maturity because no significant difference was found in these factors. Nutritional environment was probably not significantly related to the difference of HDL₂-Chol and serum lipids because the social status of the groups was similar and body fat, which responds to the nutritional condition, was not significantly different.

The increased aerobic power in trained boys, which indicates high muscle oxidative capacity and high lipoprotein lipase activity, was significantly related to high HDL-Chol (Nikkila, Taskinen, Rehunen, & Harkonen, 1978) and HDL$_2$-Chol in the present study. The physical activity levels of trained boys, estimated from heart rates during training involving soccer practice, were very high (they trained for 2 hrs above a heart rate of 160 bpm). On the contrary, mean heart rate level over 160 bpm during a 12-hr daytime measurement in untrained boys was about 30 min (Atomi, Iwaoka, Hatta, Miyashita, & Yamamoto, in press). It seems that these differences in habitual physical activity might induce a significant difference in HDL$_2$-Chol between groups.

It has been reported that adult females show higher HDL-Chol and HDL$_2$-Chol than adult males (Anderson et al., 1978). In the present study, preadolescent females showed relatively higher HDL$_2$-Chol than untrained boys, and mean values of HDL$_2$-Chol were not significantly different from that of trained boys. Further, the relationship between HDL$_2$-Chol and body fat in girls was somewhat different from those of the two groups of boys. It seems that increasing body fat in female children does not increase HDL$_3$-Chol. Estrogen may influence the serum lipids and lipoprotein levels in preadolescent females as well as in adult females. The estrogen level of preadolescent girls was somewhat higher than that of males (Zonderland et al., 1984).

CONCLUSION

Higher total cholesterol and HDL-Chol of trained boys observed in the present study might be dependent on the higher HDL$_2$-Chol. Two subfractions of HDL-Chol seem to be influenced by different factors; that is, HDL$_2$-Chol may change in relation to physical-activity level and HDL$_3$-Chol may change in relation to serum lipids and body fat in preadolescent boys. Despite high body fat and higher triglycerides in females, the levels of HDL-Chol and HDL$_2$-Chol in females were not significantly different from those of trained boys. Sex differences were observed in the lipoprotein metabolism in 10- to 12-year-old children.

REFERENCES

Anderson, D.W., Nichols, A.V., Pan, S.S., & Lindgren, F.T. (1978). High density lipoprotein distribution—Resolution and determination of three major components in a normal population sample. *Atherosclerosis, 29,* 161-179.

Atomi, Y., Iwaoka, K., Hatta, H., Miyashita, M., & Yamamoto, Y. (in press). Daily physical activity levels in preadolescent boys related to VO$_2$max and lactate threshold. *European Journal of Applied Physiology.*

Castelli, W.P., Doyle, J.T., Gordon, T., Hames, C.G., Hjortland, M.C., Hulley, S.B., Kagan, A., & Zukel, W.J. (1977). HDL cholesterol and other lipids in coronary heart disease—Cooperative lipoprotein phenotyping study. *Circulation, 55*, 767-772.

Gordon, T., Castelli, W.P., Hjortland, M.C., Kannel, W.B., & Dawber, T.R. (1977). High density lipoprotein as a protective factor against coronary heart disease. The Framingham Study. *American Journal of Medicine, 62*, 707-714.

Kraus, R.M., Lindgren, F.T., Wood, P.D., Haskell, W.L., Albers, J.J., & Cheung, M.C. (1977). Differential increase in plasma high density lipoprotein's subfractions and apolipoproteins (Apo-Lp) in runners. *Circulation, 56* (Suppl. 3), 4.

Linder, C.W., DeRant, R.H., & Mahoney, O.M. (1983). The effect of physical conditioning on serum lipids and lipoproteins in white male adolescents. *Medicine and Science in Sports and Exercise, 15*, 232-236.

Miller, G.J., & Miller, N.E. (1975). Plasma-high-density-lipoprotein concentration and development of ischemic heart disease. *Lancet, I*, 16-19.

Miller, N.E. (1978). The evidence for antiatherogenicity of high density lipoprotein in man. *Lipids, 13*, 914-919.

Nikkila, E.A., Taskinen, M.R., Rehunen, S., & Harkonen, M. (1978). Lipoprotein lipase activity in adipose tissue and skeletal muscle of runners: Relation to serum lipoproteins. *Metabolism, 27*, 1661-1671.

Okuni, M., Hayashi, K., Kiryu, S., & Yamauchi, K. (1980). Risk factors for arteriosclerosis in Japanese children. *Japanese Circulation Journal, 44*, 69-75.

Rahn, H., Fenn, W.O., & Otis, A.B. (1949). Daily variations of vital capacity, residual air, and expiratory reserve including a study of the residual air method. *Journal of Applied Physiology, 1*, 725-736.

Rhoads, C.G., Culbrandsen, C.L., & Kagan, A. (1976). Serum lipoprotein and coronary heart disease in a population study of Hawaii Japanese men. *New England Journal of Medicine, 294*, 293-298.

Smith, B.W., Sparrow, A.W., Heusner, W.W., Van Huss, W.D., & Conn, C. (1985). Serum lipid profiles of pre-teenage swimmers. *Medicine and Science in Sports and Exercise, 17*, 220.

Thorland, W.G., & Gilliam, T.B. (1981). Comparison of serum lipids between habitually high and low active pre-adolescent males. *Medicine and Science in Sports and Exercise, 13*, 316-321.

Wood, P.D., & Haskell, W.L. (1979). The effect of exercise on plasma high density lipoproteins. *Lipids, 14*, 417-427.

Zonderland, M.L., Erich, W.B.M., Peltenberg, A.L., Havekes, L., Bernink, M.J.E., & Huisveld, I.A. (1984). Apolipoprotein and lipid profiles in young female athletes. *International Journal of Sports Medicine, 5*, 78-82.

The Effects of a Season of Competitive Soccer on the Serum Lipid and Lipoprotein Cholesterol Profile of Adolescent Boys

Kevin F. Deveaux
Richard D. Bell
University of Saskatchewan, Saskatoon, Canada
Victor A. Laxdal
University Hospital, University of Saskatchewan, Saskatoon, Canada

Most industrialized nations, including Canada, still experience a high incidence of coronary heart disease as a result of the interaction of a variety of recognized risk factors including atherosclerosis. Atherosclerosis refers to the process of increasing fatty acid accumulation in the walls of smaller blood vessels with special emphasis on the coronary arteries (Kaplan & Pesce, 1984). These atherosclerotic plaques have been found in children as young as 6 to 10 years of age (Velican & Velican, 1983) and the rate of progression is thought to be risk factor dependent. Young children and adolescents possess many of the risk factors associated with the development of atherosclerosis and many authors believe that intervention designed to modify these various risk factors should begin at an early age (Gilliam, Katch, Thorland, & Weltman, 1977; Watkins & Strong, 1984; Zonderland, 1985). Unfortunately, there is a lack of research information to support the hypothesis that risk factor modification begun in childhood will reduce the incidence of coronary heart disease in later years.

One risk factor that is receiving increasing attention is physical activity. Physical activity levels are thought to be inversely related to the incidence of coronary heart disease through the effects, either directly or indirectly, on other risk factors such as obesity or the serum lipoproteins. Physical activity is thought to modify the various serum lipids and lipoproteins and, by so doing, may eventually influence the incidence of coronary heart disease (Danner et al., 1984; Gordon, Witztum, Hunninghake, Gates, & Glueck, 1983; Hooper & Noland, 1984; Kiens, Lithell, & Vessby, 1984; Stamford et al., 1984). Relatively few studies have examined the effects of physical activity programs on the serum lipid and lipoprotein profiles of children or adolescent populations (Gilliam & Burke, 1978;

174 Deveaux, Bell, and Laxdal

Linder, DuRant, Gray, & Harkess, 1979; Linder, DuRant, & Mahoney, 1983; Sady, Savage, et al., 1983; Widhalm, Maxa, & Zyman, 1978), and even fewer have investigated the effects of reduced physical activity levels on the serum lipids and lipoprotein profiles of younger populations. The general consensus at the moment seems to be that the effects of physical activity are positive but transient and are lost with the cessation or reduction in physical activity levels (Danner et al., 1984; Gilliam & Burke, 1978; Kesl, Hutchinson, & Sharp, 1984; Thompson, Cullinane, Eshleman, Sady, & Herbert, 1984).

The four lipoprotein classes are (a) chylomicrons, (b) very low density lipoprotein (VLDL), (c) low density lipoprotein (LDL), and (d) high density lipoprotein (HDL). Both VLDL-cholesterol (VLDL-C) and LDL-cholesterol (LDL-C) are thought to be related to coronary heart disease (Gordon, Castelli, & Hjortland, 1977; Lipid Research Clinic Program, 1984a, 1984b), whereas HDL-cholesterol (HDL-C) is thought to have an antiatherosclerotic effect and is therefore inversely related to the development of coronary heart disease (Brownell, Bachorik, & Ayerle, 1982; Castelli et al., 1977; Gordon et al., 1977; Miller, Thelle, Fjorde, & Mjos, 1977). The serum triglyceride concentration (TG) is also thought to be related to the development of coronary heart disease in adults (Hulley, Roseneman, & Boival, 1980) even though this relationship has not been adequately demonstrated in younger populations (Moll et al., 1983; Schrott, Clarke, & Abrahams, 1982).

PURPOSE OF THE STUDY

The purpose of this study was to investigate the effect of 8 weeks of soccer training and 6 weeks of subsequent detraining on the serum lipid and lipoprotein cholesterol levels of male adolescents. Soccer was chosen because it represents an endurance type of sport that is an integral part of the sports program of most Canadian high schools and community minor-sports programs. If soccer training can positively affect the levels of blood lipids and lipoproteins, then soccer can also be seen as having some positive health benefits that may have favorable health implications in later years.

METHODS

A total of 12 male subjects, aged 14 to 17 years, underwent 8 weeks of soccer training with comparisons made between preseason and postseason serum lipid and lipoprotein patterns. Similar comparisons were made from postseason to 6 weeks postseason in 5 subjects who decreased their physical activity level and 7 subjects who remained physically active to further determine the effect of detraining on these various serum lipid and lipoprotein profiles. The exercise program consisted of 8 weeks of soccer training, which consisted of four practices per week and one game per week. The soccer practices were, on average, 1 hr 15 min in duration and of moderate intensity.

Data were collected at the start of the soccer season, immediately following the conclusion of the soccer season, and 6 weeks after the completion of the soccer season. Resting blood samples of approximately 10 ml were taken after receiving informed parental consent, following a 12-hr fasting period, and subsequently were analyzed for total cholesterol (T-C), T-G, HDL-C, LDL-C, VLDL-C, and HDL-C/T-C ratio.

Analysis of the serum lipid and lipoprotein cholesterol profile was carried out in the Pathology Department, University of Saskatchewan Hospital. T-C was analyzed by the method of Allain, Poon, Chan, Richmond, and Fu (1974), whereas TG was analyzed by the method of Bucolo and David (1973). HDL-C was analyzed by the methods of Lopes-Virella, Stone, and Ellis (1977). VLDL-C was calculated as the TG concentration divided by 2.2 (Wilson, Abbot, Garrison, & Castelli, 1981) and LDL-C was calculated by subtracting the HDL-C and VLDL concentrations from the T-C concentration (Friedewald, Levy, & Fredrickson, 1972). Body weight (kg), sum of skinfolds (cm) according to the method of MacDougall, Wenger, and Green (1982), and a 2400-m timed-run performance (s) were also measured, as was the subject's predicted work capacity at a heart rate of 170 beats/min (PWC$_{170}$) (kgm/kg/min). A 5-day nutritional survey and a lifestyle survey were also administered at each testing session in order to monitor, as closely as possible, those external factors that might influence the serum lipid and lipoprotein cholesterol profile.

Comparisons of T-C, TG, VLDL-C, LDL-C, HDL-C, HDL-C/T-C ratio, body weight, sum of skinfolds, PWC$_{170}$, and timed run performance from preseason to postseason and from postseason to 6 weeks postseason were statistically analyzed in the detraining and non-detraining groups using the multivariate statistic MANOVA (SPSS-X, 1983). Comparison of mean and individual dietary intake of calories, fat, CHO, protein, cholesterol, and polyunsaturated and saturated fat from preseason to postseason to 6 weeks postseason was done using one-way analysis of variance (*SPSS-X User's Guide*, 1983).

RESULTS AND DISCUSSION

Work Capacity and Run Performance

The mean initial PWC$_{170}$ values for both the detraining and the non-detraining groups (16.26 kgm/kg/min and 15.14 kgm/kg/min, respectively) were slightly higher than the Canadian means as reported by Gauthier, Massicotte, Hermiston, and MacNab (1983). Similarly the mean 2400-m timed-run values of 604.2 s for the detraining group and 594.8 s for the non-detraining group were also somewhat better than average Canadian standards (Canada Fitness Survey, 1983). There were no significant (p < .05) alterations in either the physical work capacity or the timed-run performance as a result of either the soccer training program or the subsequent period of detraining. The lack of improvement in work capacity or timed-run performance probably reflected the fact that the soccer training program represented only a moderate intensity increase in a normally active lifestyle and improvements are relatively difficult to elicit when initial fitness levels are above the average (Kiens et al., 1984; Williams, Wood, Haskell, & Varnizan, 1982).

Anthropometric Parameters

Initial mean body weights for both the detraining and non-detraining group (64.5 kg and 64.3 kg, respectively) were similar to the values obtained in the Canada Fitness Survey for males 14 to 17 years of age. Interestingly, the initial mean tricep skinfold values of 8.8 mm and 8.1 mm for the detraining and non-detraining groups were somewhat lower than comparable Canadian values (Canada Fitness Survey, 1983) indicating that the soccer players in this study already possessed a relatively low degree of body fat. There were no significant alterations in either body weight or skinfold values as a result of either the soccer training or the subsequent period of detraining, which would further substantiate the fact that the soccer training program lacked the necessary intensity to significantly alter anthropometric parameters. Mean performances and anthropometric values are shown in Tables 1 and 2.

Nutrition and Lifestyle Surveys

Individual nutritional patterns were closely monitored by means of a 5-day comprehensive nutritional survey. All subjects showed consistent dietary patterns throughout the study with no significant (p < .05) alterations in percentage of fat, carbohydrate, protein, polyunsaturated fat, saturated fat, polyunsaturated-fat-to-saturated-fat ratio, or total calories consumed. As a result, it was assumed that dietary fluctuations would not be a source of possible changes in serum lipid or lipoprotein cholesterol concentrations that might have occurred. Similarly, no significant consumption of tobacco, alcohol, or drugs was reported by any of the subjects in this study.

Serum Lipid and Lipoprotein Cholesterol

Mean T-C concentrations reported in this study (3.56 mmol/l and 3.96 mmol/l for the non-detraining and detraining groups, respectively) agreed

Table 1   Mean Fitness and Body Composition Values of the Detraining and Non-Detraining Group From Preseason to Postseason

Parameter	Group	n	Pretraining M	SD	n	Posttraining M	SD	F-ratio
PWC	D	4	16.26 ±	1.51	4	17.19 ±	1.80	
(kpm/min/kg)	N	7	16.80 ±	3.73	7	16.83 ±	2.32	
	$\bar{X}_T$	11	16.60 ±	3.01	11	16.69 ±	2.06	NS
1.5-mile run (s)	D	5	604.2 ±	44.8	5	576.0 ±	40.9	
	N	5	594.8 ±	38.0	5	561.7 ±	31.2	
	$\bar{X}_T$	10	599.4 ±	36.6	10	574.7 ±	30.3	NS
Sum of skinfolds	D	5	45.16 ±	9.52	5	46.10 ±	9.77	
(mm)	N	7	46.54 ±	9.47	7	43.07 ±	7.76	
	$\bar{X}_T$	12	45.97 ±	9.07	12	44.33 ±	8.36	NS
Wt (kg)	D	5	64.49 ±	10.17	5	65.10 ±	10.06	
	N	7	64.28 ±	8.43	7	64.50 ±	8.48	
	$\bar{X}_T$	12	64.37 ±	8.74	12	64.75 ±	8.73	NS

Note. D = detrainers; N = non-detrainers; $\bar{X}_T$ = total sample.

Table 2   Mean Fitness and Body Composition Values of the Detraining and Non-Detraining Group From Postseason to 6 Weeks Postseason

Parameter	Group	n	Posttraining M	SD	n	6 weeks posttraining M	SD	F-ratio
PWC	D	4	17.19 ±	1.80	4	18.76 ±	1.85	
(kpm/min/kg)	N	7	16.83 ±	2.32	7	17.29 ±	2.38	
	$\bar{X}_T$	11	16.96 ±	2.06	11	17.82 ±	2.23	NS
1.5-mile run (s)	D	5	577.8 ±	35.7	5	594.6 ±	20.9	
	N	5	571.6 ±	27.8	5	571.6 ±	33.3	
	$\bar{X}_T$	10	574.7 ±	30.3	10	583.1 ±	28.9	NS
Sum of skinfolds	D	5	46.10 ±	9.77	5	44.04 ±	9.76	
(mm)	N	7	43.07 ±	7.76	7	42.48 ±	6.50	
	$\bar{X}_T$	12	44.33 ±	8.36	12	43.13 ±	7.64	NS
Wt (kg)	D	5	65.10 ±	10.06	5	65.10 ±	10.52	
	N	7	64.50 ±	8.48	7	64.96 ±	8.23	
	$\bar{X}_T$	12	64.75 ±	8.73	12	65.02 ±	8.79	NS

Note. D = detrainers; N = non-detrainers; $\bar{X}_T$ = total sample.

with previously reported values for similar age groups (Cresanta, Sathanur, Srinivasan, Webber, & Berenson, 1982). LDL-C values were slightly higher, especially for the detraining group, than values reported elsewhere (Cresanta et al., 1982) while HDL-C values were slightly lower. The values for VLDL-C reported in this study were surprisingly higher than those reported by Cresanta et al. (1982) but in relative agreement with values reported by Jones et al. (1980) involving Canadian subjects. As might be expected the mean TG values were also slightly higher than previously reported values (Jones et al., 1980; Tamir et al., 1980). The serum lipid and lipoprotein cholesterol profiles of the subjects in this study, however, do appear to fall into a normal range of values. Data for all serum lipid and lipoprotein cholesterol parameters are presented in Tables 3 and 4.

There is still disagreement concerning the intensity and/or duration of work required to favorably alter blood lipid profiles (Danner et al., 1984; Gaesser & Rich, 1984; Heath, Ehsani, Hagberg, Hinderliter, & Goldberg, 1983; Linder et al., 1983; Michielli, Stein, Glantz, Sardy, & Cohen, 1982; Stubbe, Hansson, Gustafson, & Nilsson-Ehle, 1983; Thomas, Adeniran, Iltis, Aquiar, & Albers, 1985; Trann, Weltman, Glass, & Mood, 1983; Widhalm et al., 1978). The lack of change in serum lipid and serum lipo-

Table 3   Mean Serum Lipid and Lipoprotein Cholesterol Values of the Detraining and Non-Detraining Group From Preseason to Postseason

Parameter	Group		Pretraining			Posttraining		F-ratio
		n	M	SD	n	M	SD	
T-Chol	D	5	3.96	± .60	5	3.82	± .76	
(mmol/L)	N	7	3.56	± .38	7	3.33	± .57	
	$\bar{X}_T$	12	3.73	± .50	12	3.53	± .64	NS
Triglycerides	D	5	.81	± .29	5	.81	± .31	
(mmol/L)	N	7	1.00	± .43	7	.78	± .18	
	$\bar{X}_T$	12	.92	± .38	12	.79	± .23	NS
VLDL-C	D	5	.34	± .13	5	.37	± .14	
(mmol/L)	N	7	.45	± .19	7	.36	± .08	
	$\bar{X}_T$	12	.42	± .17	12	.36	± .10	NS
LDL-C	D	5	2.30	± .54	5	2.18	± .55	
(mmol/L)	N	7	1.96	± .43	7	1.86	± .49	
	$\bar{X}_T$	12	2.10	± .49	12	1.99	± .52	NS
HDL-C	D	5	1.30	± .14	5	1.28	± .15	
(mmol/L)	N	7	1.16	± .13	7	1.10	± .16	
	$\bar{X}_T$	12	1.22	± .15	12	1.18	± .18	NS
T-Chol/HDL-C	D	5	3.07	± .59	5	2.97	± .47	
	N	7	3.09	± .32	7	3.04	± .42	
	$\bar{X}_T$	12	3.08	± .43	12	3.01	± .43	NS

Note.   D = detrainers; N = non-detrainers; $\bar{X}_T$ = total sample.

Table 4 Mean Serum Lipid and Lipoprotein Cholesterol Values of the Detraining and Non-Detraining Group From Postseason to 6 Weeks Postseason

Parameter	Group	Posttraining			6 weeks posttraining			F-ratio
		n	M	SD	n	M	SD	
T-Chol	D	5	3.82 ± .76		5	4.10 ± .59		
(mmol/L)	N	7	3.33 ± .57		7	3.53 ± .48		
	$\bar{X}_T$	12	3.35 ± .67		12	3.77 ± .59		NS
Triglycerides	D	5	.81 ± .31		5	.85 ± .27		
(mmol/L)	N	7	.78 ± .18		7	.86 ± .32		
	$\bar{X}_T$	12	.80 ± .23		12	.86 ± .29		NS
VLDL-C	D	5	.37 ± .14		5	.39 ± .12		
(mmol/L)	N	7	.36 ± .08		7	.39 ± .12		
	$\bar{X}_T$	12	.36 ± .10		12	.39 ± .13		NS
LDL-C	D	5	2.18 ± .55		5	2.40 ± .46		
(mmol/L)	N	7	1.86 ± .49		7	1.91 ± .61		
	$\bar{X}_T$	12	1.99 ± .52		12	2.12 ± .59		NS
HDL-C	D	5	1.28 ± .15		5	1.30 ± .16		
(mmol/L)	N	7	1.10 ± .16		7	1.21 ± .23		
	$\bar{X}_T$	12	1.18 ± .18		12	1.25 ± .20		NS
T-Chol/HDL-C	D	5	2.97 ± .48		5	3.18 ± .49		
	N	7	3.04 ± .42		7	3.04 ± .87		
	$\bar{X}_T$	12	3.01 ± .43		12	3.09 ± .72		NS

Note. D = detrainers; N = non-detrainers; $\bar{X}_T$ = total sample.

protein cholesterol levels was not surprising given the lack of change as a result of the 8-week training period. Previous authors have shown negative effects of a detraining period (Danner et al., 1984; Kesl et al., 1984; Thompson et al., 1984) but only after significant improvements were elicited as a result of a specific training program.

CONCLUSION

If soccer is a representative sporting program at the high-school level and if positive health goals are to be one of the objectives of the high-school program, more attention should be devoted to the required training intensity and duration of the various sports programs necessary to elicit positive changes in various health-related parameters such as the serum lipid and lipoprotein cholesterol levels.

Acknowledgment

This study was supported by a Research Grant (1984) from the Saskatchewan Sport and the Saskatchewan Soccer Association.

REFERENCES

Allain, C.C., Poon, L.S., Chan, C.S.G., Richmond, W., & Fu, P.C. (1974). Enzymatic determination of total serum cholesterol. *Clinical Chemistry,* **20,** 740-745.

Brownell, K.D., Bachorik, P.S., & Ayerle, R.S. (1982). Changes in lipid and lipoprotein levels in men and women after a program of moderate exercise. *Circulation,* **65**(3), 477-484.

Bucolo, D., & David, H. (1973). Quantitive determination of serum triglycerides by the use of enzymes.

Canada Fitness Survey. (1983). *Fitness and Lifestyle Canada.* Ottawa: Government of Canada, Department of Fitness and Amateur Sport.

Castelli, W.P., Doyle, J.T., Gorden, T., Hames, C.G., Hjortland, M.C., Hulley, S.B., Kagan, A., & Zukel, W.I. (1977). Cholesterol levels (HDL) and other lipids in coronary heart disease: The cooperative lipoprotein phenotyping study. *Circulation,* **55,** 767-772.

Cresanta, J.L., Sathanur, R., Srinivasan, S.R., Webber, L.S., & Berenson, G.S. (1982). Serum lipid and lipoprotein cholesterol grids for cardiovascular risk screening of children. *American Journal of Disease in Children,* **138,** 379-387.

Danner, S.A., Wieling, W., Havekes, L., Leuven, J.G., Smit, E.M., & Dunning, A.J. (1984). Effect of physical exercise on blood lipids and adipose tissue composition in young healthy men. *Atherosclerosis,* **53,** 83-90.

Friedewald, W.T., Levy, R.I., & Fredrickson, D.S. (1972). Estimation of the concentration of low-density lipoprotein cholesterol in plasma, without the use of preparative ultracentrifuge. *Clinical Chemistry,* **18,** 499-502.

Gaesser, G.A., & Rich, R.G. (1984). Effects of high and low-intensity exercise on aerobic capacity and blood lipids. *Medicine and Science in Sports and Exercise,* **16**(3), 269-274.

Gauthier, R., Massicotte, D., Hermiston, R., & MacNab, R. (1983). The physical work capacity of Canadian children, aged 7 to 17, in 1983. 2. A comparison with 1968. *Capher Journal,* (Nov.-Dec.), 4-9.

Gilliam, T.B., & Burke, M.B. (1978). Effects of exercise on serum lipids and lipoproteins in girls, ages 8 to 10 years. *Artery,* **4,** 203-213.

Gilliam, T.B., Katch, V.L., Thorland, W., & Weltman, A. (1977). Prevalence of coronary heart disease risk factors in children, 7 to 12 years of age. *Medicine and Science in Sports and Exercise,* **9**(1), 21-25.

Gordon, D.J., Witztum, J.L., Hunninghake, D., Gates, S., & Glueck, C.J. (1983). Habitual physical activity and high-density lipoprotein cholesterol in men with hypercholesterolemia. 2. The Lipid Research Clinic's primary prevention trial. *Circulation,* **67**(3), 512-520.

Gordon, T., Castelli, W.P., & Hjortland, M.C. (1977). High density lipo-protein as a protective factor against coronary heart disease: The Framingham study. *American Journal of Medicine, 62,* 707-714.

Heath, G.W., Ehsani, A.A., Hagberg, J.M., Hinderliter, E.M., & Gold-berg, A.P. (1983). Exercise training improves lipoprotein lipid profiles in patients with coronary artery disease. *American Heart Journal, 105,* 889-894.

Hooper, P.L., & Noland, B.J. (1984). Aerobic dance program improves cardiovascular fitness in men. *The Physician and Sportsmedicine, 12*(5), 132-135.

Hulley, S.B., Roseneman, R.H., & Boival, R.D. (1980). The association between triglycerides and coronary heart disease. *New England Journal of Medicine, 302,* 1383-1389.

Jones, G.J.L., Hewitt, D., Godin, G.L., Breckenridge, W.C., Bird, J., Mishkel, M.A., Steiner, G., & Little, J.A. (1980). Plasma lipoprotein levels and prevalence of hyperlipoproteinemia in a Canadian working population. *Canadian Medical Association Journal, 122,* 37-46.

Kaplan, L.A., & Pesce, A.J. (1984). *Clinical chemistry theory analysis and correlation.* St. Louis: Mosby.

Kesl, L.D., Hutchinson, W.W., & Sharp, R.L. (1984). Effects of training and detraining on maximal oxygen uptake and plasma lipoprotein cholesterol concentrations. *Medicine and Science in Sports and Exercise* (Abstract), *16*(2), 197.

Kiens, B., Lithell, H., & Vessby, B. (1984). Further increases in high density lipoprotein in trained males after enhanced training. *European Journal of Applied Physiology, 52,* 426-430.

Linder, C.W., DuRant, R.H., Gray, R.G., & Harkess, J.W. (1979). The effects of exercise on serum lipids in children. *Clinical Research* (Abstract), *27,* 797.

Linder C.W., DuRant, R.H., & Mahoney, O.M. (1983). The effect of physical conditioning on serum lipids and lipoproteins in white male adolescents. *Medicine and Science in Sports and Exercise, 15*(3), 232-236.

Lipid Research Clinic Program. (1984a). The Lipid Research Clinic's coronary primary prevention trial results. I. Reduction in incidence of coronary heart disease. *Journal of the American Medical Association, 251,* 351-364.

Lipid Research Clinic Program. (1984b). The Lipid Research Clinic's coronary primary prevention trial results. II. The relationship of reduc-tion in incidence of coronary heart disease to cholesterol lowering. *Journal of the American Medical Association, 251,* 365-374.

Lopes-Virella, M.F., Stone, P., & Ellis, S. (1977). Cholesterol determina-tion in high-density lipoproteins separated by three different methods. *Clinical Chemistry, 23*(5), 882-884.

MacDougall, J.D., Wenger, H.A., & Green, H.J. (1982). *Physiological testing of the elite athlete.* Canada: Mutual Press.

Michielli, D.W., Stein, R.A., Glantz, M., Sardy, H., & Cohen, A. (1982). The effect of different exercise training intensities on plasma cholesterol. *Medicine and Science in Sports and Exercise* (Abstract), **14**(2), 110.

Miller, N.E., Thelle, D.S., Fjorde, O.H., & Mjos, O.D. (1977). The Tromso heart study. 2. High-density lipoprotein and coronary heart disease: 3. A prospective case-control study. *Lancet,* **1**, 965-968.

Moll, P.P., Sing, C.F., Weidman, W.H., Gorden, H., Ellefson, R.D., Hodgson, M.S., & Kottke, B.A. (1983). 2. Prediction of coronary heart disease in adult relatives. *Circulation,* **67**, 127-134.

Sady, S.P., Savage, M.P., Petratis, M.M., Thompson, W.W., Berg, K., & Smith, J.L. (1983). Comparative effects of exercise training on serum lipids and lipoproteins of prepubescent boys and adult men. *Medicine and Science in Sports and Exercise* (Abstract), **15**(2), 184.

Schrott, H.G., Clarke, W.R., & Abrahams, P. (1982). Coronary heart disease mortality in relatives of hypertriglyceridemic school children. 2. The muscatine study. *Circulation,* **65**, 300-305.

SPSS-X user's guide. (1983). New York: McGraw-Hill.

Stamford, B.A., Matter, S., Fell, R.D., Sady, S., Papanek, P., & Cresanta, M. (1984). Cigarette smoking and high density lipoprotein cholesterol. *Atherosclerosis,* **52**, 73-83.

Stubbe, I., Hansson, P., Gustafson, A., & Nilsson-Ehle, P. (1983). Plasma lipoproteins and lipolytic enzyme activities during endurance training in sedentary men. 2. Changes in high-density lipoprotein subfractions and composition. *Metabolism,* **32**(12), 1120-1128.

Tamir, I., Heiss, G., Glueck, C.J., Christensen, B., Witerovich, P.K., & Rifkind, B.M. (1980). Lipid and lipoprotein distributions in white children ages 6-19 years. 2. The Lipid Research Clinic's program prevalence study. *Journal of Chronic Disease,* **34**, 27-39.

Thomas, T.R., Adeniran, S.B., Iltis, P.W., Aquiar, C.A., & Albers, J.J. (1985). Effects of interval and continuous running on HDL-cholesterol, apoproteins A-I and B, and LCAT. *Canadian Journal of Applied Sports Sciences,* **10**(1), 52-59.

Thompson, P.D., Cullinane, E.M., Eshleman, R., Sady, S.P., & Herbert, P.N. (1984). The effect of caloric restriction and exercise cessation on the serum lipid lipoprotein concentrations of endurance athletes. *Metabolism,* **33**, 943-950.

Trann, Z.V., Weltman, A., Glass, G.V., & Mood, D.P. (1983). The effects of exercise on blood lipids and lipoproteins: A meta-analysis of studies. *Medicine and Science in Sports and Exercise,* **15**(5), 393-402.

Velican, C., & Velican, D. (1983). Progression of coronary atherosclerosis from adolescents to mature adults. *Atherosclerosis, 47*, 131-144.

Watkins, L.O., & Strong, W.B. (1984). The child: When to begin preventive cardiology. *Current Problems in Pediatrics, 14*(6), 1-71.

Widhalm, K., Maxa, E., & Zyman, H. (1978). Effect of exercise upon the cholesterol and triglyceride content of plasma lipoproteins in overweight children. *European Journal of Pediatrics, 127*, 121-126.

Williams, P.T., Wood, P.D., Haskell, W.L., & Varnizan, K. (1982). The effects of running mileage and duration on plasma lipoprotein levels. *American Medical Association Journal, 247*(19), 2674-2679.

Wilson, P.W., Abbot, R.D., Garrison, R.J., & Castelli, W.P. (1981). Estimation of very low density lipoprotein cholesterol from data on triglyceride concentrations in plasma. *Clinical Chemistry, 27*, 2008-2010.

Zonderland, M.L. (1985). Lipemic risk factors and physical activity, nutrition and biological maturation. In *Lipid and Apolipoprotein Profiles in Premenarcheal Athletes. 2. The Relation with Training, Nutrition and Biological Maturation* (pp. 15-44). Netherlands: Medische Begeleiding.

Blood Pressure Response to Exercise in Adolescent Competitive Athletes

Ronald A. Dlin
Nora Hanna-Paparo
Gershon Tenenbaum
Wingate Institute, Wingate Post, Israel

Previous reports have indicated that blood pressure response to exercise may be useful in the prediction of future hypertension (Dlin, Hanne, Silverberg, & Bar-Or, 1983; Jackson, Squires, Grimes, & Beard, 1983; Wilson & Meyer, 1981). Highly trained athletes have been reported to have a higher systolic BP (SBP) response to exercise than less-trained individuals (Dlin et al., 1984; Ikuyama et al., 1979). Although previous studies have been published describing BP response in adolescents both normotensive and hypertensive (Alpert, Dover, Booker, Martin, & Strong, 1981; Falkner & Lowenthal, 1980; James et al., 1980; Nudel et al., 1980; Riopel, Taylor, & Hohn, 1979), none of these have dealt with populations regularly engaged in physical training. The present study was undertaken to describe the normal SBP response to exercise in a large population of adolescent athletes training in a variety of sports to determine whether differences in BP response between athletes and nonathletes exist in this age group and to elucidate differences, if any, that appear in SBP response between the various sport groups.

METHODS

In a review of the results of subjects who had undergone cycle ergometry testing at the Sport Medicine Unit of the Wingate Institute, 822 male athletes aged 14 to 18 years met these entry criteria: regular training in a specific sport, participation in competition, and healthy with no known chronic illnesses.

The different sport groups and the number of subjects in each group are shown in Table 1. The testing protocol included a medical history, physical examination, resting ECG, and anthropometric measurements. The subjects were then seated on a standard Monark cycle ergometer with the ECG electrodes in place. An appropriate BP cuff was placed on the right upper arm, and the ECG and BP were recorded in the seated position prior to beginning the exercise task. The exercise consisted of submaximal graded and continuous cycle ergometry, each stage lasting 3 min.

Blood pressure was recorded by manual techniques using a mercury sphygmomanometer and heart rate (HR) through the ECG recording during the last 15 s of each power load. During the BP measurement the right hand was held free of the handlebar.

Table 1 Sport Groups and Number of Subjects

Sport groups	N	% of total
Swimming	107	13
Rowing	33	4
Volleyball	57	7.0
Basketball	126	15.3
Soccer	82	10
Team handball	80	9.7
Tennis	34	4.2
Distance running	71	8.6
Cycling	46	5.6
Boxing	23	2.8
Track and field	102	12.4
Other[a]	61	7.4
Total	n = 822	100%

[a]Other includes specific sport groups with less than 20 subjects per group.

STATISTICAL ANALYSIS

Statistical analysis was carried out by computer using the SPSS package. Univariate analysis of variance with the Scheffé post hoc multiple comparison procedure was used for comparing means between individual groups. Data presented as means are based on the entire sample of subjects. When groups were compared only those groups with more than 20 subjects were included in the comparative statistics. These groups are listed in Table 1.

RESULTS

The study population was comprised of competitive athletes representing 11 different sports (see Table 1). For purposes of presentation of means for the entire age group, sports groups with fewer than 20 subjects were included as "other" but were excluded in intergroup comparisons. Anthropometric and physiological characteristics for the entire study population are presented in Table 2. The HR and SBP response for the various groups are shown in Table 3. Data are presented for three different power loads.

Table 2   Anthropometric and Physiological Characteristics of the Entire Study Population

Characteristics	M	SD
Anthropometric		
Age (yr)	15.9	1.1
Height (cm)	174.8	8.9
Weight (kg)	65.4	9.9
BSA (m²)	1.79	0.17
% fat	8.1	4.0
Physiological		
HR (bpm)	70.7	11.0
SBP (mmHg)	119.3	10.9
$\dot{V}O_2$max (max l/min)	3.9	0.8
$\dot{V}O_2$max/kg (ml/kg/min)	59.4	9.9

Table 3   Mean and *SD* for HR and SBP Response to Exercise in Various Sport Groups

Group	Parameter	HR (bpm)			SBP (mmHg)		
		100 W	200 W	250 W	100 W	200 W	250 W
Swimming	M	124	162	168	153	188	204
	SD	15	13	9	16	18	18
Rowing	M	116	156	172	156	187	197
	SD	11	13	8	18	19	14
Volleyball	M	119	159	171	158	189	194
	SD	12	12	6	18	19	10
Basketball	M	119	155	162	155	189	210
	SD	14	14	10	17	19	18
Soccer	M	120	159	169	152	181	198
	SD	14	14	11	16	15	13
Handball	M	119	157	169	151	188	205
	SD	13	15	9	18	18	17
Tennis	M	123	161	172	149	185	206
	SD	18	14	4	17	15	16
Distance running	M	118	158	171	152	186	205
	SD	15	15	9	16	21	18
Cycling	M	120	157	173	152	186	206
	SD	15	13	7	14	16	10
Boxing	M	131	161	—	140	166	—
	M	18	10		16	17	
Track and field	M	120	159	170	150	186	202
	SD	14	14	7	17	17	13
All groups[a]	M	120	158	169	153	187	203
	SD	14	14	9	17	18	15
	n	811	517	130	811	517	130

[a]Values for groups with fewer than 20 subjects are not presented individually but are included in the overall mean.

When the HR and SBP response of each of the sport groups at equivalent power loads (100, 200, and 250 W) were compared by one-way analysis of variance using the Scheffé post hoc multiple comparison procedure, no significant differences between individual groups at any of the power loads were found. However, there were groups that represent the opposite extremes for each of these variables. Boxers showed the highest HR and the lowest SBP response, whereas rowers had the lowest HR and highest SBP response to a given power load (HR 131 versus 115, SBP 140 versus 157). Because of the inherent difficulties in comparing SBP when HR varies, Figure 1 presents the mean SBP response to exercise plotted against the mean HR response. This graph represents means and 1 *SD* of each of the parameters, respectively, for the entire sample of subjects. Thus, at the peak exercise measured in this study, the mean SBP was 203 ± 15 mmHg with a range from 160 to 245 mmHg. At this level mean HR was 170 ± 9 bpm with a range from 135 to 185 bpm. As is evident from the HR, this was not maximal effort for this age group but represented submaximal exercise values.

Although differences were found in body surface area (BSA) among groups, no significant correlation was found between BSA and SBP

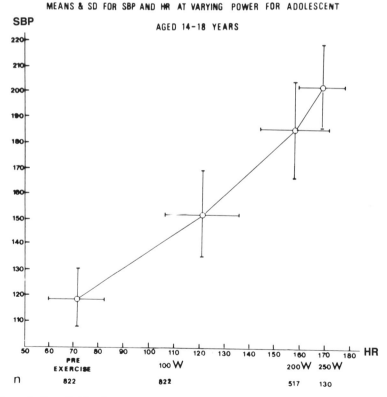

Figure 1 Systolic blood pressure (SBP) response plotted against heart rate (HR) at varying power loads for the entire population.

response, indicating that the fit for any linear regression lines would be unsatisfactory. The same was true for the correlations obtained between age and SBP response.

DISCUSSION

This study differed from other reported blood pressure studies in the literature in that it was comprised of only competitive athletes actively participating in training in a particular sport. It was also unique in that it was a large sample representing a wide range of sport activities. Mean height and weight fell within the 25th to 75th percentile as presented by Tanner, Whitehouse, and Takaishi (1966). The sample was not divided into groups by BSA because of the limited variability (mean BSA = 1.79 ± 0.17 m²). The sample was comparable to groups of larger subjects in reports on other adolescents (Alpert et al., 1981; James et al., 1980; Riopel et al., 1979).

Preexercise HR was somewhat lower (70.7 versus 87.0 bpm) than that reported by Riopel et al. (1979) in those with similar BSA and lower than the larger subjects in James et al. (1980) (70.7 versus 82.0 bpm). Preexercise SBP was similar to that shown by Riopel et al. (1979) (119 versus 118 mmHg) and slightly lower than that reported by James et al. (1980) (119 versus 120-126 mmHg).

Fitness parameters of predicted $\dot{V}O_2$max absolute and relative to body weight were more than 1 SD above the mean reported by Bar-Or (1983) in a healthy nonathletic sample of similar age, and are much higher than that shown by Fixler et al. (1979), in which 43% of the population were engaged in some physical activity.

Because absolute power loads impose a varying strain on a subject depending on the fitness level, comparison of SBP between individuals or groups performing at varying cardiovascular strain cannot be considered valid. Heart rate, because it is a good indicator of relative cardiovascular effort, is a reasonable basis for comparison. Means of SBP response to exercise are thus shown plotted against HR response in Figure 2. When the SBP and HR were plotted at the 25th and 75th percentile for the entire population along with the mean in each sport group, it can be seen (see Figure 2) that with the exception of boxers all groups fell within the 25th to 75th percentile. It would, therefore, appear that for the majority of the groups presented here the sport did not seem to be a contributing factor in the development of the SBP response in this age group even though sports requiring primarily aerobic, anaerobic, or strength were included. It would, therefore, appear unnecessary to present the SBP response of each group separately but rather as a single age group.

The boxers had been training a shorter time than the other groups (2.2 ± 1.2 versus group mean of 4.8 ± 2.7 years). This was significantly less than some but not all of the groups. Although their resting SBP was the lowest of the groups tested, it was not significantly lower than all the

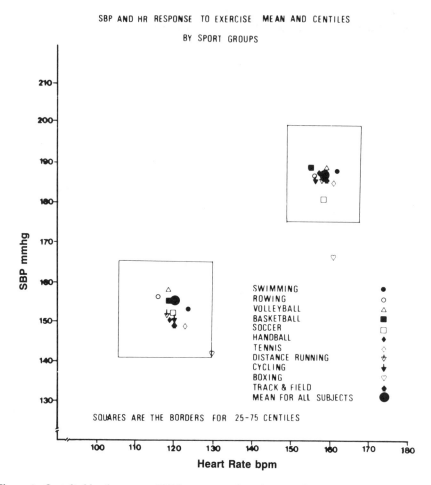

Figure 2 Systolic blood pressure (SBP) response plotted against heart rate (HR) with the mean of each group presented separately. The boxes represent the limits of the 25 to 75 percentile as shown for SBP and HR at power loads of 100 and 200 W, respectively.

groups. The same was true of BSA, which also failed to show any significant correlation with SBP response. Their $\dot{V}O_2max/kg$ was not significantly different from the other groups. It should also be noted that, whereas 70% of the overall group performed 200-W power load, only 30% of the boxers reached this level.

The data for the entire population are presented at several points of effort rather than at peak exercise as reported by others (Alpert et al., 1981; James et al., 1980; Riopel et al., 1979), as maximal levels are subject to uncontrolled variation, such as subject motivation and examiner differences in evaluating end points. The measurement of SBP at submaximal levels presents far fewer problems than measurement at maximal effort. Using Figure 1, the range of normal SBP response at a given HR can be determined for an individual suited to this population. Individuals falling outside the range can be identified and appropriate measures taken.

The BP reached at the highest power load in the present study was similar to that reported by James et al. (1980) and higher than that found by other authors (Alpert et al., 1981; Fixler et al., 1979; Nudel et al., 1980) and in fact higher than their hypertensives. When the HR at the above SBP were compared, the present study group had a markedly low HR, thus suggesting a high SBP response when compared at an equivalent work intensity. These results were very similar to those reported by Mallion et al. (1974). That group, however, included individuals in the age range 15 to 30 years. It would, therefore, appear that SBP in this athletic population was higher than that of nonathletic populations reported in the literature. Similarly a higher SBP response in water-polo players when compared within other adult populations has previously been reported (Dlin et al., 1984). Ikuyama et al. (1979) have also reported a higher SBP response in trained versus untrained men.

The reasons for the higher SBP response to exercise in this athletic population are not known at present, nor is the significance of this BP response for future health aspects clear. Changes in cardiac dimensions are known to occur with training. Left ventricular volume and wall thickness increase as a result of dynamic training (Keul, Dickhuth, Lehmann, & Staiger, 1982; Keul, Dickhuth, Simon, & Lehmann, 1981). These changes have also been observed in children engaged in competitive training (Rost, 1982). The increased end diastolic volumes with the increased ejection fractions during exercise may in part account for the higher BP recorded.

In a previous study (Dlin et al., 1984), water-polo players had a significantly higher SBP response to exercise than a control group; their muscle fiber distribution, however, was not different. The water-polo players trained more frequently and intensely and had a higher VO_2max than did the control group.

While some authors (Dlin et al., 1983; Jackson et al., 1983; Wilson et al., 1981) have reported that a high SBP response to exercise may be predictive of future hypertension, no evidence could be found of any link between sport activity in adolescence and hypertension in later life.

This study defined a normal SBP response to exercise in adolescent male athletes. The significance of a SBP response falling outside the normal range has yet to be determined in this age group. Follow-up studies of normotensive adolescents with abnormal exercise BP response should be undertaken. Longitudinal testing of adolescents undergoing both training and detraining may also contribute further to an understanding of the SBP responses to exercise and their significance.

Acknowledgments

The authors are grateful to Dinah Figenbaum for secretarial assistance and to Etty Brown, Levana Zegal, and Rivka Levy for technical assistance. This project was supported by the Israel Sports Authority of the Ministry of Education.

REFERENCES

Alpert, B.S., Dover, E.V., Booker, D.L., Martin, A.M., & Strong, W.B. (1981). Blood pressure response to dynamic exercise in healthy children—Black vs. white. *Journal of Pediatrics*, **99**, 556-560.

Bar-Or, O. (1983). *Pediatric sports medicine for the practitioner* (pp. 303-304). New York: Springer-Verlag.

Dlin, R.A., Dotan, R., Inbar, O., Rotstein, A., Jacobs, I., & Karlsson, J. (1984). Exaggerated systolic blood pressure response to exercise in a water polo team. *Medicine and Science in Sport and Exercise*, **162**, 294-298.

Dlin, R.A., Hanne, N., Silverberg, D.S., & Bar-Or, O. (1983). Follow-up of normotensive men with exaggerated blood pressure response to exercise. *American Heart Journal*, **106**, 316-320.

Falkner, B., & Lowenthal, D.T. (1980). Dynamic exercise response in hypertensive adolescents. *International Journal of Paediatric Nephrology*, **1**, 161-165.

Fixler, D.E., Laird, W.P., Browne, R., Fitzgerald, V., Wilson, S., & Vance, R. (1979). Response of hypertensive adolescents to dynamic and isometric exercise stress. *Pediatrics*, **64**, 579-583.

Ikuyama, T., Arao, T., Imano, H., Kataoka, Y., Wada, M., Sano, Y., & Osani, H. (1979). Changes in arterial blood pressure during exercise in trained young distance runners, untrained young men and trained men of middle and elderly age. *Bulletin of Physical Fitness Research Institute* (Japan), **42**, 34-46.

Jackson, A.S., Squires, W.G., Grimes, G., & Beard, E.F. (1983). Prediction of future resting hypertension from exercise blood pressure. *Journal of Cardiac Rehabilitation*, **3**, 163-168.

James, F.W., Kaplan, S., Glueck, C.G., Tsay, J., Knight, M.J.S., & Sarwar, C.G. (1980). Responses of normal children and young adults to controlled bicycle exercise. *Circulation*, **61**, 902-912.

Keul, J., Dickhuth, H.H., Lehmann, M., & Staiger, J. (1982). The athlete's heart. Hemodynamics and structure. *International Journal of Sports Medicine*, **3**, 33-43.

Keul, J., Dickhuth, H.H., Simon, G., & Lehmann, N. (1981). Effect of static and dynamic exercise on heart volume, contractibility and left ventricular dimensions. *Circulation Research*, **48** (Supp. I), 162-170.

Mallion, J.M., Debru, J.L., Mikler, F., Avegen, F., Can, G., & Muller, J.M. (1974). Mesure du profil tensionnel d'effort normal. *La Nouvelle Presse Medicale*, **3**, 2003-2006.

Nudel, D.B., Gootman, N., Brunson, S.C., Stengler, A., Shenker, R., & Gauthier, B.G. (1980). Exercise performance of hypertensive adolescents. *Paediatrics*, **65**, 1073-1078.

Riopel, D.A., Taylor, A.B., & Hohn, A.R. (1979). Blood pressure, heart rate pressure rate product, and electrocardiographic changes in healthy children during treadmill exercise. *American Journal of Cardiology,* **44,** 697-704.

Rost, R. (1982). The athlete's heart. *European Heart Journal* (Suppl. A), 193-198.

Tanner, J.M., Whitehouse, R.H., & Takaishi, M. (1966). Standards from birth to maturity for height, weight, height velocity and weight velocity: British children, 1965. *Archives of Disease in Children,* **41,** 454, 613.

Wilson, N.V., & Meyer, B.M. (1981). Early prediction of hypertension using exercise blood pressure. *Preventive Medicine,* **10,** 62-68.

Effects of an 8-Month Reducing Program on the Physical Fitness of Obese Children

Maria Gołębiowska
Tadeusz Bujnowski
Institute of Pediatrics, Medical Academy, Łódź, Poland

Obesity in children is a serious health problem and it may cause numerous diseases over time (Kostka-Trabka & Cergowska, 1966; Tatoń, 1975). The only proper treatment is to maintain a negative energy balance that can be achieved by both a suitable diet and physical activity (Gołębiowska, Chlebna-Sokół, & Tume, 1979; Gołębiowska, Chlebna-Sokół, & Weremczuk, 1979b). The aim of this study was to evaluate physical fitness in obese children based on heart rate and blood metabolites and the changes of these indices due to a reducing program.

MATERIAL AND METHODS

A total of 42 obese children (23 boys, 19 girls) aged 9 to 16 years, with mean excess weight of 38%, participated in this study and were compared with 20 normal children (10 boys, 10 girls) of the same age. Anthropometric measurements using the Martin technique (body weight and height), lean body mass (LBM), and fat mass (FM) (Pařízková, Vaneckova, Sprynarova, & Vamberova, 1971) were determined. A 6-min ergometric test with individual load, according to the PWC_{170} method ($0.8 - 2.0$ W/kg) was administered to each subject (Rutenfranz, 1968; Woynarowska & Wójcik, 1975).

Before and after the test, lactic and pyruvic acid concentrations were determined by enzymatic methods. All the tests were performed (a) before the reducing program; (b) after a 12-week summer camp that included a diet of 1,200 to 1,600 kcal/day of low fat and low carbohydrate, physical activity 8 to 10 hrs/day, and pharmacological treatment (Teronac, Sandoz); and (c) after 20 weeks of home therapy with a subcaloric diet.

RESULTS AND DISCUSSION

The body composition in the obese children was as follows: mean body mass = 71.01 kg, LBM = 46.65 kg, and FM = 24.36 kg (33.44%). The same values in the normal children were: 41.15, 32.99, and 8.16 kg (19.4%), respectively. There was a statistically significant difference between groups in all three variables ($p < .001$). According to percentage of FM these children would be classified as average obese (Kozłowski & Nazar, 1984).

Physical fitness as determined by the 6-min ergometric test was lower in the obese children than in other children of average body mass, according to Gołębiowska, Chlebna-Sokól, and Tume (1979), Gołębiowska, Chlebna-Sokól, and Weremczuk (1979), Mocellin and Rutenfranz (1971), and Paŕizková et al. (1971). Heart rates for each minute of the test (apart from the 1st min) and in recovery were significantly higher in the obese children than in the normal children (see Figure 1).

Values of PWC_{170}/kg of body mass in the obese children were significantly lower than in the children of the control group ($p < .001$). After the 12-week reducing program a significant decrease in body mass, percent FM, and LBM ($p < .001$) was observed. This was consistent with the findings of other researchers (Krawczuk-Rybakowa & Urban, 1984; Paŕizková et al., 1971; Paŕizková, 1977). After an additional 20 weeks of a noncontrolled home dieting program all of the values already mentioned increased significantly, except percent FM, which remained lower in relation to the primary value (see Figure 2).

Physical fitness determined by an ergometric test after 12 weeks of a reducing program was not changed, but after 32 weeks there was a significant decrease in heart rate and heart recovery rate (see Figure 3). It

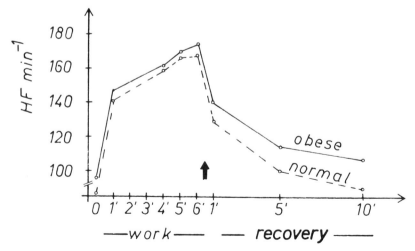

Figure 1 Heart rate during and after exercise in obese children in comparison with normal ones.

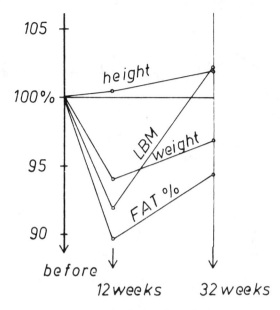

Figure 2   Anthropometric measurements during the reducing program.

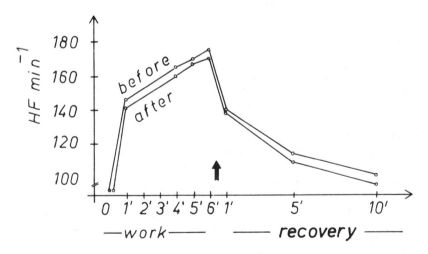

Figure 3   Heart rate during and after exercise, before and after the reducing program.

was assumed that this change was due to LBM changes during the reducing program (see Figure 2). Despite the lack of a significant increase in physical fitness after the 12-week program, PWC_{170} value (in terms of kg/body mass) increased ($p < .05$), and after 32 weeks this value decreased again as a result of the change in body mass (see Figure 4).

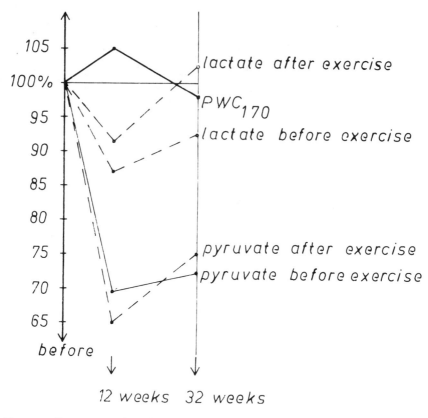

Figure 4 Comparison of PWC₁₇₀, lactate, and pyruvate before and after the reducing program.

Biochemical analyses are shown in Figure 4 of both lactic and pyruvic acid concentrations in the obese children due to the reducing program as compared with the control group. The concentrations of lactic and pyruvic acid in the obese children before the ergometric test were higher than in the normal children ($p < .02$ and $p < .001$, respectively), but after the test the values of these metabolites in both groups increased, and obese children compared with the normal ones showed a higher concentration of pyruvic acid only ($p < .001$).

After the 12-week reducing program there was a significant decrease in the concentrations of both lactic and pyruvic acids in the blood both before and after physical exercise ($p < .001$). After 20 weeks of additional dieting, however, concentrations of both acids before and after exercise increased significantly ($p < .001$). Still, they were lower than before the initiation of the reducing program (see Figure 4).

Higher values of pyruvic acid concentration in blood in obese children were observed. This condition was due to the phenomenon of excessive production or a disorder slowing the process of further modifications of this compound (Kostka-Trabka & Cergowska, 1966). Significant decreases in the concentration of pyruvic acid during the course of a reducing program can be explained by better utilization of this compound in the mitochondria. This cycle of metabolism supplies large amounts of ATP and, therefore, physical fitness is improved (Kozłowski & Nazar, 1984).

CONCLUSIONS

This program of physical activity and subcaloric diet had a favorable effect on the body as evidenced by fat mass reduction and an increase in physical fitness in obese children. The concentration of pyruvic acid in the blood after exercise in comparison with lactic acid was of greater importance for the determination of the physical working capacity of obese children.

REFERENCES

Gołębiowska, M., Chlebna-Sokół, D., & Tume, W. (1979). Influence of special summer camp on body composition and hemodynamic indices of obese children [in Polish]. *Przeglad Pediatryczny, 9*, 287.

Gołębiowska, M., Chlebna-Sokół, D., & Weremczuk, A. (1979, October). *Dependence of physical working capacity of obese children on overweight level and adolescence phase* (Abstract 263). Paper presented at the XX Congress of Pediatrics, Bratislava.

Kostka-Trabka, E., & Cergowska, D. (1966). Pickwick syndrome and pyruvic acid disorders [in Polish]. *Wiadomości Lekarskie, 9*, 315.

Kozłowski, S., & Nazar, K. (1984). Introduction to clinical physiology [in Polish]. Warszawa: Polskie Zaklady Wydawnictw Lekarskich.

Krawczuk-Rybakowa, M., & Urban, M. (1984). Influence of a low caloric diet and physical activity on anthropometric measurements [in Polish]. *Pediatria Polska, 59*, 221.

Mocellin, R., & Rutenfranz, J. (1971). Investigations of the physical working capacity of obese children. *Acta Paediatrica Scandinavica, 217* (Suppl.), 77-79.

Pařízková, J. (1977). *Body fat and physical fitness*. The Hague: Nijhoff.

Pařízková, J., Vaneckova, M., Sprynarova, S., & Vamberova, M. (1971). Body composition and fitness in obese children before and after special treatment. *Acta Paediatrica Scandinavica, 217* (Suppl.), 80-85.

Rutenfranz, J. (1968). Möglichkeiten und Grenzen der Funktionsprüfungen von Herz- und Kreislauf im Kindesalter. *Zeitschrift für Ärztliche Fortbildung, 62*, 931-938.

Tatoń, J. (1975). Obesity [in Polish]. Warszawa: Polskie Zaklady Wydawnictw Lelcarskich.

Woynarowska, B., & Wójcik, M. (1975). Estimation of physical fitness in children [in Polish]. *Pediatria Polska, 50*, 655.

Part V
Circulation

Longitudinal Study of Maximal Aerobic Power in Boys and Girls From 12 to 23 Years of Age

Han C.G. Kemper
Robbert Verschuur
Luciënne Storm-van Essen
Ronald van Aalst
University of Amsterdam and Free University,
Amsterdam, The Netherlands

In a multiple longitudinal study, "Growth, Health, and Fitness of Teenagers" (Kemper, 1985), the maximal aerobic power was measured in a group of teenagers during four consecutive years (1976 to 1980). This longitudinal study was designed (Kemper & van 't Hof, 1978) to describe the course of the physical and mental development of teenagers and to find out whether there is a period of deterioration in their health status. Within the limitations of this study, the following major conclusion was drawn. Although the amount of physical activity, especially the heavy types, diminished from 12 to 17 years of age and the eating habits, as far as the proportion of nutrients is concerned, were typically western and did not fully meet the recommendations, these changes in lifestyle were not reflected in an unfavorable development of the physical and psychological characteristics of these teenagers (Kemper et al., 1983).

To verify the prognosis that a further decline in the level of habitual physical activity after school age would result in a decrease of the maximal aerobic power, the same longitudinal sample was studied when they were in their early 20s. Therefore, in 1985 the longitudinal sample was recalled for a fifth measurement. In this article, the results of some anthropometric measurements and the measurement of maximal aerobic power are presented as part of the study, "From Teenager to Adult, Investigation into Health and Lifestyle."

METHODS

The current study was carried out with the longitudinal sample from a secondary school in Amsterdam, The Netherlands (Pius X Lyceum). A total of 102 boys and 131 girls was measured on a yearly basis during 4 consecutive years (1976 to 1980). Of the original 233 subjects, 200 came to the laboratory for one more measurement (107 girls and 93 boys). The total dropout percentage was 14.1%, but considerably more girls (18.3%) than boys (8.8%) dropped out. Table 1 gives a summary of the number of boys and girls in each of the four birth cohorts: 1961, 1962, 1963, and 1964. Because there were only 4 boys and 1 girl in the 1961 cohort, the data for these subjects were not used in the results. Subjects were classified into age groups on the basis of the date of birth being within about 6 months of that age at the selected reference date of September 15.

Table 1   Number of Boys and Girls in Each Birth Cohort From the Longitudinal Group Measured From 1976 to 1985

	1964	1963	1962	1961	Total
Boys	23	45	21	4	93
Girls	24	56	26	1	107
Total	47	101	47	5	200

All measurements were performed in a mobile laboratory using the same instruments and supervised by the same researchers over the entire period of 10 years (from 1976 to 1985) in order to avoid confounding effects. Anthropometric measurements of height, weight, and four skinfold thicknesses (biceps, triceps, subscapular, and suprailiac) were performed according to the guidelines of the International Biological Program (IBP) (Weiner & Lourie, 1969).

Maximal aerobic power ($\dot{V}O_2max$) was measured by a direct method using a standard running test on a treadmill at a constant speed of 8 km/h (Kemper & Verschuur, 1981). A procedure using a submaximal running test preceded the maximal running test (Bar-Or & Zwiren, 1975). The submaximal test consisted of a 6-min run starting with the treadmill at horizontal (0%). After 2 min the slope of the treadmill was increased to 2.5% and in the last 2 min to 5%. After a recovery period, the subject began the maximal test with a slope of 7.5% and this slope was increased every two minutes by 2.5%. The subject was encouraged to continue until complete exhaustion was reached. During the test oxygen uptake, carbon dioxide output, and ventilation volume were measured every minute by the open circuit technique. The longitudinal results are presented as mean and standard error values per age group for each cohort, separately for boys and girls.

RESULTS

Anthropometric Development

In Table 2 mean and standard deviation of the anthropometric measurements are summarized for the 1985 measurements by cohort and by sex. In Figure 1, mean heights of the three cohorts of boys and girls

Table 2   Mean and Standard Deviation of Height, Weight, and Sum of Four Skinfolds of the Boys and Girls of the Longitudinal Group, Measured in 1985

Birth cohort	Sex	Body height (cm)		Body weight (kg)		Sum of four skinfolds (mm)	
		M	SD	M	SD	M	SD
1964	Boys	180.8	7.2	71.1	8.5	34.5	11.9
	Girls	168.8	6.2	61.5	7.5	52.3	17.1
1963	Boys	182.9	6.3	71.5	7.3	36.6	12.3
	Girls	170.6	6.6	63.4	10.7	55.5	19.9
1962	Boys	183.4	4.4	70.3	7.6	34.6	19.0
	Girls	169.9	6.8	60.9	7.6	53.2	19.2

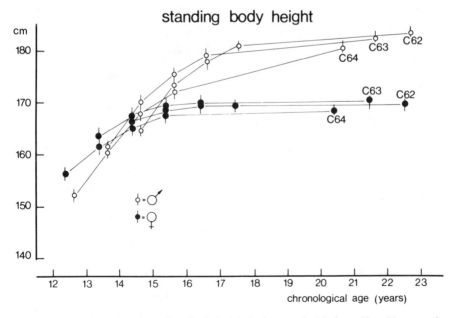

Figure 1 Development of standing body height in boys and girls from 12 to 23 years of age divided into three birth cohorts (C 62, C 63, C 64).

are shown over a chronological age span of 10 years (from 12 to 23 years of age). After school age, the girls hardly increased in height. The boys, however, were still growing, especially the youngest cohort (C 64). The mean increase from age 15/16 to age 20/21 years amounted to about 8 cm. The development of body weight, illustrated in Figure 2, shows that after school age the average increase in girls amounted to about 3 to 4 kg and in boys twice as much, about 6 to 9 kg. In Figure 3, the develop-

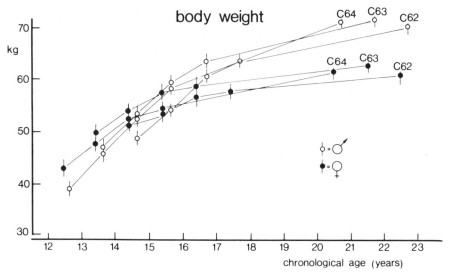

Figure 2   Development of body weight in boys and girls from 12 to 23 years of age divided into three birth cohorts (C 62, C 63, C 64).

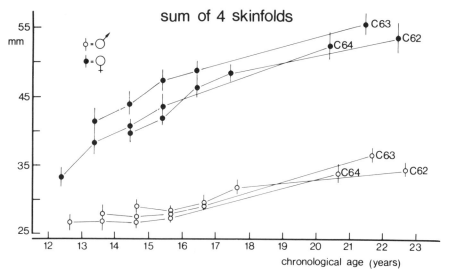

Figure 3   Development of sum of four skinfolds in boys and girls from 12 to 23 years of age divided into three birth cohorts (C 62, C 63, C 64).

mental pattern of the sum of four skinfolds is summarized. In girls, the increase was already apparent at the beginning of secondary school and continued after they left secondary school, from about 38 mm at age 12/13 to about 53 mm at age 20/23 years. In boys, the increase started after secondary-school age, from 30 mm at age 15/18 to 35 mm at age 20/23 years.

Maximal Aerobic Power

In boys, maximal aerobic power, which was measured as $\dot{V}O_2$max in l/min (see Figure 4), ceased to increase after secondary-school age except

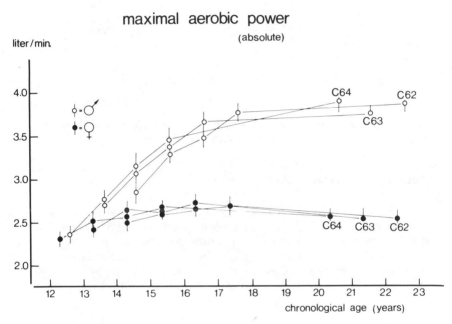

Figure 4   Development of maximal aerobic power (absolute) in boys and girls from 12 to 23 years of age divided into three birth cohorts (C 62, C 63, C 64).

in the youngest cohort (C 64), of which the mean $\dot{V}O_2$max was still increasing 0.5 l/min, from 3.4 at age 15/16 to 3.9 at age 20/21 years. In girls, the slight increase during secondary school was followed by a slight decrease in all cohorts. The $\dot{V}O_2$max of about 2.7 l/min at age 15/18 had decreased to about 2.5 l/min at age 20/23 years. Figure 5 shows the maximal aerobic power measured as $\dot{V}O_2$max relative to body weight ($\dot{V}O_2$max/BW). In boys, the decrease of $\dot{V}O_2$max/BW started after secondary school, from about 59 ml/kg · min at age 15/18 to about 54 ml/kg · min at age 20/23 years. In girls $\dot{V}O_2$max/BW decreased gradually between age 12/13 and 20/23 from about 51 ml/kg · min at age 12/13 to 41 ml/kg · min at age 20/23 years.

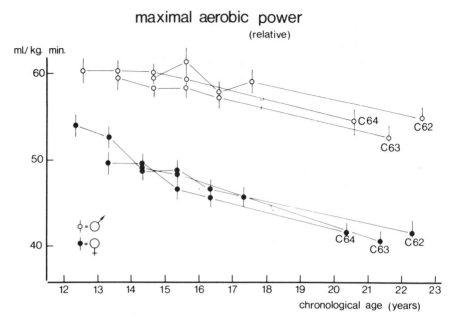

Figure 5 Development of maximal aerobic power (relative) in boys and girls from 12 to 23 years of age divided into three birth cohorts (C 62, C 63, C 64).

Running Performance on the Treadmill

Running performance was expressed as the maximal slope that could be reached on the treadmill at a running speed of 8 km/hr. Figure 6 shows that between age 12/13 and 17/18 running performance increased in boys and remained constant in girls, whereas after secondary school it decreased in boys as well as in girls, from about 15.5 to 14% in boys and in girls from 10.5 to 8.5%.

DISCUSSION

In The Netherlands, Saris (1982) collected reference data on boys and girls from a random sample in the town of Nijmegen. The boys and girls in this cross-sectional study showed the same tendencies over age as in the present study. Verschuur and Kemper (1985) found, in both boys and girls, a decline in both the amount and the intensity of habitual physical activity throughout the years of adolescence, although in boys the level of activity was higher than in girls at all ages. It was suggested that this was the reason that during school years in boys the VO_2max/BW was maintained at a relatively high level (59/l/kg · min), while in girls it decreased from 51 to 47 ml/kg · min.

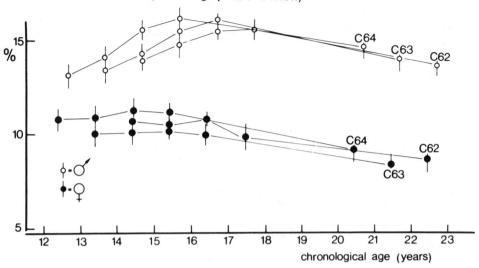

Figure 6 Development of maximal slope on a treadmill (running speed, 8 km/hr) in boys and girls from 12 to 23 years of age divided into three birth cohorts (C 62, C 63, C 64).

At that time, it was predicted that after the subjects left school physical activity would probably decline further, leading to a decrease in relative $\dot{V}O_2$max. The present results confirm that both girls and boys had a decrease of $\dot{V}O_2$max/BW. Whether this is caused by a further decrease in physical activity or the aftereffect of the decline between age 12/13 and 17/18 is still subject to further analysis of the physical activity patterns of these young adults.

Maximal aerobic power ($\dot{V}O_2$max) is a universally accepted parameter to measure current state and changes in endurance fitness. How $\dot{V}O_2$max can be expressed in relation to body size (Bailey, Ross, Mirwald, & Weese, 1978) is still a subject for discussion. The relation between $\dot{V}O_2$max and body size, however, is of considerable significance in growth and training studies on children (Mirwald & Bailey, 1985). The problem is how to determine whether changes in $\dot{V}O_2$max are the result of training, growth, or a combination of the two factors. For this study the traditional approach was chosen and $\dot{V}O_2$max was related to body weight (Bar-Or, 1982; Keul, 1982). It seems that the decrease in $\dot{V}O_2$max/BW is at least partly caused by the increase in the fat mass, resulting in higher body weight. If one assumes a certain mechanical efficiency at all ages, it is to be expected that any change in mean $\dot{V}O_2$max/BW would be reflected in a similar change in the maximal slope reached on the treadmill. During the school years, this certainly did not hold true: the mean $\dot{V}O_2$max/BW of the boys hardly changed (about 59 ml/kg • min), but they increased their maximal slope on the treadmill; the girls' $\dot{V}O_2$max/BW decreased (from 51 to 47 ml/kg • min) but the maximal slope remained constant.

Explanations for the difference in development of maximal slope and mean $\dot{V}O_2$max/BW could be: an increase in mechanical efficiency (Åstrand & Rodahl, 1977; Davies, 1980) and/or an increase in anaerobic power (Eriksson, 1972; Eriksson & Saltin, 1974). After secondary-school age, however, a decrease in $\dot{V}O_2$max/BW occurred with a decrease in maximal slope.

CONCLUSIONS

In girls, $\dot{V}O_2$max decreased after secondary-school age both in absolute and in relative terms ($\dot{V}O_2$max/BW). In boys, $\dot{V}O_2$max increased slightly after school age in absolute value as a result of their height growth. The relative value, however, started to decrease after they left secondary school. After secondary school, the maximal slope reached on the treadmill at a speed of 8 km/h started to decrease. In girls, the increase in fat mass, measured as the sum of four skinfolds, started during secondary school and continued until adult age (20/23 years). In boys, the increase started after they left secondary school.

REFERENCES

Åstrand, P.-O., & Rodahl, K. (1977). *Textbook of work physiology* (2nd ed.). New York: McGraw-Hill.

Bailey, D.A., Ross, W.D., Mirwald, R.L., & Weese, C. (1978). Size dissociation of maximal aerobic power during growth in boys. In J. Borms & M. Hebbelinck (Eds.), *Pediatric work physiology* (pp. 140-151) (Medicine and Sport Science, Vol. 11). Basel: Karger.

Bar-Or, O. (1982). Physiologiche Gesetzmässigkeiten Sportlicher Aktivität beim Kind. In H. Howald & E. Hahn (Eds.), *Kinder und Leistungssport* (pp. 18-30). Basel: Birkhäuser.

Bar-Or, O., & Zwiren, L.D. (1975). Maximal oxygen consumption test during arm exercise—Reliability and validity. *Journal of Applied Physiology*, **38**, 424-426.

Davies, C.T.M. (1980). Metabolic cost of exercise and physical performance in children with some observations on external loading. *European Journal of Applied Physiology*, **45**, 95-102.

Eriksson, B.O. (1972). Physical training, oxygen supply and muscle metabolism in 11- to 13-year-old boys. *Acta Physiologica Scandinavica*, **384** (Suppl.).

Eriksson, B.O., & Saltin, B. (1974). Muscle metabolism during exercise in boys age 11 to 16 years compared to adults. *Acta Pediatrica Belgica*, **28** (Suppl.), 257-265.

Kemper, H.C.G. (Ed.). (1985). *Growth, health and fitness of teenagers. Longitudinal research in international perspective* (Medicine and Sport Science, Vol. 20). Basel: Karger.

Kemper, H.C.G., Dekker, H.J.P., Ootjers, M.G., Post, B., Snel, J., Splinter, P.G., Storm-van Essen, L., & Verschuur, R. (1983). Growth and health of teenagers in the Netherlands: Survey of multidisciplinary longitudinal studies and comparison to recent results of a Dutch study. *International Journal of Sports Medicine, 4*, 202-214.

Kemper, H.C.G., & van 't Hof, M.A. (1978). Design of a multiple longitudinal study of growth and health of teenagers. *European Journal of Pediatrics, 129*, 147-155.

Kemper, H.C.G., & Verschuur, R. (1981). Maximal aerobic power in 13- and 14-year-old teenagers in relation to biological age. *International Journal of Sports Medicine, 2*, 97-100; 261-262.

Keul, J. (1982). Zur Belastbarkeit des Kindlichen Organismus ans biochemischer sicht. In M. Howald & E. Hahn (Eds.), *Kinder und Leistungssport* (pp. 31-49). Basel: Birkhäuser.

Mirwald, R.L., & Bailey, D.A. (1985). *Longitudinal analysis of maximal aerobic power in boys and girls by chronological age, maturity and physical activity*. Report of the College of Physical Education. Saskatoon, Canada: University of Saskatchewan.

Saris, W.H.M. (1982). *Aerobic power and daily physical activity in children with special reference to methods and cardio-vascular risk indicators*. Thesis, Nijmegen, Katholieke Universiteit.

Verschuur, R., & Kemper, H.C.G. (1985). The pattern of daily physical activity. In H.C.G. Kemper (Ed.), *Growth, health and fitness of teenagers: Longitudinal research in international perspective* (pp. 169-186) (Medicine and Sport Science, Vol. 20). Basel: Karger.

Weiner, J.S., & Lourie, J.A. (Eds.). (1969). *Human biology, a guide to field methods* (IBP handbook, No. 9). Oxford: Blackwell.

Maximal Aerobic Power
in Early and Late Maturing Teenagers

Han C.G. Kemper
Robbert Verschuur
Jan W. Ritmeester
University of Amsterdam and Free University,
Amsterdam, The Netherlands

In the field of growth and development, a distinction can be made between two fundamentally different types of ages, chronological age and biological age. Chronological age refers to the number of years a person has lived since birth. This parameter is convenient but has a number of shortcomings as an indicator of maturity. This is especially true during puberty when, due to the wide variation in the onset of pubertal changes, children of the same chronological age can show marked variations in all facets of growth and development. The concept of the biological age of a child provides an improved measure of maturation: It measures the progress along the road of life anatomically, physiologically, and mentally (Cheek, 1968).

However, no single measure of maturity can assess the overall developmental status of a child, and no single event can be used to distinguish between early and late maturation over an age range of from 10 to 16 years. Single events that have been used frequently are: (a) age of menarche (Marshall, 1978), (b) body structure development index (Koinzer, Enderlein, & Herforth, 1981), and (c) age of peak height velocity (Cunningham, Paterson, Blimkie, & Donner, 1984; Mirwald, Bailey, Cameron, & Rasmussen, 1981; Rutenfranz et al., 1982). A series of consecutive developmental events such as calcification of bones or teeth has been proposed as more refined estimators of maturity. The purpose of the present article is to focus on one of these systems, the skeletal maturity, measured repeatedly during puberty in the same individuals.

In a multiple longitudinal study on the growth and health of teenagers (Kemper, 1985; Kemper & Van 't Hof, 1978), skeletal age was measured on a yearly basis as an indication of the biological maturation of a group of growing Dutch youngsters. Maximal oxygen uptake was also measured to evaluate the health status of these youngsters with respect to their endurance fitness (Kemper et al., 1983). This longitudinal study was designed to describe the course of the physical and mental development of teenagers and to find out whether there is a period of deterioration in their health status. In order to explain changes in development, measurements were taken concurrently of skeletal age.

METHODS

The current study was carried out at a secondary school in Amsterdam, The Netherlands (Pius X Lyceum). The teenagers who started with the 1st year of this longitudinal study were 307 pupils of the first and second form of the school. A total of 102 boys and 131 girls were measured yearly during 4 consecutive years. The total dropout percentage of the study was 24.1% (girls, 17.6%; boys, 31.1%). Of these only 2.6% refused to continue participation in the course of the 4 years. The other pupils dropped out because of transfer to other residences and/or types of school. In Table 1, the number of boys and girls in each chronological age group is indicated for the 1st year of the investigation. Informed consent for this investigation was given by the pupils, by their parents, and by the school directory. All testing took place during regular school hours in a mobile laboratory placed near the school.

Table 1   Number of Boys and Girls in the Longitudinal Group Divided into Chronological Age Groups in the First Year of the Study

| Sex | Chronological age (yr) | | | | Total |
	12	13	14	15	
Boys	26	48	24	4	102
Girls	31	68	31	1	131
Total	57	116	55	5	233

Biologic Maturation

Biologic age was estimated from radiographs of the left hand and wrist, taken yearly (Kemper & Verschuur, 1981). Ratings of 20 bones of the hand and wrist according to the Tanner-Whitehouse II Method (Tanner, Whitehouse, Marshall, Healy, & Goldstein, 1975) were assigned by comparing the ossification stage of each bone with plates, diagrams, and descriptions of the bone in question. With the aid of the Utilis 15/18 (Enraf-Nonius, Delft, The Netherlands) X-ray apparatus, photographs were taken of the hand with the palm faced downward. To restrict the radiation to the child's left hand, a wooden box was used, covered on the inside with lead. The opening for the hand at the base of the box was covered by flexible lead-filled rubber (see Figure 1). The X-ray tube at the top of the

Figure 1 Radiograph of the left hand, taken in the mobile research unit with X-ray tube in box covered with lead restricting radiation.

box was centered at a distance of 80 cm above the hand, which lay on an Osray T-4 (Agfa-Gevaert, Amsterdam, The Netherlands) double-wrapped film. Exposure time varied from 0.3 to 0.5 s, with a tube voltage of 53 kV, thus restricting the local radiation to less than 30 mR. All radiographs were rated by the same examiner (C.v.d.B.), who had been trained to use the Tanner-Whitehouse II method at the Institute of Child Health (Prof. Dr. J. Tanner) of the University of London. In Table 2, a frequency distribution of skeletal age is given for boys and girls separately.

Table 2   Number of Boys and Girls in the Longitudinal Group by Skeletal Age

Biological age group	Girls	Boys	Total
10	3	3	6
11	8	7	15
12	31	41	72
13	115	47	162
14	122	62	184
15	57	116	173
16	184	75	259
17	—	24	24
18	—	28	28

Early Versus Late Maturers

During puberty considerable differences exist between teenagers in maturation as determined from radiographs. Therefore, boys and girls participating in this study were divided into a group of early maturers (EM), a group of late maturers (LM), and a group with a mean maturation (MM). The general criteria for assigning the subjects to one of the groups were as follows: EMs were those whose skeletal age compared to their chronological age was advanced by more than 3 months; LMs were those subjects whose skeletal age compared to their chronological age was retarded by more than 3 months. MMs were those subjects who could not be assigned to either EM or LM group. Because there were four annual measurements and girls on the average are fully mature at 16 years and boys 2 years later at age 18 years, the criteria were different for each sex and age group. These criteria are illustrated in more detail in Figure 2 for boys and Figure 3 for girls. The number of boys and girls in the 3 maturation groups are summarized in Table 3.

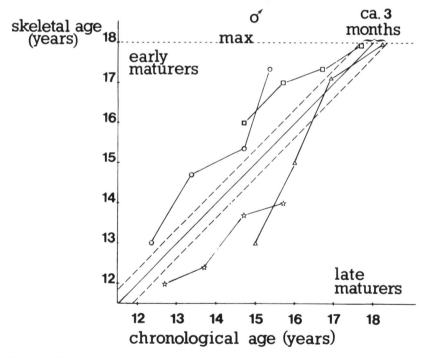

Figure 2   Illustration of the criteria used for assigning boys to late and early maturing groups based on measurement of skeletal age in 4 consecutive years.

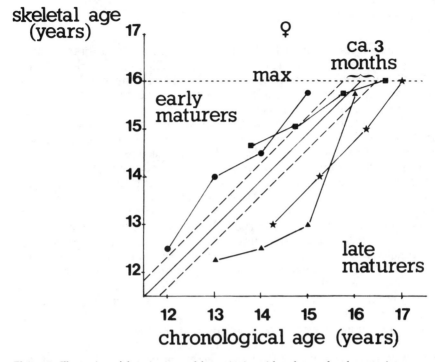

Figure 3 Illustration of the criteria used for assigning girls to late and early maturing groups based on measurement of skeletal age in 4 consecutive years.

Table 3 Number of Boys and Girls in the Three Skeletal Maturation Groups by Chronological Age

Chronological age group (yr)	Boys			Girls		
	Early	Mean	Late	Early	Mean	Late
12	9	8	9	12	8	11
13	31	24	16	35	29	34
14	37	32	26	39	44	46
15	40	33	28	39	44	47
16	31	25	19	27	37	35
17	8	9	11	(4)	15	13
18	(2)	(1)	(1)		(1)	

Note. Numbers in parentheses are not used in the results.

Maximal Aerobic Power

Maximal aerobic power ($\dot{V}O_2$max) was measured by a direct method using a standard running test on a treadmill. The pupils were asked not to eat 1.5 hr prior to testing. $\dot{V}O_2$max was measured during the treadmill test and used as the criterion for maximal aerobic power. A procedure with a submaximal test preceding a maximal test was used that was a slightly modified method of Bar-Or and Zwiren (1975). The submaximal test consisted of three 2-min runs at a constant speed of 8 km/hr with an increasing slope of 0%, 2.5%, and 5%, respectively. During practice and this submaximal test, the subjects acquainted themselves with running on a treadmill, as well as the mouthpiece plus nose clip. At the same time, they were warming up. After a short period of rest (approximately 10 to 15 min), running was continued on the treadmill at the same constant speed of 8 km/hr. In this maximal test, the slope was increased every 2 min by 2.5% or 5% depending on the heart rate of the pupil. This maximal test was continued until complete exhaustion was reached. Each boy or girl was stimulated to exercise to his or her maximum by verbal encouragements. The criteria used for exhaustion was a heart rate of 90% of the maximal heart rate according to age and a respiratory exchange ratio of more than 1.0.

Oxygen uptake was analyzed throughout the test by the open circuit technique. Expired air was collected in a 10 l, high-speed, low-resistance dry gasometer (Parkinson-Cowan CD4) via a two-way, low-resistance breathing valve (Terpoorten, Coronel Laboratory, Amsterdam, The Netherlands) with a dead air space of 35 ml. Samples of mixed expired air were continuously withdrawn from the gasometer, dried by tampons (Amira Extra) and analyzed for F_EO_2 by a paramagnetic oxygen analyzer (Servomex) and F_ECO_2 by an infrared carbon dioxide analyzer (Mijnhardt). The gasometer, two gas analyzers, and a number of electronic calculators were incorporated into a movable 19-in. unit, called an Ergo-Analyzer (Mijnhardt B.V., Odijk, The Netherlands), which continuously and automatically analyzed the expired air collected and printed out the calculated oxygen uptake (STPD). Measurement of the oxygen uptake with the Ergo-Analyzer system was comparable to the classical method of collecting expired air in Douglas bags and analyzing CO_2 and O_2 content with the Scholander technique (Kemper, Binkhorst, Verschuur, & Vissers, 1976; Saris, 1982).

RESULTS

Anthropometric variables such as height (see Figure 4) and fat mass (see Figure 5) show that early maturers, both boys and girls, were taller and had a higher percentage of fat mass than late maturers. In body height, the differences between EMs and LMs disappeared when both groups approached the age of full maturity: girls from age 14/15 years

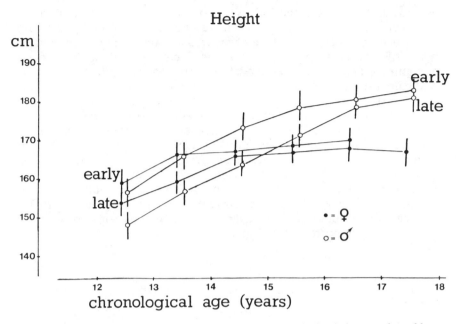

Figure 4 Development of mean body height in boys and girls divided into early and late maturing groups.

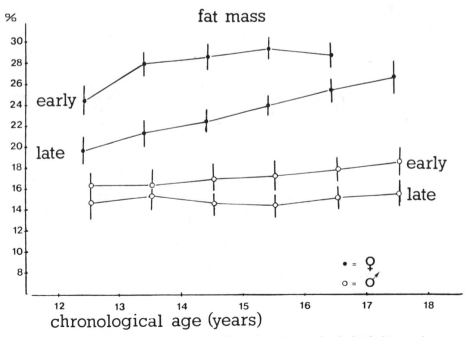

Figure 5 Development of mean percentage of body fat in boys and girls divided into early and late maturing groups.

onward and boys from age 16/17 years onward. Percentage of fat mass, however, tended to remain higher in early maturers in both sexes. The differences in mean percentage of fat was greater in girls than boys in both EMs and LMs. In girls, the fat mass increased with age regardless of maturation group. In boys, the fat mass remained reasonably constant.

Maximal aerobic power (see Figure 6) exhibited a pattern that was comparable to general height growth: In boys and girls EMs had higher $\dot{V}O_2max$ than LMs. These differences tended to disappear at full maturation. Figure 7 shows $\dot{V}O_2max$ calculated per kilogram of body weight ($\dot{V}O_2max/BW$). Taking into account $\dot{V}O_2max$ relative to body mass, the picture was reversed. Early maturing girls showed lower mean values of $\dot{V}O_2max$ at all ages. Early maturing boys had lower mean values of $\dot{V}O_2max$ from age 13 years onward. Both groups of boys had a tendency to maintain their aerobic power through the years from age 13 to 18, whereas both groups of girls experienced a decrease in their aerobic power as they progressed to full maturity.

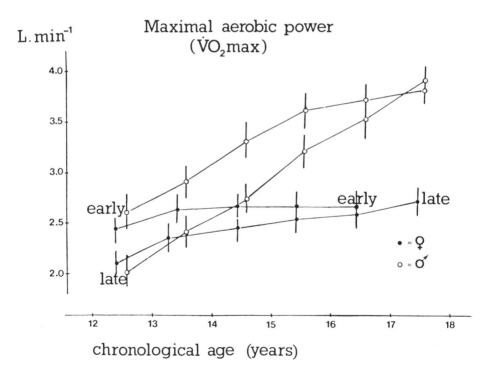

Figure 6 Development of mean maximal aerobic power ($\dot{V}O_2max$) in boys and girls divided into early and late maturing groups.

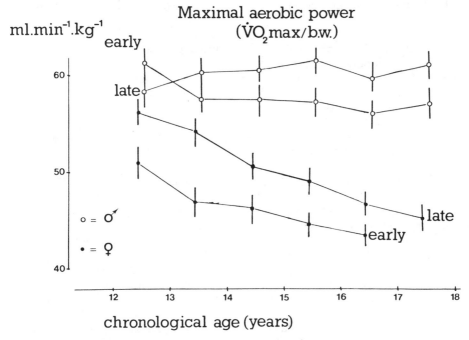

Figure 7 Development of mean maximal aerobic power ($\dot{V}O_2$max) relative to body mass in boys and girls divided into early and late maturing groups.

DISCUSSION

Several studies have provided information about the relationship between skeletal age and cardiorespiratory endurance based on cross-sectional observations (Hollman & Bouchard, 1970; Koinzer, 1978; Koinzer et al., 1981; Szabo, Doka, Aport, & Somogyvari, 1972). Studies of maturation groups, based on longitudinal observations, have not been done up until now to our best knowledge. An earlier study (Kemper et al., 1975) provided evidence that there was no relationship between chronological age and increase in skeletal age over a period of 10 months (the individual increase varied between 0 months and 25 months). Skeletal development of some individuals seems to vary. In the present study it appeared that the criterion for early or late maturers in terms of 3 months advanced or delayed compared to chronological age over a period of 4 years was difficult to maintain. A high percentage of boys and girls showed a developmental pattern that was characterized by initial retardation followed by advancement at the end of the 4-year period with respect

to chronological age and vice versa. Three reasons can be proposed for
this:

- Biological development is not a gradual but more a discontinuous
  process depending on the individual.
- Measurement error occurred in establishing skeletal age (Roche, 1978).
  (Reliability, however, was enhanced by comparing the radiographs of
  the same individuals with those from the preceding years.)
- Girls reach full maturity at about age 16 years and boys at age 18 years.
  EMs had already reached maturity in the 2nd or 3rd year of measure-
  ment, and as a consequence were no longer early maturers.

In Table 4 the chronological ages of the 3 maturation groups in the 1st
year of measurement are compared. In boys and girls, the mean chronological ages were almost equal in all maturation groups with a mean of
13 years. Therefore, differences in maturity cannot be caused by systematic
differences in chronological ages. Mean skeletal age on the average was
slightly advanced: in boys 5 months (13.0 versus 13.4 years) and in girls
6 months (13.0 versus 13.5 years). This can be explained by secular trends:
The radiographs were compared with the standards of Tanner et al. (1975)
that are based on a British population of 3,000 children measured during
the 1950s.

During puberty the increase in height shows the same pattern as the
increase in maximal aerobic power. The height increase with chronological age is greater in boys than in girls. Also, the development in early
and late maturers is equal: At 12/13 years of age EMs have significantly
greater height and VO$_2$max than LMs, but at age 16/17 years the differences have disappeared. The development of maximal aerobic power
apparently increases proportionally to body dimensions. At age 12/13
years, when body height in late maturers was less than in early maturers,

Table 4   Mean (M) and Standard Deviation (SD) of Chronological and Skeletal Age of
Maturation Groups of Boys and Girls in the First Year of Measurement

	Maturation group	N	Chronological age M	SD	Skeletal age M	SD
Boys	Early	40	13.1	0.7	14.2	1.1
	Mean	33	13.0	0.7	13.3	0.9
	Late	28	13.0	0.7	12.5	1.0
	Total	101	13.0	0.7	13.4	1.0
Girls	Early	39	13.0	0.7	14.0	0.7
	Mean	45	12.8	0.5	13.7	0.6
	Late	47	13.1	0.6	12.7	1.0
	Total	131	13.0	0.6	13.5	0.8

$\dot{V}O_2$max was also less. But when teenagers were fully grown and both late and early maturers had achieved the same body height, the difference in $\dot{V}O_2$max had also disappeared.

So far these results are in agreement with the cross-sectional results of Hollman & Bouchard (1970) and Rutenfranz et al. (1982). However, if $\dot{V}O_2$max is related to body weight, LMs show significantly higher $\dot{V}O_2$max/BW than EMs at all ages. The finding that biologically older boys and girls have lower $\dot{V}O_2$max/BW is in accordance with the higher percentage of body fat in the early maturers over the whole age range. A higher percentage of fat mass increases body weight and represents an extra load upon the oxygen transport system. From the results it seems that LMs have absolute $\dot{V}O_2$max values equal to EMs, but that the mean $\dot{V}O_2$max/BW values are lower in EMs, caused by a higher percentage of body fat. The lower mean $\dot{V}O_2$max/BW values in EMs could be caused by the fact that they are socialized away from sport activities at a younger chronological age, and as a consequence they show less habitual physical activity, resulting in lower $\dot{V}O_2$max/BW.

CONCLUSIONS

$\dot{V}O_2$max in early and late maturers increases proportionally with body height. At the age of 16/17 years (girls) or 17/18 years (boys), when most of the teenagers are fully mature, the differences have disappeared. In their teens, $\dot{V}O_2$max relative to body weight is lower in early maturers than in late maturers. This can be explained by the higher percentage of body mass in both boys and girls in the early maturing group as compared to the late maturers.

Acknowledgments

This study is part of the study, Growth and Health of Teenagers, a multiple longitudinal study carried out in Amsterdam at the University of Amsterdam in The Netherlands. This study is a mutual research project of the Coronel Laboratory for Occupational and Environmental Health (Prof. Dr. R.L. Zielhuis), Laboratory of Psychophysiology (Prof. Dr. P. Visser), and the Working Group of Exercise Physiology and Health (Prof. Dr. H.C.G. Kemper).

This research has been financially supported by grants from the Dutch Prevention Fund (Project Number 28-289a), Foundation for Educational Research (Project Number 0255), and Dutch Heart Foundation (Project Number 76.051-79.051) in The Hague, The Netherlands.

We acknowledge all the members of the project team, the teachers of physical education, and last but not least, the pupils of the Pius X Lyceum (Amsterdam) who served as our subjects.

REFERENCES

Bar-Or, O., & Zwiren, L.D. (1975). Maximal oxygen consumption test during arm exercise—Reliability and validity. *Journal of Applied Physiology*, **38**, 424-426.

Cheek, D.B. (1968). *Human growth. Body composition, cell growth, energy, and intelligence.* Philadelphia: Lea & Febiger.

Cunningham, D.A., Paterson, D.H., Blimkie, C.J.R., & Donner, A.P. (1984). Development of cardiorespiratory function in circumpubertal boys: A longitudinal study. *Journal of Applied Physiology*, **56**, 302-307.

Hollman, W., & Bouchard, C. (1970). Untersuchen über die Beziehungen zwischen chronologischen und biologischen Alter zu spiroergometrischen Messgroessen, Herzvolumen, anthropometrische Daten und Skeletmuskelkraft bei 8-18 jährigen Jungen. *Z. Kreisl-Forschung*, **59**, 160-176.

Kemper, H.C.G. (Ed.). (1985). *Growth, health and fitness of teenagers. Longitudinal research in international perspective* (Medicine and Sport Science, Vol. 20). Basel: Karger.

Kemper, H.C.G., Binkhorst, R.A., Verschuur, R., & Vissers, A.C.A. (1976). Reliability of the Ergo-Analyzer. *Journal of Cardiovascular Pulmonary Technology*, **4**, 27-30.

Kemper, H.C.G., Dekker, H.J.P., Ootjers, M.G., Post, B., Snel, J., Splinter, P.G., Storm-van Essen, L., & Verschuur, R. (1983). Growth and health of teenagers in The Netherlands: Survey of multidisciplinary longitudinal studies and comparison to recent results of a Dutch study. *International Journal of Sports Medicine*, **4**, 202-214.

Kemper, H.C.G., & van 't Hof, M.A. (1978). Design of a multiple longitudinal study of growth and health in teenagers. *European Journal of Pediatrics*, **129**, 147-155.

Kemper, H.C.G., & Verschuur, R. (1981). Maximal aerobic power in 13- and 14-year-old teenagers in relation to biologic age. *International Journal of Sports Medicine*, **2**, 97-100; 261-262.

Kemper, H.C.G., Verschuur, R., Ras, K.G.A., Snel, J., Splinter, P.G., & Tavecchio, L.W.C. (1975). Biological age and habitual physical activity in relation to physical fitness in 12- and 13-year-old schoolboys. *Zeitschrift für Kinderheilkunde*, **119**, 169-179.

Koinzer, K. (1978). Zu den Unterschieden der ergometrischen Leistungsfähigkeit und der Sauerstoffaufnahmefähigkeit bei 10- bis 14jährigen Kindern und Jugendlichen in Abhängigkeit vom biologischen Entwicklungsstand. *Medizin und Sport*, **18**, 184-188.

Koinzer, K., Enderlein, G., & Herforth, G. (1981). Untersuchungen zur Abhängigkeit der W_{170} vom Kalenderalter, vom biologischen Entwicklungsstand und vom Übungszustand bei 10- bis 14jährigen Jungen und Mädchen mittels dreifaktorieller Varianzanalyse. *Medizin und Sport, 21,* 201-206.

Marshall, W.A. (1978). Puberty. In F. Falkner & J.M. Tanner (Eds.), *Human growth 2. Postnatal growth* (pp. 141-181). New York: Plenum Press.

Mirwald, R.L., Bailey, D.A., Cameron, N., & Rasmussen, R.L. (1981). Longitudinal comparison of aerobic power in active and inactive boys aged 7.0 to 17.0 years. *Annals of Human Biology, 8,* 405-414.

Roche, A.F. (1978). Bone growth and maturation. In F. Falkner & J.M. Tanner (Eds.), *Human growth 2. Postnatal growth* (pp. 327-355). New York: Plenum Press.

Rutenfranz, J., Lange Andersen, K., Seliger, V., Ilmarinen, J., Klimmer, F., Kylian, H., Rutenfranz, M., & Ruppel, M. (1982). Maximal aerobic power affected by maturation and body growth during childhood and adolescence. *European Journal of Pediatrics, 139,* 106-112.

Saris, W.H.M. (1982). *Aerobic power and daily physical activity in children with special reference to methods and cardio-vascular risk indicators.* Thesis, Katholieke Universiteit, Nijmegen.

Szabo, S., Doka, J., Apor, P., & Somogyvari, K. (1972). Die Beziehungen zwischen Knochenlebensalter, funktionellen anthropometrischen Daten und der aeroben Kapazität. Schweirische *Zeitschrift für Sportmedizin, 20,* 109-115.

Tanner, J.M., Whitehouse, R.H., Marshall, W.A., Healy, M.J.R., & Goldstein, H. (1975). *Assessment of skeletal maturity and prediction of adult height (TW 2 method).* London: Academic Press.

Maximal Oxygen Consumption of Children (6 to 18 Years) Predicted From Maximal and Submaximal Values in Treadmill and Bicycle Tests

Robert A. Binkhorst
University of Nijmegen, Nijmegen, The Netherlands
Wim H.M. Saris
University of Limburg, Maastricht, The Netherlands
Annemieke M. Noordeloos
Martin A. van 't Hof
Anton F.J. de Haan
University of Nijmegen, Nijmegen, The Netherlands

Maximal oxygen consumption ($\dot{V}O_2max$) generally is considered to be a valid measure of the functional capacity of the cardiorespiratory system. Its measurement, however, needs special equipment for the determination of gas exchange values, for example, Douglas bags and analyzers for O_2 and CO_2 or an on-line system that is automatized to determine the necessary values. Not all institutes in which the cardiorespiratory system is examined during exercise have access to such devices. In those cases, the state of functioning can be determined by means of assessing maximal power, or by power at a heart rate of 170 (W_{170}), or by predicting $\dot{V}O_2max$ from maximal power or from heart rates at submaximal loads. In children, few data are available with respect to the use of submaximal exercise tests in the prediction of $\dot{V}O_2max$ (Saris, de Koning, Elvers, de Boo, & Binkhorst, 1984). Therefore, in a study on reference values of $\dot{V}O_2max$ in about 300 children aged 6 to 18 years (Saris, Noordeloos, Rignalda, van 't Hof, & Binkhorst, 1985), data were also collected during bicycle ergometer and treadmill tests to develop prediction formulas from maximal and submaximal nongaseous values.

METHOD

A total random sample of 143 boys and 136 girls (even year groups, 6 to 18) from the Nijmegen community took part in the study. It should be noted that each of the age groups had a standard deviation of only $\pm$ 2 weeks. All children had a health examination; no contraindications to performing a maximal test were found. The parents after being informed about the test gave their approval.

A bicycle ergometer test with a stepwise increasing load of 20 W $\cdot$ min^{-1} at 60 rpm was performed by the subjects in the age groups 12 to 18 years only, whereas the Bruce protocol on a treadmill was performed by all subjects. Oxygen consumption was measured either by means of Douglas bags and gas analyses of O_2 (Servomex, type AO 272, Taylor Servomex, England) and CO_2 (Uras, Hartmann und Braun, West Germany) or an automatized system (Oxycon IV, Mijnhardt, Odijk, The Netherlands) that was calibrated with the Douglas bag method. Heart rate was calculated from the ECG.

To predict $\dot{V}O_2$max with the values of the bicycle test, maximal power (Max-W) and power at a heart rate of 170 (W_{170}) were used. For the Bruce Test, maximal time (Max-T) and time at a heart rate of 170 (T_{170}) were used; Max-T of each individual was rounded off to whole minutes to coincide with the times for filling Douglas bags or the Oxycon. In the development of the prediction formulas, the most important intervening factors were considered to be age, sex, and body mass (BM). W_{170} and T_{170} were estimated for individuals by linear regression with the dependent variable, heart rate, and the independent variable, power (bicycle test) or time (Bruce Test).

Bicycle Test

For statistical reasons of normality and variance stabilization, a logarithmic transformation of $\dot{V}O_2$max was used for predicting. A stepwise linear regression with dependent variable ln ($\dot{V}O_2$max) and independent variables age, body mass, sex, and Max-W resulted in a final linear regression equation with dependent variable ln ($\dot{V}O_2$max) and independent variable Max-W. The same procedure was followed for predicting ln ($\dot{V}O_2$max) using W_{170}.

Bruce Test

To correct for the influence of body mass on the $\dot{V}O_2$max, $\dot{V}O_2$max $\cdot$ BM^{-1} was chosen for prediction. Stepwise linear regression analysis with the dependent variable $\dot{V}O_2$max $\cdot$ BM^{-1} and independent variables Max-T, age, and sex yielded a final regression equation with dependent variable $\dot{V}O_2$max $\cdot$ BM^{-1} and independent variables Max-T and sex. For predicting $\dot{V}O_2$max $\cdot$ BM^{-1} the same procedure was followed leading to a similar regression equation.

RESULTS AND DISCUSSION

In Tables 1 and 2, the data are presented for the measured V̇O₂max, the best-fitting prediction formula, the predicted V̇O₂max, and the differences between measured values and predicted values. These data are all related to the age groups of boys and girls. All subjects performed the Bruce Test but only the 12- to 18-year-olds bicycled. The number of subjects that walked and cycled was not always the same because occasionally data for a subject were not collected properly or the subject did not perform maximally (no leveling off of heart rate, R lower than 1.1, or Max-HR lower than minus 2 SD of age-related Max-HR, according to Åstrand, 1952).

V̇O₂max for girls in Table 1 show the well-known trend with age, that is, a trend of plateauing at the ages of 16 and 18 years. Boys, however, still increase their maximum at these ages. In Table 2, it is shown that V̇O₂max • BM^{-1} for each of the sexes over the whole range remains at about the same level, boys higher than girls, although the oldest girls showed a tendency of a decrease that might have been due to the increase

Table 1 Maximal Oxygen Consumption (l • min⁻¹) on the Bicycle Test for Boys and Girls of Different Ages

					Difference		
Age (yr)	N	Measured V̇O₂max		Max-W V̇O₂max		W₁₇₀ V̇O₂max	
		M	SD	M	SD	M	SD
12							
Boys	13	1.85	0.32	0.04	0.18	−0.12	0.31
Girls	21	1.59	0.30	−0.06	0.18	−0.18	0.17
14							
Boys	22	2.48	0.38	0.09	0.17	0.02	0.32
Girls	22	2.01	0.36	−0.02	0.19	−0.04	0.28
16							
Boys	22	3.20	0.44	−0.01	0.24	0.25	0.46
Girls	18	2.22	0.34	0.03	0.22	−0.11	0.30
18							
Boys	18	3.34	0.30	0.00	0.23	0.24	0.48
Girls	18	2.14	0.35	0.00	0.14	0.06	0.20

Note. Measured values and the differences between measured and predicted values are given. Formula using maximal power: ln (V̇O₂max) = 0.162 + 0.00484 Max-W (r = 0.95). Using power at heart rate 170: ln (V̇O₂max) = −0.145 + 0.0058 W₁₇₀ (r = 0.86). (See text for further explanation.)

Table 2 Maximal Oxygen Consumption (l · min⁻¹) on the Bruce Test for Boys and Girls of Different Ages

Age (yr)	N	Measured $\dot{V}O_2$max		Difference Max-T $\dot{V}O_2$max		T_{170} $\dot{V}O_2$max	
		M	SD	M	SD	M	SD
6							
Boys	19	46.5	5.0	−1.7	4.6	−3.9	5.2
Girls	17	44.3	4.3	0.7	4.1	−0.2	4.2
8							
Boys	20	50.1	5.7	1.7	4.5	−0.2	6.1
Girls	21	44.6	4.6	0.5	4.0	−0.4	4.6
10							
Boys	24	52.2	5.1	1.2	4.0	0.7	4.5
Girls	17	46.8	4.8	1.9	3.6	2.4	4.1
12							
Boys	18	50.4	6.2	0.2	4.5	0.0	5.7
Girls	23	45.0	6.2	0.5	5.1	1.3	6.0
14							
Boys	22	51.1	5.4	0.1	4.2	0.2	5.3
Girls	23	44.7	4.2	0.4	2.9	1.1	4.1
16							
Boys	23	53.8	6.6	0.0	3.9	2.7	5.2
Girls	17	42.0	4.2	−1.0	2.4	−2.2	3.7
18							
Boys	17	51.3	4.2	−2.1	4.1	−0.2	3.7
Girls	18	41.2	5.1	−3.2	3.9	−2.5	4.6

Note. Formula using maximal time of exercise (min): for boys $\dot{V}O_2$max · BM⁻¹ = 19.6 + 2.43 Max-T; for girls = 17.0 + 2.43 Max-T (r = 0.76). Using time at heart rate 170: for boys $\dot{V}O_2$max · BM⁻¹ = 39.4 + 1.29 T_{170}; for girls = 34.2 + 1.29 T_{170} (r = 0.61). (See text for further explanation.)

in percentage of body fat. Because $\dot{V}O_2$max related to sex and age has been discussed at length recently (Saris et al., 1985), this aspect of the results will not be discussed in detail here. Emphasis will be placed on the prediction of $\dot{V}O_2$max.

The best-fitting prediction formulas for the bicycle test (Table 1) do not contain factors for sex, age, or BM, because these factors did not contribute to a more precise prediction. This confirms the general finding that oxygen consumption on a bicycle ergometer is rather independent of BM over a wide range of BMs. The predicted $\dot{V}O_2$max from Max-W over the whole age range shows a mean difference with the actual $\dot{V}O_2$max ranging from −0.06 to 0.09 l · min⁻¹, whereas the standard deviation ranges from 0.14 to 0.24 l · min⁻¹. For the prediction using W_{170} these values are considerably higher, that is, −0.18 to 0.25 and 0.17 to 0.48, respectively, for the mean difference and its standard deviation.

With respect to the Bruce Test (see Table 2) it is shown that $\dot{V}O_2$max • BM^{-1} is predicted from linear formulas for each sex separately; age did not contribute significantly to prediction. The formulas for boys and girls, respectively, do have the same (regression) slope but significantly (analysis of covariance) different intercepts. This means that $\dot{V}O_2$max • BM^{-1} for boys at a certain Max-T or T_{170} is higher than for girls. It was hypothesized that one formula for this weight-bearing exercise would fit both sexes because $\dot{V}O_2$max is expressed per BM. It was not clear what the reason for this finding might have been; it may have been that girls walked somewhat more efficiently or the finding was a statistical artifact. Furthermore, the differences might have been smaller by using lean BM. The values predicted with both formulas showed a considerable overestimation for the extreme age groups. This might mean that the relationship with age in fact is not linear; a systematically lower value of $\dot{V}O_2$max • BM^{-1} at these ages compared with the younger ages (Table 2) most probably caused this effect.

The prediction from Max-T showed a range for the mean difference of -3.2 to 1.9 ml • kg^{-1} • min^{-1} and a standard deviation ranging from 2.9 to 5.1. Using T_{170} the values were -3.9 to 2.7 for the mean and 3.7 to 6.1 for the standard deviation.

From Tables 1 and 2, it can easily be seen that the standard deviation of the predicted values using W_{170} or T_{170} lie between 10% and 20% of the measured $\dot{V}O_2$max. There is no literature available to compare these findings for both sexes and over the age range of 6 to 18 years. In general, however, prediction of $\dot{V}O_2$max from submaximal data for children of smaller age groups do show a standard deviation of at least 10% (Franz, Wiewel, & Mellerowicz, 1984; Woynarowska, 1980).

Prediction using Max-W or Max-T (see Tables 1 and 2) show that the mean predicted $\dot{V}O_2$max differed less than using the submaximal values W_{170} or T_{170}. For Max-W the standard deviation (about 0.2 l • min^{-1}) of the predicted $\dot{V}O_2$max was 6% for the oldest boys and 13% for the youngest girls, thus covering the whole range. Kuipers (1983) showed a similar value (5%) for 20- to 30-year-old subjects.

The level of the standard deviations of the differences for the prediction with Max-T was 11% for the whole age range, which was smaller than when using T_{170}. The mean of the predicted mean value for the whole age range differed 0.1 ml • kg^{-1} • min^{-1} from the measured $\dot{V}O_2$max • BM^{-1} but showed large differences for the 18-year-old boys and girls. The value of 11% confirmed the findings of Cumming, Everatt, and Hastman (1978) who found for their group a value of 10% when predicting $\dot{V}O_2$max from Max-T.

CONCLUSION

Formulas were developed to predict $\dot{V}O_2$max for bicycle and treadmill tests (Bruce) for both sexes over the age range of 6 to 18 years. The standard deviation of the predicted values using submaximal data (i.e., W_{170} or T_{170} was between 10% and 20% of the measured $\dot{V}O_2$max. The formulas using maximal data (i.e., Max-W or Max-T) showed that this standard deviation is around 10%. It is therefore strongly advised not to use prediction formulas for an accurate individual $\dot{V}O_2$max determination.

Acknowledgment

This study was subsidized by The Netherlands Heart Foundation, Grant No. 79.015.

REFERENCES

Åstrand, P.-O. (1952). *Experimental studies of physical working capacity in relation to sex and age*. Copenhagen: Munksgaard.

Cumming, G.R., Everatt, D., & Hastman, L. (1978). Bruce treadmill test in children: Normal values in a clinic population. *The American Journal of Cardiology, 41*, 69-75.

Franz, I.-W., Wiewel, D., & Mellerowicz, H. (1984). Comparative measurements of $\dot{V}O_2$max and PWC_{170} in schoolchildren. In H. Löllgen & H. Mellerowicz (Eds.), *Progress in ergometry: Quality control and test criteria* (pp. 60-64). Berlin, New York: Springer-Verlag.

Kuipers, H. (1983). *Variability of physiological responses to exercise*. Haarlem: De Vrieseborch.

Saris, W.H.M., de Koning, F., Elvers, J.W.H., de Boo, T., & Binkhorst, R.A. (1984). Estimation of W_{170} and maximal oxygen consumption in young children by different treadmill tests. In J. Ilmarinen & I. Välimäki (Eds.), *Children and sport* (pp. 86-92). Berlin, New York: Springer-Verlag.

Saris, W.H.M., Noordeloos, A.M., Rignalda, B.E.M., van 't Hof, M.A., & Binkhorst, R.A. (1985). Reference values for aerobic power of healthy 4- to 18-year-old Dutch children. In R.A. Binkhorst, H.C.G. Kemper, & W.H.M. Saris (Eds.), *Children and exercise XI* (pp. 151-160) (International Series on Sport Sciences, Vol. 15). Champaign, IL: Human Kinetics.

Woynarowska, B. (1980). The validity of indirect estimations of maximal oxygen uptake in children 11 to 12 years of age. *European Journal of Applied Physiology, 43*, 19-23.

A Longitudinal Study of Muscular Strength and Cardiorespiratory Fitness in Girls (13 to 18 Years)

Jan A. Vos
Wim Geurts
Tom Brandon
Robert A. Binkhorst
University of Nijmegen, Nijmegen, The Netherlands

This study was part of a more extensive project undertaken and performed on girls in two secondary schools, the MAVO school and the LHNO school in Eindhoven and Nijmegen, respectively, in The Netherlands. The purpose of the project was to provide data on aspects of muscular strength development of large muscle groups, cardiorespiratory fitness, and body composition changes over a 4-year period in a group of children. In cooperation with school physicians and physiotherapists, deviations in physical development and posture in the subjects were controlled 2 times a year, but treatments, exercises, and results of this part of the investigation will not be discussed in this article.

MAVO pupils study principally theoretical school subjects and are prepared for jobs in shops, offices, banks, and other businesses or continue their studies on a higher level, for example, in technical or other schools. LHNO pupils spend their days partly in theoretical courses and to a large extent in practice of applied domestic sciences such as housekeeping. Only a few pupils continue their studies after 17 or 18 years of age; thus, after leaving this school of domestic sciences, many girls work in shops or at housekeeping. Both groups represent the largest percentage of pupils in their age groups (13 to 18 years) but little information about their physiological development exists. Thus, it seemed of value to conduct a longitudinal study of this type.

METHODS

Both schools were situated in lower socioeconomic areas of the two cities. The MAVO girls were 12.5 years of age and the LHNO girls were

13.2 years of age when the investigation began. They were members of the same class per school type and involved in the same pattern of school activities. In the first 3 years at the 4-year schools they received 3 hours a week of physical education and in the final year 2 hours a week. (One school period was 50 minutes.) In the MAVO group, 35 subjects were involved in anthropometric and bicycle ergometer tests and 14 in the strength measurements for all 4 years. In the LHNO group, 30 subjects finished all of the experimental tests.

Height

Height was measured with a wall-mounted stadiometer to the nearest 0.5 cm. Light upward pressure under the jaw and occiput by one hand provided maximum extension of the spine.

Body Fat

Body fat as a fraction of total body mass was assessed by the four skin-fold caliper method (Holtain type) following Durnin and Womersley (1974).

Aerobic Power

Exercise was performed on the Monark bicycle ergometer with saddle height adapted to the child. Each child exercised with a pedaling frequency of 50 rpm at a submaximal load for 6 min and maintained a steady state heart rate in a range of about 130 to 170 beats/min. Åstrand's (1960) method to predict VO_2max was used.

Strength

The "perfect" muscle test would be one that measures in one trial the maximum forces throughout the whole range of movement of the joints. Because of fatigue, the last part of any test cannot be maximal, and thus no such ideal muscle test exists. Asmussen (1959) stated that the general maximal static strength of the muscles of the body should not be evaluated from measurements in one single muscle group but from an application of a battery of selected, well-standardized tests (Kroemer, 1970).

All forces in the test battery were measured by means of the deformation of a steel rod recorded by strain gauges, a Wheatstone bridge, and a recording potentiometer after amplification. The maximal force was the peak value of three well-exerted trials (Vos, 1976). The battery consisted of

1. arm flexion, right and left arms measured separately. The angle between the upper and lower arm was about 90° during force exertion, while standing in an erect position and flexing at the elbow.
2. both arms extension. In a standing position, the subject pushed as strongly as possible on a steel rod with both arms in front of her.
3. trunk flexion and extension. In a fixed, standing position, the subject pushed with the upper part of her body against a wooden shelf mounted on a steel rod, either in front or behind her, in order to measure, respectively, trunk flexion or extension.
4. both legs extension. Sitting on a rolling seat that could be fixed at an optimal leg length, the subject extended both legs against a foot plate fixed on a steel rod to which strain gauges were fixed. During maximal effort both legs were almost fully extended.
5. hand-grip strength. Right and left hands were measured separately by an adjustable dynamometer (Bettendorf, Belgium).
6. one dynamic strength test, either the Vertical Jump or the Sargent Test. This test measured the height in centimeters that a subject reached after jumping as high as possible from a standing position with both legs.

RESULTS

The results are presented descriptively. No statistical analyses for comparing groups were applied because the results mostly were so clear that statistical tests were not considered to be necessary.

Physical characteristics of the LHNO girls (n = 30) and MAVO girls (n = 35) are given in Figures 1 and 2. All SDs are not presented in the figures because it was felt this would make the figures too confusing and, furthermore, the differences in SD between one measurement and the other at different ages were very small. In Figures 1 and 2 one can note that the MAVO girls finished their maturation about half a year earlier than the LHNO girls. In mean body fat, there was no clear difference between the two groups (see Figure 3). In VO_2max, a decrease started at the age of about 14 to 15 years; especially remarkable in this respect is the LHNO group after the age of 15.5 years (see Figure 4).

Of the MAVO group (n = 35), 14 girls were randomly selected to be examined for the strength of their large muscle groups. These data are expressed in Newtons per kilogram of body weight ($N \cdot kg^{-1}$). According to de Koning (1984), this type of expression corrects for differences in body dimensions when comparing groups of individuals (see Figures 5 to 9). In general, maximal static strength in flexion and extension of

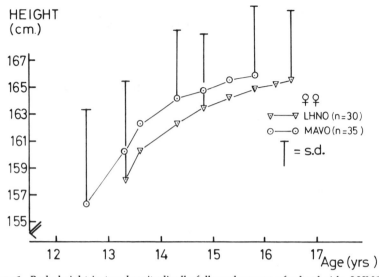

Figure 1 Body height in two longitudinally followed groups of school girls. LHNO is a school for domestic sciences and MAVO a more theoretical middle school. Mean values and 1 *SD* are given.

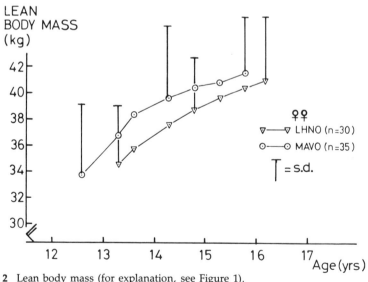

Figure 2 Lean body mass (for explanation, see Figure 1).

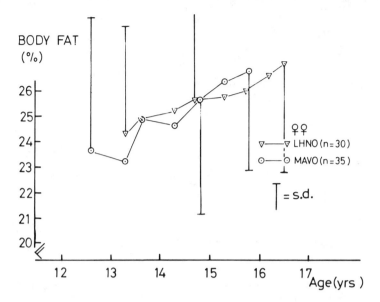

Figure 3 Body fat (for explanation, see Figure 1).

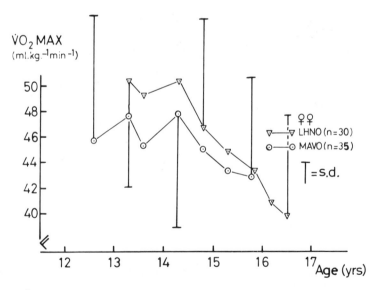

Figure 4 $\dot{V}O_2$max in ml per kg body mass per minute (for explanation, see Figure 1).

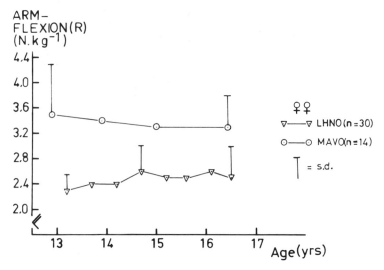

Figure 5 Maximal static arm flexion forces of the right arm expressed in N/kg body mass (for explanation, see Figure 1).

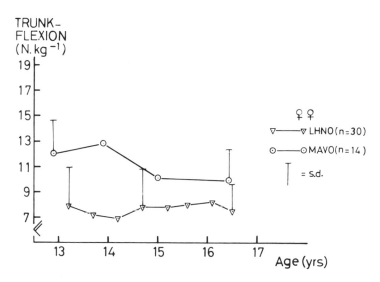

Figure 6 Maximal static force in trunk flexion are expressed in N/kg body mass (for explanation, see Figure 1).

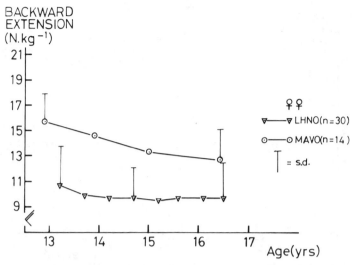

Figure 7 Maximal static force in backward extension expressed in N/kg body mass (for explanation, see Figure 1).

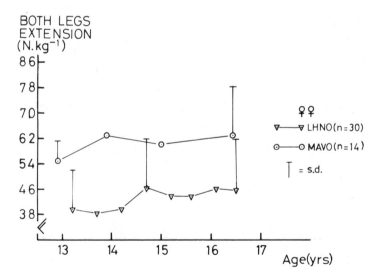

Figure 8 Maximal static force in both legs extension expressed in N/kg body mass (for explanation, see Figure 1).

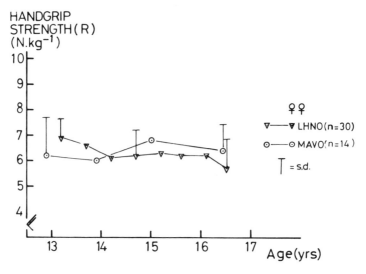

Figure 9   Hand grip strength for right and left hands (for explanation, see Figure 1).

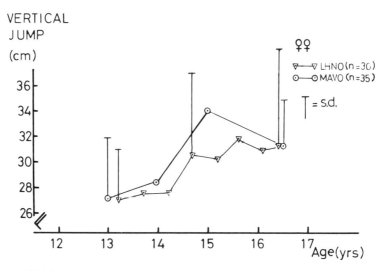

Figure 10   Height in vertical jump (or Sargent Jump) (for explanation, see Figure 1).

large muscle groups was at the same level at all ages or decreased slightly. The MAVO girls (n = 14) as a mean were about 30% stronger than the LHNO group (n = 30) in all muscle groups except hand-grip strength and vertical jump performance (see Figure 10).

DISCUSSION

Aerobic power assessment is of practical importance as a measure of cardiorespiratory and circulation function and later as a measure of preparedness for sport and/or occupation and is utilized in some cases as a diagnostic tool in disease or rehabilitation work. Maximal aerobic power is affected by age, training, sex, and genetic endowment. Selection of the subjects, different test procedures, and socioeconomic background are important causal factors for differences between results of various studies. Aerobic power in girls has seldom been measured in longitudinal studies; thus these data were compared with data from cross-sectional studies. The data of Seliger and Bartunek (1976), Saris (1982) using the Bruce treadmill protocol, Kemper and Verschuur (1981) who also measured a group of high-school girls, and Massicotte, Gauthier, and Markou (1985) who like Seliger tested subjects on a bicycle ergometer are similar to these data on VO_2max per kilogram showing a general level of 45 to 50 ml $\cdot$ kg^{-1} $\cdot$ min^{-1}. Comparing the data at the age of 16 years, the LHNO girls showed a larger decrease than the MAVO girls and also than the data collected by Massicotte and Seliger (see Table 1). This could be the effect of being physically inactive at this age of life. Increases in height of 8 to 10 cm in almost 3.5 years in both groups and increases in body weight of 11 to 12 kg in the same period did not result in improvement in their relative strength that at the age of 16 years was rather low for the LHNO group. Strength per kilogram of body weight or per kilogram of lean body mass remained at about the same level or decreased slightly during the 4 years at the schools (see Figure 5 to 9). The most striking difference was the fact that the LHNO group showed a 30% lower force in large muscle groups than the MAVO girls. This was perhaps the reason that often these girls complained during exercises that they did not have strength enough to finish an exercise or sport activity. Comparative data on static muscular strength do not exist in the literature to the best of our knowledge.

CONCLUSION

The longitudinal data on VO_2max of girls 12 to 17 years of age showed a remarkable decrease at older ages for the LHNO school. Furthermore, their maximal static force was about 30% lower than that of girls at a different type of school. Because this group represented a large school population, these findings might have consequences for preventive health care in The Netherlands and provide at least an indication that further and larger studies should be done with respect to physical fitness of these groups.

Table 1   Mean Values of Anthropometric Data and Aerobic Power in Girls (Bicycle Ergometer Tests)

Data source	Age (yr)	N	Height (cm)	Weight (kg)	Lean BM (kg)	$\dot{V}O_2max$ ($l \cdot min^{-1}$)	$\dot{V}O_2max$ ($ml \cdot kg^{-1} \cdot min^{-1}$)	$\dot{V}O_2max$ ($ml \cdot kg_{LBM}^{-1} \cdot min^{-1}$)	Body fat (%)
Seliger (1976)	13	—	157.4	47.1	37.1	1.69	38.6	45.6	21.0
Massicotte (1985)	13	21	157.5	46.3	34.7	2.19	47.2	63.1	25.0
Vos (1977) MAVO	13	77	158.3	46.6	35.2	2.10	45.2	59.7	23.9
Vos (1985) LHNO	13	30	158.0	45.7	34.6	2.25	50.4	66.1	24.3
Seliger (1976)	14	—	160.9	51.6	41.0	1.83	38.2	44.6	20.6
Massicotte (1985)	14	21	161.2	51.6	38.7	2.41	46.8	62.3	25.0
Vos (1977) MAVO	14	77	163.0	51.7	38.7	2.36	45.7	60.9	24.7
Vos (1985) LHNO	14	30	162.2	50.4	37.5	2.44	50.0	66.4	25.1
Seliger (1976)	15	—	162.6	54.3	43.5	1.94	37.9	44.6	20.2
Massicotte (1985)	15	19	162.5	53.9	39.3	2.43	45.1	61.8	27.0
Vos (1977) MAVO	15	77	164.7	54.4	40.7	2.46	45.3	60.4	25.2
Vos (1985) LHNO	15	30	164.3	53.6	39.6	2.36	44.8	59.9	25.7
Seliger (1976)	16	—	163.5	56.1	45.0	2.01	37.6	44.7	20.0
Massicotte (1985)	16	19	162.8	54.8	40.0	2.45	44.6	61.3	27.0
Vos (1977) MAVO	16	77	165.2	55.4	41.1	2.45	44.2	59.6	25.8
Vos (1985) LHNO	16	30	165.4	56.1	40.9	2.25	40.9	55.0	26.5

Note. MAVO = a more theoretical middle school; LHNO = a more practical domestic sciences school. Total $N = 77$ in the MAVO group including the longitudinal group ($n = 35$) and a longitudinal group ($n = 42$) started one year later.

REFERENCES

Asmussen, E. (1959). *Communications, No. 5.* Hellerup, Denmark: Danish National Association for Infantile Paralysis.

Åstrand, I. (1960). Aerobic work capacity in men and women with special reference to age. *Acta Physiologica Scandinavica,* **49** (Suppl.), 1-92.

de Koning, F.L.H.A. (1984). *Force and speed of human muscle.* Unpublished thesis, Nijmegen, The Netherlands.

Durnin, J.V.G.A., & Womersley, J. (1974). Body fat assessed from total body density and its estimation from skinfold thickness. *British Journal of Nutrition,* **37**, 77-86.

Kemper, H.C.G., & Verschuur, R. (1981). Maximal aerobic power in 13- and 14-year-old teenagers in relation to biologic age. *International Journal of Sports Medicine,* **2**, 97.

Kroemer, K.H.E. (1970). Human strength: Terminology, measurement and interpretation of data. *Human Factors,* **12**(3), 297-313.

Massicotte, D.R., Gauthier, R., & Markou, P. (1985). Prediction of $\dot{V}O_2$max from the running performance in children aged 10-17 years. *Journal of Sports Medicine,* **25**, 10-17.

Saris, W.H.M. (1982). *Aerobic power and daily physical activity in children.* Unpublished thesis, Nijmegen, The Netherlands.

Seliger, V., & Bartunek, Z. (1976). *Mean values of various indices of physical fitness in the investigation of Czechoslovak population aged 12 to 55 years.* Praha: CSSR Association of Physical Culture.

Vos, J.A. (1976). *Static and dynamic strength measurements* [in Dutch]. Unpublished thesis, Gent, Belgium.

Vos, J.A. (1977). *Development in physical characteristics in boys and girls of 13 to 17 years* [in Dutch] (Report). University of Nijmegen, Nijmegen, The Netherlands.

Longitudinal Observations of the Effects of the Training Process on Pupils in Sport Classes

Hilda Svátková
Kazimír Feriencik
Eva Slováková
Jozef Liška
Institute of National Health, Bratislava, Czechoslovakia

Accelerated growth in children and young people has long been accepted as a positive reflection of improved socioeconomic and hygienic conditions of countries (Drobná & Drobný, 1978). However, it is necessary to answer the question whether the accelerated development can be considered unambiguously as a positive phenomenon. It appears that the accelerated body development does not proceed uniformly and optimally in all aspects, and the increased body size is not always accompanied by adequate development of functional abilities. This report includes an analysis of selected indices observed for some time in pupils of sport classes of ice hockey and athletics in Bratislava.

METHOD

During the 1978 to 1982 period, 361 pupils were examined, including 223 pupils from ice hockey classes and 138 from athletics, the pupils being 11 to 14 years old (in the fifth to the eighth grades of basic schools). Comparisons were made of the pupils from Bratislava with the pupils from Brno who were engaged in ice hockey (Placheta, 1980) as well as with Czechoslovakian children not active in sports (Seliger & Bartunĕk, 1977).

RESULTS

Functional Indices

The highest values of maximum oxygen intake expressed in terms of kilograms of body mass ($\dot{V}O_2$max/kg) were found for Bratislava ice-hockey players; the next higher oxygen intake values were for the ice-hockey players from Brno. It can be seen from Figure 1 that the sporting pupils had increasing values (ice hockey) and almost steady values (athletics), respectively; the values decreased in the nonsport population during their development. Statistically significant differences were found in favor of ice-hockey players in all the age groups (see Figure 1). The values of maximum oxygen pulse ($\dot{V}O_2$max/HR) showed the sport pupils markedly higher until they were 14 years old, when the Czechoslovakian nonsport population caught up to them (see Figure 2).

The results of the working capacity values (W_{170}) in relation to age were unexpected. Though the values in pupils of sport classes increased, the nonsport pupils were ahead of them already when 12 years old, and by the time they were 14 years old they showed even greater differences, which were higher (see Figure 3). The results were similar when the working capacity values expressed in terms of kilograms of body mass (W_{170}/kg) were computed, only the nonsport population exceeded the best sport pupils (ice-hockey classes) as late as between the 13th and 14th years (see Figure 4).

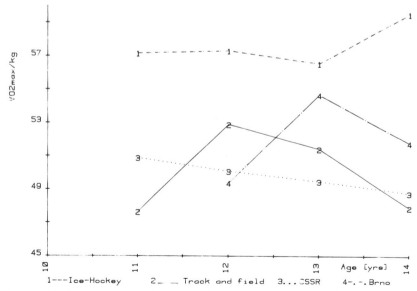

Figure 1 Maximum oxygen intake expressed in terms of kg body mass ($\dot{V}O_2$max/kg) versus age.

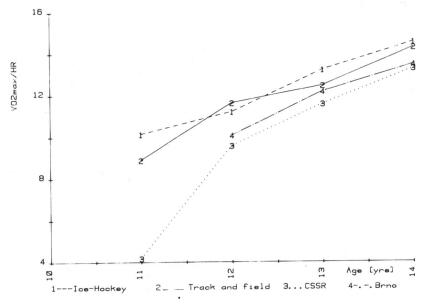

Figure 2 Maximum oxygen pulse ($\dot{V}O_2$max/HR) versus age.

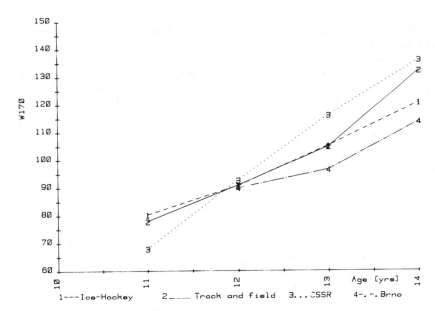

Figure 3 Working capacity (W_{170}) versus age.

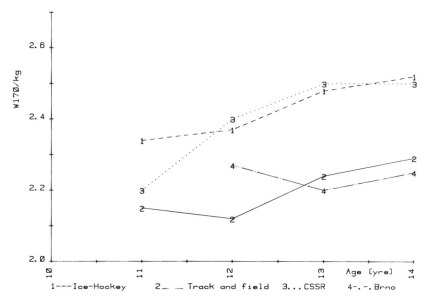

Figure 4   Working capacity expressed in terms of kg body mass (W_{170}/kg) versus age.

Anthropometric Indices

Higher values for body mass in pupils of athletics classes with age were quite evident when compared with ice-hockey participants. The difference was statistically significant in the 12-, 13-, and 14-year-old pupils. The children of the nonsport population had lower values in all of the age groups (see Figure 5). The mean values of lean body mass (kilograms) at all ages were found to be highest in the pupils of athletics classes, and the difference was statistically significant in 12-, 13-, and 14-year-old pupils (see Figure 6).

DISCUSSION

The results of long-term observation of pupils attending sport classes answered some questions regarding selection of talented young people. More pupils with greater body mass were grouped in the athletics classes than in the ice-hockey classes. This would be a recommended situation if physical body development were in accordance with functional development, but the contrary is true. The body mass of 36% of the individuals in the track and field classes were one to two sigmas higher (7.5 to 15 kg) than the mean of children of the same age in the general Czechoslovakian population. Only 13% of the pupils in the ice-hockey classes surpassed the population mean of Czechoslovakian children by as much as 1 sigma (7.5 kg).

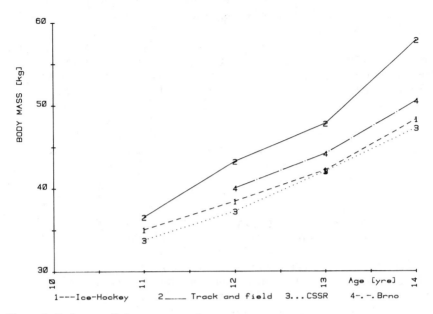

Figure 5 Body mass (kg) versus age.

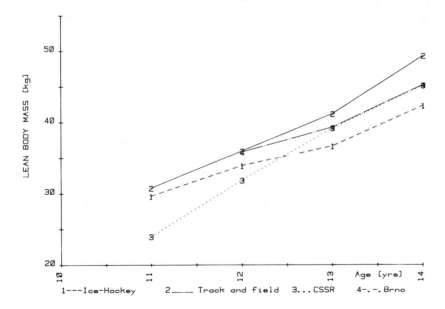

Figure 6 Lean body mass (kg) versus age.

On the other hand, in the case of maximum oxygen intake expressed in terms of kilograms of body mass ($\dot{V}O_2$max/kg), only 23% of the athletic group surpassed the mean nonsport population by 1 sigma or more. A total of 47% of the ice-hockey players surpassed the $\dot{V}O_2$max values of the nonsport group by 1 sigma or more. It follows from the analysis that functional indices increasingly lag behind the increase in body mass in the athletes as compared with ice-hockey players. The lower values of working capacity (W_{170} and W_{170}/kg) in the pupils of sport classes observed when compared with the nonsport children indicate an insufficient level of general training capacity in both the groups (athletics and ice-hockey players). Several authors have also confirmed increasing absolute values in untrained pupils, but decreasing values of $\dot{V}O_2$max/kg with age (Bink & Wafelbakker, 1968; Lorenz & Leupold, 1968).

Pupils in football classes in Bratislava were not found to have higher values of W_{170} and W_{170}/kg than the control nonsport group (Hájková, Horniak, Handzo, Korček, & Poláčková, 1981; Hájková, Horniak, Handzo, Minarovjech, & Korček, 1981; Horniak, Hájková, Handzo, Novotná, & Minarovjech, 1981). Also, values of functional indices were reported in adolescent footballers to be approximately the same as in the Czechoslovakian nonsport population, indicating an insufficient level of general training capacity (Handzo & Novotná, 1979).

On the other hand, several researchers have reported a positive effect of training on the functional development of children and young people (Horniak & Hájková, 1976; Svátková & Neščáková, 1979). It would seem that favorable results of the training process depend markedly on correct selection.

CONCLUSION

Observations have shown that the problem of excessive weight, encountered in children of good health, was more marked in pupils of sport classes. It was shown that 36% of pupils attending athletics classes and 13% of pupils attending ice-hockey classes surpassed the nonsport population of children in body mass by 1 to 2 sigmas. The children with excessive weight did not lose their increased mass even during several years of training in sport classes.

REFERENCES

Bink, B., & Wafelbakker, F. (1968). Physical working capacity at maximum levels of work, of boys 12-18 years of age. *Zeitschrift für Ärztliche Fortbildung,* **62**, 957-961.

Drobná, M., & Drobný, I. (1978). *Evolutionary anthropology.* Bratislava: Univerzita Komenského.

Hájková, M., Horniak, E., Handzo, P., Korček, F., & Poláčková, M. (1981). Effect of soccer training on the somatic ability of pupils. *Proceedings of the Scientific Council of the Central Committee of the Czechoslovak Union of Physical Training, 12*, 305-310.

Hájková, M., Horniak, E., Handzo, P., Minarovjech, V., & Korček, F. (1981). Functional and motoric indices of young footballers. *Lékar a Tělesná Výchova, 3*, 23-25.

Handzo, P., & Novotná, E. (1979). Health viewpoints of the transition of adolescents to adult teams in soccer. *Tréner, 1*, 5-7.

Horniak, E., & Hájková, M. (1976). Relation between the heart volume and some functional indices in youth, adults, and sportsmen. *Proceedings of the Scientific Council of the Slovak Central Committee of the Czechoslovak Union of Physical Training, 4*, 119-136.

Horniak, E., Hájková, M., Handzo, P., Novotná, E., Minarovjech, V. (1981). Four-year observation of somatic development of football class pupils. *Proceedings of the Scientific Council of the Central Committee of the Czechoslovak Union of Physical Training, 12*, 283-288.

Lorenz, K., & Leupold, W. (1968). "Physical Working Capacity" und spiroergometrische Untersuchungsergebnisse im Kindesalter. *Zeitschrift für Ärztliche Fortbildung, 62*, 942-945.

Placheta, Z. (1980). *Youth and physical activity*. Brno: Univerzita J.E. Purkyně.

Seliger, V., & Bartuněk, Z. (1977). *Somatic ability of 12 to 55 year old inhabitants in the ČSSR*. Prague: Karlova Univerzita.

Svátková, H., & Neščáková, E. (1979). Development of the functional ability of pupils of sport classes. *Proceedings of the Scientific Council of the Slovak Central Committee of the Czechoslovak Union of Physical Training, 30*, 38-54.

Svátková, H., Neščáková, E., & Liska, J. (1980). Somatic and functional development of pupils of sport classes in Bratislava. *Československá Hygiena, 1*, 13-21.

The Effects of 20-Min Steady State Running on the 2-Min Recovery Heart Rate Response

Frederick W. Kasch
Michel C. Biederman
Jackie Jo Ehmer
Virginia M. Drennan
Mark R. Hilty
Joseph S. Erlichman
Thomas J. Albrecht
University of Colorado, Boulder, Colorado, USA

In order for exercise prescription to be safe and effective, it must be administered as carefully as any other therapeutic medium. The use of heart rate (HR) as a guide and control of exercise intensity has been used almost universally in various training and fitness programs. A recovery HR of 120 beats/min has been used as a means of monitoring athletes during interval training (Reindell, Roskamm, & Gerschler, 1962; Roskamm, Reindell, & Keul, 1962). Adult-fitness and cardiac-rehabilitation programs in the USA have used a modification of the postexercise HR of 120 beats/min. This has usually been done at 2-min postexercise and after a 20-min or longer steady state activity, such as jogging or swimming. Little, if any, data are available as to the validity of the latter method. This study proposed to test the hypothesis that the 2-min recovery HR would return to 120 beats/min after a 20-min steady state treadmill run. The 20-min run conforms to the requirements of the American College of Sports Medicine (ACSM, 1978) for quantitative and qualitative changes due to training in healthy adults.

METHOD

Eleven healthy young men 18 to 21 years old (M 19.5 years) were given a $\dot{V}O_2$max treadmill test using the protocol of Costill and Fox (1969) on one day, followed by a 20-min steady state treadmill run at about 70% of $\dot{V}O_2$max on a subsequent day. Hereafter, the max test will be referred to as T1 and the 20-min steady state test as T2. Table 1 gives the descriptive data for the subjects. Each subject reported to the laboratory a minimum

Table 1   Descriptive Data of the Subjects ($N = 11$)

Age (yr)	Height (cm)	Weight (kg)	HR rest (beats/min)	HR max (beats/min)
19.5	179	72.6	57.7	198.9
(0.94)	(9.4)	(11.8)	(6.9)	(8.8)

Note.   Means (and SD).

of 2 hrs postabsorptive and signed an informed consent as approved by the University of Colorado, Human Subjects Committee. Oral temperatures and resting blood pressures were normal in all subjects. Each person was weighed and his height measured while clad in running trunks. Next, each one was prepared for ECG recording using a skin abrasive and a modified CM5 lead system (Ellestad, 1976). This was followed by the necessary test instructions, familiarization with the test equipment, and a 4- to 5-min warm-up on the treadmill, followed by a short rest period. Next, the subject mounted the treadmill and the predetermined speed was gradually increased to the required rate. The treadmill speed was calibrated for each and every test.

$\dot{V}O_2$ was determined by the Douglas bag method (Consolazio, Johnson, & Pecora, 1963) with aliquots of expired air analyzed using Godart CO_2 and O_2 meters that had been calibrated by Scholander (1947) span gases. Air volumes were measured with a Parkinson-Cowan dry gas meter that was calibrated with a Tissot gasometer. The necessary volume corrections were made for STPD. Heart rates were monitored continually with an oscilloscope and recorded for 10 to 15 s each minute throughout each test and for at least 2 min of recovery. The HR percentage was calculated as net HR by the Karvonen method (Karvonen, Kentala, & Mustala, 1957).

RESULTS

$\dot{V}O_2$max (T1) averaged 4.31 ($\pm$ 0.78) l/min and 59.6 ($\pm$ 3.5) ml/min^{-1} • kg^{-1}, whereas the $\dot{V}O_2$ for T2 averaged 3.00 l/min and 41.6 ($\pm$ 6.4) ml/min^{-1} • kg^{-1}, or 70% of maximal. The HR at several points during T2 are illustrated in Figure 1. The 2-min recovery HR averaged 122.4 ($\pm$ 14.8) after T2, or 2% above the hypothesized 120 beats/min. This was 59% of the 20-min HR of 167 beats/min during T2. The 1-min post-T2 HR was 138 ($\pm$ 17.0) beats/min (73%). Figure 2 illustrates the HR percentages during T2. The HRs 1 and 2 min after $\dot{V}O_2$max (T1) were 166 (77%) and 141 (59%) beats/min, respectively. Although these HRs were considerably higher in absolute numbers, the percentages were nearly identical to the 1- and 2-min recovery HR in T2. This is readily apparent as seen in Figure 3.

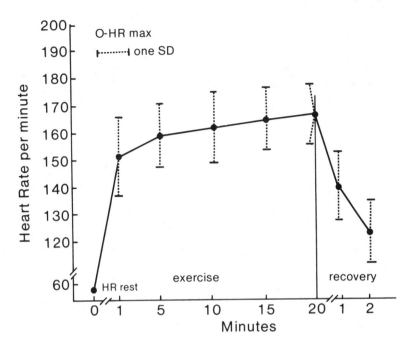

Figure 1 Exercise and recovery HR during 20-min steady state run.

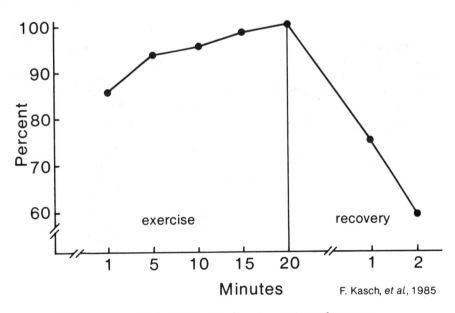

F. Kasch, *et al,* 1985

Figure 2 HR percentages during 20-min steady state exercise and recovery.

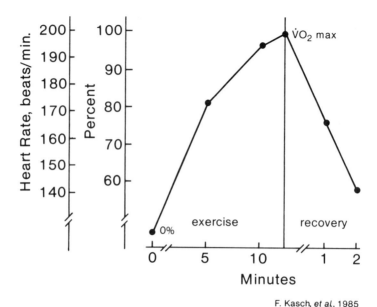

F. Kasch, et al, 1985

Figure 3 Heart rate and HR percentages during $\dot{V}O_2$max recovery.

DISCUSSION

By comparison, four men aged 27 years ($\pm$ 2.3) tested under identical conditions had 2-min recovery HRs of 110 ($\pm$ 6.8), or 57%, of the 153 HR at the 20th min of T2. This was very close to the 60% found in the younger subjects. The HR percentages during and after 20-min steady state treadmill exercise were nearly identical, as can be seen by Figure 4.

It has been reported (Wilt, 1968) that the recovery HR during interval training should return to 120 beats/min, or 66% of the exercise HR, prior to resuming the subsequent interval. It appears that with either maximal or submaximal running the HR returns to approximately 60%, as seen by the results of both the younger (Group A) and older (Group B) subjects in the present experiment (see Figure 4). The use of a percentage or ratio may be a more valid method of determining the 2-min recovery HR, particularly in view of the fact that HR max declines with age. In addition to age differences, a ratio would more likely be valid for persons with an abnormally high or low HR max or to allow for environmental or diurnal differences. The following formula may suffice to determine a more precise 2-min recovery HR:

Steady State HR $-$ (HR rest) $\times$ 60% + (HR rest) = 2-min recovery HR

The findings of this study also produced some data of further interest. The prediction of $\dot{V}O_2$ may be calculated from the horizontal running rate

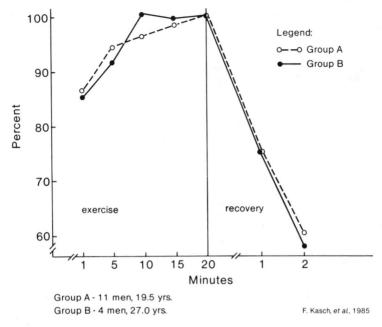

Figure 4 Comparison of HR percentages with steady state during exercise and recovery for 2 groups.

in m/min within the range of 150 to 300 m/min (Balke, 1960); for example, the running rate averaged 200 m/min during steady state. Using the formula

$$\dot{V}O_2 \text{ ml/min}^{-1} \cdot \text{kg}^{-1} = \text{Run rate} - (150) \times 0.18 + (33.3)$$

we find the VO₂ is 42.3, compared to 41.6 ml/min⁻¹ · kg⁻¹ by direct measurement.

A more simplified formula is:

$$\dot{V}O_2 \text{ ml/min}^{-1} \cdot \text{kg}^{-1} = \text{Run rate (m/min)} \times 0.2 + (3, 2, 1)$$

when the result is in the decrement of 30, 40, or 50, respectively. Using this formula gives a result of 42.0 ml/min⁻¹ · kg⁻¹ at 200 m/min running rate. The formulae are valuable and have practical application in determining the $\dot{V}O_2$ or energy cost of horizontal running if the rate per minute is known and ranges between 150 and 300 m/min.

CONCLUSION

It was found that the 2-min recovery HR of relatively young subjects was approximately 60% of the 20-min steady state running HR and not a fixed HR of 120 beats/min, as hypothesized. These data may have application to other age levels than those reported herein.

REFERENCES

American College of Sports Medicine. (1978). Position statement on the recommended quantity and quality of exercise for developing and maintaining fitness in healthy adults. *Medicine and Science in Sports*, **10**(3), VII-X.

Balke, B. (1960). *The effect of physical exercise on metabolic potential, a crucial measure of physical fitness, exercise and fitness.* Chicago: Athletic Institute.

Consolazio, C.F., Johnson, R.E., & Pecora, L.J. (1963). *Physiological measurements of metabolic functions in man.* New York: McGraw-Hill.

Costill, D.L., & Fox, E.L. (1969). Energetics of marathon running. *Medicine and Science in Sports*, **1**, 81-86.

Ellestad, M.H. (1976). *Stress testing.* Philadelphia: F.A. Davis.

Karvonen, M.J., Kentala, E., & Mustala, O. (1957). The effects of training on heart rate. *Annales Medicinae Experimentalis et Biologiae Finniae*, **35**, 307-315.

Reindell, H., Roskamm, H., & Gerschler, W. (1962). *Das Intervall-Training* (p. 67). München: Barth.

Roskamm, H., Reindell, H., & Keul, J. (1962). Die Lehre der Leichtathletik. In H. Reindell, H. Roskamm, & W. Gerschler (Eds.), *Das Interval-Training* (pp. 72-81). Munich: Barth.

Scholander, P.F. (1947). Analyzer for accurate estimation of respiratory gases in one-half cubic centimeter samples. *Journal of Biological Chemistry*, **167**, 235-250.

Wilt, F. (1968). Training for competitive running. In H.B. Falls (Ed.), *Exercise physiology* (pp. 395-414). New York: Academic Press.

The Fallacy of the Heart Rate Response to Exercise in Evaluating Exercise Performance in Children Operated on for Tetralogy of Fallot

Tony M. Reybrouck
Maria L. Weymans
Hugo J. Stijns
Lucas G. Van der Hauwaert
University of Leuven, Leuven, Belgium

Exercise performance capacity has frequently been evaluated by assessing the heart rate (HR) response to exercise. However, in patients operated on for tetralogy of Fallot (TF), a reduced HR response has been observed during graded exercise, compared to normal children (Bjarke, 1975; Wessel et al., 1980). However, because maximal exercise performance capacity remains subnormal even many years after surgery (Bjarke, 1975; Wessel et al., 1980), the reliability of exercise performance tests based on HR response may be questioned. The purpose of the present study was to evaluate such tests and to compare them with a recently introduced index of cardiorespiratory performance capacity, the ventilatory threshold (Reybrouck, Ghesquiere, Cattaert, Fagard, & Amery, 1983; Wasserman, Whipp, Koyal, & Beaver, 1973), which is independent of HR response. The ventilatory threshold has been defined as the highest exercise intensity at which pulmonary ventilation ($\dot{V}_E$) ceases to increase linearly with increasing oxygen uptake ($\dot{V}O_2$). Above this exercise intensity, a disproportionate increase in $\dot{V}_E$ relative to $\dot{V}O_2$ is found.

METHODS

A total of 26 boys were evaluated 1 to 10.4 years (M 4.6 ± 2.5) after surgical correction of TF. Mean age at correction was 5.7 ± 2.8 years. There were 10 patients who had previously undergone either a Blalock-Taussig operation (7 patients) or a Waterston anastomosis (3 patients) at a mean age of 1.7 ± 1.4 years. All patients were asymptomatic. None was taking medication. Children younger than 5 years and patients with mental retardation were excluded. Also excluded were those with significant residual lesions. The postoperative ECG showed sinus rhythm in all patients and a right bundle branch block in all except one case. At the time of the exercise test, age varied from 5 to 17 years ($M = 10$ year). When the data for height and weight were expressed as percentiles and compared with a standard reference grid (Stuart & Meredith, 1946) 3 out of the 26 patients were below the 3rd percentile for height and 6 of 26 for weight.

Habitual Level of Physical Activity

By means of a standardized questionnaire, information was obtained about the number of hours of sport participation, other leisure-time activities, and how the patients moved to and from the school. The number of hours of physical activity were cumulated as a score. When repeated within a time lapse of 1 month the scores were highly reproducible ($r = 0.90$).

Testing Procedure

A motor-driven treadmill was used because this type of exercise has been shown to be suitable for children as young as 4 years of age (Cumming, 1979). The treadmill was set at a speed of 4.8 km/h for children younger than 6 years and 5.6 km/h for children above 6 years of age (Chandramouli, Ehmke, & Lauer, 1975). The inclination was increased stepwise 2%/min until a HR of 170 beats/min was reached. The electrocardiogram from a bipolar lead was recorded during the last 15 s of each treadmill inclination without stopping the treadmill. The children were not allowed to touch the guard rail.

Respiratory variables were measured by the open-circuit method. The patients breathed through a low resistance two-way valve with small dead space. Expired gas was collected every minute in Douglas bags. The volume of expired air was measured by a dry gas meter and the concentrations of O_2 and CO_2 were determined by electronic gas analyzers. Measured variables were the ventilatory minute volume ($\dot{V}_E$, L/min), oxygen uptake ($\dot{V}O_2$, ml/min), and carbon dioxide ouput ($\dot{V}CO_2$, ml/min); derived from these were the respiratory gas exchange ratio ($R = \dot{V}CO_2/\dot{V}O_2$), the ventilatory equivalent for O_2 ($\dot{V}_E/\dot{V}O_2$), and the ventilatory equivalent for CO_2 ($\dot{V}_E/\dot{V}CO_2$). The exercise intensity was expressed as $\dot{V}O_2$ (ml O_2/min/kg), because a linear relationship was found between $\dot{V}O_2$ and the percentage of treadmill inclination. Exercise performance was assessed by determination of the ventilatory threshold, expressed as O_2/min/kg.

This break point of the $\dot{V}_E$ during incremental exercise was checked through reference to the exercise intensity, at which (a) the $\dot{V}CO_2$ began to increase nonlinearly, (b) the ventilatory equivalent for O_2 ($\dot{V}_E/\dot{V}CO_2$) continuously increased without a concomitant increase in the ventilatory equivalent for CO_2 ($V_E/\dot{V}CO_2$), (c) the fractional concentration of O_2 in the mixed expired air (FEO_2) progressively increased, and (d) an excess rise of the respiratory gas exchange ratio (R) occurred (Caiozzo et al., 1982; Reybrouck et al., 1983). The exercise intensity or $\dot{V}O_2$ reached at a HR of 170/min ($\dot{V}O_2$170) was measured. The values for ventilatory threshold and $\dot{V}O_2$170 in patients were compared with values obtained in 234 healthy children (Reybrouck, Weymans, Stijns, Knops, & Van der Hauwaert, 1985). The results of a homogeneous subgroup of 11 boys operated on for TF were analyzed in more detail and compared with those in normal children with comparable weight and height.

Statistical Analysis

When the mean values of different groups were compared, the grand mean was used. The dispersion of the data is given by the standard error of the mean and for normal children also by the 95% confidence limits. Differences between the frequency of subnormal values for ventilatory threshold and $\dot{V}O_2$170 were calculated by a sign test or a chi-square test.

RESULTS

Exercise Performance Capacity

The ventilatory threshold that could be determined in 22 of the 26 patients operated on for TF was significantly lower than that in healthy children matched for sex and weight. It averaged $76.5 \pm 14.4\%$ of the normal mean value. In 22 of these boys the $\dot{V}O_2$170 was also determined; the mean value was normal and averaged $94.6 \pm 15.6\%$ of the value in healthy peers. When compared to the 95% confidence limits in normal children, a significantly larger fraction of patients showed a subnormal value for ventilatory threshold (73%) than for $\dot{V}O_2$170 (41%).

Heart Rate – O_2 Uptake of Patients Operated On for TF and Healthy Children

Comparative studies were performed in a homogeneous subgroup of 11 boys in the 5- to 8-year-old age group. During graded submaximal exercise, for the same inclination on the treadmill, 5 of the 11 boys had a HR below the normal limit (defined as the normal mean value $-$ 1 SD) throughout all exercise levels. Individual values for these patients and the normal mean value $\pm$ 1 SD obtained in healthy children, matched for sex and body weight, are represented in Figure 1. Mean HR was significantly lower ($p < .001$) in the TF patients ($M = 144$ beats/min) than in healthy children matched for sex and body weight ($M = 159$ beats/min).

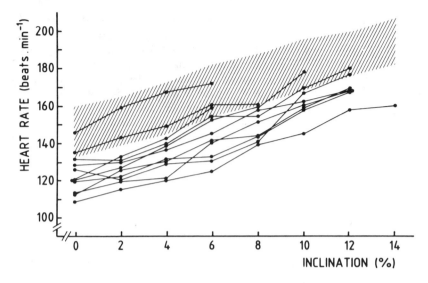

Figure 1 Individual values for heart rate response during graded treadmill exercise in 11 boys (aged 5 to 8 years) operated on for tetralogy of Fallot. The normal range (defined as $M \pm 1\ SD$) is shown by the shaded area. The exercise intensity is expressed by the inclination (%) of the treadmill belt. From Reybrouck et al., in press, *American Heart Journal*.

Significant differences ($p < .001$) were also found when the mean HR values in these patients were compared with those for corresponding $\dot{V}O_2$ in healthy children matched for sex, age, and height.

Habitual Level of Physical Activity

The habitual level of physical activity, expressed as a score, was significantly lower in patients operated on for TF than in healthy children matched for sex and body weight. It averaged 3.74 (range 1.5 to 6.5) units in the patients compared to 4.37 (3.3 to 6.9) in age-matched healthy children. When expressed as a percentage of the normal value, the mean value averaged 84.9% ± 28.3.

DISCUSSION

Although a lower-than-normal HR response to exercise could be theoretically interpreted as indicating a high physical performance capacity, the results of our study show that this criterion can be misleading in patients operated on for TF. In 8 of the 22 patients in whom both tests were performed, the ventilatory threshold was subnormal, whereas VO_2170 was normal. This is in agreement with previous studies, in which normal values in postoperative TF patients have been reported for exercise tests based on HR response to exercise, such as the PWC_{170} (Mocellin & Bastanier, 1976; Strieder, Aziz, Zaver, & Fellows, 1975; Wessel et al., 1980).

By contrast, studies that are not based on HR response to exercise, such as VO_2max or maximal exercise duration, usually show a subnormal exercise capacity after correction of TF (Mocellin, Bastanier, Hofacker, & Bühlmeyer, 1976; Wessel et al., 1980). Similarly, in the present series the ventilatory threshold, a test that is independent of HR response to exercise, remained subnormal 1 to 10 years ($M = 4.6$) after correction of TF.

The finding of a reduced HR response to exercise in the present series of postoperative TF patients is in agreement with previous observations (Bjarke, 1975; James et al., 1976; Wessel et al., 1980). In patients operated on for TF, a reduced HR response to exercise may be misleading, because this relative bradycardia is not compensated for by an increased stroke volume, as found in endurance-trained athletes (Åstrand & Rodahl, 1977). In these patients stroke volume during exercise has been shown to be considerably lower than in age- and sex-matched healthy subjects (Epstein et al., 1973), and consequently cardiac output and maximal oxygen uptake may be markedly decreased (Mocellin et al., 1976). The reason for this inability of most patients to increase their HR during exercise is unclear. Several hypotheses have been postulated, such as an adaptive feedback mechanism inducing a longer diastole (Bjarke, 1975); the presence of conduction disturbances, for example, right bundle branch block (Bjarke, 1975); or an impaired autonomic nervous system (Wessel et al., 1980).

An important factor contributing to the reduction of exercise performance in patients operated on for TF is restriction of physical activity. In fact, the habitual level of physical activity in these patients was significantly lower than in healthy controls. If hypoactivity is a major factor determining the reduced exercise capacity, patients should be strongly encouraged to perform more dynamic physical activity, unless specifically contraindicated (e.g., because of rhythm disturbances).

CONCLUSION

The present study shows that assessing exercise capacity by using the HR response during exercise, in patients operated on for TF, may be seriously misleading. When exercise capacity is measured by determination of the ventilatory threshold, a subnormal exercise performance capacity is found in the majority of the patients. Therefore, it is not recommended to evaluate exercise performance by measuring HR response, but to analyze gas exchange during exercise in patients operated on for TF.

REFERENCES

Åstrand, P.-O., & Rodahl, K. (1977). *Textbook of work physiology* (2nd ed.). New York: McGraw-Hill.

Bjarke, B. (1975). Oxygen uptake and cardiac output during submaximal and maximal exercise in adult subjects with totally corrected tetralogy of Fallot. *Acta Medica Scandinavica, 197*, 177-187.

Caiozzo, V.J., Davis, J.A., Ellis, J.F., Azus, J.L., Vandagriff, R., Prietto, C.A., & McMaster, W.C. (1982). A comparison of gas exchange indices used to detect the anaerobic threshold. *Journal of Applied Physiology, 53*, 1184-1189.

Chandramouli, B., Ehmke, D.A., & Lauer, R.M. (1975). Exercise-induced electrocardiographic changes in children with congenital aortic stenosis. *Journal of Pediatrics, 87*, 725-730.

Cumming, G.R. (1979). Maximal supine exercise haemodynamics after open heart surgery for Fallot's tetralogy. *British Heart Journal, 41*, 683-691.

Epstein, S.E., Beiser, D.G., Goldstein, R.E., Rosing, D.R., Redwood, D.R., & Morrow, A.G. (1973). Hemodynamic abnormalities in response to mild and intense upright exercise following operative correction of an atrial septal defect or tetralogy of Fallot. *Circulation, 47*, 1065-1075.

James, F.W., Kaplan, S., Schwartz, D.C., Chon, T.C., Sandker, M.J., & Naylor, V. (1976). Response to exercise in patients after total surgical correction of tetralogy of Fallot. *Circulation, 54*, 671-679.

Mocellin, R., & Bastanier, C. (1976). Validity of W_{170} as a measure of physical performance capacity in assessment of children with heart disease. *European Journal of Pediatrics, 123*, 223-239.

Mocellin, R., Bastanier, C., Hofacker, W., & Bühlmeyer, K. (1976). Exercise performance in children and adolescents after surgical repair of tetralogy of Fallot. *European Journal of Cardiology, 4*, 367-374.

Reybrouck, T., Ghesquiere, J., Cattaert, A., Fagard, R., & Amery, A. (1983). Ventilatory thresholds during short- and long-term exercise. *Journal of Applied Physiology, 55*, 1694-1700.

Reybrouck, T., Weymans, M., Stijns, H., Knops, J., & Van der Hauwaert, L. (1985). Ventilatory anaerobic threshold in healthy children. Age and sex differences. *European Journal of Applied Physiology, 54*, 278-284.

Strieder, D.J., Aziz, K., Zaver, A.G., & Fellows, K.E. (1975). Exercise tolerance after repair of tetralogy of Fallot. *Annals of Thoracic Surgery, 19*, 397-405.

Stuart, H.C., & Meredith, H.V. (1946). Use of body measurements in the school health program. *American Journal of Public Health, 36*, 1365-1386.

Wasserman, K., Whipp, B.J., Koyal, S.N., & Beaver, W.L. (1973). Anaerobic threshold and respiratory gas exchange during exercise. *Journal of Applied Physiology, 35*, 236-243.

Wessel, H.U., Cunningham, W.J., Paul, M.H., Bastanier, C.K., Muster, A.J., & Idriss, F.S. (1980). Exercise performance in tetralogy of Fallot after intracardiac repair. *Journal of Thoracic and Cardiovascular Surgery, 80*, 582-593.

Oxygen Transport and Cardiac Output Regulation Measured by Electrical Impedance Cardiography During Non-Steady State Exercise

Jiří Radvanský
Jan Vávra
Miloš Máček
Charles University, Prague, Czechoslovakia

The non-steady state of work during childhood is interesting from several points of view:

- The non-steady state represents a classical model situation for biofeedback and regulation dynamics of principal cardiorespiratory parameters.
- The non-steady state rather than the steady state is a typical attribute of spontaneous physical activity of children (Máček & Vávra, 1980).
- Noninvasive methods must be used to maintain strict physiological conditions.
- Only a few noninvasive techniques of cardiovascular examination can be used during exercise because suitable techniques must not require exact cooperation of the examined person and must be able to be used repeatedly (Gollan, Kizakewich, & McDermott, 1978; Weissman et al., 1982).

The last point is, in fact, the main reason for the lack of information concerning the non-steady exercise state in children. Considering all of these facts, an attempt was made to calculate the relationship between oxygen uptake and cardiac output during the nonsteady state by parallel use of two methods: (a) oxygen consumption evaluation using the Douglas bag method and (b) stroke volume evaluation by means of electrical impedance cardiography (EIC). It would then be possible to calculate the a-v oxygen difference by dividing the oxygen consumption by a given cardiac output. In this preliminary study, the problems dealt with concerned the EIC data processing and the trends of the obtained parameter dynamics. The good correlation between the values obtained through the EIC and comparable measurements obtained with dye dilution and other techniques is now well established, as is the reproducibility of these values (Gabriel, Atterhog, Oro, & Ekelund, 1976). Methodological aspects of impedance measurement and its clinical use are discussed in another presentation that appears in this publication (Vávra, Radvanský, Sazima, & Vaněk, 1986).

METHOD

Oxygen consumption was evaluated by collecting the expired air in small Douglas bags that were changed every 15 s. Gas analysis was done by a paramagnetic Beckmann oxygen analyzer and an infrared CO_2 analyzer. Gas volumes were obtained using a Tissot spirometer.

To compensate for the deterioration of the impedance signal by artifacts from movement, computer averaging of the EIC signal was used. A semi-automatic method of processing was preferred to fully automatic evaluation in order to allow exclusion of the most deteriorated parts of the EIC curve. The first derivative of the EIC signal was processed in these steps:

1. Analog-to-digital conversion of the EIC and 1 lead of the ECG.
2. Signing the peak r waves on the ECG.
3. Averaging (gating) of 15 heart cycles of the EIC curve (see Figure 1, raw impedance curve).

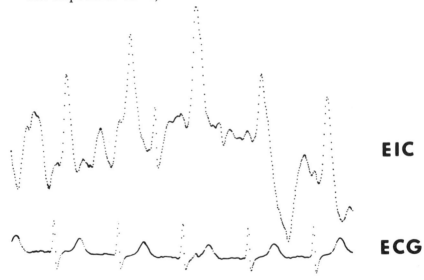

EIC

ECG

Figure 1   Raw data recorded during exercise—1 lead of ECG and the first derivative of the electrical impedance curve are plotted versus time.

4. Signing of the three key points on an averaged EIC curve (see Figure 2): U point—start of ventricular ejection; Z point—peak flow velocity in the root of the aorta; and X point—end of the ventricular ejection.

Averaging was repeated in 12-s intervals. The stroke volume calculation was done using a formula published by Kubicek, Karnegis, Patterson, Witsoe, and Matson (1966):

$$SV = p \cdot LVET \cdot (L/Z_o) \cdot (1/Z_o) \cdot dZ/dt \text{ max}$$

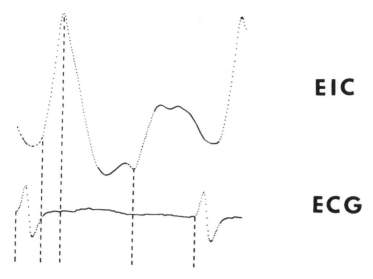

EIC

ECG

Figure 2   The mean of 15 heart cycles of the preceding signal.

where p = resistance of the blood (taken as 135 Ohms • cm), L = distance of inner electrodes (cm), Z_o = basal impedance of the thorax (Ohm), dZ/dt max = difference of y coordinates of U and Z key points.

The subjects were 3 healthy children aged 8.5, 9.0, and 9.5 years, 2 girls and 1 boy, all engaged in sports training. Their $\dot{V}O_2$max were slightly above the mean population values—60 ml/kg/min for the boy, 50 and 51 for the girls.

Before the examination, the children were repeatedly invited for preliminary examinations in order to become used to the laboratory milieu and personnel. They underwent exercise tests but without the evaluation of the data. During the third and fourth sessions, they underwent four non-steady state exercise ergometric tests at the level of load of 1.5 w/kg lasting 6 min. $\dot{V}O_2$ and EIC data were measured separately. At least 30 min of break time was given during the two exercise tests.

RESULTS

To compare raw and averaged EIC curves, see Figures 1 and 2. The shape of the averaged curve in its systolic part was very similar to the curve of the resting conditions. The key points are easily visible. The mean stroke volume (SV) changes are shown in Figure 3. Even the absolute values of the stroke volumes, from 30 to 45 ml, seem to be in the range of normal values as reported by Krovetz, McLoughlin, Mitchell, and Schiebler (1967).

The arteriovenous oxygen difference, cardiac output, and $\dot{V}O_2$ changes (absolute and relative) are shown in Figures 4 and 5. Notice the initial

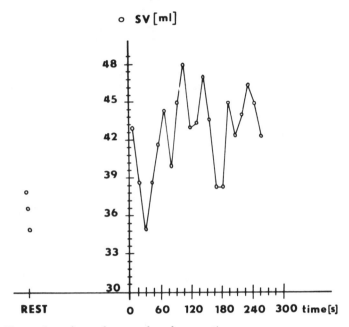

Figure 3 The stroke volume changes plotted versus time.

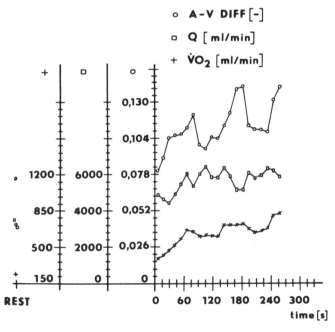

Figure 4 Dynamics of oxygen consumption, a-v difference, and cardiac output at rest and during exercise (start of exercise at time = 0).

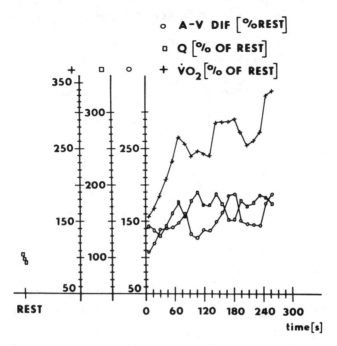

Figure 5 The parameters expressed in percentage of mean resting values.

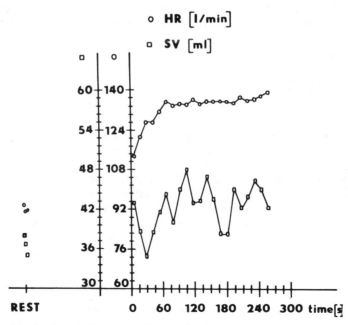

Figure 6 Heart rate and stroke volume plotted versus time (rest values are on left side of figure).

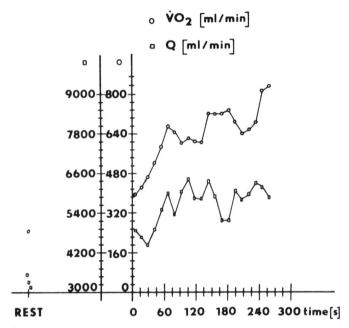

Figure 7 $\dot{V}O_2$ and cardiac output dynamics.

increase of a-v difference and subsequent slow oscillations. To compare the mean SV and HR dynamics, see Figure 6. Note the SV gap at the end of the 3rd min. $\dot{V}O_2$ and cardiac output dynamics are shown in Figure 7.

DISCUSSION

No references could be found for the non-steady state exercise, cardiovascular physiological parameters related to the age group of 9 years, with the exception of FH. The principal reasons are clear. Young children, although able to undergo exercise tests, are not able to cooperate in activities other than those they are accustomed to in everyday life. All the exercise tests must be done completely noninvasively to avoid any discomfort. Even a mouthpiece of a Douglas bag caused during a first session a heavy hyperventilation with a respiratory quotient at rest over 1.1. $\dot{V}O_2$ used for the a-v difference evaluation was that obtained during the third session.

The $\dot{V}O_2$ kinetics were characterized by large oscillations around the mean, single-exponential curve. Such kinetics were in agreement with the authors' unpublished analysis of $\dot{V}O_2$ kinetics of 13-year-old boys that revealed a significant correlation between height of oscillations around the exponential course and maximal aerobic capacity. Similar high amplitude oscillations were evident in the dynamics of SV changes. A possibility of systematic error cannot be fully rejected in this preliminary study, but it is improbable that three or four adjacent erroneously deviated values of SV would lie on the same line (see Figure 5). In our opinion, these oscillations can be considered as a range of possible SV physiological values for a given child and situation.

REFERENCES

Gabriel, S., Atterhog, J.H., Oro, L., & Ekelund, L.G. (1976). Measurement of cardiac output by impedance cardiography in patients myocardial infarction. Comparative evaluation of impedance and dye dilution methods. *Scandinavian Journal of Clinical and Laboratory Investigation*, **36**, 29-34.

Gollan, F., Kizakewich, P.N., & McDermott, J. (1978). Continuous electrode monitoring of systolic time intervals during exercise. *British Heart Journal*, **40**, 1390-1396.

Krovetz, L.J., McLoughlin, T.G., Mitchell, M.B., & Schiebler, G.L. (1967). Hemodynamic findings in normal children. *Paediatric Research*, **1**, 122-130.

Kubicek, W.G., Karnegis, J.N., Patterson, R.P., Witsoe, D.A., & Matson, R.H. (1966). Development and evaluation of an impedance cardiac output system. *Aerospace Medicine*, **37**, 1208-1212.

Máček, M., & Vávra, J. (1980). The adjustment of oxygen uptake at the onset of exercise: A comparison between prepubertal boys and young adults. *International Journal of Sports Medicine*, **1**, 70-72.

Vávra, J., Radvanský, J., Sazima, V., & Vaněk, J. (1986). Electrical impedance cardiography as a noninvasive technique in exercise testing. In J. Rutenfranz, R. Mocellin, & F. Klimt (Eds.), *Children and exercise XII* (pp. 383-393) (International Series on Sport Sciences, Vol. 16). Champaign, IL: Human Kinetics.

Weissman, M., Jones, P.W., Oren, A., Lamarra, N., Whipp, B.J., & Wasserman, K. (1982). Cardiac output increase and gas exchange at start of exercise. *Journal of Applied Physiology*, **52**, 236-244.

Essential Cardiovascular and Respiratory Determinants of Physical Performance at Age 12 to 17 Years During Intensive Physical Training

Günter Koch
Free University, West Berlin, Federal Republic of Germany
Leif Fransson
Central Hospital, Karlskrona, Sweden

Information is scanty about the development of the cardiovascular and respiratory parameters essential for oxygen transport, and thus physical performance, during the years of rapid growth. Most data available are confined to maximal oxygen uptake and stem from cross-sectional studies (Åstrand, 1952; Davies, Barnes, & Godfrey, 1972; Kemper & Verschuur, 1980). Extensive longitudinal studies including the analysis of cardiovascular and respiratory parameters in addition to maximal oxygen uptake are restricted to training periods of short duration (Eriksson & Koch, 1973; Koch & Eriksson, 1973a, 1973b; von Döbeln & Eriksson, 1972). Most studies involving longer training periods, such as 22 months (Daniels & Oldridge, 1971) and 32 months (Ekblom, 1969), were confined to the effect of physical training on maximal oxygen uptake alone.

The present study involved a group of boys who were selected for a longitudinal study because of their high motivation for sports and exercise and the high intensity of physical activity they displayed. Its purpose was to describe the development of some cardiorespiratory functions particularly important for oxygen transport and physical performance under the influence of intensive physical training from prepuberty to young adulthood. Emphasis was placed on the cardiovascular and ventilatory responses to submaximal and maximal exercise including muscle blood flow and static and dynamic lung volumes. In addition, at postpubertal ages, plasma and blood volumes and submaximal and maximal adrenergic activity in terms of plasma catecholamines were studied. Preliminary results of this investigation have been published previously (Koch, 1978, 1980a, 1980b).

METHODS

A total of 9 boys participated with their parents' consent in this longitudinal study. Initially, they were 11.9 ± 0.2 (range 11.8 – 12.3) years of age. They were reevaluated at exactly 12-month intervals during the subsequent 5 years. At the age of 15 years, however, 2 of the boys declined to participate in the annual examination; the total number of subjects since that time was only 7. Some relevant anthropometric data are given in Table 1.

Prior to the initial examination, all the boys were highly motivated by a strong interest in physical exercise and sports and participated regularly in different sport activities such as soccer, running, badminton, and ice hockey. They could be considered well trained judging from their maximal oxygen uptake (M = 59.5 ml/kg BW). After the initial evaluation at age 12 they were encouraged to continue at the same level or, preferably, even to increase physical training. Training was supervised and coordinated by an experienced physical-education instructor with whom the boys were familiar from the school. An evaluation of the average intensity of physical training performed during 40-week periods, according to the boys' own records, is given in Table 2.

On all occasions, the boys were evaluated using identical techniques and under identical conditions. The sequence of the different examination routines was also exactly the same. The methods used are only briefly described here, details having been reported elsewhere (Eriksson & Koch, 1973; Koch, 1974; Koch & Eriksson, 1973a, 1973b; Koch, Johansson, & Arvidsson, 1980; Koch & Röcker, 1977).

Exercise Tests

The submaximal and maximal exercise tests were performed on two consecutive days with the boys seated on an electrodynamically braked bicycle ergometer (Elema). During the *submaximal test*, work was started at 40 W and loads were increased stepwise by 40 W until a pulse rate of at least 180 bpm was reached. The boys exercised for 6 min at each work load. W_{170} was calculated by interpolation.

During the *maximal exercise test*, the boys exercised for 3 min at a low work load and for 6 min at a work load corresponding to 60% of their maximal capacity. They were then allowed to rest for about 30 to 60 s sitting on the bicycle (the time required for injection of Xe-133 for measurement of muscle blood flow). Subsequently they continued for about 2 min at a high submaximal (about 80% of maximal) and finally for 1 to 2 min at the maximal load that had been predicted from the pulse response during the previous submaximal exercise. In most cases, this test was repeated and the highest value of oxygen uptake obtained was used. Heart rates were obtained by continuous ECG recordings. Ventilation and

Table 1 Body Height and Weight at Different Ages (Means ± SD)

	Age of subjects (yr)					
	12	13	14	15	16	17
Height (cm)	150.0 ± 4.3	156.2 ± 5.0	164.1 ± 5.0	174.0 ± 4.5	179.8 ± 4.5	180.6 ± 4.9
Weight (kg)	39.2 ± 4.0	43.2 ± 4.1	50.8 ± 7.9	59.2 ± 7.8	61.6 ± 7.0	70.6 ± 7.9

Table 2   Intensity of Physical Training During 40-Week Periods (Excluding Holidays)

		Age of subjects (yr)		
		11 to 12	13 to 14	15 to 16
Total number of days/week[a]	$M \pm SD$	4.6 ± 0.6	4.6 ± 0.5	3.7 ± 1.0
of physical exercise	Range	3.8 - 5.3	3.8 - 5.3	1.6 - 4.9
Number of days/week[a] of running	$M \pm SD$	1.7 ± 1.2	1.6 ± 1.7	1.5 ± 1.3
exercise (average 3.5 km/session,	Range	0.4 - 4.5	0.2 - 5.3	0.1 - 3.9
interval training)				

Note. In addition, all subjects participated in school gymnastics (mainly ball games) 3 hr/week.
[a]Calculated according to the boys' records.

oxygen uptakes were measured by the Douglas bag technique, blood pressures by the Riva Rocci cuff method. The O_2 and CO_2 were determined according to Scholander, and lactate in arterialized blood by an enzymatic method.

Muscle Blood Flow (MBF)

MBF was measured with the 133-Xenon clearance method, that is, by determination of the clearance rate of 133-Xenon after injection into the muscle to be studied (Clausen & Lassen, 1971). These determinations were made in two different situations on 2 consecutive days:

1. After 2 to 3 min of ischemic work in the tibialis anterior muscle; that is, the subject flexed and extended his foot against a resistance with a pressure cuff inflated to above 200 mmHg applied around the thigh. Maximal MBF occurs immediately after release of the cuff pressure concomitant with the reactive hyperemia induced by tissue hypoxia and acidosis.
2. In the vastus lateralis muscle during successive submaximal and maximal bicycle ergometer exercise in the sitting position (Koch, 1978).

Spirometry

A Bernstein spirometer was used for determination of static and dynamic lung volumes. The residual volume was determined by the closed helium equilibration method. Gas distribution and closing volume were evaluated by the nitrogen single breath test.

Plasma Volume, Total Hemoglobin, and Intravascular Protein Masses

The blood samples were obtained in the morning, the boys having fasted overnight. Plasma volume was determined by use of ^{125}I-tagged human serum albumin (RISA) with the 10-min distribution space taken as the plasma volume. Hemoglobin was measured by the spectrophotometric hemoglobin cyanide method and hematocrit by the microcapillary technique. Total blood volume and the total amount of hemoglobin (THb) were calculated from plasma volume by means of the hematocrit and hemoglobin values, respectively (Koch, 1966). Total serum protein concentrations were measured by the biuret method, albumin according to the radial immunodiffusion principle. The intravascular protein masses (IPM) were obtained by multiplying the respective protein concentrations by the plasma volume.

Sympathetic-Adrenergic Activity

Adrenergic activity was assessed by measuring levels of circulating catecholamines and of plasma renin activity (PRA) at rest, during steady state submaximal exercise, and during maximal exercise. Catecholamines were determined by means of an enzymatic single isotope method (Koch et al., 1980), PRA by radioimmunoassay (Fyhrqvist, Sovery, Puutula, & Stenman, 1976).

RESULTS

Submaximal and Maximal Exercise

W_{170} determined during submaximal exercise increased steadily from 106 ± 25 W and 109 ± 18 W at ages 12 and 13, respectively, to 216 ± 30 W at age 17. The highest rate of increase was observed at transition from 13 to 14 and 15 years, that is, during puberty. The significant increase of W_{170} was due to a steady reduction of pulse rate during exercise at respective work loads. Conversely, maximal heart rates remained unchanged at about 200 beats/min (see Table 3 and Figure 1). Maximal work load and maximal oxygen uptake (see Table 3 and Figure 2) showed a similar steady increase as W_{170} from age 12 to 13 ($\dot{V}O_2$max 2.4 l) to age 17 ($\dot{V}O_2$max 4.4 l); however, maximal oxygen uptake per kilogram of body weight (see Table 3 and Figure 2) did not reveal any significant change throughout the entire period, although there was a tendency toward slightly higher $\dot{V}O_2$ values after puberty.

Table 3 Maximal Exercise

Variable	Age (yr)					
	12	13	14	15	16	17
Work load (W)	169 ± 29	224 ± 15***	279 ± 27***	322 ± 43**	358 ± 52**	364 ± 42
Pulse rate	197 ± 6	200 ± 6	196 ± 5	197 ± 11	197 ± 8	195 ± 8
Respiratory rate	49 ± 9	53 ± 8	43 ± 3*	56 ± 9*	49 ± 7*	40 ± 4*
Systolic BP (mmHg)	160 ± 8	172 ± 8***	175 ± 14	184 ± 16*	187 ± 15	199 ± 20*
Diastolic BP (mmHg)	76 ± 3	81 ± 3	72 ± 3	74 ± 4		
Lactate (mM/l)	7.0 ± 1.4	6.3 ± 1.3	5.6 ± 0.8*	5.1 ± 0.8	6.0 ± 0.7*	
Lactate (mM/l)[a]	9.3 ± 2.6	8.8 ± 1.4	9.4 ± 1.7	5.8 ± 0.8	7.7 ± 0.8*	
$\dot{V}E$ (l)	109.3 ± 16.8	120.7 ± 17.6**	107.4 ± 9.2***	127.0 ± 20.8**	112.0 ± 15.0	119.0 ± 15.8
$\dot{V}O_2$ (l)	2.33 ± 0.31	2.46 ± 0.24	2.92 ± 0.40*	3.50 ± 0.59*	4.00 ± 0.68*	4.35 ± 0.38
$\dot{V}O_2$ (ml/kg BW)	59.5 ± 6.1	56.8 ± 9.7	58.5 ± 8.0	61.8 ± 8.9	65 ± 5	62 ± 6
$\dot{V}E/\dot{V}O_2$	47.2 ± 6.5	49.7 ± 4.0	36.6 ± 3.7***	37.1 ± 3.9*	30.8 ± 3.6*	27.4 ± 4.9*

Note. Means and standard deviations of some circulatory and respiratory data obtained during maximal exercise at different ages.
[a]4 min postexercise.
*$p < .05$; **$p < .01$; ***$p < .001$; in comparison with preceding examination.

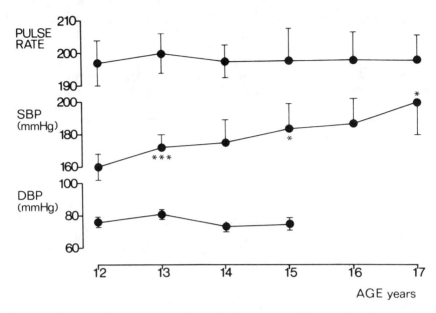

Figure 1 Means and standard deviations of pulse rates, systolic and diastolic pressures during maximal exercise at different ages. *$p < .05$; **$p < .01$; ***$p < .001$; concerning changes from preceding examination.

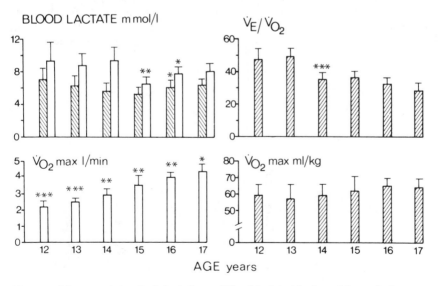

Figure 2 Means and standard deviations of blood lactate (shadowed bars: during maximal exercise; open bars: 4 min after cessation of exercise), total and relative maximal oxygen uptake and ventilation equivalent during maximal exercise at different ages (for significance of asterisks, see Figure 1).

Ventilation during maximal work was approximately at the same level despite significantly increasing work loads; the ventilation equivalent ($\dot{V}E/\dot{V}O_2$) during exercise was significantly lower after the age of 14, not only during maximal work conditions (see Table 3 and Figure 2) but also during submaximal exercise. Systolic blood pressures during maximal work increased steadily from 160 mmHg at age 12 to 200 mmHg at age 17. Diastolic blood pressure was unchanged. Maximal blood lactate, both during maximal exercise and 4 min after cessation of maximal exercise, decreased after the age of 14 (see Table 3 and Figure 2).

Muscle Blood Flow

MBF (Figure 3) both during maximal and submaximal bicycle exercise and during ischemic work showed a tendency toward lower values with increasing age, particularly with regard to MBF during submaximal and maximal bicycle work between the ages of 13 and 14 years. Conversely, postexercise MBF was virtually unchanged during the entire period.

Lung Dimensions and Ventilatory Capacity

Lung volumes (vital capacity, functional residual capacity [FRC], and total lung capacity [TLC]) and volume dependent ventilatory capacity (maximal voluntary ventilation, forced inspiratory, and expiratory volumes per second) showed a steady and significant increase throughout the entire observation period, at least until the age of 16 (see Table 4). However, when corrected for body growth by dividing by height[3] (von

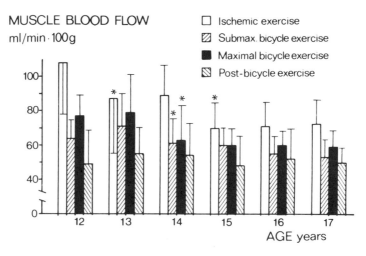

Figure 3 Means and standard deviations of muscle blood flow (average values of right and left leg) in the vastus lateralis muscle during bicycle ergometer exercise seated and in the anterior tibialis muscle after ischemic exercise in the supine posture (for significance of asterisks, see Figure 1).

Table 4 Static and Dynamic Lung Volumes

Variable	Age (yr)				
	13	14	15	16	17
VC (l)	3.44 ± 0.36	4.01 ± 0.40***	4.98 ± 0.01**	5.82 ± 0.32**	6.11 ± 0.57**
VC/VC pred (%)	89 ± 8	97 ± 7	89 ± 11	97 ± 3	103 ± 8
FRC (l)	1.63 ± 0.27	2.04 ± 0.47	2.29 ± 0.35*	2.81 ± 0.42**	2.98 ± 0.49
RV (l)	0.57 ± 0.15	0.94 ± 0.41	0.87 ± 0.19	0.92 ± 0.28*	1.17 ± 0.22*
TLC (l)	4.00 ± 0.46	4.96 ± 0.78**	5.67 ± 0.82**	6.75 ± 0.58	7.28 ± 0.59**
FRC/TLC (%)	41 ± 3	41 ± 4	41 ± 4	42 ± 5	41 ± 5
RV/TLC (%)	14 ± 3	18 ± 5	15 ± 2	14 ± 3	16 ± 3
MVV (l)	108 ± 15	125 ± 13**	156 ± 18**	208 ± 28**	240 ± 57
FEV 1.0 (l)	3.02 ± 0.45	3.40 ± 0.62	4.42 ± 0.53**	5.47 ± 0.20**	5.40 ± 0.63
FEV/FEV pred (%)	103 ± 9	98 ± 14	92 ± 8	108 ± 4	108 ± 11
FEV/VC (%)	87 ± 7	84 ± 9	89 ± 3*	94 ± 3	88 ± 4
FIV 1.0 (l)	3.08 ± 0.33	3.15 ± 0.67	4.50 ± 0.61**	5.64 ± 0.43***	5.79 ± 0.64
FIV/VC (%)	90 ± 12	88 ± 14	91 ± 5	97 ± 3	95 ± 3
SBT (% N$_2$)	1.0 ± 0.4	1.3 ± 0.9	0.9 ± 0.9	1.1 ± 0.5	1.0 ± 0.7
CLV/VC (%)	9.4 ± 0.9	6.3 ± 2.2**	7.9 ± 1.7	5.6 ± 1.8	7.2 ± 3.9

Note. Means and standard deviations of some spirometric data obtained at different ages (VC = vital capacity; FRC = functional residual capacity; RV = residual volume; TLC = total lung capacity; MVV = maximal voluntary ventilation; FEV 1.0 = forced expiratory volume per second; FIV 1.0 = forced inspiratory volume per second; SBT = single breath test; CLV/VC = closing volume in relation to vital capacity.

*$p < .05$; **$p < .01$; ***$p < .001$; in comparison with preceding examination.

Table 5   Plasma Volume and Intravascular Proteins

Variable	Boys (n = 8) 14 to 15 yr	Boys (n = 7) 17 yr	Men (n = 10) 17 to 20 yr	Men (n = 6) 24 to 30 yr
Weight (kg)	52.4 ± 8.0	70.6 ± 7.9	69.6 ± 3.9	61.7 ± 2.1
Height (cm)	166 ± 8	180 ± 5	182 ± 6	175 ± 4
Plasma volume (l)	3.10 ± 0.61**	3.47 ± 0.37	3.57 ± 0.32	3.87 ± 0.54
Plasma volume (ml/kg)	59.1 ± 12.0	49.1 ± 9.8	51.3 ± 4.0	59.4 ± 5.9
THb (g)	656 ± 12.9	784 ± 51	907 ± 97	885 ± 128
THb (g/kg)	12.6 ± 1.9	11.1 ± 1.8	13.0 ± 1.0	14.4 ± 2.0
Hemoglobin (g/l)	134 ± 9	148 ± 5	144 ± 6	137 ± 4
Total protein (g/l)	65.6 ± 2.9	67.9 ± 2.1	68.1 ± 2.0	68.5 ± 2.1
Total protein mass (g/kg)	3.9 ± 0.6	3.7 ± 0.5	3.5 ± 0.3	4.2 ± 0.3
Albumin (g/l)	41.8 ± 1.7*	45.4 ± 1.5	46.3 ± 1.8	44.4 ± 2.3
Albumin mass (g/kg)	2.5 ± 0.4	2.6 ± 0.3	2.4 ± 0.2	2.7 ± 0.3

Note. Means and standard deviations of some anthropometric data, plasma volume, hemoglobin (THb = total amount of hemoglobin), total plasma protein, and albumin in 4 groups of subjects—the group of boys at ages 14 to 15 and 17 years, respectively, and two groups of endurance-trained adults (Koch & Röcker, 1977).

*p < .05; **p < .01; boys versus adults.

Döbeln & Eriksson, 1972), these increases could be shown to be entirely due to changes in body dimensions.

Plasma Volume, Total Hemoglobin, and Intravascular Protein Masses

The boys had significantly larger plasma volumes, total amounts of hemoglobin, and blood volumes than children with normal physical activity (see Figure 4). They had also significantly larger intravascular protein masses (see Table 5) in relation to body weight than normally active children (Koch & Röcker, 1977); total intravascular protein and albumin masses were of the same order as in endurance-trained young men aged 17 to 30 years (Koch & Röcker, 1977, see Table 5).

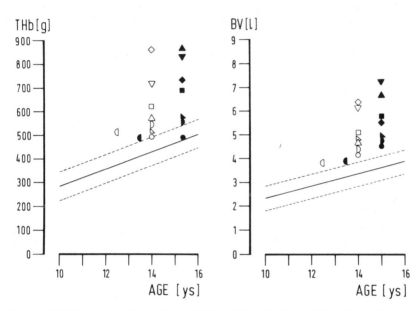

Figure 4   Total amount of hemoglobin (THb) and blood volume of boys in relation to age at two different examinations (open and closed symbols respectively) approximately 1 year apart. Continuous line and dashed lines denote regression line ± 1 standard error of estimate for boys aged 5 to 16 years with normal physical activity (Koch, 1966).

Sympathetic-Adrenergic Activity

Plasma norepinephrine (NE), epinephrine (E), and dopamine (D) increased during exercise in parallel with the work intensity, peak values being attained at the highest load or immediately after cessation of exercise (see Figure 5). Maximal levels of NE, E, and D, respectively, were approximately 15, 10, and 3 times higher than basal (resting) ones. Ten

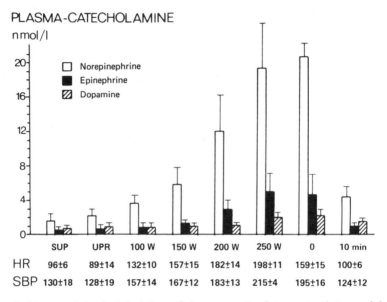

PLASMA-CATECHOLAMINE
nmol/l

□ Norepinephrine
■ Epinephrine
▨ Dopamine

	SUP	UPR	100 W	150 W	200 W	250 W	0	10 min
HR	96±6	89±14	132±10	157±15	182±14	198±11	159±15	100±6
SBP	130±18	128±19	157±14	167±12	183±13	215±4	195±16	124±12

Figure 5 Means and standard deviations of plasma norepinephrine, epinephrine, and dopamine at rest in the supine and upright positions as well as during submaximal and near maximal exercise, and after exercise, in the boys at age 15 to 16 years. PR = pulse rate; SBP = systolic blood pressure.

minutes after work, NE and D were still significantly higher than the initial resting values, whereas E had approached basal levels. The increase from basal (resting) values of heart rate and systolic blood pressure in relation to the increase of NE and E, respectively, was significantly smaller in the boys than in a group of normotensive adults aged 22 to 34 years (Koch et al., 1980; see Figures 6 and 7).

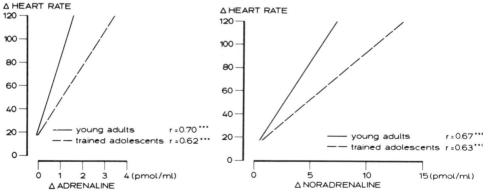

Δ HEART RATE

—— young adults   r = 0.70 ***
−− trained adolescents   r = 0.62 ***

Δ ADRENALINE

Δ HEART RATE

—— young adults   r = 0.67 ***
−− trained adolescents   r = 0.63 ***

Δ NORADRENALINE

Figure 6 Increase from basal values in heart rate in relation to increase in plasma epinephrine (upper panel) and norepinephrine during submaximal work (r = coefficient of correlation). The group of young adults consists of 16 normotensive subjects aged 22 to 34 years (Koch et al., 1980).

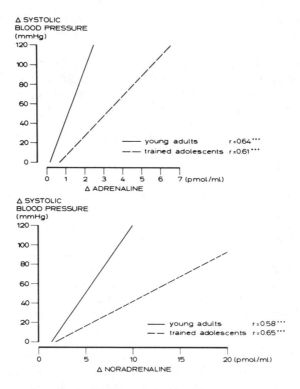

Figure 7 Increase from basal values in systolic blood pressure in relation to increase in plasma epinephrine and norepinephrine during submaximal work (symbols and subject groups as in Figure 6).

DISCUSSION

Cardiorespiratory Function

At the time the boys were selected to enter the study, they already had a high aerobic capacity. Their initial average maximal oxygen uptake appears to be higher than any value reported for boys of corresponding age prior to specific training (Eriksson, 1972). In view of the level of the initial maximal $\dot{V}O_2$ (59.5 ± 6.1 ml/kg) it is not surprising that the relative maximal oxygen uptake did not show any further substantial increase during the three subsequent years despite continued high levels of physical activity. This would imply that 60 ml/kg corresponds to the average upper limit of aerobic capacity attainable at 12 to 15 years of age. The figure of 60 ml/kg is in good agreement with the results obtained in specific training studies; thus, boys aged 11 years studied by Ekblom (1969) increased their relative maximal oxygen uptake from 53.9 to 59.4 ml/kg after 6 months of training; it was 58.1 ml/kg after 32 months. The group of 14 boys aged between 10 and 15 years studied by Daniels & Oldridge (1971) started with 59.5 ml/kg; after 22 months of training (middle-distance runners' training program) they had a maximal oxygen uptake of 58.3 ml/kg.

At the transition from 13 to 14 years of age the boys revealed, during both submaximal and maximal exercise, a striking decrease in ventilation when related to oxygen uptake (ventilation equivalent, $\dot{V}E/\dot{V}O_2$), compared to ages 12 and 13 years (see Figure 2). After 14 years, the ventilation equivalent was of the same order as that seen in normal adults. This might suggest a change in control of breathing during exercise, occurring concomitantly with the important changes that take place in hormonal homeostasis at puberty. At prepuberty, the boys' ventilation equivalent was significantly higher than that observed in another group of boys aged 11 to 12 years (Koch & Eriksson, 1973a), although a 5-month training period actually resulted in an increase of the ventilation equivalent from 28.9 ± 4.0 to 35.1 ± 4.6 ($p < .01$) in these boys. The significant increase of the ventilation equivalent during training in this latter group suggests that the ventilation equivalent is positively correlated with maximal oxygen uptake, at least at this young age. Actually, the present group had not only higher ventilation equivalents, but also revealed a significantly higher maximal oxygen uptake (60 ml/kg versus 42 and 48 ml/kg before and after the 5-month training period, respectively).

Maximal heart rates remained unchanged at about 200 beats/min. Whereas systolic blood pressures rose from about 160 mmHg at age 12 to 200 mmHg at age 17 years, diastolic blood pressure remained unchanged at about 70 to 80 mmHg (see Figure 1). The dramatic increase in total maximal oxygen uptake with unchanged maximal pulse rate reflects mainly the increase of maximal cardiac output because of a significant rise in stroke volume as reflected by the considerable increase in the systolic-diastolic blood pressure amplitude. The increase of stroke volume was apparently primarily due to normal growth and physical maturation (see Figure 1), but most probably the high intensity of physical exercise by itself promotes, and presumably accelerates, the increase in maximal stroke volume. Thus an increase of maximal stroke volume by roughly 15% has been shown to occur in 11- to 12-year-old boys during 5 months of physical training (Eriksson & Koch, 1973).

The increase of lung dimensions and ventilatory capacity could be entirely explained by normal maturation. This was also evident from the fact that static and dynamic lung volumes expressed in relation to predicted values were unchanged (see Table 4).

Muscle Blood Flow

MBF both during maximal and submaximal bicycle work in the vastus lateralis muscle decreased significantly at the transition from 13 to 14 years. The values obtained at the age of 14 years were practically identical with those reported for 25-year-old men of normal fitness (Clausen & Lassen, 1971; Nordenfeld, 1974). There was also a tendency toward lower MBF in the anterior tibialis muscle after ischemic work, especially from 12 to 13 and from 14 to 15 years of age.

Prepubertal (Eriksson & Koch, 1973) and to a lesser degree pubertal boys (Eriksson, Grimsby, & Saltin, 1979) have been shown to have a slightly lower cardiac output than young adults; they also tend to have a slightly higher arterial-mixed venous oxygen (a-vO$_2$) difference, at least at submaximal exercise levels. Apparently because of a smaller effective muscle mass in the prepubertal boys, a lower proportion of cardiac output is distributed to the working muscle, but blood flow per unit of muscle mass is higher. These differences apparently tend to vanish after the age of 14 years when muscle development accelerates during puberty. After the age of 15 years, when muscle mass had markedly increased in all the subjects, relative muscle blood flows tended even to be lower than in young men with normal physical activity and fitness (Clausen & Lassen, 1971; Nordenfeld, 1974). Most probably, this was due to the extensive physical training that the boys continued to have. It is well established that normally the blood flow required by the skeletal muscles during exercise at identical work loads decreases after training, while the density of the mitochondria and the oxidative enzyme capacity increase (Koch, 1978).

Blood lactate concentration during maximal work at the age of 12 to 13 years was identical with that observed in the 11- to 13-year-old boys after training (Eriksson & Koch, 1973). There was a tendency toward lower peak lactate values at the age of 14 and particularly 15 years compared with 13 and 12 years (Figure 2). This is in agreement with the observation of higher muscle but lower blood lactate concentrations during heavy exercise following physical training in boys aged 11 to 13 years (Eriksson, Gollnick, & Saltin, 1973). The significant decrease of blood lactate during maximal exercise observed after puberty most probably reflects changes in muscle metabolism and muscle fiber distribution. Enhanced glycolytic and oxidative capacity, together with changes in fiber distribution, have been shown to be induced by training in this age group (Eriksson et al., 1973). However, the changes in peak blood lactate might also be explained by other mechanisms. Both increased extraction of lactate by other tissues, such as the myocardium, and the disproportional expansion of plasma volumes observed in endurance-trained subjects (Koch & Röcker, 1977) would tend to lower lactate levels.

Plasma Volume

At postpubertal age (14 to 16 years) the boys showed the same pattern of adaptive increases of plasma and blood volumes, total amounts of hemoglobin, and plasma proteins as endurance-trained adult athletes (Koch & Röcker, 1977). However, because of the disproportionate increase of plasma volumes, total protein concentration and, in particular, albumin concentrations, the hemoglobin concentration and the hematocrit were lower (see Table 5). These adjustments imply a higher water-binding capacity of the plasma, lower blood viscosity, and lower oncotic pressures and represent a definite advantage for thermoregulation and perfusion in terminal vascular beds. Hence, they contribute to improvement of the circulatory system's ability to sustain heavy exercise.

Adrenergic Activity

Activation of the sympathetic system is the most important control mechanism in the hemodynamic adjustment to physical exercise. Epinephrine is mainly released from the adrenal medulla and norepinephrine from the sympathetic nerve endings. Although plasma levels of catecholamines are the result of very complex processes, circulating catecholamines appear to reflect adrenergic activity in a reliable way, in particular during exercise (Cryer, 1976; Koch et al., 1980). At the age of 15 to 17 years, the present adolescents had significantly higher peak norepinephrine and epinephrine levels and higher plasma renin activity (Koch et al., 1980) than young normotensive adults and hence smaller increments of heart rate and systolic blood pressure in relation to the increase of norepinephrine and epinephrine, respectively, in association with exercise.

These findings suggest a lower degree of adrenoceptor sensitivity and/or receptor density. They are consistent with the results of recent studies, using specific radioligand techniques for the quantitative evaluation of adrenoceptors, that demonstrate a significant positive correlation of the density of $ß_2$-adrenoceptors with age and mean blood pressure (Middeke, Remien, & Holzgreve, 1984) and a negative correlation between the density of ß ($ß_1$ + $ß_2$)-adrenoceptors and the degree of aerobic capacity (Butler, O'Brien, O'Malley, & Kelly, 1982). Similar data concerning the density of α-adrenoceptors are not available, although α-receptors, by mediating norepinephrine vascular effects, are more important for blood pressure regulation than are ß-adrenoceptors. It is particularly noteworthy that the adolescents in the present series resembled young borderline hypertensives (Koch, 1980b) with respect to the relationship between heart rate and blood pressure rise and the increase of catecholamines. Possible clinical implications of these findings are difficult to evaluate; the relationship between adrenergic activity, adrenoceptor sensitivity, and high blood pressure is a complex one and is still not well understood.

Although it is fairly well established that young borderline hypertensives normally have a high output circulation due to, or associated with, high circulating catecholamines (Koch, 1980b; Messerli et al., 1982), it is not known if they have increased plasma catecholamine levels prior to the onset of hypertension, that is, during adolescence. Apparently, prospective studies of the relationship between blood pressure and the activity of the sympathetic system in terms of both circulating catecholamines and the density of different types of adrenoceptors, starting during childhood, are necessary in order to better define the role of the adrenergic system as a possible causative factor in essential hypertension.

REFERENCES

Åstrand, P.-O. (1952). *Experimental studies of physical working capacity in relation to sex and age.* Copenhagen: Munksgaard.

Butler, J., O'Brien, M., O'Malley, K., & Kelly, J.G. (1982). Relationship of ß-adrenoceptor density to fitness in athletes. *Nature, 298,* 60-62.

Clausen, J.P., & Lassen, N.A. (1971). Muscle blood flow during exercise in normal man studied by the 133-Xenon clearance method. *Cardiovascular Research, 5,* 245-250.

Cryer, P.E. (1976). Isotope—Derivate measurements of plasma norepinephrine and epinephrine in man. *Diabetes, 25,* 1071-1078.

Daniels, J., & Oldridge, N. (1971). Changes in oxygen consumption of young boys during growth and running training. *Medicine and Science in Sports, 3,* 161-165.

Davies, C.T.M., Barnes, C., & Godfrey, S. (1972). Body composition and maximal exercise performance in children. *Medicine and Science in Sports, 9*(2), 191-214.

Ekblom, B. (1969). Effect of physical training in adolescent boys. *Journal of Applied Physiology, 27,* 350-358.

Eriksson, B.O. (1972). Physical training, oxygen supply and muscle metabolism in 11- to 13-year-old boys. *Acta Physiologica Scandinavica, 384* (Suppl.), 1-124.

Eriksson, B.O., Gollnick, P.D., & Saltin, B. (1973). Muscle metabolism and enzyme activities after training in boys 11 to 13 years old. *Acta Physiologica Scandinavica, 87,* 106-114.

Eriksson, B.O., Grimby, G., & Saltin, B. (1979). Cardiac output and arterial blood gases during exercise in pubertal boys. *Journal of Applied Physiology, 31,* 348-351.

Eriksson, B.O., & Koch, G. (1973). Effect of physical training on the hemodynamic response during submaximal and maximal exercise in 11- to 13-year-old boys. *Acta Physiologica Scandinavica, 87,* 27-39.

Fyhrqvist, F., Sovery, P., Puutula, L., & Stenman, U.-H. (1976). Radioimmunoassay of plasma renin activity. *Clinical Chemistry, 22*(2), 250-258.

Kemper, H.C.G., & Verschuur, R. (1980). Measurement of aerobic power in teenagers. In K. Berg & B.O. Eriksson (Eds.), *Children and exercise IX* (pp. 55-63) (International Series on Sport Sciences, Vol. 10). Baltimore: University Park Press.

Koch, G. (1966). Determination of total amount of hemoglobin, blood volume and red cell volume. In H. Opitz & F. Schmid (Eds.), *Handbuch der Kinderheilkunde* [Handbook of Pediatrics] (pp. 265-272). Berlin, Heidelberg, New York: Springer-Verlag.

Koch, G. (1974). Muscle blood flow after ischemic work and during bicycle ergometer work in boys aged 12 years. *Acta Paediatrica Belgica*, **28** (Suppl.), 29-39.

Koch, G. (1978). Muscle blood flow in prepubertal boys. Effect of growth combined with intensive physical training. *Medicine and Sport*, **11**, 39-46.

Koch, G. (1980a). Aerobic power, lung dimensions, ventilatory capacity, and muscle blood flow in 12- to 16-year-old boys with high physical activity. In K. Berg & B.O. Eriksson (Eds.), *Children and exercise IX* (pp. 99-107) (International Series on Sport Sciences, Vol. 10). Baltimore: University Park Press.

Koch, G. (1980b). Adrenergic activity at rest and during exercise in normotensive boys and young adults, and in hypertensive patients. In K. Berg & B.O. Eriksson (Eds.), *Children and exercise IX* (pp. 375-383) (International Series on Sport Sciences, Vol. 10). Baltimore: University Park Press.

Koch, G., & Eriksson, B.O. (1973a). Effect of physical training on pulmonary ventilation and gas exchange during submaximal and maximal work in boys aged 11 to 13 years. *Scandinavian Journal of Clinical and Laboratory Investigation*, **31**, 87-94.

Koch, G., & Eriksson, B.O. (1973b). Effect of physical training on anatomical R-L shunt at rest and pulmonary diffusing capacity during near-maximal exercise in boys 11 to 13 years old. *Scandinavian Journal of Clinical and Laboratory Investigation*, **31**, 95-103.

Koch, G., Johansson, U., & Arvidsson, E. (1980). Radioenzymatic determination of epinephrine, norepinephrine and dopamine in 0.1 ml plasma samples. Plasma catecholamine response to submaximal and maximal exercise. *Journal of Clinical Chemistry and Clinical Biochemistry*, **18**, 367-372.

Koch, G., & Röcker, L. (1977). Plasma volume and intravascular protein masses in trained boys and fit young men. *Journal of Applied Physiology*, **43**(6), 1085-1088.

Messerli, F.H., Ventura, H.O., Reisin, E., Dreslinski, G.R., Dunn, F.G., MacPhee, A.A., & Frohlich, E.D. (1982). Borderline hypertension and obesity: Two prehypertensive states with elevated cardiac output. *Circulation*, **66**, 55-61.

Middeke, M., Remien, J., & Holzgreve, H. (1984). The influence of sex, age, blood pressure and physical stress on ß-$_2$-adrenoceptor density of mononuclear cells. *Journal of Hypertension*, **2**, 261-264.

Nordenfeld, I. (1974). Blood flow of working muscles during autonomic blockade of the heart. *Cardiovascular Research*, **8**, 1227-1231.

von Döbeln, W., & Eriksson, B.O. (1972). Physical training, maximal oxygen uptake and dimensions of the oxygen transporting and metabolizing organs in boys 11 to 13 years of age. *Acta Paediatrica Scandinavica*, **61**, 653-662.

Part VI
Respiration

Bronchial Reactivity Measured by EIA-Test and PC$_{20}$-Histamine: A Comparison of Two Methods

Kai Håkon Carlsen
Ragnhild Bech
Svein Oseid
Eli Schrøder
Children's Asthma and Allergy Institute, Oslo, Norway

The basic prerequisite of asthma is thought to be nonspecific bronchial hyperreactivity (Boushey, Holtzman, Sheller, & Nadel, 1980). The various factors precipitating asthmatic attacks are thought to exert their effect via this hyperreactivity. Several procedures have been introduced to measure nonspecific bronchial hyperreactivity, among them inhalation of nebulized histamine and physical exercise tests. Exercise-induced asthma (EIA) has been shown to be associated with increased plasma levels of histamine (Morgan, Moodley, Phillips, & Davies, 1983). This study was a preliminary one performed to examine the degree to which nonspecific bronchial hyperreactivity as measured by histamine inhalation tests and by physical exercise tests (treadmill) corresponded to each other.

METHOD

Bronchial responsiveness was measured in 18 patients (11 boys and 7 girls) between 6 and 17 years of age by two different methods and the results were compared. The patients had all been diagnosed as suffering from bronchial asthma. In two patients, the asthmatic symptoms had not been present for 2 years. The patients were classified according to their antiasthmatic drug treatment with scores increasing from 0 for no treatment up to 6 for treatment with systemic steroids, as shown in Table 1.

The reaction to inhaled histamine was measured by the method introduced by Cockcroft, Ruffin, Dolovich, & Hargreave (1977): provocation concentration 20 of histamine (PC$_{20}$). Histamine chloride, phosphate-buffered to pH 7.4, in doubling concentrations from 0.03 mg/ml to a maximum of 32 mg/ml, was nebulized by a PARI$^{(R)}$ nebulizer, with a stated mist-droplet size of 0.5 to 5 μ and nebulization speed of 0.13 ml/min, and

Table 1 Classification of Patients According to the Antiasthmatic Drug Treatment

Treatment	Score	N
None	0	4
Disodium cromoglycate inhaled (DSCG)	1	2
Beta-2-agonist	2	3
Beta-2-agonist + sustained release theophylline	3	2
Beta-2-agonist + sustained release theophylline + DSCG inhaled	4	2
Beclomethasone inhaled[a]	5	4
Systemic steroids[a]	6	1

[a]In addition to several of the drugs above.

inhaled by tidal breathing for 2 min after an initial inhalation of phosphate-buffered saline. Forced expired volume in first second (FEV_1) was measured before, 0.5 min after, and 1.5 min after each inhalation. Two measurements of FEV_1 were made each time, and the best was selected. The greatest reduction in FEV_1 of the postchallenge measurements was used. The concentration of histamine causing a fall of 20% in FEV_1 as compared with the postsaline value was called PC_{20}. The results were plotted on a semilogarithmic dose-response diagram, and the exact PC_{20} was determined by interpolation on the dose-response curve. EIA was measured by running on a treadmill set at 4° gradient with a steady state heart rate of at least 170 beats/min (in the submaximal range) (Oseid & Haaland, 1978). Running was performed at a constant speed for 6 min in stable environmental conditions (relative humidity of the air, 55% to 66%; temperature, 20 °C to 22 °C). FEV_1 was measured before running, immediately after, and 3, 6, 10, and 15 min after running. The best of two efforts of FEV_1 was used. The results were expressed as the bronchial lability index (BLI), that is, the largest fall in FEV_1 from the initial measurement, divided by the initial FEV_1, slightly modified after Godfrey, Silverman, and Anderson (1973). Patients with BLI > 10% were considered to have exercise-induced asthma (EIA).

The children participating in the study were examined in periods with baseline lung function and without the use of bronchodilators. Theophylline was stopped at least 72 hours before the tests, and beta-2-agonists at least 8 hours before. The results were evaluated by the Spearman rank correlation (r_s = rank correlation coefficient) and the Wilcoxon-Mann-Whitney Rank Test for two samples (W-M-W). Differences were considered to be significant at a level of 5% ($p < .05$).

RESULTS

The results of PC_{20}, BLI, FEV_1 in percentage of predicted value (Zapletal, Paul, & Samánek, 1977), and the FEV_1/FVC ratio are given in Table 2 (FVC = forced vital capacity). Mean PC_{20} was 4.2 mg/ml with a range from 0.08 to 32 mg/ml. Mean BLI was 20.0% with a range from 1.2% to 64%. FEV_1 in percentage of predicted value and the FEV_1/FVC ratio were all within normal limits. A positive correlation was found between PC_{20} and BLI in the same patients ($r_s = 0.70$; $p < .01$) (see Figure 1). All patients with EIA were also bronchial hyperreactive to histamine with a PC_{20} below 2 mg/ml, whereas another 4 patients with PC_{20} below 2 mg/ml showed no signs of EIA under the conditions tested (see Figure 1 and Table 2).

No positive correlation was found between FEV_1 in percentage of predicted value and hyperreactivity to histamine ($r_s = 0.13$; $p > .05$). There was a positive correlation between the FEV_1/FVC ratio and PC_{20} ($r_s = 0.53$; $p < .05$). No positive correlation was found between BLI and the FEV_1/FVC

Table 2   Values of PC_{20}, BLI, and Lung Function Tests in Children With Bronchial Asthma

Age (yr)	Sex	PC_{20} (mg/ml)	BLI (%)	FEV_1 (% of predicted)	FEV_1/FVC
12	Boy	0.1	10	110	0.85
12	Boy	9	1.2	98	0.82
10	Boy	0.65	2.7	121	0.86
13	Girl	0.53	42.5	90	0.87
7	Boy	16	2.3	96	0.82
8	Girl	3.85	8.2	84	0.83
11	Girl	0.68	35	109	0.88
14	Boy	3.94	3	97	0.87
11	Boy	0.37	64	90	0.79
11	Girl	0.58	6.2	84	0.80
6	Girl	0.6	2	126	0.87
6	Boy	0.46	64	106	0.85
12	Boy	1.85	1.4	87	0.88
12	Boy	0.08	18	83	0.78
11	Girl	4.5	5	98	0.93
12	Girl	1.05	30.4	104	0.91
12	Boy	0.095	61.3	72	0.80
17	Boy	32	2		0.095

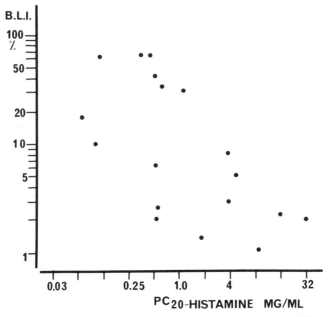

Figure 1   The relationship between bronchial lability index (BLI) measured by running on treadmill and PC$_{20}$-histamine. A significant correlation was found between the BLI and the PC$_{20}$: r_s = 0.70 ($p < .01$).

ratio (r_s = 0.29, $p > .05$), or between BLI and FEV$_1$ in percentage of predicted value (r_s = 0.22, $p > .05$). The patients with EIA did not have a higher distribution of the FEV$_1$/FVC ratio (W-M-W, $p > .05$) or FEV$_1$ in percentage of predicted value (W-M-W; $p > .05$) than patients without EIA. A positive correlation was found both between the antiasthmatic treatment score and PC$_{20}$ (r_s = 0.66, $p < .05$), and the BLI (r_s = 0.62, $p < .05$) (see Table 2).

DISCUSSION

The relationship between PC$_{20}$ and BLI in the present study confirmed that both methods may be used as a measure of the nonspecific bronchial reactivity as previously reported (Hargreave et al., 1981). Figure 1 shows that the histamine test discriminated better than the EIA-test. Whereas the values of PC$_{20}$ showed a distribution throughout the whole scale, only 8 patients showed signs of EIA on the treadmill test. These 8 patients had clearly enhanced bronchial hyperreactivity as measured by PC$_{20}$ (PC$_{20}$ < 2 mg/ml). Seven patients had PC$_{20}$ between 0.25 mg/ml and 1 mg/ml, whereas their BLI varied from 2% to 64%. The PC$_{20}$ seemed better related to the degree of illness than the BLI, as was also reported by Bhagat and Grunstein (1984). They were able to discern between 2 groups of asthmatic patients by means of the PC$_{20}$ to histamine and methacholine, but not by exercise tests. In the present study, the PC$_{20}$ seemed to be better related to the lung function as measured by the FEV$_1$/FVC ratio than the BLI. On the other hand, the BLI may be taken as a measure of the impairment of physical activity caused by the asthmatic state. A further increase in the duration of the steady state running on the treadmill might possibly increase the sensitivity of the EIA test.

EIA is thought to be effected by mediator release from mast cells located in the submucosal layers of the bronchi. The mediator release usually has been regarded as a result of heat exchange across the bronchial mucosal wall (Strauss, McFadden, Ingram, Deal, & Jaeger, 1978). Recent findings suggest that a change in surface osmolarity of the bronchial lumen may be important in initiating bronchoconstriction during exercise in some patients (Anderson, 1983). The differences in BLI among patients with the same degree of bronchial reactivity, as measured by the PC$_{20}$, may reflect different pathogenetic mechanisms in the asthma (Bhagat & Grunstein, 1984).

Both the BLI as measured by EIA tests and the PC$_{20}$ are valuable tools in assessing the condition of the patient and the degree of asthma. This was confirmed by the relationship between the two measures of bronchial hyperreactivity and the antiasthmatic treatment score, showing that the patient's need for drug therapy correlated well with the nonspecific bronchial hyperreactivity. The evaluation of the patient by means of these two methods may therefore help the physician in determining a more optimal treatment for the patient both in regard to the drug therapy and the participation of the patient in play and sport, but further modifications of these methods may give additional information.

REFERENCES

Anderson, S.D. (1983). Current concepts of exercise-induced asthma. *Allergy*, **38**, 289-302.

Bhagat, R.G., & Grunstein, M.M. (1984). Comparison of responsiveness to methacholine, histamine, and exercise in subgroups of asthmatic children. *American Review of Respiratory Disease*, **129**, 221-224.

Boushey, H.A., Holtzman, M.J., Sheller, J.R., & Nadel, J.A. (1980). Bronchial hyperreactivity. *American Review of Respiratory Disease*, **121**, 389-413.

Cockcroft, D.W. Ruffin, R.E., Dolovich, J., & Hargreave, F.E. (1977). Allergen induced increase in non-allergic bronchial reactivity. *Clinical Allergy*, **7**, 503-513.

Godfrey, S., Silverman, M., & Anderson, S. (1973). Problems of interpreting exercise-induced asthma. *Journal of Allergy and Clinical Immunology*, **52**, 199-209.

Hargreave, F.E., Ryan, G., Thomson, N.C., O'Byrne, P.M., Latimer, K., Juniper, E.F., & Dolovich, J. (1981). Bronchial responsiveness to histamine or methacholine in asthma: Measurement and clinical significance. *Journal of Allergy and Clinical Immunology*, **68**, 347-355.

Morgan, D.J.R., Moodley, I., Phillips, M.J., & Davies, R.J. (1983). Plasma histamine in asthmatic and control subjects following exercise: Influence of circulating basophils and different assay techniques. *Thorax*, **38**, 771-777.

Oseid, S., & Haaland, K. (1978). Exercise studies on asthmatic children before and after regular physical training. In B. Eriksson & B. Furberg (Eds.), *Swimming medicine, IV* (pp. 32-41) (International Series on Sport Sciences, Vol. 6). Baltimore: University Park Press.

Strauss, R.H., McFadden, E.R., Jr., Ingram, R.H., Jr., Deal, E.C., Jr., & Jaeger, J.J. (1978). Influence of heat and humidity on the airway obstruction induced by exercise in asthma. *Journal of Clinical Investigation*, **61**, 433-440.

Zapletal, A., Paul, T., & Samánek, M. (1977). Die Bedeutung heutiger Methoden der Lungenfunktionsdiagnostik zur Feststellung einer Obstruction der Atemwege bei Kindern und Jugendlichen. *Zeitschrift für Erkrankungen der Atmungsorgane*, **149**, 343-371.

Transcutaneous and End-Tidal PO$_2$ and PCO$_2$ During Rest and Maximal Exercise in Children and Adolescents

Hans U. Wessel
Jeffrey J. Sroka
Milton H. Paul
The Children's Memorial Hospital, Chicago, USA

During the past decade transcutaneous (tc) O$_2$ and CO$_2$ measurements have been expanded beyond a monitoring application in the newborn and infant. One area of interest has been exercise testing (Borgia & Horvath, 1978) because transcutaneous monitoring is noninvasive and potentially provides continuous estimates of arterial PO$_2$ and PCO$_2$. Most previous studies in adults have reported comparisons of PtcO$_2$ with intermittent determinations of PaO$_2$ (Hughes, Gray, & Hutchinson, 1984; Kentala & Repo, 1984; Kornum, Oxhoj, & Nielsen, 1982; Löllgen, von Nieding, Kersting, & Just, 1979; McDowell & Thiede, 1980; Schonfeld et al., 1980). Three studies have dealt with PtcCO$_2$ (Kentala & Repo, 1984; Kornum et al., 1982; Seiff, Mahutte, Percorraro, & Light, 1983). The results indicated a linear relationship of PtcO$_2$ to PaO$_2$, with large differences between studies and individuals, suggesting that PaO$_2$ cannot be predicted from PtcO$_2$ with sufficient accuracy (Kornum et al., 1982). There are multiple reasons for the large absolute differences, some technical and some biological. The latter include differences in skin blood flow, skin O$_2$ consumption, and skin thickness. However, the reported data suggest that changes of PtcO$_2$ accurately reflect PaO$_2$ changes during exercise (Kentala & Repo, 1984; Schonfeld et al., 1980).

In this study, the time course of transcutaneous and end-tidal (et) PO$_2$ and PCO$_2$ before, during, and after progressive maximal exercise were compared. It was postulated that a linear relationship existed between end-tidal and transcutaneous measurements. Such linear correlations would (a) provide an indirect estimate of the link between transcutaneous and arterial PO$_2$ and PCO$_2$ and (b) establish that PtcO$_2$ and PtcCO$_2$ vary as a function of the ventilatory response to exercises because PetO$_2$ and PetCO$_2$ are directly linked to ventilation.

Assuming that end-tidal approximates alveolar PO_2 and PCO_2 (Stout, Wessel, & Paul, 1981), then under steady state:

$$PetCO_2 = 0.115 \ \dot{V}CO_2/\dot{V}_A$$

$$PetO_2 = PIO_2 - (P_B - 47)\dot{V}O_2/\dot{V}_A + PIO_2(1 - R)\dot{V}O_2/\dot{V}_A$$

where $PetCO_2$, $PetO_2$ (kPa), and $\dot{V}CO_2/\dot{V}_A$, $\dot{V}O_2/\dot{V}_A$ (ml STPD/L BTPS). Ignoring P_B and R, transcutaneous and end-tidal PO_2 were correlated with $\dot{V}O_2/\dot{V}_A$ and transcutaneous and end-tidal PCO_2 with $\dot{V}CO_2/\dot{V}_A$. We compared $PtcO_2$ to $PetO_2$ and $PtcCO_2$ to $PetCO_2$, and $PaCO_2$ computed as (Jones & Campbell, 1982):

$$PaCO_2 = 5.5 + PetCO_2 \ 0.9 - .022 \ \dot{V}_T$$

METHOD

A total of 109 patients were studied (age range 7 to 57 years) (see Table 1). Each underwent lung function studies and maximal cycle exercise with progressive work rate increments of 1-min duration (non-steady state work, NSSW) or of 4-min duration (steady state work, SSW). $PtcO_2$ and $PtcCO_2$ were measured with the radiometer transcutaneous system after 1 point calibration (see Table 2). The heated electrodes (44 °C) were applied to the volar surface of the forearm. Heart rate, ECG, and in some cases SaO_2 by earpiece oximetry were monitored continuously. Systemic

Table 1 Study Patients by Diagnosis

Diagnosis	N
TET, PS, VSD, ASD	16
AS, IHSS, Coarctation	37
TGV, TA, DORV, Truncus Arteriosus	10
Thalassemia, sickle cell disease, myocardiopathy	13
Mitral valve disease	6
Pulmonary disease	7
Miscellaneous: Chest pain, dyspnea, palpitation, arrhythmia, RBBB, Levocardia, Kawasaki disease, sinus tachyc., normals	20
Total	109

Note. TET = tetralogy of Fallot; PS = pulmonic stenosis; VSD, ASD = ventricular or atrial septal defect; AS = valvar aortic stenosis; IHSS = idiopathic hypertrophic subaortic stenosis; TGV = transposition of the great vessels; TA = tricuspid atresia; DORV = double outlet right ventricle; RBBB = right bundle branch block.

Table 2   Mean Values (N = 109) of End-Tidal (et) and Transcutaneous (tc) PO$_2$ and PCO$_2$

Variable	Rest 3rd min	Exercise 1st min	Last min	Recovery 4th min
PO$_2$				
et	14.1 ± 1.0	13.4 ± 1.1	14.4 ± 0.8	15.4 ± 0.6
tc	9.3 ± 1.5	9.3 ± 1.6	10.1 ± 1.6	10.7 ± 1.6
Δ(et-tc)	4.8 ± 1.8***	4.2 ± 1.9***	4.3 ± 1.8***	4.6 ± 1.7***
PCO$_2$				
et	4.8 ± 0.6	5.0 ± 0.6	5.3 ± 0.7	4.7 ± 0.5
a	4.9 ± 0.5	5.0 ± 0.5	5.1 ± 0.6	4.7 ± 0.5
tc	4.9 ± 0.6	4.9 ± 0.6	5.1 ± 0.8	4.6 ± 0.6
Δ(et-tc)	0.0 ± 0.8	0.2 ± 0.9**	0.3 ± 1.1*	0.1 ± 0.5
Δ(a-tc)	0.1 ± 0.5	−0.2 ± 0.5**	0.0 ± 0.7	−0.1 ± 0.5*
Δ(et-a)	−0.1 ± 1***	0.0 ± 0.1	0.1 ± 0.2***	−0.1 ± 0.1***

Note.   Mean ± SD of absolute values and differences of end-tidal (et) and transcutaneous (tc) PO$_2$ (kPa) and of et, tc, and computed arterial (a) PCO$_2$ (kPa).
*p ≤ .05; **p ≤ .01; ***p ≤ .001; p values of differences by paired comparison.

blood pressure was measured intermittently. Ventilation and pulmonary gas exchange was determined breath-by-breath (Wessel, Stout, & Paul, 1979). All 1-min ventilation and gas exchange data represent the average of all breaths during each minute, whereas the transcutaneous values represent the instantaneous digital readouts at the end of the corresponding minute. Linear regressions were based on all exercise and 1 to 4 recovery minutes. Regressions were computed for pooled patient data and for each individual. The latter were expressed in terms of the mean ± 1 SD of regression slopes, intercepts, correlation coefficient (r), and SE of the slope (SE_{SL}) (see Table 3). The significance of slope differences was computed:

$$z = (SL[1] - SL[2])/(SE_{SL1}{}^2 + SE_{SL2}{}^2)^{-1/2}$$

Partial pressure differences (see Table 2) were evaluated by paired comparison.

RESULTS

The average PtcO$_2$ was significantly less than PetO$_2$ ($p < .001$) at rest, during exercise, and recovery (see Table 2). However, both increased from rest to the end of exercise and further during recovery. The average PetCO$_2$, PaCO$_2$, and PtcCO$_2$ also increased from rest to the end of exercise but then fell slightly below resting levels during recovery. Although

Table 3 Linear Regressions of End-Tidal (et) and Transcutaneous (tc) PO_2 and PCO_2 on Ventilation ($\dot{V}O_2/\dot{V}_A$, $\dot{V}CO_2/\dot{V}_A$)

Equation	Linear regression		r	SE_{SL}
4	$PetO_2 = -.094\ \dot{V}O_2/\dot{V}_A + 18.6$		.995	.003
	SD $\pm.006$	± 0.3	$\pm.01$	$\pm.003$
5	$P_{tc}O_2 = -.059\ \dot{V}O_2/\dot{V}_A + 12.8$		.791	.016*
	SD $\pm.046$	± 2.6	$\pm.230$	$\pm.018$
6	$P_{tc}O_2 = .591\ PetO_2 + 1.7$		.782	.171
	SD $\pm.481$	± 6.9	$\pm.226$	$\pm.189$
7	$PetCO_2 = .114\ \dot{V}CO_2/\dot{V}_A + .004$		.999	.001
	SD $\pm.003$	$\pm.05$	$\pm.003$	$\pm.002$
8	$P_{tc}CO_2 = .055\ \dot{V}CO_2/\dot{V}_A + 2.5$		.719	.019**
	SD $\pm.038$	± 1.7	$\pm.234$	$\pm.014$
9	$P_{tc}CO_2 = .489\ PetCO_2 + 2.4$		.733	.182
	SD $\pm.333$	± 1.8	$\pm.220$	$\pm.180$
10	$P_{tc}CO_2 = 0.677\ PaCO_2 + 2.0$		.711	.234
	SD ± 1.04	± 2.3	$\pm.214$	$\pm.208$

Note. Linear relationship of end-tidal (et) and transcutaneous (tc) PO_2 and PCO_2 (kPa) to $\dot{V}O_2/\dot{V}_A$ and $\dot{V}CO_2/\dot{V}_A$ (ml STPD/L BTPS), respectively; and linear relationship of $P_{tc}O_2$ to $P_{et}O_2$ and $P_{tc}CO_2$ and computed $PaCO_2$; r = correlation coefficient; SE_{SL} = standard error of the regression slope SD 1 standard deviation.
*$p \leqslant .05$ for slope difference between equations 4 and 5; **$p < .01$ for slope difference of equations 7 and 8.

the average differences $\Delta P(et\text{-}tc)CO_2$ and $\Delta P(a\text{-}tc)CO_2$ were small, all comparisons had large SDs. Pooling exercise and recovery minutes of all studies, only 334/509 (65.6%) measurements of $\Delta P(a\text{-}tc)CO_2$ were within $\pm$ 0.4 kPa for the steady state work protocol. For the non-steady state work protocol, 342/642 (53.3%) comparisons were within $\pm$ 0.4 kPa. Overall, $\Delta P(a\text{-}tc)PCO_2$ was within $\pm$ 0.53 kPa ($\pm$ 4 torr) in 813/1151 (70.7%) comparisons.

On the average, neither $PtcO_2$ nor $PtcCO_2$ changed from rest to the end of the 1st min of exercise, whereas the average $PetO_2$ decreased and $PetCO_2$ increased (see Table 2). The lack of change is due to the delay time between alveolar space and skin, and the different response time of the measurement systems. Hyperventilation and O_2 or CO_2 breathing indicated a delay time of approximately 20 and 60 s for $PtcO_2$ and $PtcCO_2$, respectively. The systems response differed approximately 600 fold, the mass spectrometer having a 90% response time of < 100 msec as compared to approximately 1 min for the transcutaneous electrodes. Even though no attempts were made to adjust for these delays, Table 3 indicates for individual cases a highly linear relationship of $PtcO_2$ and $PtcCO_2$ to $\dot{V}O_2/\dot{V}_A$ and $\dot{V}CO_2/\dot{V}_A$, respectively. Consequently, there was a similar highly linear relationship between $PtcO_2$ and $PetO_2$ and $PtcCO_2$ and $PetCO_2$ or

$PaCO_2$. For correlations between $PtcO_2$ and $PetO_2$ the correlation coefficient (r) was $\leqslant$ .50 in only 14/109 patients (12.8%). In the case of $PtcCO_2$ versus $PaCO_2$, r was $\leqslant$ .50 in 17/109, or 15.6%.

The $PetO_2$ and $PtcO_2$ response from rest to exercise to recovery was similar to the average response shown in Table 2 in 96/109 (88.1%) patients. $PtcCO_2$ was stable or increased by < .27 kPa (2 torr) in 61%. The increase exceeded 0.67 kPa (5 torr) in 14.8%. During recovery $PtcCO_2$ and $PetCO_2$ decreased rapidly to or below resting levels.

Distinctly different responses were seen (a) in patients with severe pulmonary vascular disease or diminished pulmonary blood flow with or without intracardiac shunt and (b) in patients with symptomatic interstitial pulmonary disease. At rest $PtcO_2$ in these patients was generally low and began to fall progressively with the onset of exercise.

In patients with right to left shunts, $PtcO_2$ frequently continued to fall after termination of exercise and then gradually returned to resting levels. All cardiac patients with this $PtcO_2$ response manifested marked hyperventilation at rest (high $PetO_2$, low $PtcCO_2$, $PetCO_2$, and $\dot{V}O_2/\dot{V}_A$). With exercise $PetO_2$ increased, and $PetCO_2$ and $\dot{V}O_2/\dot{V}_A$ decreased progressively. The low $PtcCO_2$ did not change. In interstitial pulmonary disease $PtcO_2$ usually leveled off before the end of exercise followed by a rapid rise above resting levels during recovery. Transcutaneous and end-tidal PCO_2 either remained stable in the pulmonary patients or rose with exercise.

DISCUSSION

The majority of these patients had no evidence of impaired arterial oxygenation or CO_2 retention and showed the same $PtcO_2$ and $PtcCO_2$ response to maximal exercise as subjects free of pulmonary or cardiac disease. These data confirm previous observations of $PtcO_2$ and $PtcCO_2$ changes during exercise. They provide quantitative evidence that individual differences in the ventilatory response contribute significantly to the variations of transcutaneous PO_2 and PCO_2 during maximal exercise testing. In keeping with previous studies, the data suggest that continuous transcutaneous measurements accurately reflect changes of arterial PO_2 and PCO_2. However, absolute values of arterial PO_2 or PCO_2 cannot be predicted with sufficient accuracy to replace direct arterial measurements.

CONCLUSION

It is concluded that the interpretation of transcutaneous PO_2 and PCO_2 data is enhanced by simultaneous evaluation of ventilation and pulmonary gas exchange on a breath-by-breath basis.

Acknowledgment

Supported in part by the Richard J. Daley II Memorial Pulmonary Research Fund.

REFERENCES

Borgia, J.F., & Horvath, S.M. (1978). Transcutaneous, noninvasive PO_2 monitoring in adults during exercise and hypoxemia. *Pflügers Archiv,* **377**, 143-145.

Hughes, J.A., Gray, B.J., & Hutchinson, D.C.S. (1984). Changes in transcutaneous oxygen tension during exercise in pulmonary emphysema. *Thorax,* **39**, 424-431.

Jones, N.L., & Campbell, E.J.M. (1982). *Clinical exercise testing.* Philadelphia: Saunders.

Kentala, E., & Repo, U.K. (1984). Feasibility of cutaneous blood gas monitoring during exercise stress testing. *Annals of Clinical Research,* **16**, 40-46.

Kornum, M., Oxhoj, H., & Nielsen, G. (1982). Transcutaneous versus arterial oxygen tension during exercise in chronic pulmonary disease. *Clinical Physiology,* **2**, 521-528.

Löllgen, H., von Nieding, G., Kersting, F., & Just, H. (1979). Transcutaneous measurement of PO_2 in adults: Exercise testing and monitoring in acute myocardial infarction. *Medical Progress through Technology,* **6**, 43-52.

McDowell, J.W., & Thiede, W.H. (1980). Usefulness of the transcutaneous PO_2 monitor during exercise testing in adults. *Chest,* **78**, 853-855.

Schonfeld, T., Sargent, C.W., Bautista, D., Walters, M.A., O'Neal, M.H., Platzker, A.C.G., & Keens, T.G. (1980). Transcutaneous oxygen monitoring during exercise stress testing. *American Review of Respiratory Disease,* **121**, 457-462.

Seiff, K.H., Mahutte, C.K., Percorraro, F.G., & Light, R.W. (1983). The relationship between transcutaneous and arterial PCO_2 during exercise. *American Review of Diagnostics,* **3**, 87-90.

Stout, R.L., Wessel, H.U., & Paul, M.H. (1981). Validity of breath-by-breath PaO_2 and $PaCO_2$ from end-tidal samples. *Federation Proceedings,* **40**, 357.

Wessel, H.U., Stout, R.L., & Paul, M.H. (1979). Minicomputer based system for breath-by-breath analysis of ventilation and pulmonary gas exchange. *Procedures of the Fourth Annual Conference on Computers in Cardiology* (pp. 97-102). Long Beach, CA: IEEE Computer Society.

Part VII
Locomotor Apparatus

Isokinetic Strength and Flexibility Characteristics in Preadolescent Boys

David A. Brodie
Janice Burnie
Roger G. Eston
Jon A. Royce
University of Liverpool, Liverpool, England

Isokinetic strength testing and training is well documented in the literature (Hislop & Perrine, 1967; Perrine, 1968; Thistle, Hislop, Moffroid, & Lowman, 1966); yet it is still the mode of exercise least familiar to work physiologists. Training techniques have tended to use more conventional modes of exercise, causing the muscles to contract either isometrically or isotonically. A limitation of isokinetics has partially been the very specialized equipment required to perform truly isokinetic movement, and even then controversy exists over the definition of the term *isokinetic exercise*. The controversy relates to whether isokinetic refers to a constant angular velocity of the limb or to a constant linear velocity of muscle contraction. Hinson, Smith, and Funk (1979) presented a mathematical argument to show that when the angular velocity of a limb is held constant it is not accompanied by a uniform rate of linear muscular contraction. Their definition concurs with a constant angular rate of limb movement and is supported by other workers including De Lateur et al. (1972); Moffroid, Whipple, Hofkosh, Lowman, and Thistle (1969); and Thistle et al. (1966). Hislop and Perrine (1967), on the other hand, consider the contractile rate of muscle fibers and therefore define isokinetics in relation to a constant rate of muscular contraction. Hubbard (1979) in response to Hinson et al. (1979) suggested that the term *isokinetic* should be reserved for exercise programs using constant velocity devices, but Hubbard may have been under the misconception that isokinetic devices move the segment attached to the device at a constant velocity throughout the range of motion. Hinson correctly established that isokinetic instrumentation does not move the body segment, but provides a time-constant resistance to movement. Movement occurs as a consequence of active muscular contraction, but this contraction may not be of constant velocity, even though the limb movement is constant. This controversy indicates the necessity for a clear definition, and this is clarified somewhat by the design of isokinetic equipment, which is generally associated with a limb moving at a constant angular velocity.

For the purposes of this study Perrine's (1969) patented definition was used. This included the statement that "the speed of an exercise movement is allowed to accelerate essentially unopposed by resistance forces from zero to a preset or predetermined rate of speed, and any magnitude of muscular force tending to accelerate the exercise movement beyond the predetermined rate of speed is counteracted by the system." Thus, regardless of the force exerted, the resistive force will exactly balance or accommodate the muscular force applied. There will consequently be no net force remaining and, in accordance with Newton's First Law, no acceleration of the limb.

Isokinetic measurement thus permits a quantitative examination of various principles relating to the nature of muscular contraction, including the magnitude and rate at which tension develops. Force-velocity relationships have been investigated for almost 50 years (Dern, 1947, Hill, 1938, 1970; Perrine, 1969; Wilkie, 1949), but isokinetic dynamometers (e.g., Cybex II system) have facilitated the measurements of torque, average power, and torque acceleration energy. Only one report was found in the literature (Davies et al., 1980) that describes shoulder flexion and extension at a range of limb velocities, and this applied only to adults. The aim of this study was thus to present values for preadolescent boys for isokinetic strength measures and range of motion at different limb velocities. These values were then compared with other joints and with adults.

METHODS

A total of 24 preadolescent males of mean age 11.72 (± 0.40) years were recruited from a local school. The subjects and their parents provided informed consent following the guidelines of the American College of Sports Medicine and the 1975 Declaration of Helsinki. The selection criteria required that the boys not be involved in any specific strength-training program beyond their normal school curriculum activities. None was familiar with isokinetic strength testing or training and there was no history of significant illness or injury in any of the children. The subjects had a mean weight of 38.4 ± 7.4 kg, a mean height of 147.9 ± 7.1 cm, and a percentage of body fat using a standard regression equation (Parizkova, 1961) of 17.9 ± 4.8%. Height, weight, and skinfold measurements followed the procedure recommended by the Canadian Association of Sports Sciences (MacDougall, Wenger, & Green, 1982).

The isokinetic measurements were made on the left side using a Cybex II isolated joint testing system (Cybex Division, Lumex, Ronkonkoma, NY). An upper body testing table was employed so that the dynamometer could be placed in line with the shoulder joint. Prior to testing, the Cybex II was calibrated using the recommended procedure. Each subject was familiarized with the equipment by extending and flexing the shoulder joint through the full range of movement at each test speed. The test protocol required each subject to perform six repetitions of the shoulder flexion-extension movement pattern at each velocity. The Cybex II lever arm was adjusted to the appropriate length for each subject's arm. Subjects were given standardized instructions verbally and all were motivated by the test administrator to encourage maximum effort throughout the complete range of motion on each repetition. The six test velocities were randomly ordered so that each subject was measured at 0.52 rads s⁻¹ (30 deg s⁻¹), 1.04 rads s⁻¹ (60 deg s⁻¹), 1.56 rads s⁻¹ (90 deg s⁻¹), 2.09 rads s⁻¹ (120 deg s⁻¹), 2.62 rads s⁻¹ (150 deg s⁻¹), and 3.15 rads s⁻¹ (180 deg s⁻¹).

Test results were obtained using the Cybex Data Reduction Computer interfaced with the dual channel recorder and dynamometer to give a data printout with standard format for each subject. This system provided a number of isokinetic measures, but this study considered only peak torque (Tp), average power (P), "torque acceleration energy" (TAE), reciprocal muscle group ratio (RMGR), and maximum range of motion (ROM max). Peak torque, measured in Newton-meters, was the maximum torque generated by the subject throughout one series of repetitions. Average power, measured in Watts, was taken to be a measure of work rate per unit of time.

Torque acceleration energy, measured in joules, was taken to be an "in vivo" measure of the recruitment rate of motor units during the initial phase of torque production. Previously measurements of this nature were taken from the slope of the rising torque curve in isometric tests or by taking torque at some specific time along the baseline of the torque curve. Time to peak torque has also been used as an indicator of motor unit recruitment rate but often this is only measuring the relationship of test speed and starting position to optimal joint position rather than muscular quickness. TAE measures the energy expended in terms of the work performed in the first .125 s of torque production (as defined by Cybex Division, Lumex).

Reciprocal muscle group ratios were expressed as a ratio of flexors divided by extensors for Tp, P, and TAE. This gave an indication of the relative isokinetic capabilities of the muscle groupings controlling the shoulder joint in uni-planar movement. Maximum range of movement was the aggregate angular displacement of arm movement from full flexion to full extension in the sagittal plane, measured in degrees, using the Cybex II dynamometer.

RESULTS

The means and standard deviations for Tp, P, TAE, RMGR, and ROM max for each velocity are shown in Table 1. Mean values for Tp ranged from 10.6 to 16.5 Newton-meters, for P from 2.9 to 11.9 W, for TAE from 0.2 to 1.7 joules, for RMGR from 84% to 142%, and for ROM max from 202° to 209°.

Table 1 Means (and *SD*) of Isokinetic and Range of Motion Values for Each Velocity

Variable	Velocity (rads s^{-1})					
	0.52	1.04	1.56	2.09	2.62	3.15
Tp (Nm)						
Extension	16.5 (5.7)	13.7 (4.4)	13.4 (4.3)	13.2 (4.9)	13.4 (4.6)	10.6 (4.4)
Flexion	14.3 (5.0)	14.3 (5.3)	12.5 (4.8)	12.9 (5.0)	13.5 (7.4)	11.8 (7.8)
P (W)						
Extension	2.9 (1.5)	5.0 (2.7)	6.8 (4.3)	8.6 (4.5)	11.5 (6.9)	9.3 (6.0)
Flexion	2.9 (1.4)	5.8 (2.8)	7.4 (4.0)	9.6 (5.5)	11.9 (6.9)	10.0 (6.7)
TAE (J)						
Extension	0.17 (0.09)	0.43 (.19)	0.82 (.41)	1.14 (.51)	1.50 (.97)	1.74 (1.10)
Flexion	0.16 (.13)	0.35 (.20)	0.60 (.40)	0.96 (.56)	1.15 (.67)	1.45 (1.12)
RMGR, Tp (%)	92.2 (30.4)	105.2 (34.3)	96.2 (28.2)	96.7 (27.1)	99.7 (31.8)	111.1 (39.7)
RMGR, P (%)	112.7 (51.2)	121.9 (47.4)	121.6 (63.2)	110.1 (27.6)	115.2 (59.2)	142.6 (119.9)
RMGR, TAE (%)	126.0 (114.7)	95.1 (60.8)	84.2 (54.3)	112.9 (78.5)	90.4 (70.9)	88.0 (36.8)
ROM max (degrees)	202 (5.1)	204 (7.7)	208 (8.0)	208 (9.4)	208 (10.3)	208 (10.3)

A one-way analysis of variance using the Statsease microcomputer program (Clarke, 1981) produced the F values and levels of significance shown in Table 2. These refer to the significant differences between the six limb velocities. The ANOVA indicated that limb velocity had a significant effect ($p < .01$) on the values for Tp in extension, for P in extension and flexion, and for TAE in extension and flexion, but was nonsignificant for RMGR, Tp in Flexion, and ROM max.

Table 2 Mean Values (N = 109) of End-Tidal (et) and Transcutaneous (tc) PO$_2$ and PCO$_2$

Variable	Rest 3rd min	Exercise 1st min	Last min	Recovery 4th min
PO$_2$				
et	14.1 ± 1.0	13.4 ± 1.1	14.4 ± 0.8	15.4 ± 0.6
tc	9.3 ± 1.5	9.3 ± 1.6	10.1 ± 1.6	10.7 ± 1.6
Δ(et-tc)	4.8 ± 1.8***	4.2 ± 1.9***	4.3 ± 1.8***	4.6 ± 1.7***
PCO$_2$				
et	4.8 ± 0.6	5.0 ± 0.6	5.3 ± 0.7	4.7 ± 0.5
a	4.9 ± 0.5	5.0 ± 0.5	5.1 ± 0.6	4.7 ± 0.5
tc	4.9 ± 0.6	4.9 ± 0.6	5.1 ± 0.8	4.6 ± 0.6
Δ(et-tc)	0.0 ± 0.8	0.2 ± 0.9**	0.3 ± 1.1*	0.1 ± 0.5
Δ(a-tc)	0.1 ± 0.5	−0.2 ± 0.5**	0.0 ± 0.7	−0.1 ± 0.5*
Δ(et-a)	−0.1 ± 1***	0.0 ± 0.1	0.1 ± 0.2***	−0.1 ± 0.1***

Note. Mean ± SD of absolute values and differences of end-tidal (et) and transcutaneous (tc) PO$_2$ (kPa) and of et, tc, and computed arterial (a) PCO$_2$ (kPa).
*$p \leqslant .05$; **$p \leqslant .01$; ***$p \leqslant .001$; p values of differences by paired comparison.

Thus, it was appropriate to apply a Newman-Keuls post hoc multiple comparisons test to the variables showing significant velocity differences. The results have been summarized in Table 3 with the levels of significance indicated between each paired comparison. Tp in extension has been omitted because the significant ANOVA was caused by a single pair, the difference between velocities 0.52 and 3.15 rads s^{-1}. These were the extremes of the velocities used, thus indicating that a simple ANOVA can provide a slightly distorted picture of the underlying effects.

Average power in flexion showed significant differences between the lowest velocity and all others. As the velocity increased the differences between those differing by 0.52 rads s^{-1} became progressively less. A similar trend was observed for average power in extension. Torque acceleration energy in extension showed significant differences between most of the pairs, whereas TAE in flexion only showed significant differences between the three lower velocities and the two higher velocities.

Table 3 Linear Regressions of End-Tidal (et) and Transcutaneous (tc) PO$_2$ and PCO$_2$ on Ventilation ($\dot{V}O_2/\dot{V}_A$, $\dot{V}CO_2/\dot{V}_A$)

Equation	Linear regression		r	SE_{SL}
4	$P_{et}O_2 = -.094 \, \dot{V}O_2/\dot{V}_A + 18.6$		.995	.003
	SD ±.006	±0.3	±.01	±.003
5	$P_{tc}O_2 = -.059 \, \dot{V}O_2/\dot{V}_A + 12.8$		.791	.016*
	SD ±.046	±2.6	±.230	±.018
6	$P_{tc}O_2 = .591 \, PetO_2 + 1.7$		.782	.171
	SD ±.481	±6.9	±.226	±.189
7	$P_{et}CO_2 = .114 \, \dot{V}CO_2/\dot{V}_A + .004$		.999	.001
	SD ± .003	±.05	±.003	±.002
8	$P_{tc}CO_2 = .055 \, \dot{V}CO_2/\dot{V}_A + 2.5$		.719	.019**
	SD ± .038	±1.7	±.234	±.014
9	$P_{tc}CO_2 = .489 \, PetCO_2 + 2.4$		.733	.182
	SD ±.333	±1.8	±.220	±.180
10	$P_{tc}CO_2 = 0.677 \, PaCO_2 + 2.0$		.711	.234
	SD ±1.04	±2.3	±.214	±.208

Note. Linear relationship of end-tidal (et) and transcutaneous (tc) PO$_2$ and PCO$_2$ (kPa) to $\dot{V}O_2/\dot{V}_A$ and $\dot{V}CO_2/\dot{V}_A$ (ml STPD/L BTPS), respectively; and linear relationship of $P_{tc}O_2$ to $P_{et}O_2$ and $P_{tc}CO_2$ and computed PaCO$_2$; r = correlation coefficient; SE_{SL} = standard error of the regression slope; SD 1 standard deviation.
*$p \leqslant .05$ for slope difference between equations 4 and 5; **$p < .01$ for slope difference of equations 7 and 8.

DISCUSSION

A review of the literature revealed no published data on isokinetic measures of shoulder extension-flexion in children. These data are thus presented as an initial contribution to normative values, although they are restricted in sample size and age. The only published work on isokinetic shoulder extension-flexion relates to U.S. cross-country skiers (Davies et al., 1980), and so absolute comparisons are limited, although changes with velocity and reciprocal muscle group ratios may be of interest.

The shoulder flexion-extension values for the skiers are presented in Figure 1, and the characteristic reduction in peak torque as velocity increased can be observed. It was not possible to calculate the significant differences between velocities from the published data, but Figure 1 indicates that large differences in velocity are needed to show changes. This was corroborated in the present study with peak torque in extension. It was not possible to compare average power and torque acceleration energy with other studies because the Davies study reports peak torque and reciprocal muscle group ratios only. The reciprocal muscle group ratios for peak torque are compared in Figure 2, and it can be seen that

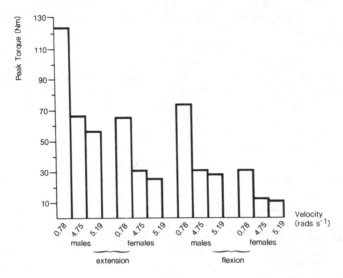

Figure 1 Peak torque at different velocities for cross-country skiers (data from Davis et al., 1980).

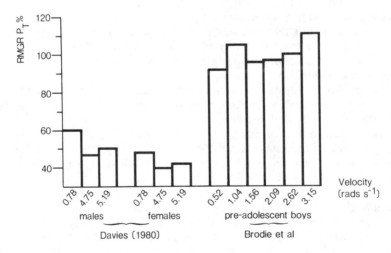

Figure 2 Reciprocal muscle group ratios for peak torque comparing Davies et al. (1980) with the present study.

the children showed considerably higher values at all velocities. This indicated that there was little difference in the peak torque generated by the flexors and the extensors of the shoulder at a young age whereas adults showed much more relative development of the extensors (Davies et al., 1980). The musculoskeletal developmental process thus appears to favor the shoulder extensors. This discrepancy between children and adults is an important observation because of the potential relationship between muscular imbalance and subsequent incidence of injury.

Goslin and Charteris (1979) indicated that substantial deviation from the normal extensor-flexor equilibrium could predispose an individual toward injury. This observation was based on the knee flexor-extensors (hamstring-quadriceps), but the principle may be equally valid for the shoulder joint, particularly in competitive sports involving the upper body. Goslin & Charteris (1979) suggested that a range of 66% to 30% is the extreme of normality. The adult shoulder data of Davies et al. (1980) falls within these limits, but the children of the present study ranged from 90% to 111%, which is considered pathological by Goslin and Charteris (1979). This emphasizes the necessity for using age-related data and demonstrates the dangers of assuming that children have relative musculature characteristics similar to adults.

The paucity of data on reciprocal muscle group ratios makes comparison difficult, particularly as most studies report RMGR for peak torque only, for the knee joint, and at no more than two velocities (Alexander & Molnar, 1973; Bailey, 1980; Burkett, 1970; Gilliam, Villanacci, Freedson, & Sady, 1979; Klein & Allman, 1969; Molnar & Alexander, 1973; Morris, Lussier, Bell, & Dooley, 1983). The predominance of quadriceps over hamstring values is clearly related to the greater contractile muscle volume. The data of Davies et al. (1980) seemed to support this for the adult shoulder joint, but in children the muscles used in extension seemed to generate the same torque, average power, and torque acceleration energy as the flexors. It is likely that as children mature they develop relatively more contractile muscle volume in the extensors of the shoulder joint. It is possible that adults also use more ancillary muscles in the action of upper arm extension.

An alternative strategy is to make comparisons among similarly aged boys, but necessarily using different joint complexes. It can be seen from Figure 3 that in both extension and flexion there was a trend for a faster velocity to cause a decrease in peak torque, but it was much more pronounced in the knee than the other joints. The relationship between peak torque and angular velocity has been well established (e.g., Ingemann-Hansen & Halkjaer-Kristensen, 1979; Moffroid & Whipple, 1970), but once again the relationship is based extensively on the knee joint and adult populations. Figure 3 illustrates that the same statement cannot be made for the elbow and shoulder, and so the force-velocity relationships in children for joints other than the knee may need reassessment. Decreases in torque production at increasing limb velocities, when they occur, have been attributed to the different contractile velocity capabilities of individual muscle fibers (Hill, 1970; Pipes & Wilmore, 1975). It has been suggested that in a muscle contracting at a given velocity only fibers with an individual contractile velocity equal to or greater than the contractile velocity of the total muscle would be capable of contributing to the total tension within the muscle. Thus, at slow muscle contractile velocities, the peak torque is greater because more individual fibers have the contractile velocity capability to contribute to the total tension in the

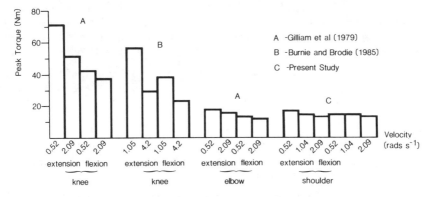

Figure 3 Comparative values of peak torque from similarly aged boys.

muscle. Conversely, as the contractile rate of the total muscle increases, it exceeds the maximum contractile velocity of many of the individual fibers. These cannot contribute to the total tension in the muscle and the peak torque is subsequently reduced. Any decrease in torque produced by increased limb velocity has implications for training and rehabilitation programs.

Training should be speed specific, and studies such as Moffroid and Whipple (1970) and Smith and Melton (1981) have indicated that training at high limb velocities will have a positive transfer to activities performed at lower velocities. There appears to be little or no transfer of training, however, to activities demanding limb velocities in excess of training velocity. As this study showed no differences in torque production at varying velocities it would appear, at least for preadolescent boys, that the shoulder (and elbow if one takes account of the study by Gilliam et al., 1979) does not require velocity-related training or rehabilitation. Although this applies when the objective is to increase peak torque, the same would not follow for the development of tension within the muscle, as indicated by torque acceleration energy. Our studies, Burnie and Brodie (unpublished data) and the present one, indicated consistently that TAE is velocity dependent. It is assumed that motor units recruited at high limb velocities are only those that are capable of high contractile velocities. This would account for the apparent increase in the rate of motor unit recruitment or TAE with increased limb velocities. Thus, if the intention is to improve specifically the rate of motor unit recruitment, the specificity of velocity should be considered.

CONCLUSION

This study has presented initial isokinetic data on preadolescent boys, comparing and contrasting them with values for adults' shoulders and children's knees. Preadolescent boys show velocity differences in average power and torque acceleration energy, but not in the other isokinetic variables. These differences indicate the importance of treating children separately from adults in terms of testing, training, and rehabilitation.

REFERENCES

Alexander, J., & Molnar, G.E. (1973). Muscular strength in children: Preliminary report on objective standards. *Archives of Physical Medicine and Rehabilitation,* **54,** 424-427.

Bailey, D. (1980). Strength in balances common in young gridders. *USSA News,* **4,** 5-8.

Burkett, L.N. (1970). Causative factors in hamstring strains. *Medicine and Science in Sports,* **2** (Spring), 39-42.

Clarke, B. (1981). *Statsease computer program.* Nottingham, England: Leicester Computer Centre.

Davies, G.J., Halbach, J.W., Carpenter, M.A., Scheid, D.T., Reinbold, T.R., Brandt, J.A., Tesch, J.C., Kirkendall, D.T., & Wilson, P.K. (1980). A descriptive muscular power analysis of the United States cross country ski team. *Medicine and Science in Sports and Exercise,* **12,** 141.

De Lateur, B., Lehmann, J.F., Warren, C.G., Stonebridge, J., Funita, G., Cokelet, K., & Egbert, H. (1972). Comparison of effectiveness of isokinetic and isotonic exercise in quadriceps strengthening. *Archives of Physical Medicine and Rehabilitation,* **53,** 60-64.

Dern, R. (1947). Forces exerted at different velocities in human arm movements. *American Journal of Physiology,* **15,** 415-437.

Gilliam, T.B., Villanacci, J.F., Freedson, P.S., & Sady, S.P. (1979). Isokinetic torque in boys and girls ages 7 to 13: Effect of age, height and weight. *Research Quarterly,* **50,** 599-609.

Goslin, B.R., & Charteris, J. (1979). Isokinetic dynamometry: Normative data for clinical use in lower extremity (knee) cases. *Scandinavian Journal of Rehabilitation Medicine,* **11,** 105-109.

Hill, A.V. (1938). Heat of shortening and dynamic constants of muscle. *Proceedings of the Royal Society of Medicine,* **126,** 136-195.

Hill, A.V. (1970). *First and last experiments in muscle mechanics.* London: Cambridge University Press.

Hinson, M.N., Smith, W.C., & Funk, S. (1979). Isokinetics: A clarification. *Research Quarterly,* **50,** 30-35.

Hislop, H.J., & Perrine, J.J. (1967). The isokinetic concept of exercise. *Physical Therapy,* **47,** 114-117.

Hubbard, A.W. (1979). Comments on isokinetics. *Research Quarterly,* **50,** 528-530.

Ingemann-Hansen, T., & Halkjaer-Kristensen, J. (1979). Force-velocity relationships in the human quadriceps muscles. *Scandinavian Journal of Rehabilitation Medicine, 11*, 85-89.

Klein, K.K., & Allman, F.L. (1969). *The knee in sports.* Austin, TX: Jenkins.

MacDougall, J.D., Wenger, H.A., & Green, H.J. (1982). *Physiological testing of the elite athlete.* Mutual Press.

Moffroid, M.T., & Whipple, R.H. (1970). Specificity of speed of exercise. *Physical Therapy, 50,* 12.

Moffroid, M., Whipple, R., Hofkosh, J., Lowman, E., & Thistle, H. (1969). A study of isokinetic exercise. *Physical Therapy, 49,* 735-747.

Molnar, G.E., & Alexander, J. (1973). Objective, quantitative muscle testing in children: A pilot study. *Archives of Physical Medicine and Rehabilitation, 54,* 224-228.

Morris, A., Lussier, L., Bell, G., & Dooley, J. (1983). Hamstring/quadriceps strength ratios in collegiate middle-distance and distance runners. *The Physician and Sportsmedicine, 11* (10), 71-77.

Parizkova, J. (1961). Total body fat and skinfold thickness in children. *Metabolism, 10,* 794-807.

Perrine, J.J. (1968). Isokinetic exercise and the mechanical energy potentials of muscle. *Journal of Health, Physical Education, Recreation, 39,* 40-44.

Perrine, J.J. (1969, September 9). *Isokinetic exercise process and apparatus* (3.465 and 592). U.S. Patent Office.

Pipes, T.V., & Wilmore, J.H. (1975). Isokinetic vs isotonic strength training in adult men. *Medicine and Science in Sports, 7,* 262-274.

Smith, M.J., & Melton, P. (1981). Isokinetic versus isotonic variable-resistance training. *American Journal of Sports Medicine, 9,* 275-279.

Thistle, H.G., Hislop, H.J., Moffroid, M., & Lowman, E.W. (1966). Isokinetic contraction: A new concept of resistive exercise. *Archives of Physical Medicine and Rehabilitation, 48,* 279-282.

Wilkie, D.R. (1949). The relation between force and velocity in human muscle. *Journal of Physiology (London), 110,* 249-280.

Relationships Among Some Muscle Functions, Aerobic Power, and Age During Childhood and Adolescence in Czechoslovakian Children

Jiřina Máčková
Postgraduate Medical and Pharmaceutical Institute,
Prague, Czechoslovakia
Miloš Máček
Jan Vávra
Laboratory for Physical Fitness Research, Prague, Czechoslovakia
Joseph Rutenfranz
Hannegret Kylian
Institute of Occupational Health at the University of Dortmund,
Dortmund, West Germany
Kristian Lange Andersen
Laboratorium for Miljofysiologi, Oslo, Norway

The increasing frequency of disorders of the locomotor system resulting in back pain has been observed in recent years in children. A number of factors were found, but quite common for this kind of disorder was the lifestyle of an industrial society, which lacks locomotor activity of sufficient variety or intensity. The present lifestyle loads the postural muscle system more and neglects the phasic one. The purpose of this study was to determine the relationships between these clinical symptoms and the degree of physical fitness in children.

METHOD

The status of the locomotor system of a randomized sample of children and their physical fitness expressed as $\dot{V}O_2$max were examined with a sport activity score. The subjects and study design are described in another report to which the reader is referred for details (Máček et al., 1985). A total of 120 boys and girls, aged 8, 12, and 16 years, were studied twice in 2 years. The children, living in a rural community, enjoyed a favorable lifestyle with regard to nutrition and habitual physical activity.

$\dot{V}O_2$max was determined using the Douglas bag method; physical activity was expressed as a sport activity score according to the method of Ilmarinen and Rutenfranz (1980). The system of Janda tests (1979) was used for evaluation of shortening of the main postural muscles and hypermobility in some regions of the body.

Means and standard deviation were obtained for all variables. Paired t-tests were used to test significant differences between repeated measurements, and the student t-test was used to test significant differences between age groups. The interrelationships between the status of the locomotor system and variables of physical fitness were calculated in the form of a correlation matrix, separately for boys and girls, pooling together all age groups.

RESULTS

In boys, the number of shortened muscles had increased with age when the same individuals were retested after 2 years, except for the group aged 16 to 18 years, as shown in Figure 1. In girls, the number of shortened

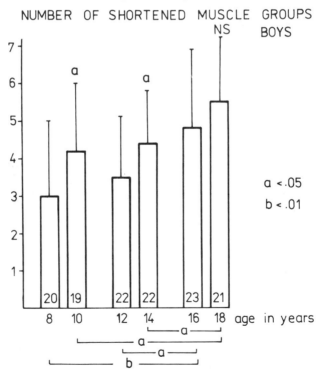

Figure 1   Means and SD of the number of shortened muscle groups in boys. Student t-test for independent means at 8, 12, and 16 years of age. Paired t-test for repeated measurements at 8 to 10, 12 to 14, and 16 to 18 years.

muscles increased only until the age of 12 years, after which a decreasing tendency was noted (see Figure 2). The hamstrings were most often shortened, in 90% of boys and 75% of girls. Less frequently, other muscle groups were affected, such as the iliopsoas, rectus femoris, trapezius, and levator scapulae in boys and girls and the gastrocnemius and pectoralis major mainly in boys.

The number of the regions with hypermobility in boys increased with age in the same individuals after 2 years. In the cross-sectional comparison, the number increased until the age of 12 years, after which the number of hypermobile regions was less (see Figure 3). In contrast, the absolute number of regions affected by hypermobility in girls was higher than in boys, and the increasing tendency was found in the longitudinal study as well as in the cross-sectional observations in various age groups (see Figure 4).

The most involved regions on the upper part of body were the shoulder girdle and also the elbow in the girls. On the lower part of body the hypermobility was most pronounced in the hip joint in girls and younger boys. The lumbosacral region was also affected more in the girls.

A significant relationship was not found between the frequency of shortened muscles and $\dot{V}O_2$max and the sport activity score. Only in the group of 12-year-old girls was a positive correlation found between the frequency of shortened muscles and $\dot{V}O_2$max (see Figure 5) and the sport activity score (see Figure 6) that was close to statistical significance.

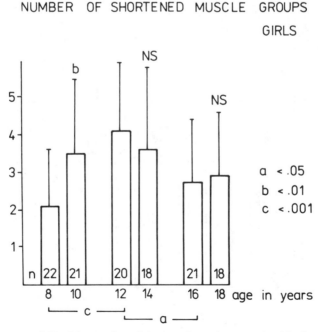

Figure 2   Means and SD of the number of shortened muscle groups in girls. Student t-test for independent means at 8, 12, and 16 years of age. Paired t-test for repeated measurements at 8 to 10, 12 to 14, and 16 to 18 years.

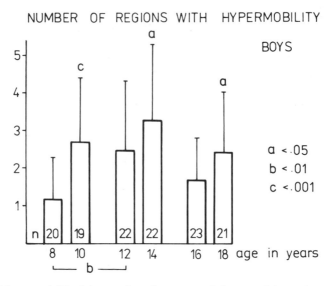

Figure 3 Means and *SD* of the number of regions with hypermobility in boys. Student *t*-test for independent means at 8, 12, and 16 years of age. Paired *t*-test for repeated measurements at 8 to 10, 12 to 14, and 16 to 18 years.

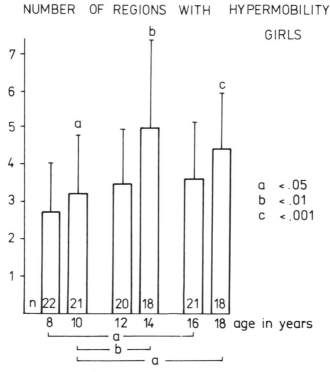

Figure 4 Means and *SD* of the number of regions with hypermobility in girls. Student *t*-test for independent means at 8, 12, and 16 years of age. Paired *t*-test for repeated measurements at 8 to 10, 12 to 14, and 16 to 18 years.

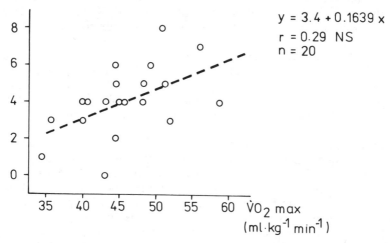

Figure 5 The number of shortened muscle groups plotted against V̇O₂max in girls at 12 years of age.

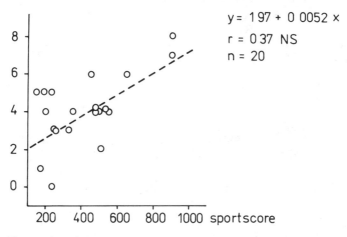

Figure 6 The number of shortened muscle groups plotted against sport activity score in girls at 12 years of age.

DISCUSSION

Information is lacking on the frequency of this phenomenon in normal children. These results are not in agreement with Kendall and Kendall (1948), who found the lowest frequency of hypermobility in 12- and 13-year-old boys and girls, respectively. On the other hand, Micheli (1979) described similar decreases in flexibility in boys in early adolescence.

Máčková, Javůrek, Máček, and Vávra (1985) described a lower frequency of shortened muscles in children engaged in sport training in comparison with the group of children with normal physical activity. The opposite was found concerning the frequency of hypermobility in these trained children.

In this study with a randomized nonselected sample of children with different levels of physical activity, higher relationships between age and shortened muscle and hypermobility were found. The explanation for these findings is difficult. The groups of children engaged in sports were highly selected. The intensity of training was relatively high and the duration was about 12 hours or more per week. It is important to note most of the children practiced stretching exercises regularly as a part of the training lessons. This was assumed to be an effective way of preventing muscle tightness and resulting muscle imbalances.

The physical activity in the present sample was much higher due to favorable conditions in their rural community than for normal children living in large towns. In spite of this, the variety of physical activity and relatively high physical fitness did not provide a sufficient protection from muscle imbalances and hypermobility, without special compensatory exercises. These must be included in the training methods and in school gymnastic lessons.

REFERENCES

Ilmarinen, J., & Rutenfranz, J. (1980). Longitudinal studies of the changes in habitual physical activity of school children and working adolescents. In K. Berg & B.O. Eriksson (Eds.), *Children and exercise IX* (pp. 149-159) (International Series on Sport Sciences, Vol. 10). Baltimore: University Park Press.

Janda, V. (1979). *Muskelfunktionsdiagnostik [Diagnostics of muscle function]*. Heidelberg: Verlag für Medizin, E. Fischer.

Kendall, H.O., & Kendall, F.P. (1948). Normal flexibility according to age groups. *Journal of Bone and Joint Surgery*, **30**, 690-694.

Máček, M., Rutenfranz, J., Lange Andersen, K., Masopust, J., Vávra, J., Klimmer, F., Kylian, H., Daněk, K., Máčková, J., Flöring, R., & Ottmann, W. (1985). Favourable levels of cardio-vascular health and risk indicators during childhood and adolescence. *European Journal of Pediatrics*, **144**, 360-367.

Máčková, J., Javůrek, J., Máček, M., & Vávra, J. (1985). A longitudinal study of the locomotor system in trained children. In R.A. Binkhorst, H.C.G. Kemper, & W.H.M. Saris (Eds.), *Children and exercise XI* (pp. 319-322) (International Series on Sport Sciences, Vol. 15). Champaign, IL: Human Kinetics.

Micheli, L.J. (1979). Low back pain in the adolescent: Differential diagnosis. *American Journal of Sports Medicine*, **7**, 362-365.

Back Pain and Skeletal Conditions During Intensive Training in Children and Adolescents

Miroslav Kučera
Charles University, Prague, Czechoslovakia

The problem of the relationship between physical load during sports training and the origin of back pain has recently been drawing considerable interest. The quality and quantity of physical load, often novel and unilaterally oriented, is one of the causes of frequent spinal disorders. Back pain is becoming one of the typical civilization diseases, the essence of which is in disproportion to the quality and quantity of the movement of the organism, past and present, and to the genetically created needs for movement. Whereas movement was earlier characterized by a dynamic form of work, especially of the musculoskeletal system, the current way of life leads to a predominance of static forms of motion. Retaining one position, especially during long periods of standing or sitting, represents a typical load causing larger or smaller local overloads due to isometric contractions of the postural muscles. This is responsible for the generation of maladaptive mechanisms in areas where the load is largest, frequently already the site for later degenerative changes. For an organism, and especially a young organism, it is important that this process not originate either under the maximum loads of unilateral sports practice or during apparent inactivity, such as static sitting and standing. In other words, excessive sports practice, unilaterally oriented with maximum performances, is equally as great a risk as long periods of sitting in school without the possibility of compensatory relaxation by equalizing movement during school intermissions and during the course of lessons.

The spinal system is complicated and operates in harmony and mutual cooperation with the individual parts of the whole organism. Figure 1 shows how the primary effect is reflected in the spine, where it may be manifest as the first and frequently predominating symptom, which may even obscure the basic disease. To function, the spine needs dynamic movement that not only maintains it in working condition but, at the same time, helps to develop it. At birth, the spine is straight; the lifting of the suckling's head generates cervical lordoses, sitting creates thoracic kyphosis, and mastering the upright supine position is responsible for the generation of lumbar lordosis. This demonstrates quite distinctly the function of movement in ontogenesis; however, movement is also im-

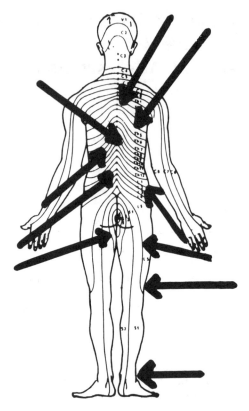

Figure 1   Localization of the primary effect, which is often manifested as back pain.

portant in the subsequent stages, but not as much. If the movement is not adequate, painful syndromes as well as other organic afflictions occur. This is due, on the one hand, to unilateral and maximum physical load (a prototype is power-sports practice) and, on the other, to insufficient movement stimulation. Apart from these general factors, the following also contribute to the difficulties and pathology:

- Hereditary factors—in particular, spinal pains, Scheuermann's disease, poor posture, and inbred disorders, especially of the hip joint
- Evolution of the musculoskeletal system and the organism as a whole; the basic stages of evolution and their course, special orientation to movement manifestations and their retardation or acceleration (Berger et al., 1984; Bierich, 1985; Ogden, 1984)
- Muscle functions—the disorders and especially the disproportion between the functions of the separate groups: imbalance, hypertrophy, atrophy, innervation disorders, and so on (Janda, 1974)
- Anthropometric indexes—comparison of the dynamics of the growth process with standards (Prokopec, Suchy, & Tittelbachova, 1973; Willner & Johnson, 1983)

- General illnesses—especially diseases of the musculoskeletal system and recording of all diseases requiring long-term hospitalization (Kučera, Čermak, & Javurek, 1979; Stein, Krahl, & Klimt, 1980)
- Disorders of the function of internal organs and their impact on the spine
- Injuries
- Microtrauma
- The movement regimen, its quality and quantity

Back pains and functional disorders are frequent even during ontogenesis. Various authors report different frequencies in the population. For example, in the list of sick-leave illnesses in Czechoslovakia in 1983, back pain is second to respiratory diseases and amounts to 10.72% of all diagnoses. This is also one of the most frequent causes of sportsmen being absent from sports practice.

METHOD

The results of examining the condition of children who were members of sports clubs or school centers, and who were subject to specialized sports practice, were processed. All the children were examined twice a year. Special attention was devoted to the condition of the musculoskeletal system, especially the spine. The usual clinical method was used to analyze the anatomical and functional arrangement. A special device, designed to show the deviations of the spinal axis (see Figure 2), was

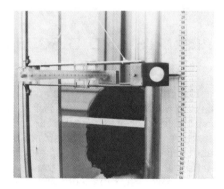

Figures 2a and 2b Instrument for recording deviations of the spinal axis.

used to record postural values. Where back pains, functional disorders, or significant deviations of the spinal axis were observed, x-ray examination was indicated in two projections, centered in the middle of the discovered symptom.

The total number of examined children, aged 11 to 14 years, was 1,912. The other part of the investigation concerned the same group of children, who continued with their sports practice and who reached the age of 15 to 17 years. There were 435 of these children. The investigation and analysis criteria were the same. The sports involved were athletics, gymnastics, football, swimming, Nordic skiing, ice hockey, handball, canoeing, basketball, and figure skating. This group of children had practiced their sport for more than 5 years. In the third group were medical students (aged 18 to 20 years) in the first year of their medical studies. The fourth group was a control group of adult men in their fifth and sixth decades. Their numbers were 33 and 30, respectively. The former were patients after myocardial infarction who were sent to the clinic for functional tests; the latter were patients of a polyclinic sent for examination because of various deviations of the musculoskeletal system (Table 1).

Table 1 Patients With Spinal Disorders

Group	Age (yr)	N	Scoliosis (%)	Scheuermann's disease (%)	Spinal disorders (%)
Sport clubs	11 to 14	1,912	18.9	4.6	30.08
Sport clubs	15 to 17	435	17.9	6.4	30.90
Medical students	18 to 20	2,724	21.2	3.15	12.5
Veteran athletes	40 to 59	30	66.0	25.0	56.0
Cardiacs	40 to 59	33	69.6	27.2	66.6

RESULTS AND DISCUSSION

The spinal system is affected considerably by insufficient as well as excessive movement activity. For some sports it is even possible to identify typical loci minoris resistentiae (see Figure 3). These areas are where the force vectors (of stress and strain) are centered and where the forces cause acute as well as chronic damage. Figure 4 shows the pattern of pressures acting when the body axis changes its position. This provides the justification for comprehensive examinations of children before they are assigned to any sports activity (or employment), with special regard for the nature of the expected load. The selection process is justified on the basis of examining 2,347 children of both sexes. A total of 30% of the children had difficulties—mostly spinal pains. Moreover, 40% of these pains were caused by organic changes in the musculoskeletal system. That is why it is always necessary to determine the cause precisely once the symptom of the pain has been discovered. This is important for preventing secondary changes. The process of the formation of the spine and other bones is long term, and protective regimens are important, especially at the time of maximum growth, during adolescence. Growth terminates at various stages, the latest in the so-called "carrier" bones (see Figure 5). The fact that this sample showed a relatively low number of Scheuermann's disease in both groups of child population, only 4.6%, can be explained by the system of selection. The normal population displays a higher frequency of occurrence of this disease as reported in the literature (Blazek, Streda, Čermak, & Skallova, 1985, report 25.0%), and the values in the present study show 25.0% resp. 27.2% (see Table 2). Under continuing sports load, only a higher percentage of spinal disorders in adolescent children was found; the other frequencies, including Scheuermann's disease, did not differ statistically from that reported for the normal population. In analyzing the results, Scheuermann's disease has to be considered a serious condition requiring the adjustment of the movement regimen of all children. Its adequacy must be evaluated as an important factor responsible for chronic damages in adulthood. This

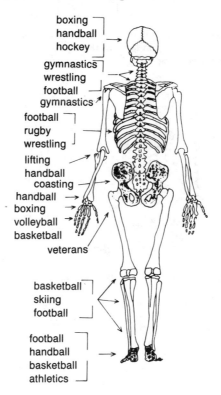

Figure 3 Typical loci minoris resistentiae in some sports.

334 Kučera

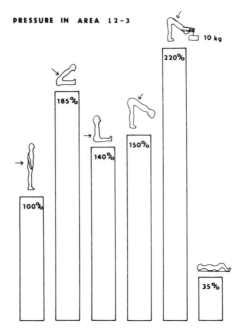

PRESSURE IN AREA L 2-3

Figure 4 Pattern of pressure in areas L2 and L3 while standing, sitting in forward flexion of 45°, sitting, standing in forward flexion of 45°, and standing in forward flexion of 45° with a weight of 10 kg.

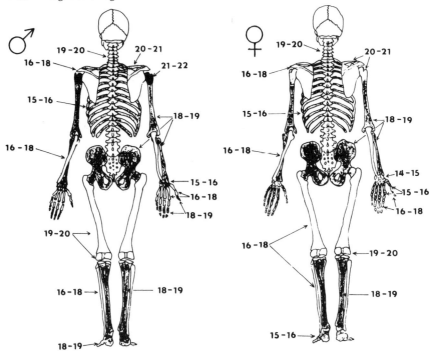

Figure 5 The end of ossification (in years) in males (a) and females (b).

Table 2   Patients With Spinal Disorders

Group	Age (yr)	N	Positive radiographic identification	Scheuermann's disease (%)	Scoliosis (%)
Sport clubs	11 to 14	575	234	51.3	46.0
Sport clubs	15 to 17	135	57	46.3	44.1
Medical students	18 to 20	333	314	25.8	27.1
Veteran athletes	40 to 59	17	24	25.0	66.0
Cardiacs	40 to 59	22	29	27.2	69.6

protective regimen, eliminating overload, results in the elimination of microtraumatization (restricting local overloading due to static, long-term and unilateral load, and to jumping). Moreover, the principles of correct evolution of the organism in every child have to be considered.

CONCLUSION

In ontogenesis, the spinal system undergoes important changes that are affected directly by movement activity. For this effect to be positive, it is necessary to adhere to the following:

1. Correct selection of individuals for the appropriate activity
2. Consistent and regular medical examinations and evaluations of growth dynamics and evolution
3. Practice to be carried out in accordance with the growth and evolution principles

The adequacy of the load due to movement is a prerequisite for harmonic growth and evolution, and spinal disorders require individual analysis and approach. Any deviation from the adequacy principle will cause a maladaptational reaction of the organism with the consequences often resulting in secondary changes. Spinal pains in children are always a warning signal and require detailed examination.

REFERENCES

Berger, W., Dietz, V., Hufschmidt, A., Jung, R., Mauritz, K.-H., & Schmidtbleicher, D. (1984). Haltung und Bewegung beim Menschen. *Physiologie, Pathophysiologie, Gangentwicklung und Sporttraining*. Berlin, New York: Springer-Verlag.

Bierich, J.R. (1985). Das Wachstum in der Pubertät [Growth in Puberty]. *Pädiatrie und Pädologie*, **20**, 7-19.

Blažek, O., Středa, A., Čermak, V., & Skallova, O. (1985). Scheuermann's disease: A roentengenologist's point of view [in Czech]. *Lekar a TV*, **3**, 24-26.

Janda, V. (1974). *Examination of mobility* [in Czech]. Praha: Avicenum.

Kučera, M., Čermak, V., & Javurek, J. (1979). Back pain in athletes [in Czech]. *Lekar a TV*, 4-22.

Ogden, J.A. (1984). Growth slowdown and arrest lines. *Journal of Pediatric Orthopedy*, **4**, 409-515.

Prokopec, M., Suchy, J., & Tittelbachova, S. (1973). Anthropometric data of Czech child population [in Czech]. *Ceskoslovenska Pediatrie*, **28**, 341-346.

Stein, W., Krahl, H., & Klimt, F. (1980). Orthopädische Erkrankungen und Schulsport. *Orthopedic Diseases and Schoolsport*, **11**, 522-534.

Willner, S., & Johnson, B. (1983). Thoracic kyphosis and lumbar lordosis during the growth period in children. *Acta Paediatrica Scandinavica*, **72**, 873-878.

Sagittal Spinal Curves in Young Finnish Cross-Country Skiers and Control Children

Seppo T. Mahlamäki
Heikki A. Pekkarinen
University of Kuopio, Kuopio, Finland

Cross-country skiing is a popular sport activity, especially in the Nordic countries. Preprogrammed training often is started during adolescence. However, the effects of extensive cross-country skiing on the musculo-skeletal systems have not been studied systematically. In previous studies concerning adolescent cross-country skiers it has been proposed that cross-country skiing might cause deepening of the lumbar lordosis (Mahlamäki, Pekkarinen, & Hänninen, 1982).

The determination of sagittal spinal curves by simple visual observation is not accurate, although it has some restricted validity when performed by an experienced examiner. Lateral radiographic examination of the spine cannot be used for screening studies in the determination of the ranges of spinal curves. Recently, a simple device, the spinal pantograph, has been developed and has proven to be both an accurate and an inexpensive way to analyze the spinal curves in the sagittal plane (Willner, 1981).

In this study, an attempt was made to determine the effects of competitive cross-country skiing on the ranges of thoracic kyphosis and lumbar lordosis in adolescence.

METHODS

The ranges of thoracic kyphosis and lumbar lordosis were examined with a spinal pantograph. The 388 children in the study were between the ages of 12 and 16 years and comprised six subgroups: skier boys (n = 120), rural control boys (n = 48), urban control boys (n = 48), skier girls (n = 79), rural control girls (n = 45), and urban control girls (n = 48). All of the subgroups were matched by age. Most skiers had been involved in preprogrammed training for at least 3 years.

To determine the sagittal spinal curves, each child was positioned in front of the pantograph and the contour of the spine was recorded as the pantograph wheel was moved along the body. The estimation of thoracic kyphosis and lumbar lordosis was made by drawing tangents to the curves that deviated maximally from the vertical plane (see Figures 1a and 1b). The proximal angle was the measure of the thoracic kyphosis and the distal angle was that of the lumbar lordosis. The method was developed and tested in Malmö, Sweden, and has proven to be accurate and to have good reproducibility (Willner, 1981). The statistical analysis was made by student *t*-tests and by analysis of variance.

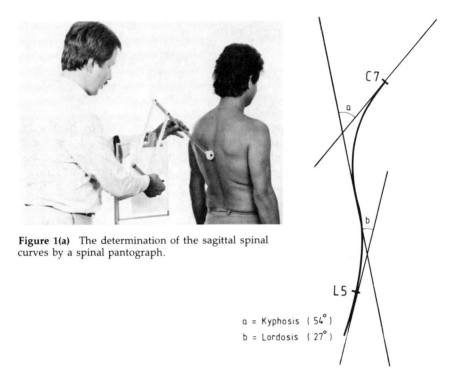

Figure 1(a) The determination of the sagittal spinal curves by a spinal pantograph.

a = Kyphosis (54°)
b = Lordosis (27°)

Figure 1(b) Method of recording the degrees of kyphosis and lordosis.

RESULTS

The values for thoracic kyphosis in each subgroup are presented in Figure 2. There were no significant differences among the groups. The values for lumbar lordosis are presented in Figure 3. The girls had deeper lordosis than the boys. The mean degrees of thoracic kyphosis and lumbar lordosis in five different age groups for each subgroup are presented in Figures 4 to 6 (boys) and in Figures 7 to 9 (girls).

There were no differences among the subgroups. In boys, the highest mean degree of kyphosis was found at the age of 16 ycars in all three

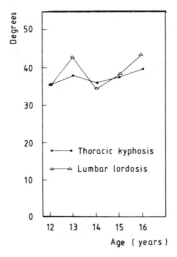

Figure 2 Degrees ($M \pm SD$) of thoracic kyphosis in all subjects (1), skier boys (2), rural control boys (3), urban control boys (4), skier girls (5), rural control girls (6), and urban control girls (7).

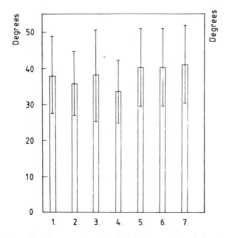

Figure 3 Degrees ($M \pm SD$) of lumbar lordosis in all subjects (1), skier boys (2), rural control boys (3), urban control boys (4), skier girls (5), rural control girls (6), and urban control girls (7).

groups. In girls, the kyphosis was highest at the age of 14 years in both rural and urban control groups, but in skiers at the age of 16 years. The mean degree of thoracic kyphosis was 43.1° in 16-year-old skier girls and 30.0° in rural control girls at the same age. The difference was statistically significant ($p < .01$). Analysis of variance, however, showed no significant differences among the groups.

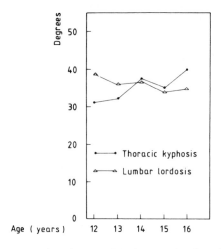

Figure 4 Mean degrees of kyphosis and lordosis in skier boys between the ages of 12 and 16 years.

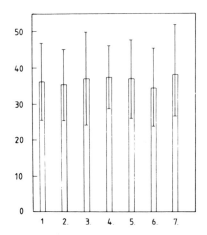

Figure 5 Mean degrees of kyphosis and lordosis in rural control boys between the ages of 12 and 16 years.

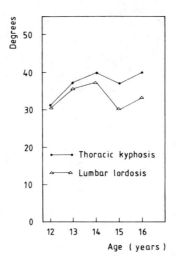

Figure 6 Mean degrees of kyphosis and lordosis in urban control boys between the ages of 12 and 16 years.

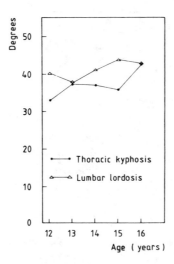

Figure 7 Mean degrees of kyphosis and lordosis in skier girls between the ages of 12 and 16 years.

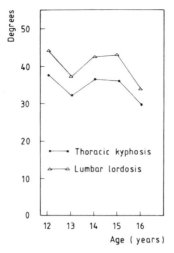

Figure 8 Mean degrees of kyphosis and lordosis in rural control girls between the ages of 12 and 16 years.

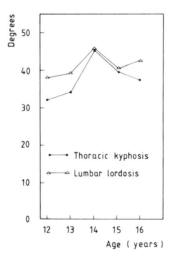

Figure 9 Mean degrees of kyphosis and lordosis in urban control girls between the ages of 12 and 16 years.

The highest degrees of lordosis were found generally in younger age groups. An exception was the group of rural control boys, in which the highest degree (43.6°) was noted at the age of 16 years. The highest mean degree of lumbar lordosis was found in 14-year-old urban girls (46°).

DISCUSSION

The method used in the determination of spinal sagittal curves has been shown to be reliable. The correlation with the values determined from radiographs was very high, especially in the case of thoracic kyphosis (Willner, 1981). In this study, the mean degree of thoracic kyphosis was highest in the oldest age group (16 years) in all three groups of boys. In each age group these results were generally comparable to those found in a study of Willner and Johnson (1983).

In girls, both control groups had the highest mean degree of kyphosis at the age of 14 years. This was the case also in the Swedish study (Willner & Johnson, 1983). In skier girls, the findings differed from those of control girls. Skier girls had the highest degree of kyphosis at the age of 16 years, and also in general their mean values of thoracic kyphosis corresponded with those of the boys.

Lordosis was more prominent in girls than in boys. This was the case also in the study of Willner and Johnson (1983). The highest degrees were found at the age of 16 years in rural boys. In all other groups, the highest values for lumbar lordosis were noticed between the ages 13 and 15 years. The differences between the groups were not statistically significant at any age level.

It is evident that the degrees of lumbar lordosis and thoracic kyphosis will change physiologically during the growing period and adolescence. A relationship between the growth velocity and degrees of sagittal spinal curves has been suggested. According to Willner and Johnson (1983), the kyphosis is least pronounced during the slow growth period. A statistical correlation has also been found between kyphosis and lordosis in adolescence (Willner & Johnson, 1983). The results of this study are in accordance with those of Willner and Johnson.

The mean degrees found in this study for thoracic kyphosis and lumbar lordosis were regarded as normal. Compared to the degrees presented by Willner and Johnson (1983), the mean degrees are higher in some age groups of each subgroup. However, a large variation must be considered as normal but, if a pathological situation is suspected, a follow-up should be arranged.

In cross-country skiing, mostly flexion-type movements of the trunk are performed against resistance. The effects of this type of movement on the shape of the vertebral column during adolescence should be systematically studied.

CONCLUSION

The spinal pantograph proved to be a suitable device for determining the degrees of the sagittal spinal curves in this study. No systematic differences were found, however, in the mean degrees of the sagittal spinal curves between the cross-country skiers and the control groups.

REFERENCES

Mahlamäki, S., Pekkarinen, H., & Hänninen, O. (1982). Low back disorders of adolescent Finnish cross-country skiers [in Finnish]. *Finnish Sports and Exercise Medicine, 1*, 62-65.

Willner, S. (1981). Spinal pantograph—A non-invasive technique for describing kyphosis and lordosis in the thoraco-lumbar spine. *Acta Orthopaedica Scandinavica, 52*, 525-529.

Willner, S., & Johnson, B. (1983). Thoracic kyphosis and lumbar lordosis during the growth period in children. *Acta Paediatrica Scandinavica, 72*, 873-878.

Part VIII
Physical Performance and Motor Learning

Age Dependency in the Development of Motor-Test Performance

János Mészáros
János Mohácsi
Róbert Frenkl
Hungarian University of Physical Education, Budapest, Hungary
Tamás Szabó
Iván Szmodis
Központi Sportiskola, Budapest, Hungary

In order to correctly evaluate the changes in the motor performance of regularly trained young athletes, the effects of spontaneous development must also be known. Only then can any actual functional improvement due to training be assessed with some degree of accuracy. The biological status of the developing child or adolescent exerts its influence not only on body size and physiological functions, but also on performance, though hereditary factors, inborn abilities, and the extent of physical activity naturally cannot be neglected, either.

Despite the importance of biological developmental status, the Hungarian studies reporting the changes in motor performance have rather consistently used calendar age as a grouping criterion (Mészáros & Szmodis, 1977; Mohácsi, Farkas, & Mészáros, 1983; Szabó, 1977). Only a few reports include biological age estimates among the variables (Szabó & Mészáros, 1980; Wahlstab & Dóka, 1970).

METHOD

The test scores in the 30-m dash, 1,200-m run, standing long jump, and fistball throw were studied relative to age in 562 regularly trained ball players and in 2,312 school children who were only active physically during curricular lessons of physical education (termed nonathletes). Chronologically, all of these children were between 10 and 15 years of age. Their morphological age was also obtained in order to utilize it as an independent variable. This age estimate based on stature, body mass, and Conrad's plastic index (Conrad, 1963) has been reported to be valid. Because this method has been discussed elsewhere (Mészáros, Mohácsi, & Szabó, 1983; Mészáros, Szmodis, Mohácsi, & Szabó, 1984), details will not be given here. The dependence of these motor test scores on age was studied by linear regression analysis. Correlation coefficients were compared by using z-transformations. Differences between the respective means were subjected to the student t-test using a probability level of 5% for statistical significance.

RESULTS AND DISCUSSION

Before the results of the regression analysis are presented, the groups are briefly described by the means of the variables.

The means of stature and of body mass in the respective peer groups of different physical activity levels were very similar. Both the means and within-group variance were rather close to the results found in comparable but much larger national samples (Mészáros & Mohácsi, 1983; Mészáros, Szmodis, & Mohácsi, 1979; Szmodis, Mészáros, & Szabó, 1976). The obtained mean values for growth types (Conrad, 1963) of the nonathletic age groups corresponded almost totally to the Hungarian standards. The children trained in ball games had more leptomorphic metric indices than their nonathletic peers, whereas their plastic index (referring to the developmental status of the musculoskeletal system) exceeded significantly, in every age group, the plastic index of the nonathletes.

Because of the fixed limits in classifying the subjects into age groups, the means of the chronological ages were not different. On the other hand, morphologically the ball players were consistently older. Consequently, the difference between morphological and chronological ages was also statistically significant in the athletic groups.

Because the plastic index is known to be closely related to both morphological and bone age (Mészáros & Mohácsi, 1983), older morphological age and larger plastic index convey the same meaning, namely, that the athletic children were more advanced physically than their peers. Their more linear body build, on the other hand, could not be attributed to biological factors. It was regarded as being due to the selection principles of the coaches. The same selection procedure was assumed to have led to the fact that the ball players were morphologically older than their chronological age and than their peers.

The athletic children performed better in the motor tests. Because the employed tests were closer to track and field exercises than to those involved in playing a ball game, the better performances had to be explained by the general effects of regular athletic training.

Table 1 summarizes the regression parameters in relation to chronological as well as morphological age. The observed improvement in performance could be quite well approximated by a straight line using either morphological or chronological age as a predictor. Several significant

Table 1 Regression Parameters in Relation to Ages

Variable	b	a	r	s_b
Nonathletes				
DA/30	−0.19	7.88	−0.46	0.40
DA/FBTH	3.55	−8.93	0.47	7.41
DA/1,200	−15.49	531.01	−0.35	45.72
DA/SLJ	6.64	98.97	0.32	21.67
MA/30	−0.34	9.68	−0.66	0.40
MA/FBTH	3.15	−3.47	0.59	7.32
MA/1,200	−12.25	488.72	−0.33	16.02
MA/SLJ	5.94	108.62	0.34	7.76
Athletes				
DA/30	−0.17	7.25	−0.67	0.27
DA/FBTH	3.80	−6.89	0.66	8.81
DA/1,200	−15.39	488.55	−0.80	24.07
DA/SLJ	10.48	55.58	0.67	17.96
MA/30	−0.17	7.57	−0.80	0.27
MA/FBTH	3.85	−7.01	0.75	8.11
MA/1,200	−15.45	493.15	−0.89	20.20
MA/SLJ	10.50	56.09	0.76	6.11

Note. DA = decimal age; 30 = 30-m dash; FBTH = fistball throw; 1,200 = 1,200-m run; SLJ = standing long jump; MA = morphological age; b = regression coefficient; a = y intercept; r = correlation coefficient; s_b = standard error of regression.

differences have been found, however, between the respective correlation coefficients used as a measure for the goodness of fit. It was found that in general the relationship of motor score to age was the weakest for chronological age in the nonathletic groups and the strongest for morphological age in the players' groups. Another consistent trend was that motor performance was more closely related to morphological age than to chronological age in both the athletic and the nonathletic groups.

The inference drawn from the analysis of regression slopes and intercepts was that these age-dependent regression lines were in fact parallel. The scatter around the regression lines was smaller when morphological age was used as the independent variable. Further, the lines of the athletic children showed a shift to the right along the age axis, because as mentioned they were morphologically older in all of the age groups.

These observations appeared quite obvious and according to expectation until analyses of the series of means and the age trend of the rates of change were undertaken. These are shown in Figures 1 to 4, in which means are indicated at the top and the respective rates of change at the bottom. To keep the plots more lucid, the symbols depicting variability were omitted. The possible changes expected to occur by 17 or 18 years of age are plotted as dotted lines for the nonathletic children relative to

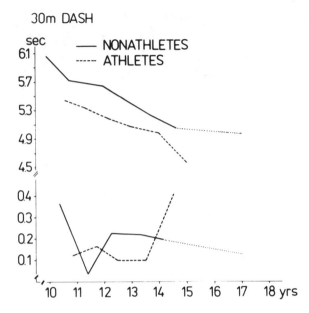

Figure 1 Means and rates of change of 30-m dash versus age.

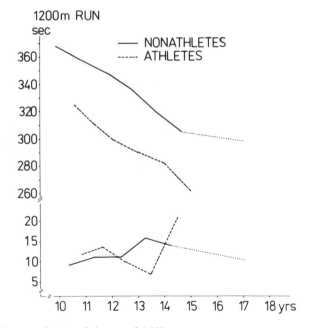

Figure 2 Means and rates of change of 1,200-m run versus age.

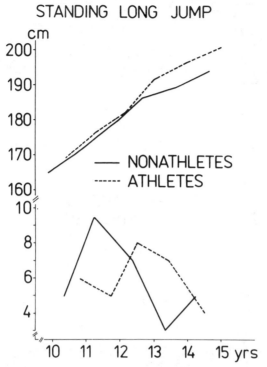

Figure 3   Means and rates of change of standing long jump versus age.

the national standards for the running events. It can be seen that the apparent parallel trend of the means was in part due to the fitting of a straight line. Actually the distance between the means was increasing, although not linearly, and therefore a considerable gap might be expected to develop by the age of 18 years.

The results obtained for the respective rates of change differed for the athletic and nonathletic subjects. While for the fistball throw the trends of the two groups were approximately the same (see Figure 4), in the other three tests the players' rates of change appeared to mirror those of the nonathletes. The differences in the trends of the means could be interpreted relatively easily. It must be a general conditioning effect of regular physical training that was manifested in the test scores. The marked difference in the rate of change is worth giving a second look. One of the possible interpretations may be that strength, endurance, and motor coordination follow different paths in individuals of different habitual physical activity. In the light of reports of qualitatively different functions in physically well-conditioned people from those in sedentary individuals (Frenkl, 1984), this assumption cannot be ruled out completely.

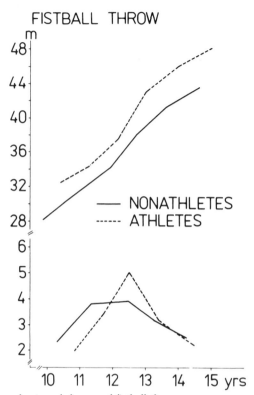

Figure 4 Means and rates of change of fistball throw versus age.

Another possible explanation would assume a similar course of development in physical abilities, but with different rates of change and different points of time for reaching the respective levels of performance. On first consideration, this assumption does not provide any immediate reason for the mirror-image trends described. In dealing with this aspect, however, one has to take the morphologically older age of the players into account. Regular physical training at this young age usually speeds up the rate of development in physical abilities. So, for instance, players were able to run 30 m as fast at the age of 13 years as nonathletes of 15 years, or the fistball was only thrown as far by the 15-year-old nonathletic child as by a player of 13 years of age. This kind of reasoning obviously holds between certain age limits only. Athletic children with a training history of 5 to 6 years sometimes have better performance scores at the age of 15 years than nonathletic adults. Consistent with this reasoning, if the plots of the rates of change are shifted by 1.5 to 2.5 years along the age axis, their course becomes much more similar for the two activity groups.

REFERENCES

Conrad, K. (1963). *Der Konstitutionstypus* (2nd ed.). Berlin: Springer-Verlag.

Frenkl, R. (1984). Sport és életkor. In R. Frenkl (Ed.), *Sportorvostan* (pp. 417-429). Budapest: Sport.

Mészáros, J., & Mohácsi, J. (1983). *The assessment of biological development and adult stature on the basis of the growth curves of Hungarian urban youth* [in Hungarian]. Unpublished doctoral thesis, Budapest.

Mészáros, J., Mohácsi, J., & Szabó, T. (1983, September). *Assessment of biological development by anthropometric variables.* Paper presented at Pediatric Work Physiology XI, Papendal, The Netherlands.

Mészáros, J., & Szmodis, I. (1977). Indices of physique and motor performance in pupils attending schools with a special physical education curriculum. In O.G. Eiben (Ed.), *Growth and development, physique* (pp. 253-260). Budapest: Akadémiai Kiadó.

Mészáros, J., Szmodis, I., & Mohácsi, J. (1979). The relationship of physique with physical education and sport training [in Hungarian]. *A Sport és Testnevelés Időszerü Kérdései*, **20**, 15-38.

Mészáros, J., Szmodis, I., Mohácsi, J., & Szabó, T. (1984). Prediction of final stature at the age of 11 to 13 years. In J. Ilmarinen & I. Välimäki (Eds.), *Children and sport* (pp. 31-36) (Paediatric Work Physiology). Berlin, New York: Springer-Verlag.

Mohácsi, J., Farkas, A., & Mészáros, J. (1983). The relationship of chronological age and motor test scores [in Hungarian]. *A Testnevelés Tanitása*, **2**, 51-53.

Szabó, T. (1977). The selection system for sport events in the central school of sports. I [in Hungarian] (pp. 3-54). Budapest: Utánpótlásnevelés, KSI.

Szabó, T., & Mészáros, J. (1980). Relationship of bone age, physical development and athletic performance at the age 11 to 12 years. *Anthropológiai Közlemények*, **24**, 263-267.

Szmodis, I., Mészáros, J., & Szabó, T. (1976). Relationships of indices of physique and function in children, adolescents and youths [in Hungarian, abstract in English]. *Testnevelés és—Sportegészségügyi Szemle*, **17**, 255-272.

Wahlstab, S., & Dóka, J. (1970). The importance of bone age in adolescent track and field athletes [in Hungarian]. *TF Tudományos Közleményei, Testnevelési Föiskola*, **4**, 287-290.

Physical Ability
of Deaf and Blind Children

Roy J. Shephard
Graham R. Ward
Mary Lee
University of Toronto and Variety Village, Toronto, Canada

Several authors have suggested previously that blind students have a low level of physical fitness, but that sensory deprivation encourages vigorous physical activity in the deaf, giving them a normal or above-average physical working capacity (Cumming, Goulding, & Baggley, 1971; Jankowski & Evans, 1981; Sündberg, 1982). Studies of blind students have described delays in the appearance of various motor skills (Adelson & Fraiberg, 1974; Winnick & Short, 1982); poor balance, gait, and locomotion (Buehl, 1979; Emes, in press); and low scores on the Kraus-Weber test (Seelye, 1983), in addition to a poor physical working capacity and maximum oxygen intake.

Details of disability, test methodology, and available programs of physical education have been sketchy in many of these reports. However, it has been widely hypothesized that the poor showing of the blind students is not due to any inherent limitation of capability, but rather to an overprotection by teachers and parents (Warren, 1976). We have now explored these points in a substantial sample of adolescent students, both deaf and blind, testing the latter in the fall, in the spring (after 4 months' participation in a rigorous program of endurance training), and again in the fall after a two-month vacation during which they were living with their parents.

METHODS

The deaf students (15 male and 14 female volunteers aged 13.5 ± 2.4 years) all had sufficient disability to require a hearing aid, but none had multiple disorders. A total of 15 were attending special classes within the Metropolitan Toronto School System, and the remaining 14 were enrolled at a residential school east of Toronto, generally returning to their homes on weekends. At the residential school, two 30-min periods of physical education were required per week, and this was also true for most of the students in the Toronto school system.

All of the blind students (10 males and 8 females aged 11 to 18 years) were attending a residential school for the blind west of Toronto; again, the majority returned to their homes for the weekends. Only 3 students had minimal light perception; the remainder were totally blind. However, no subject had any other organic disabilities. The school had a strong interest in physical education and offered four 45-min periods of vigorous endurance activity per week. In addition, the students were encouraged to explore the spacious grounds on their own, and occasional visits to town were made with a guide, to teach the use of a cane. During the period from November to March, three additional 60-min periods of endurance activity were given per week by the two physical education specialists at the school, to examine whether the fitness of the children could be further increased. Final tests were made the following September, after the students had spent a 2-month summer vacation with their parents.

Standard test methodology (Weiner & Lourie, 1981) was used throughout this study. Observations included the thickness of four skinfolds (biceps, triceps, subscapular, and suprailiac), direct measurements of maximal oxygen intake (made on a progressive cycle ergometer test, with 16.7 W increments of power output every minute to subjective exhaustion), PWC_{170}, and the distance run in 12 min. Questionnaires explored attitudes regarding leisure and perceived obstacles to physical activity.

RESULTS

Deaf Students

The physical characteristics and fitness status of the deaf students are summarized in Table 1. Subjects were a little shorter than the national average for their peers and also had a greater than desirable body fat, as estimated by the equations of Durnin and Womersley (1974). Only 7 of the 15 boys, and 5 of the 14 girls, reached the traditional definition of a plateau in the maximum oxygen intake test (oxygen consumption increasing by less than 2 ml/kg • min for a 16.7 W increment of power output). A total of 7 of the remaining subjects were judged to have fallen short of their true maximum on the basis of (a) a low maximum heart rate, (b) a low respiratory exchange ratio, or (c) a large shortfall of oxygen consumption relative to the maximum predicted by use of the Åstrand (1960) nomogram. Data for these individuals have been extrapolated in linear fashion to a maximum heart rate of 195 beats/min; this resulted in an upward adjustment of maximum oxygen intake of 3% in the boys and 4% in the girls. Other data (for PWC_{170} and distance run) are also presented in Table 1.

Table 1 **Physical Characteristics and Fitness Data for Deaf Students ($M \pm SD$)**

Variable	Male	Female
Age (yr)	13.5 ± 2.1	13.5 ± 2.7
Height (cm)	155.8 ± 10.3	152.0 ± 10.5
Body mass (kg)	45.3 ± 9.7	45.3 ± 12.3
Lean mass (kg)	37.0 ± 7.2	33.5 ± 7.2
Skinfolds ($\Sigma 4$) (mm)	31.9 ± 16.4	41.7 ± 17.3
Estimated body fat (%)	18.4 ± 4.4	26.0 ± 6.0
Maximum oxygen intake (ml · $kg^{-1}min^{-1}$)	42.1 ± 8.3	35.6 ± 6.5
	(43.6 ± 7.7)[a]	(37.0 ± 5.8)[a]
Maximum heart rate (beats · min^{-1})	188.0 ± 10.0	186.0 ± 10.0
Maximum respiratory gas exchange ratio	1.07 ± 0.11	1.10 ± 0.10
Δ Åstrand (ml · $kg^{-1}min^{-1}$)	5.2 ± 4.8	5.0 ± 4.4
Maximum power output (W)	153.0 ± 41.0	130.0 ± 25.0
	(153.0 ± 39.0)[a]	(135.0 ± 26.0)[a]
(W · kg^{-1})	3.34 ± 0.67	2.84 ± 0.57
	(3.45 ± 0.59)[a]	(2.93 ± 0.47)[a]
12 min run (km)	1.93 ± 0.44	1.70 ± 0.45
PWC_{170} (W)	112.1 ± 34.1	95.5 ± 27.4
(W · kg^{-1})	2.43 ± 0.54	2.02 ± 0.27

[a]Values extrapolated to heart rate of 195 beats/min^{-1} in 4 boys and 3 girls with low maximum heart rate, low maximum respiratory gas exchange ratio, and large difference from Åstrand prediction.

Blind Students

Physical characteristics and fitness data for the blind students are given in Table 2. In both sexes, a substantial deficit of height existed relative to normally sighted Canadians of the same age. In the girls, body fat was comparable with that seen in the deaf students, but the boys were a little thinner than those with hearing disabilities.

A total of 5 of the 10 boys, and 6 of the 8 girls, satisfied the criterion of an oxygen plateau. These individuals showed slightly higher values for maximum oxygen intake, respiratory gas exchange ratio, and a lesser discrepancy relative to the Åstrand prediction than did those who failed to reach a plateau (see Table 3). The fairly high initial aerobic power of the sample was confirmed by the PWC_{170} data, and although the distance run in 12 min was lower than in adults, it compared quite favorably with healthy children of the same age (see Table 2).

The response to the 4-month training program was generally small. Both sexes tended to lose fat (significantly so in the boys), and an associated small increase of body mass implied an accumulation of lean tissue. The increase in maximum oxygen intake was nonsignificant, but the increase in the power output at exhaustion in both sexes was significant (10%),

Table 2 Initial Characteristics of the Blind Children and Responses to a 4-Month Endurance Training Program ($M \pm SD$)

Variable	Males				Females			
	Initial value	After 4/12 training	Δ	After 2/12 vacation	Initial value	After 4/12 training	Δ	After 2/12 vacation
Height (cm)	165.2 ±8.4	165.9 ±8.0	0.7 ±1.0	168.6 ±6.8	153.8 ±5.2	154.6 ±5.1	0.8 ±0.9	153.9 ±4.2
Body mass (kg)	55.1 ±8.8	56.4 ±7.6	1.3 ±2.5	58.5 ±6.4	49.5 ±5.8	49.9 ±4.9	0.4 ±1.5	49.1 ±4.2
Skinfold thickness (Σ4) (mm)	26.9 ±6.7	24.1 ±4.5	-2.8* ±3.0	24.8 ±4.0	43.0 ±11.6	40.3 ±10.2	-2.7 ±4.6	47.8 ±15.9
Body fat (%)	16.1 ±3.0	14.9 ±2.2	-1.2* ±1.2	14.7 ±2.0	26.0 ±3.4	25.2 ±3.1	-0.8 ±1.4	27.1 ±3.9
Lean body mass (mg · cm^{-3})	10.2 ±0.8	10.5 ±0.6	0.3 ±0.4	10.3 ±0.7	10.2 ±0.8	10.1 ±0.7	-0.1 ±0.4	10.1 ±0.4
Maximum oxygen intake[a] (ml · kg^{-1}min^{-1})	50.4 ±7.5	51.7 ±6.8	1.3 ±4.2	44.9 ±6.7	37.0 ±6.3	38.0 ±5.0	1.0 ±2.5	33.8 ±3.7
Maximum heart rate (beats · min^{-1})	188 ±9				181 ±10			
Maximum respiratory gas exchange ratio	1.15 ±0.08				1.07 ±0.13			
Discrepancy from Åstrand prediction (l · min^{-1})	-0.07 ±0.48				-0.32 ±0.34			
Maximum power[a] (W)	196 ±39	215 ±33	18* ±18		130 ±27	144 ±30	14* ±14	
PWC$_{170}$ (kp · m · min^{-1}kg^{-1})	16.6 ±2.6	15.7 ±2.6	-0.9 ±1.8		12.8 ±2.0	11.9 ±2.5	-0.9 ±1.5	
12-min distance (km)	2.50 ±0.34	2.51 ±0.26	0.01 ±0.12	2.52 ±0.35	2.08 ±0.31	2.22 ±0.29	0.18 ±0.09**	2.09 ±1.36

[a] $n = 8$ for girls.

*$p < .05$; **$p < .001$.

Table 3   Comparison Between Present Data and Earlier Reported Values for Maximum
Oxygen Intake of Blind Children

Source	Age (yr)	Reported maximum oxygen intake (ml • kg⁻¹min⁻¹)	
		Boys	Girls
Cumming et al. (1971)	8 to 12	44.6	37.4
	13 to 17	44.6	33.6
Jankowski & Evans (1981)	4 to 18	29.0[a]	29.0[a]
Sündberg (1982)	8 to 14	45.3	36.8
Present study			
All subjects	11 to 18	49.8	37.0
"Good" maxima	11 to 18	53.2	36.0

[a]Average, both sexes.

and the girls also showed a 7% increase in running speed. Over the summer vacation, some of these gains were lost. The females showed a moderate but variable (and therefore statistically nonsignificant) increase of body fat, and both sexes showed a significant 13% to 14% decrement of maximum oxygen intake. The females also showed a 10% decrease in their 12-min running distance.

DISCUSSION

The sample of deaf students (see Table 4) had a physical working capacity very comparable to that described by Cumming et al. (1971). However, it was not outstanding relative to other Canadian students of similar age, and thus the hypothesis that sensory deprivation stimulates physical activity was rejected. In this group, some evidence existed that physical activity was impeded by difficulties of communication and that they could have profited from an enhanced exercise program.

The data also fail to support the concept that physical working capacity is necessarily poor in blind students. When a school has an adequate activity program, the standards attained may be at least as good as for normally sighted individuals. If this is not the case, the implication is that the school's program of physical education needs strengthening. In this sample, the standard school program was of sufficient quality that little was gained from an additional 3 hours of endurance training per week. However, this is not evidence that children are untrainable; indeed, the students lost a substantial proportion of their physical condition over the subsequent summer vacation period. Responses to the activity questionnaire indicated a considerable decrease in daily exercise on returning

Table 4 Comparison of Present Data With an Earlier Study (Cumming et al., 1971) of Deaf Children

Variable	Boys			Girls		
	Present sample 13.5 yr	Cumming et al. 8 to 12 yr	13 to 17 yr	Present sample 13.5 yr	Cumming et al. 8 to 12 yr	13 to 17 yr
Height (cm)	155.8	144	164	152.9	149	161
Body mass (kg)	45.3	37.3	57.2	45.3	46.3	52.3
Body fat (%)	18.4	16.0	18.0	26.0	25.5	23.4
PWC$_{170}$ (W • kg^{-1})	2.43	2.38	2.50	2.02	1.90	1.95
Maximum oxygen intake (ml • kg^{-1}min^{-1}STPD)	42.1 (43.6)[a]	43.8	45.2	35.6 (37.0)[a]	37.0	37.6

[a]Extrapolating presumed low values for 4 boys and 3 girls.

home, the main reason being a lack of sighted guides. If physical condition is to be maintained when students leave their special schools, they should learn activities that can be pursued on their own, without special facilities or equipment.

When blind students ran on a track with a guide rail, their mechanical efficiency (as judged from the ratio of VO_2max to 12-min distance) appeared to be similar to that of other young people of the same age. The deficit of stature was also intriguing. On average, the blind students were 5 cm shorter than expected. In some samples, defects of growth have been blamed upon associated endocrine disorders such as cretinism, but these students were otherwise healthy. It may be that growth was inhibited by a lack of physical activity during the period prior to enrollment in the special school (tuition began at the age of 5 years); however, since the age of 5 years, exercise patterns have been as extensive as in any other group of children.

CONCLUSION

Vigorous programs of physical activity seem desirable for both deaf and blind students. If such programs are provided, fitness status is comparable with that of other children.

Acknowledgment

This research was supported in part by research grants from Health and Welfare Canada and from the Bickell Foundation.

REFERENCES

Adelson, E., & Fraiberg, S. (1974). Gross motor development in infants blind from birth. *Child Development, 45*, 114-126.

Åstrand, I. (1960). Aerobic work capacity in men and women with special reference to age. *Acta Physiologica Scandinavica, 49* (Suppl. 169), 1-92.

Buehl, A.N. (1979). The effects of creative dance movement on large muscle control and balance in congenitally blind children. *Journal of Visual Impairment and Blindness, 73*, 127-133.

Cumming, G.R., Goulding, D., & Baggley, G. (1971). Working capacity of deaf, and visually and mentally handicapped children. *Archives of Disease in Childhood, 46*, 490-494.

Durnin, J.V.G.A., & Womersley, J. (1974). Body fat assessed from total body density and its estimation from skinfold thickness. *British Journal of Nutrition, 37*, 77-86.

Emes, C. (in press). Modifying motor behavior of blind children for participation in sport and physical activity. In C. Sherrill (Ed.), *Sport for the disabled*. Champaign, IL: Human Kinetics.

Jankowski, L.W., & Evans, J.K. (1981). The exercise capacity of blind children. *Journal of Visual Impairment and Blindness, 75*, 248-251.

Seelye, W. (1983). Physical fitness of blind and visually impaired Detroit public school children. *Journal of Visual Impairment and Blindness, 77*, 117-118.

Sündberg, S. (1982). Maximal oxygen uptake in relation to age in blind and normal boys and girls. *Acta Paediatrica Scandinavica, 71*, 603-608.

Warren, D.H. (1976). Blindness and early development: What is known and what needs to be studied. *New Outlook for the Blind, 70*, 5-16.

Weiner, J.S., & Lourie, J.A. (1981). *Practical human biology*. Oxford, U.K.: Blackwell Scientific.

Winnick, J.P., & Short, F.X. (1982). *The physical fitness of sensory and orthopaedically impaired youth*. Report to special education programs. Washington, DC: U.S. Department of Education.

Anthropometric Measures of Young Finnish Cross-Country Skiers and Control Children

Heikki A. Pekkarinen
Seppo T. Mahlamäki
University of Kuopio, Kuopio, Finland

Currently athletic training and competition are commonly accepted as not retarding the physical growth and development of youngsters (Malina, Meleski, & Shoup, 1982). The differences found in anthropometric measurements when comparisons are made between young athletes in different sports and also between athletes and nonathletes are believed to be based mainly on genetic growth regulation (Peltenburg et al., 1984) and to be the results of a selection process by the youngster, by parents and coaches, or by both (Malina et al., 1982).

Swimmers and gymnasts are probably the most studied young athletes, when considering growth. Both boy and girl swimmers have been found to be taller than nonathletic boys and girls of similar age (Andrew, Becklake, Guleria, & Bates, 1972; Malina et al., 1982). Girl gymnasts (Bernink, Erich, Peltenburg, Zonderland, & Huisveld, 1983) and also boy gymnasts (Buckler & Brodie, 1977) usually have been reported to be shorter than nonathletes of a similar age. Both of these groups probably benefit from their particular physique in their sports, even though a youngster's anthropometric characteristics alone do not determine successful performance (Malina et al., 1982).

In cross-country skiing, there is no obvious anthropometrically determined "skier type," at least so far. This might also be one reason for the popularity of cross-country skiing in Nordic countries for all age groups. In this study, an attempt was made to evaluate the growth characteristics of young cross-country skiers and compare them to those of normally active school children of similar age.

METHOD

A total of 441 school children in eastern Finland, aged 10 to 14 years, volunteered for this study in the spring of 1982. The skier group consisted of 133 boys and 100 girls, most of them from rural areas, and all members of cross-country ski teams. The rest of the children were divided into rural and urban control groups, 52 boys and girls in each group. About half of the boys and a third of the girls in both control groups were members of sport clubs.

Height and weight were measured according to IBP-recommendations (Tanner, Hiernaux, & Jarman, 1969), using a light aluminum anthropometer connected to a Seca balanced weighing scale (Vogel & Halke, West Germany). The body mass index (BMI) was calculated. Triceps, biceps, subscapular, and suprailiac skinfolds (Durnin & Womersley, 1974) were measured with the Lange skinfold caliper (Cambridge Scientific Industries, Maryland). The measurements took place in the schools during normal school days. They were repeated in 1983 and 1984. During the follow-up, the total dropout was 9%.

The statistical analysis was performed at the University of Kuopio using the SPSS-program (Morrison, 1982). Pearson product-moment correlation coefficients were calculated for assessing the year-to-year correlations between the anthropometric measures. The differences between the groups were tested with an analysis of variance and Scheffe's test when significant F-ratios were found.

RESULTS

The year-to-year correlations (1982-1983, 1983-1984) for all subjects in height were .98 and .97. In weight, the correlations were .96 and .95, respectively (see Table 1). For skinfold measures, the correlations varied from .81 to .87, with the sum of four skinfolds having higher correlations than single skinfold measures. Among the single skinfolds, the subscapular thickness had the highest year-to-year correlations. No major differences were found in correlations among the groups, although the correlations in skinfold measures in skier boys were a little lower than in the other groups.

The initial measures and the yearly growth of each age group are presented in Table 2. In boys, the differences were not significant between the skiers and rural controls. For the urban boys, however, the growth in the second year, and the total growth during the two follow-up years, was greater ($p < .05$) than in skier boys. Between the two control groups, the differences were not statistically significant. For girls, no statistical differences in growth were found among the groups. The corresponding results in weight are presented in Table 3. The differences among the groups were not statistically significant in either sex. In the body mass index (see Table 4) no major differences were found among the groups. In the first measurements, BMI in rural boys was higher ($p < .05$) than in skier boys, but during the follow-up the difference disappeared.

In the beginning of the study, skier boys had significantly lower sum of four skinfolds than boys in the control groups (see Table 5). In girls the trend was similar, even though the differences were not statistically

Table 1 Pearson Correlation Coefficients Between the Yearly Measures in Height, Weight, and Four Skinfolds (Triceps, Biceps, Subscapular, Suprailiac) in Young Cross-Country Skiers and Control Children

	1982-1983				1983-1984				1982-1984			
	T	S	RC	UC	T	S	RC	UC	T	S	RC	UC
Boys												
Height	.98	.99	.99	.98	.97	.98	.98	.97	.91	.95	.95	.93
Weight	.96	.97	.98	.97	.95	.97	.97	.97	.90	.95	.94	.93
Triceps	.81	.69	.80	.82	.85	.79	.91	.82	.72	.59	.73	.70
Biceps	.82	.70	.86	.85	.85	.70	.90	.87	.77	.39	.75	.86
Subscapular	.86	.48	.90	.90	.85	.69	.84	.82	.78	.57	.86	.80
Suprailiac	.83	.71	.87	.83	.82	.68	.91	.85	.76	.57	.87	.83
Sum of skinfolds	.87	.67	.89	.87	.86	.72	.92	.85	.81	.59	.86	.83
Girls												
Height	.98	.97	.98	.97	.97	.96	.97	.96	.91	.88	.92	.88
Weight	.96	.94	.97	.95	.95	.95	.86	.93	.90	.89	.83	.87
Triceps	.81	.81	.77	.79	.85	.85	.82	.69	.72	.68	.72	.57
Biceps	.82	.77	.73	.82	.85	.84	.83	.71	.77	.82	.76	.78
Subscapular	.86	.85	.86	.91	.85	.87	.82	.81	.78	.75	.73	.83
Suprailiac	.83	.82	.82	.85	.82	.82	.81	.76	.76	.76	.73	.69
Sum of skinfolds	.87	.87	.86	.90	.86	.87	.85	.79	.81	.78	.80	.85

Note. T = all boys and girls; S = skiers; RC = rural controls; UC = urban controls.

Table 2 Initial Height and the Yearly Increase in Height (M ± SD; mm) in Young Cross-Country Skiers and Control Children

Age (yr)		Skiers						Rural controls						Urban controls				
	n	1982	n	82-83	n	83-84	n	1982	n	82-83	n	83-84	n	1982	n	82-83	n	83-84
Boys																		
10	32	1410±51	30	52±7	28	50±11	11	1389±46	11	52±9	11	63±22	10	1436±31	10	58±16	8	72±24
11	20	1477±65	19	60±20	16	62±21	10	1470±50	10	58±8	10	70±18	11	1480±51	11	65±25	11	64±18
12	30	1494±67	29	68±23	26	67±21	11	1530±76	10	73±23	9	78±27	10	1525±76	10	72±21	10	79±16
13	21	1603±89	20	75±28	20	55±23	10	1569±88	10	80±17	9	57±19	11	1579±78	10	67±17	9	64±19
14	30	1689±84	28	52±22	27	25±17	10	1684±64	10	60±19	8	26±24	10	1622±90	10	72±25	10	53±27
Total	133	1532±125		61±22		50±24	52	1526±118		64±19		60±27	52	1529±94		67±21		66±22*
		1982 to 1984 = 110±39						1982 to 1984 = 124±38						1982 to 1984 = 133±35*				
Girls																		
10	24	1437±57	20	67±16	20	63±16	10	1402±58	9	69±21	9	66±11	10	1450±65	10	71±13	9	62±15
11	19	1490±62	16	71±10	16	46±19	10	1464±72	10	61±22	10	47±24	10	1487±70	10	74±13	10	40±15
12	19	1561±71	18	53±22	17	29±21	12	1608±78	9	45±22	9	22±18	13	1519±62	12	61±15	12	36±12
13	22	1583±45	17	34±17	13	15±12	10	1605±64	10	38±23	9	16±14	10	1623±59	10	35±16	9	15±11
14	16	1637±52	16	22±11	13	9±9	10	1640±39	10	15±4	9	1±5	9	1617±41	8	22±5	8	4±6
Total	100	1535±91		50±24		36±26	52	1546±112		45±27		31±28	52	1536±90		54±24		33±23
		1982 to 1984 = 88±46						1982 to 1984 = 76±51						1982 to 1984 = 85±44				

*p < .05 (vs. skiers).

Table 3 Initial Weight and the Yearly Increase in Weight ($M \pm SD$; kg) in Young Cross-Country Skiers and Control Children

Age (yr)	Skiers			Rural controls			Urban controls		
	1982	82-83	83-84	1982	82-83	83-84	1982	82-83	83-84
Boys[a]									
10	33.2± 3.9	2.8±1.4	3.5±1.3	32.4± 4.7	3.4±1.4	4.9± 1.9	36.7±5.8	4.3±2.5	4.5±2.3
11	36.3± 5.2	3.9±2.1	4.4±2.7	39.4± 7.0	3.8±2.0	5.5± 2.6	39.4±5.0	3.3±2.3	4.9±2.6
12	38.7± 6.0	4.8±2.4	6.2±2.2	43.7± 7.8	5.6±3.6	6.8± 3.8	40.9±5.5	5.7±3.1	5.2±1.4
13	46.8± 9.1	7.0±4.7	6.3±4.1	45.1± 5.6	6.2±2.2	5.7± 2.4	46.1±7.9	5.5±2.7	4.9±3.2
14	55.6± 7.5	5.2±2.9	4.5±3.4	58.6± 9.2	3.7±1.7	3.9± 2.6	48.8±9.6	5.9±2.1	6.3±3.3
Total	42.1±10.6	4.6±3.1	4.9±3.0	43.6±11.0	4.5±2.5	5.4± 2.7	42.4±8.0	4.9±2.7	5.2±2.6
	1982 to 1984 = 9.4±4.1			1982 to 1984 = 9.8±3.9			1982 to 1984 = 10.2±4.0		
Girls[a]									
10	35.2± 5.7	5.0±2.6	5.0±2.2	31.8± 4.7	3.3±1.7	4.8± 2.7	35.9±4.7	3.6±1.9	5.7±2.2
11	39.1± 6.6	6.0±2.9	5.1±2.1	36.7± 7.7	5.0±3.2	8.0±11.3	39.4±6.3	5.1±1.5	3.9±2.5
12	43.5± 6.7	4.3±3.2	4.6±2.3	51.9±12.7	4.1±4.0	3.2± 3.6	42.0±8.3	6.4±2.3	3.5±4.3
13	48.5± 7.0	3.6±2.2	2.3±2.8	45.4± 4.8	2.2±2.7	3.4± 3.2	49.1±8.5	2.7±3.0	2.5±2.8
14	50.2± 4.9	2.4±3.3	3.2±4.1	55.5± 4.7	2.1±2.2	1.3± 2.1	49.5±5.0	2.3±2.7	2.6±1.0
Total	42.8± 8.4	4.2±3.0	4.2±2.9	44.5±11.7	3.3±3.0	4.2± 6.1	43.0±8.4	4.2±2.7	3.7±3.0
	1982 to 1984 = 8.6±4.5			1982 to 1984 = 7.6±6.8			1982 to 1984 = 7.8±4.2		

[a]Number of subjects same as in Table 2.

Table 4   Body Mass Index (BMI, kg/m²) in 1982, 1983, and 1984 in Young Cross-Country Skiers and Control Children

Age (yr)	Skiers			Rural controls			Urban controls		
	1982	1983	1984	1982	1983	1984	1982	1983	1984
Boys[a]									
10	16.6±1.2	16.7±1.5	17.4±1.6	16.8±1.8	17.2±2.0	17.9±2.0	17.7±2.3	18.2±2.5	18.9±2.2
11	16.6±1.5	17.0±1.7	17.2±1.6	18.2±2.9	18.5±3.2	19.1±3.8	17.9±1.6	17.8±1.6	18.3±2.1
12	17.2±1.4	17.7±1.5	18.4±1.7	18.6±2.1	18.6±1.9	19.6±2.0	17.5±1.4	18.2±2.1	18.4±1.7
13	18.1±1.9	19.0±2.2	19.8±2.2	18.3±1.5	18.9±1.6	19.4±1.2	18.4±2.1	19.0±2.5	19.5±2.8
14	19.4±1.7	19.9±2.0	20.8±2.0	20.5±2.1	20.4±2.0	20.9±2.0	18.4±1.8	18.9±1.7	19.9±1.9
Total	17.6±1.9	18.0±2.1	18.8±2.3	18.4±2.3*	18.7±2.4	19.3±2.5	18.0±1.8	18.4±2.1	19.0±2.2
Girls[a]									
10	17.0±2.4	17.7±3.1	18.3±3.5	16.1±1.8	15.8±1.6	16.7±1.9	17.0±1.2	17.0±1.5	18.0±2.0
11	17.5±1.8	18.2±2.3	19.2±2.6	17.0±2.1	17.8±2.5	20.0±4.3	17.8±2.3	18.2±2.4	18.9±2.5
12	17.8±1.9	18.2±1.6	19.3±1.8	19.8±3.3	20.5±3.1	21.0±2.5	18.1±3.0	19.4±3.0	20.0±3.0
13	19.4±2.8	19.9±2.7	20.4±2.6	17.6±1.3	17.6±0.8	18.7±1.2	18.5±2.2	18.8±1.6	19.5±1.5
14	18.7±1.2	19.1±1.5	20.1±1.6	20.7±2.1	21.1±2.2	21.5±2.6	19.0±2.1	19.6±2.1	20.1±2.4
Total	18.0±2.3	18.6±2.4	19.3±2.6	18.3±2.8	18.6±2.8	19.6±3.2	18.1±2.3	18.6±2.4	19.3±2.4

[a]Number of subjects same as in Table 2.
*$p < .05$ (vs. skiers).

Table 5 Initial Sum of the Four Skinfolds (Triceps, Biceps, Subscapular, Suprailiac) and the Yearly Change in the Sum (mm) in Young Cross-Country Skiers and Control Children

Age (yr)	Skiers			Rural controls			Urban controls		
	1982	82-83	83-84	1982	82-83	83-84	1982	82-83	83-84
Boys[a]									
10	28.1± 8.9	1.3± 8.1	0.2± 6.2	31.0±14.2	6.5± 7.5	-0.2± 8.7	34.7±17.5	11.7±13.0	-7.4±12.8
11	27.8±10.0	0.5±10.5	-2.1± 9.8	39.9±23.2	7.5±12.1	10.0± 7.7	35.3±12.7	2.2± 7.3	-0.9± 9.7
12	28.0± 8.3	-0.4± 5.9	1.1± 8.2	34.1±16.0	1.6± 7.8	-4.2± 8.6	35.1± 7.1	6.6±17.2	-11.8±12.8
13	27.3± 5.7	-1.6± 5.3	3.1± 6.1	30.5±13.9	3.7± 9.9	-4.3±12.4	44.3±22.5	2.7±10.0	-7.8±11.3
14	31.1± 9.4	-0.9± 8.2	1.8± 9.3	41.3±21.2	-4.0± 8.7	-2.5± 3.9	32.2±11.0	-0.6± 5.7	2.9± 9.6
Total	28.6± 8.6	-0.1± 7.7	0.9± 8.0	35.2±17.9*	3.1± 9.8	-1.9± 8.6	36.5±15.3*	4.5±11.7*	-4.6±12.0*
		1982 to 1984 = 1.3±9.4			1982 to 1984 = 1.3±11.0			1982 to 1984 = 0.3±10.9	
Girls[a]									
10	36.5±14.6	8.6±12.7	-3.5±13.0	36.9±16.5	-0.1± 4.4	-0.5±12.0	37.7± 7.3	4.2± 4.4	-0.8±11.8
11	39.3±14.9	7.1±14.7	4.7±11.5	36.4±10.8	10.0±15.6	1.9±16.1	43.6±14.1	9.0± 7.8	-4.2±11.1
12	37.4±14.6	3.7± 8.2	6.7± 5.4	49.1±20.7	11.6±11.5	3.2±15.0	42.3±20.5	13.7±16.3	-0.3±22.3
13	41.2±16.7	6.7±10.4	0.8±12.9	36.5±12.0	0.5±10.2	4.7±13.2	42.0± 8.5	5.9± 9.1	2.8± 7.4
14	40.2± 8.0	3.1± 8.0	1.3± 9.0	57.6±24.2	10.2±13.0	-0.8± 9.4	47.2±14.8	8.1±10.5	1.1± 5.4
Total	38.8±14.2	5.9±11.1	1.8±11.2	43.5±19.1	6.4±12.1	1.7±12.9	42.3±14.1	8.4±10.8	-0.4±13.5
		1982 to 1984 = 8.1±14.0			1982 to 1984 = 7.9±13.8			1982 to 1984 = 8.1±11.5	

Note. A "−" preceding a value signifies a decrease.

[a]Number of subjects same as in Table 2.

*$p < .05$ (vs. skiers).

significant. During the study the differences between the groups remained quite stable. The yearly change in the sum of four skinfolds between skier and urban control boys was different ($p < .05$). However, because of the opposite directions of changes in consecutive years, there were no statistical differences between the groups in total changes in the sum of four skinfolds. In girls, differences in changes during the follow-up were not statistically significant.

DISCUSSION

The skill level of the skier group was good to excellent. Some were top national level skiers in their age groups; others did not train regularly but were on teams and participated in a few competitions during the winter season. The most active skiers participated in more than 20 competitions during the winter season. The most active skiers participated in a few competitions during the winter. Among the controls, the percentage of subjects who were members of a sport club was quite similar to that reported previously in Finland (Telama & Laakso, 1983). Many of the boys in the control groups were on soccer and ice-hockey teams, which are especially popular at this age in eastern Finland. On the other hand, only a few of the control subjects were involved in endurance training.

Differences in anthropometry among the groups were not major. The differences found in the increase of height during the follow-up between skier and urban control boys can be explained mostly by the greater growth of the older group of urban boys. At the end of the follow-up, however, no differences in height were found in that age group either. In general, the height and weight data of this study were quite similar to those reported in a recent Finnish growth study (Ojajärvi, 1982). During puberty, both the boys and the girls are taller and heavier than 10 years ago in Finland.

The sum of the skinfolds, and thus the amount of subcutaneous fat, was less in skiers at the beginning of the study. That might have been due to training, which usually involves development of endurance. On the other hand, the differences among the groups remained quite unchanged during the study. Thus, the differences noticed can also be due to selection of certain types of children for endurance training. The selection obviously takes place at quite an early age. In girls, the differences in the sum of four skinfolds between skiers and controls were not as great as in boys. It may also be that girl skiers in these age groups are not training hard enough to affect the body fat.

CONCLUSION

These results support the findings of Malina et al. (1982) that physical growth is not affected by training. Young cross-country skiers do not differ much anthropometrically from other school children. In traditional cross-country skiing, the size of the body has not been a major determinant for success. The new skating-like style of cross-country skiing, however, will probably result in the determination of a "skier type" and then the emphasis will be on the selection of youth.

REFERENCES

Andrew, G.M., Becklake, M.R., Guleria, J.S., & Bates, D.V. (1972). Heart and lung functions in swimmers and nonathletes during growth. *Journal of Applied Physiology*, **32**, 245-251.

Bernink, M.J.E., Erich, W.B.M., Peltenburg, A.L., Zonderland, M.L., & Huisveld, I.A. (1983). Height, body composition, biological maturation and training in relation to socio-economic status in girl gymnasts, swimmers, and controls. *Growth*, **47**, 1-12.

Buckler, J.M.H., & Brodie, D.A. (1977). Growth and maturity characteristics of schoolboy gymnasts. *Annals of Human Biology*, **4**, 455-463.

Durnin, J.V.G.A., & Womersley, J. (1974). Body fat assessed from total body density and its estimation from skinfold thickness: Measurements on 481 men and women aged from 16 to 72 years. *British Journal of Nutrition*, **32**, 77-97.

Malina, R.M., Meleski, B.W., & Shoup, R.F. (1982). Anthropometric, body composition, and maturity characteristics of selected school-age athletes. *Pediatric Clinics of North America*, **29**, 1305-1323.

Morrison, N.K. (1982). *The SPSS batch system for the Dec PDP-11* (2nd ed.). New York: McGraw-Hill.

Ojajärvi, P. (1982). *The adolescent Finnish child*. A longitudinal study of the anthropometry, physical development and physiological changes during puberty [in Finnish with English summary]. Unpublished doctoral dissertation, University of Helsinki.

Peltenburg, A.L., Erich, W.B.M., Zonderland, M.L., Bernink, M.J.E., Van Den-Brande, J.L., & Huisveld, I.A. (1984). A retrospective growth study of female gymnasts and girl swimmers. *International Journal of Sports Medicine*, **5**, 262-267.

Tanner, J.M., Hiernaux, J., & Jarman, S. (1969). Growth and physique studies. In J.S. Weiner & J.A. Lourie (Eds.), *Human biology. A guide to field methods* (pp. 1-76) (IPB handbook, No. 9). Oxford: Blackwell.

Telama, R., & Laakso, R. (1983). Leisure-time physical activity. In Health habits among Finnish youth [in Finnish with English summary]. Publications of the National Board of Health, Finland Health Education, Series original reports **4**, 212-213.

Growth Selection of Young Boys Participating in Different Sports

Leo Leif Österback
Jukka Viitasalo
University of Jyväskylä, Jyväskylä, Finland

Today, children start serious athletic training at earlier ages than ever before. This has led to an increasing interest in the possible effects of strenuous exercise on growth. However, hardly any scientific publications about growth and biological development of children participating in different sport activities can be found (Peltenburg et al., 1984).

Evidence concerning the effects of exercise on bone growth is conflicting. A certain minimum of physical activity is necessary to support normal growth (Bailey, Malina, & Rasmussen, 1978). The possible negative effects of strenuous exercise are still unknown. Lamb et al. (1969) reported that forced swimming in prepubertal rats resulted in reduced length of tibias and femora but similar data for children are difficult to find. Kato and Ishiko (1966) reported reduced epiphyseal growth in the lower extremities of Japanese children who were exposed to strenuous physical labor. These children had to carry excessive loads on their shoulders and this was thought to reduce stature. On the other hand, these children lived in quite a poor environment, which could affect growth. There are also some data that suggest an increase in stature with physical training, but no consistent evidence has been found (Malina, 1979).

Young male athletes often tend to be maturationally advanced as compared to nonathletes. These differences seem more apparent in sports or positions within sports where size is important (Bailey et al., 1978). Young athletes are a highly selected group, usually chosen on the basis of size and skill. Larger size is an advantage in a number of sports and can be a limiting factor in others (Bailey et al., 1978). According to Malina (1979) regular physical activity does not accelerate or retard skeletal maturity. Those advanced at one age are most likely to be advanced at later ages, and vice versa (Malina, 1984). The differences in body size and maturity seen in different sports are either mainly based on genetic factors or show effects of strenuous training. The aim of this study was to examine growth selection of young boys in different sports.

METHOD

Growth selection may be explained by examining body height, skeletal age, and predicted adult height in boys participating in ice hockey, basketball, apparatus gymnastics, and wrestling. The subjects of this study, by age and sport, are shown in Table 1. Mean ages of the ice-hockey players, apparatus gymnasts, and wrestlers did not differ; the basketball players were younger. A postal questionnaire was used to collect information on the training background of the subjects. All of the boys had participated in regular sports training for an average of 4.5 years (see Table 2). The ice-hockey players had started their training earlier than had the wrestlers and basketball players. At the time of the study (spring, 1985) they trained 3 to 4 times a week (see Table 2). The gymnasts and ice-hockey players trained more often than basketball players and wrestlers.

Body height was measured with an accuracy of 0.1 cm. Skeletal age was estimated from radiographs of the left hand and wrist following the procedures of Greulich and Pyle (1959). Mean skeletal age determined

Table 1 Subjects of the Study by Age and Sport

Group	N	Age (yr) M ± SD
Ice-hockey players	50	13.8 ± 0.3
Apparatus gymnasts	26	13.9 ± 2.2
Basketball players	41	12.5 ± 0.5
Wrestlers	60	13.9 ± 2.2
Total	177	13.6 ± 1.7

Table 2 Participation in Regular Training

Group	Years M ± SD	Exercises/week M ± SD
Ice-hockey players	5.7 ± 1.4	3.8 ± 0.9
Apparatus gymnasts	4.7 ± 2.2	4.3 ± 1.4
Basketball players	3.7 ± 1.6	3.0 ± 0.8
Wrestlers	3.8 ± 2.9	2.8 ± 0.9

by the same physician in two assessments was used in further calculations. These estimations were highly correlated (Pearson's product-moment correlation coefficient $r = .99$). Adult height was predicted from the tables of Bayley and Pinneau (1952) using separately both assessments of skeletal age. These adult-height predictions were also highly correlated (Pearson's product-moment correlation coefficient $r = .95$).

The intergroup tests were conducted using analysis of variance (ANOVA) procedures in association with the multiple comparison LSD test. In comparing only two groups, the student t-test was used.

RESULTS

Mean body height grouped by sport is shown in Table 3. The ice-hockey players were taller than apparatus gymnasts and wrestlers, but no difference was found between basketball players and the other groups. Mean skeletal age did not differ significantly from mean chronological age among the ice-hockey and basketball players. A statistically significant difference was observed between mean skeletal and chronological age of the gymnasts and the wrestlers (see Table 4). When comparing skeletal age among the sport groups (chronological age – skeletal age) the gymnasts were skeletally delayed as compared to basketball and ice-hockey players, and the wrestlers were delayed as compared to basketball players (see Figure 1).

Predicted adult height was significantly greater among basketball players than in any of the other groups studied (see Figure 2). Even the hockey players were predicted to be taller than the gymnasts and the wrestlers. Because the gymnasts and the wrestlers were skeletally delayed as compared to the other groups and as compared to their own chronological age, they were divided by age into a younger group (age beneath the mean) and an older group (age above the mean) (see Table 5). The younger groups seemed to be more delayed skeletally (see Table 6), but in predicted adult height there were no differences (see Table 7).

Table 3 Mean Height Grouped by Sport

Group	n	Height (cm) $M \pm SD$	Significance (LSD test)
Ice-hockey players	48	164.7 ± 6.9	$p < .001$
Apparatus gymnasts	26	153.7 ± 13.0	
Basketball players	41	159.4 ± 7.3	$p < .001$
Wrestlers	59	155.8 ± 15.2	

Note. One-way ANOVA $F = 7.45$; $p < .001$.

Table 4 Chronological and Skeletal Age by Sport

Group	Chronological age (yr) M ± SD	Skeletal age (yr) M ± SD	Significance
Ice-hockey players	13.8 ± 0.3	13.6 ± 0.9	ns
Apparatus gymnasts	13.9 ± 2.2	12.9 ± 2.7	p < .001
Basketball players	12.5 ± 0.5	12.5 ± 1.2	ns
Wrestlers	13.9 ± 2.2	13.3 ± 2.8	p < .001

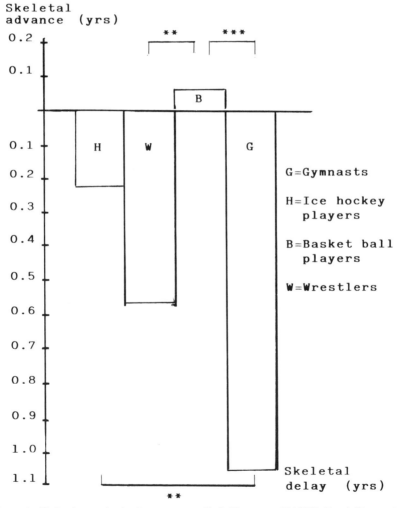

Figure 1 Skeletal maturity in the groups studied. [One-way ANOVA F = 6.67, p < .001; significance levels (LSD multiple comparisons) p < .01**, p < .001***]

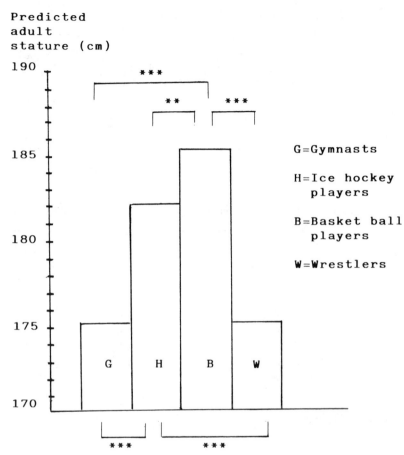

Figure 2 Predicted adult height in the groups studied. [One-way ANOVA F = 34.51, p < .001; significance levels (LSD multiple comparisons) p < .01**, p < .001***]

Table 5 Gymnasts and Wrestlers Divided Into Two Subgroups by Age

Group	N	Age (yr) M ± SD
Younger athletes (< the mean)		
Gymnasts	17	12.5 ± 0.7
Wrestlers	30	12.1 ± 1.4
Total	47	12.2 ± 1.2
Older athletes (> the mean)		
Gymnasts	9	16.7 ± 1.2
Wrestlers	30	15.7 ± 1.1
Total	39	15.9 ± 1.2

Table 6 Skeletal Delay in Younger and Older Gymnasts and Wrestlers

| Group | Skeletal delay (yr ± SD) | | Significance |
	Younger M ± SD	Older M ± SD	
Gymnasts	1.18 ± 1.30	0.82 ± 0.85	ns
Wrestlers	0.87 ± 0.91	0.27 ± 1.26	$p < .05$
Total	0.98 ± 1.06	0.40 ± 1.19	$p < .05$

Table 7 Predicted Adult Height in Younger and Older Gymnasts and Wrestlers

| Group | Predicted adult height (cm) | | Significance |
	Younger M ± SD	Older M ± SD	
Gymnasts	176.0 ± 6.1	174.1 ± 4.4	ns
Wrestlers	175.0 ± 5.4	175.7 ± 6.1	ns
Total	175.3 ± 5.6	175.3 ± 5.8	ns

DISCUSSION

These results are difficult to interpret for many reasons. Only children participating in different types of sport have been compared. Thus, a representative control group is lacking. Comparison of body height between the basketball players and the other groups was not warranted because of the age difference. This difference could have also affected the results of skeletal age and predicted adult height. Furthermore, the groups differed in training history and training frequency, which also confuses the results.

Despite these shortcomings, some clear selected traits can be seen in these boys. Gymnasts and wrestlers were smaller and skeletally delayed as compared to ice-hockey and basketball players and they even seemed to remain smaller as adults. The results for the gymnasts were in agreement with the findings of Buckler and Brodie (1977) and Österback, Lintunen, Rahkila, and Silvennoinen (1984). Even basketball players seemed to be a selected group, though in the opposite direction. They were predicted to be 10.0 cm taller than wrestlers and gymnasts and even 3.5 cm taller than ice-hockey players as adults. The skeletal delay seen in wrestlers and gymnasts was smaller in the older groups, but no differences between younger and older gymnasts and wrestlers existed in predicted adult height.

CONCLUSION

These results suggest that selection for different sports happens very early. The selected traits in these gymnasts and wrestlers were as profound in the younger groups (12 years) as in the older groups (16 years). Thus, selection mainly seemed to be based on genetic factors. It was not possible to evaluate the effects of physical exercises on these developmental factors on the basis of this cross-sectional study.

REFERENCES

Bailey, D.A., Malina, R.M., & Rasmussen, R.L. (1978). The influence of exercise, physical activity, and athletic performance on the dynamics of human growth. In F. Falkner & J.M. Tanner (Eds.), *Human growth*. Vol. 2. Postnatal growth (pp. 475-505). New York: Plenum Press.

Bayley, N., & Pinneau, S.R. (1952). Tables for predicting adult height from skeletal age: Revised for use with the Greulich-Pyle hand standards. *Journal of Pediatrics*, **40**, 423-441.

Buckler, J.M.H., & Brodie, D.A. (1977). Growth and maturity characteristics of schoolboy gymnasts. *Annals of Human Biology*, **4**, 455-463.

Greulich, W.W., & Pyle, S.I. (1959). *Radiographic atlas of skeletal development of the hand and wrist* (2nd ed.). Stanford, CA: Stanford University Press.

Kato, S., & Ishiko, T. (1966). Obstructed growth of children's bones due to excessive labor in remote corners. In K. Kato (Ed.), *Proceedings of the International Congress of Sport Sciences* (p. 479). Tokyo: Japanese Union of Sport Sciences.

Lamb, D.R., Van Huss, W.D., Carrow, R.E., Heusner, W.W., Weber, J.C., & Kertzer, R. (1969). Effects of prepubertal physical training on growth, voluntary exercise, cholesterol and basal metabolism in rats. *Research Quarterly*, **40**, 123-133.

Malina, R.M. (1979). The effects of exercise on specific tissues, dimensions, and functions during growth. *Studies in Physical Anthropology*, **5**, 21-52.

Malina, R.M. (1984, October). *Biological maturity status of young athletes*. Paper presented at the ICSPE Congress "Child and sport," Urbino, Italy.

Österback, L., Lintunen, T., Rahkila, P., & Silvennoinen, M. (1984). Urheilevien lasten sukupuolinen kypsyys ja luustoikä [Biological maturation in physically active children]. *Liikunta ja tiede*, **21**, 252-258.

Peltenburg, A.L., Erich, W.B.M., Zonderland, M.L., Bernink, M.J.E., Van Den-Brande, J.L., & Huisveld, I.A. (1984). A retrospective growth study of female gymnasts and girl swimmers. *International Journal of Sports Medicine*, **5**, 262-267.

Part IX
Miscellaneous

Electrical Impedance Cardiography as a Noninvasive Technique for Exercise Testing of Children

Jan Vávra
Jiri Radvanský
Václav Sazima
Jindřich Vaněk
Charles University, Prague, Czechoslovakia

Recently, several changes have occurred in the methods for the clinical examination of the cardiovascular system because of their wide applicability:

1. An increasing application of noninvasive techniques that are administered not only in accordance with ethical principles but also in keeping with the requirements of the physiological conditions during the examination.
2. The increasing application of exercise testing in order to reveal functional restrictions not noticeable at rest.
3. The application of these methods in uncooperative subjects, such as preschool children.

These three requirements are fully accomplished by electrocardiography (ECG) and also by electrical impedance cardiography (EIC). As shown in Figure 1, the current and the pickup electrodes are placed on the skin and the impedance changes resulting from the heart action are recorded. How hemodynamic changes alter the electrical impedance in the thoracic body segment is not entirely clear, but the physiological and clinical contribution of this technique has been verified in many studies by comparisons with other techniques for cardiac examination, both invasive and noninvasive.

The upstroke point (U) represents the end of the isovolumic phase and the beginning of the ejection phase of systole (see Figure 2). Point Z stands for the moment of maximal velocity of blood flow in the aortic root (see the comparison with the curve of transcutaneous aortovelography). Point X represents the moment very nearly at the final closing of the aortic valve, that is, the end of the ventricular systole. From these key points, the respective systolic time intervals can be measured with simultaneous recording of the ECG.

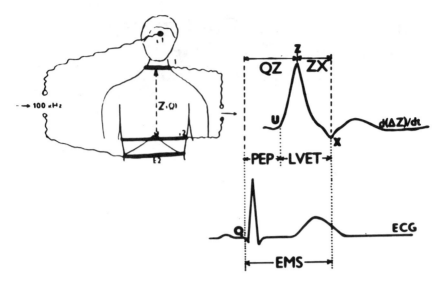

Figure 1   The electrodes for measurement of transthoracic electrical impedance and the measurement of systolic time intervals. (PEP = preejection period; LVET = left ventricle ejection time; EMS = electromechanical systole.)

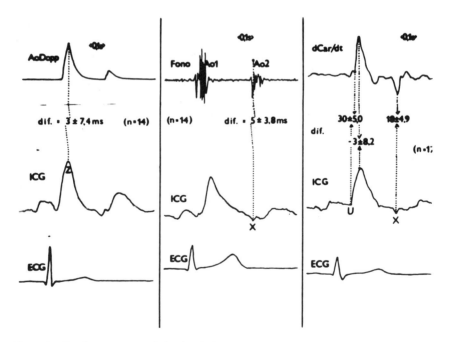

Figure 2   Simultaneous recording of EIC, the curve of aortovelography, the phonocardiogram, and the curve of the first derivative of the carotidogram.

From a comprehensive study on a healthy population of various ages, the normal values of the systolic time intervals were estimated at rest and during uninterrupted exercise of stepwise increments of intensity (Vávra, Sova, & Máček, 1982). From this study, two items with practical consequences should be stressed. The change in body position from supine to standing entails the prolongation of the isovolumic phase as represented by the preejection period and by the shortening of the left ventricle ejection time (see Figures 3 and 4). This is the consequence of impeded venous return with lesser filling of the heart. The prolongation of the preejection period is hardly apparent in children under 10 years of age, being more conspicuous in pubertal children and adults. This is most probably the effect of small body size as well as of the relatively higher blood volume in the younger age groups. From this experience, it follows

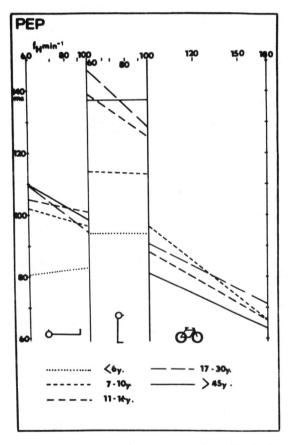

Figure 3 The preejection period (PEP) in the supine and standing body positions at rest and during uninterrupted bicycle exercise in the sitting position.

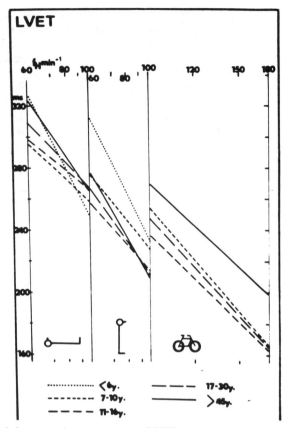

Figure 4   The left ventricular ejection time (LVET).

that the shifts of the preejection period and the left ventricle ejection time before standing could be useful in the evaluation of response to orthostatic stress. In subjects with a large increase in the heart rate after standing, the prolongation of preejection period was more accentuated and also the amplitude of the impedance curve was much lower than in the supine position (see Figure 5). Thus the EIC can be helpful in recognition of orthostatic lability.

With increasing age, the total electromechanical systole is of longer duration, which is more conspicuous at higher workloads. This systole takes about two thirds of the heart cycle in younger age groups, but more than three quarters after 45 years of age (see Figure 6). It follows that the time of diastole is more curtailed in the elderly. This finding must be respected because diastole is the time interval for providing the blood supply to the myocardium and changes in the coronary vessels occur at this age.

Having obtained normal values of the systolic time intervals in healthy populations, the values were investigated in patients suffering from various diseases in order to ascertain the possibility of EIC in the clinical

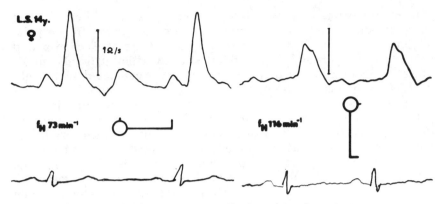

Figure 5   The decrease of the EIC curve amplitude under orthostatic stress.

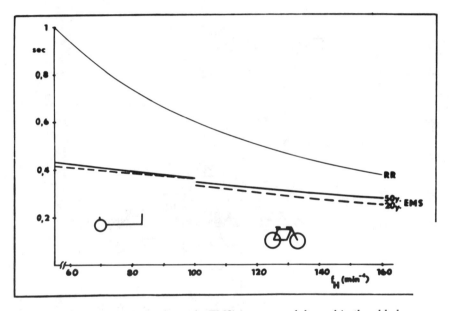

Figure 6   The electromechanical systole (EMS) in young adults and in the elderly.

medicine. The preejection period is taken as an indirect indicator of myocardial contractility with high correlation with some other indicators such as the dP/dt max, V_{cfs}, and others (Ahmed, Levinson, Schwartz, & Ettinger, 1972; Mohapatra, 1981; Parisi, Tow, Felix, & Sasahara, 1977; Steibigel, Babitt, Fox, & Warbasse, 1970). Presented here are some of our experiences in this field, focusing on the young age groups for which the literature is relatively scant.

Among more than 800 children with various congenital heart diseases subjected to an exercise test (patients in the Centre of Pediatric Cardiology,

University Hospital in Prague Motol), there were 31 children with the transposition of large arteries after Mustard correction. In the great majority of these patients, the resting values of the preejection period were already significantly higher than in healthy children (see Figure 7). The explanation could be that the driving force is generated by the right ventricle, which is not equipped to work against pressure, but another cause could be tricuspid regurgitation, which is often found in these patients. In the present group, the regurgitation of a hemodynamic significance was shown in 3 subjects only, and thus this factor could not have been the main cause for prolongation of the preejection period. It follows that the preejection period must be increased because of the inability of the right ventricle to meet the demands of the systemic circulation. This finding makes the benefits of heart surgery for a long lifespan a little uncertain.

Pediatric cardiology must deal with a number of children with a diagnosis of cardiomyopathy. We have examined 32 patients with an exercise

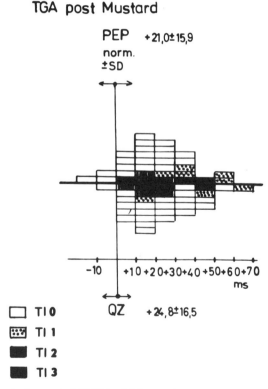

Figure 7   The preejection period (PEP) in children with transposition of great arteries after the Mustard correction. (TI_0 = children without any regurgitation; TI_1 = very short regurgitation; TI_2 = holosystolic regurgitation hemodynamic nonsignificant without propagation; TI_3 = holosystolic regurgitation with propagation to the right atrium.)

test. Presented here is a longitudinal study of a boy of 14 years of age. He came to the exercise laboratory with a clinical diagnosis of congestive cardiomyopathy, but he was without any complaints. He was able to walk upstairs without any discomfort, ride a bicycle, and participate in football with his schoolmates. His preejection period at rest and during exercise was slightly but not significantly longer than normal. As a surprising statement, the mechanical pulsus alternans was detected by means of the impedance curve in the form of alternating amplitude of the main systolic wave (see Figure 8). This pulsus alternans was present at rest in the standing position only, not in the supine position, and thus was not detected in the standard medical examination. This finding was confirmed by palpation of the peripheral pulse. The pulsus alternans persisted at work loads of lower intensity on the bicycle but disappeared at higher work loads, reappearing after a while during recovery (see Figure 9). The follow-

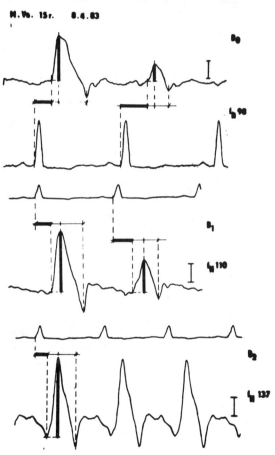

Figure 8 The picture of mechanical pulsus alternans on the impedance curve. (B_0 = sitting on bicycle at rest; B_1 = work load of 1 W per kg/BW; B_2 = work load of 2 W per kg/BW.)

M.Va. 15r.   12.7.83

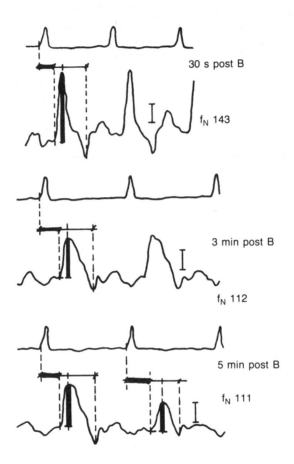

30 s post B

f_N 143

3 min post B

f_N 112

5 min post B

f_N 111

Figure 9 The reappearance of pulsus alternans during the recovery.

up of this boy showed a progressive deterioration of the systolic time intervals, such as the prolongation of the preejection period and shortening of the left ventricle ejection time, implying a progressively impaired myocardial function (see Table 1). This progress was discovered by the analysis of the impedance curve morphology, namely from the successive decrease in the systolic wave amplitude indicating a progressively decreasing stroke volume (see Figure 10). The last impedance curve was recorded during cardiogenic shock, when the curve had a quite disrupted outline. It should be stressed that the noninvasive impedance examination contributed to better understanding of the pathophysiological background of the disease, hardly accessible by other methods.

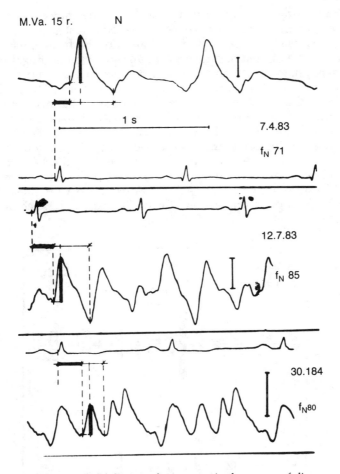

Figure 10   The deterioration of the impedance curve in the course of disease.

Table 1   The Values (msec) of the Preejection Period (PEP) and the Left Ventricle Ejection Time (LVET) in the Course of the Disease (MVa; 15 yr)

	PEP	LVET
8.4.83	118	283
12.7.83	145	239
30.1.84	166	152
Normal values	103	281

An interesting application of the systolic time interval is with thyropathies (see Figure 11). The preejection period at rest is distinctly shorter in thyrotoxicosis as a result of an excitation of the heart muscle due to a surplus of the thyroid hormones. A more significant finding occurs during exercise, namely, the normalization of these preejection period values. In some cases, even the prolonged values were found. The explanation might be in the latent thyrotoxic cardiomyopathy that becomes evident under physical work loads only, with increased demands on the heart. This latent disturbance of heart function is assumed to be revealed by impedance cardiography only, because of its applicability during uninterrupted exercise. Moreover, the measurements of the systolic time interval proved to be useful in following up these patients under treatment.

In this contribution, only a few pediatric examples were presented, yet this area offers great opportunity for further research, such as that by

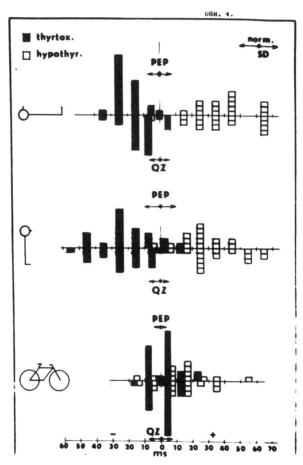

Figure 11 The values of the preejection period (PEP) and (QZ) in thyropathies. QZ includes the PEP plus the initial ejection phase.

Radvanský, Vávra, and Máček (1986) in a study of beat-by-beat analysis of heart function under non-steady state conditions in the initial phase of exercise. The EIC was sometimes helpful in the analysis of some arrhythmias in children; moreover, although the morphology of the impedance curve is not yet fully understood, it may in the future contribute to the knowledge of hemodynamic events during the heart cycle in health and disease.

REFERENCES

Ahmed, S.S., Levinson, G.E., Schwartz, C.J., & Ettinger, P.O. (1972). Systolic time intervals as measures of the contractile state of the left ventricular myocardium in man. *Circulation,* **46,** 559-571.

Mohapatra, S.N. (1981). *Noninvasive cardiovascular monitoring by electrical impedance technique.* London: Pitman Medical.

Parisi, A.F., Tow, D.E., Felix, W.R., & Sasahara, A.A. (1977). Noninvasive cardiac diagnosis. I to III. *New England Journal of Medicine,* **296,** 316-320; 368-374; 427-432.

Steibigel, R.T., Babitt, H.I., Fox, S.M., & Warbasse, J.R. (1970). Quantitative evaluation of the first derivate of the impedance cardiogram. *Circulation,* **42** (Suppl.), III-65.

Radvanský, J., Vávra, J., & Máček, M. (1986). Oxygen transport and cardiac output regulation measured by electrical impedance cardiography. In J. Rutenfranz, R. Mocellin, & F. Klimt (Eds.), *Children and exercise, XII* (pp. 267-273). (International Series on Sport Sciences, Vol. 16). Champaign, IL: Human Kinetics.

Vávra, J., Sova, J., & Máček, M. (1982). Effect of age on systolic time intervals at rest and during exercise on a bicycle ergometer. *European Journal of Applied Physiology,* **50,** 71-78.

Dynamic Exercise Echocardiography in Children

Eva-Maria Oyen
Gregor Ingerfeld
Klaus Ignatzy
Peter E. Brode
Johanniter Childrens Hospital,
St. Augustin, Federal Republic of Germany

To evaluate the myocardial status before and after surgery in congenital heart disease, the determination of myocardial left ventricular reserve during exercise is of great interest. Because echocardiography has proven to be a useful noninvasive method for obtaining left ventricular parameters during bicycle exercise in adults (Alpert, Bloom, & Olley, 1980; Crawford, White, & Amon, 1979; Sold, Zwehl, Neuhaus, & Kreuzer, 1979; Sugishita & Koseki, 1979), an effort was made to determine left ventricular function in children from M-Mode echocardiography during supine bicycle exercise.

METHOD

Because of the lack of reference values for normal boys and girls of different age groups in the literature, 110 untrained healthy children aged 6 to 14 years were first investigated (60 boys, 50 girls). Before exercise, heart diseases were excluded by clinical investigation, ECG, and echocardiography. The children were fixed to the table with special equipment that prevented them from sliding backward during pedaling and that could be adjusted to each child's height (see Figure 1). Exercise was performed with an electrically braked bicycle ergometer (Lode Instrumenten) positioned at the end of the table. The periods of exercise lasted 3 min at levels of 6, 9, 12, and 15 kpm/min/kg body weight, respectively.

M-Mode echocardiography measurements were taken before exercise; during a short rest after each period of exercise; and 1, 2, and 3 min after the last exercise period. At the time of measurements, the children were asked to breathe normally. M-Mode echocardiograms of the left ventricle

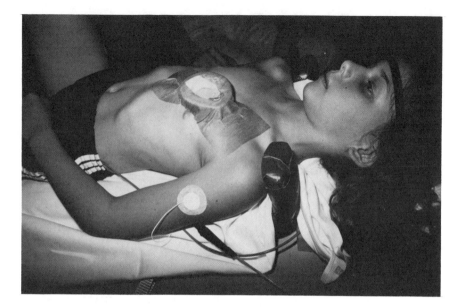

Figure 1   The attachment on the table that fixes the child's shoulder and the plastic ring on chest for fixation of the transducer.

were recorded at the level of chordae tendineae during expiration. Recorded simultaneously were ECG (lead II), phonocardiogram (PCG) from the second or fifth intercostal space, and blood pressure. Echocardiography was performed with the ATL Mark 500 with a handheld 3.5 MHz transducer that was held in position by a surrounding soft plastic ring attached to the child's chest with self-sticking tape. The position was controlled in the 2-D-echo on the oscilloscope throughout the procedure. Blood pressure was measured automatically with an oscillometer (Dinamap/Criticon). In 10 of the original 120 children measurements could not be obtained because of the poor quality of the echocardiograms. Some children were investigated twice with good reproducibility of their data by different independent observers. Because size and development at any age varied significantly in probands, patients were divided into three groups according to body surface area (see Table 1). Mean values and standard deviations for all obtained data within each group were calculated separately for boys and girls. Student t-tests for unpaired data were used to assess the statistical differences between groups. Differences were considered significant at $p < .05$.

On the basis of this investigation, 25 children with left-sided heart disease were investigated according to the protocol already described. Most of them accomplished the whole exercise program. Some children participated in only part of the protocol because of exhaustion or ventricular dysfunction. The data were compared with those of the normal children with the same body surface area.

Table 1 Groups and Numbers of Investigated Children According to Body Surface Area (BSA)

Group	BSA (m²)	Total N	Boys n	Girls n
I	0 – 1.0	48	23	25
II	1.1 – 1.4	34	21	13
III	> 1.4	28	16	12

RESULTS

The rise in heart rate and blood pressure during exercise was significantly higher in females (from 85 to 170 beats/min) than in males (from 80 to 145 beats/min). Blood pressure was higher in Groups II and III than in Group I. Similar results were also found by Rutenfranz and Mocellin (1968). The left ventricular enddiastolic diameter changed only minimally during and after exercise, but the endsystolic diameter decreased during exercise, with the highest shortening rate in Group III (statistically not significant at a level of $p < .05$). Fractional shortening during exercise rose from $37 \pm 4\%$ to $46 \pm 4\%$ with no significant differences among the three groups (see Figure 2). Significant differences ($p \leqslant .01$) among the groups were found in the increase of velocity of circumferential fiber shortening (Vcf) (see Figure 3). In Group I, this rose from 1.30 to 2.50 circ/s (92%), in Group II from 1.26 to 2.52 circ/s (100%), and in Group III from 1.16 to 2.68 circ/s (130%).

After exercise, heart rates declined more rapidly than did Vcf. Consequently the ratio of Vcf/HR showed an increase in the 1st min of rest before it slowly normalized. The cardiac patients showed different reactions to exercise according to the degree of their disease (see Figure 4). This was most evident in those patients with left ventricular pressure overload. Patients with a mild form of a disease had elevated fractional shortening and a higher Vcf/HR ratio at rest than normals. They demonstrated the same tendencies as normals during and after exercise, although on a higher level (see Figure 4). In contrast, some patients with left ventricular pressure overload showed a decrease in fractional shortening and Vcf/HR at higher exercise levels and, accordingly, a more intensive rise after exercise. This reaction probably indicates left ventricular dysfunction. Fractional shortening and Vcf of patients with VSD mostly were within the normal range; only two of these children had significantly lower fractional shortening than normal subjects.

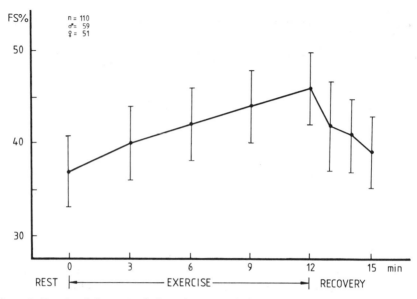

Figure 2 Fractional shortening before, during, and after exercise. Mean values ± *SD* for all investigated healthy children.

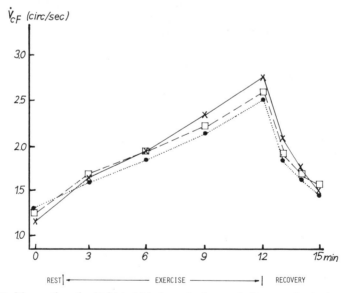

Figure 3 Mean values for Vcf (circ/s) before, during, and after exercise in three groups of normal children according to body surface area. ●·· ·● ≤ 1.1 m²; ☐– – –☐ = 1.1 – 1.4 m²; ✗——✗ > 1.4 m².

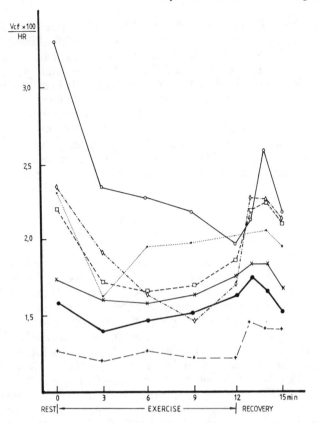

Figure 4 Typical Vcf/HR change in children with left-sided heart disease compared to mean values for all healthy children. ●——● +---+ = VSD; X——X = mean value of children with mild aortic stenosis; ◇–·–◇ = aortic stenosis; Δd 45 mmHg; ●···● = aortic stenosis Δd 70 mmHg; o——o = aortic stenosis Δd 80 mmHg; □– – –□ = aortic stenosis + incompetence.

DISCUSSION

The echocardiographic left ventricular function parameters of healthy children in different age groups in this study correlated well with the scattered data in the literature. The rise in blood pressure and heart rate was significantly higher in females (see also Mocellin, Rutenfranz, & Buhlmeyer, 1970). In all children, the increase in stroke volume was mainly achieved by an increase in left ventricular contraction rather than by increasing preload (see Sold et al., 1979). The values of the larger children (Group III) approximated those found in adults (Sold et al., 1979; Sugishita & Koseki, 1979). In the recovery period, heart rate and blood pressure normalized earlier than did fractional shortening and Vcf. This was also found by Sold et al. (1979) in adults. It became evident that, in the first phase of exercise, cardiac output mainly increased due to heart rate. With further increase in the work load, an increase occurred in ventricular contraction and ejection volume and, consequently, the increases of Vcf and fractional shortening were higher than that of heart rate. and size of the children, left ventricular function parameters were investigated in relation to the heart rate measured at the same time, with the ratio:

$$\frac{\dot{V}cf \times 100}{HR}$$

This ratio was found to be more independent of age and body surface area and better demonstrated an inadequate rise in heart rate during exercise in children with left-sided heart disease. It also demonstrated that, in normal individuals, after-exercise heart rate is sooner normalized than Vcf and fractional shortening. This reaction can be explained by different sympathetic and vagotonic influences immediately after exercise.

In some children with left-sided heart disease, the increase in cardiac ouput was mainly accomplished by a rise in heart rate. However, in other children, dilatation of the left ventricle at a certain exercise level took place. This was considered to be an expression of myocardial damage with a lack of left ventricular myocardial reserve. Such a phenomenon has also been described in older people and in individuals with coronary artery disease or cardiomyopathy (Alpert et al., 1980; Sugishita et al., 1979). These same authors found higher Vcf and fractional shortening at rest and during exercise in children with left ventricular pressure overload without myocardial disease. These findings were confirmed in this study. Those children with congenital heart disease and normal left ventricular function during bicycle exercise were supposed to have a mild form of heart disease and were not considered candidates for immediate cardiac surgery.

In contrast, we are inclined to recommend immediate cardiac surgery to all patients with signs of impaired myocardial reserve. Finally, it is believed that the described left ventricular function parameters are suitable for follow-up studies to determine the result of cardiac surgery.

REFERENCES

Alpert, B.S., Bloom, K.R., & Olley, P.M. (1980). Assessment of left ventricular contractility during supine exercise in children with left-sided cardiac disease. *British Heart Journal*, **44**, 703-710.

Crawford, M.H., White, D.H., & Amon, K.W. (1979). Echocardiographic evaluation of left ventricular size and performance during handgrip and supine and upright bicycle exercise. *Circulation*, **59**, 1188-1196.

Mocellin, R., Rutenfranz, J., & Bühlmeyer, K. (1970). Untersuchungen über die körperliche Leistungsfähigkeit gesunder und kranker Heranwachsender. IV. *Zeitschrift für Kinderheilkunde*, **108**, 265-287.

Rutenfranz, J., & Mocellin, R. (1968). Untersuchungen über die körperliche Leistungsfähigkeit gesunder und kranker Heranwachsender. I. *Zeitschrift für Kinderheilkunde*, **103**, 109-132.

Sold, G., Zwehl, W., Neuhaus, K.L., & Kreuzer, H. (1979). Echokardiographische Dimensionen des linken Ventrikels unter Ergometerbelastung: Untersuchungen an gesunden Probanden. *Zeitschrift für Kardiologie*, **68**, 802-808.

Sugishita, Y., & Koseki, S. (1979). Dynamic exercise echocardiography. *Circulation*, **60**, 743-752.

Heat-Stress Reactions
of the Growing Child

Claus Piekarski
Peter Morfeld
Bernhard Kampmann
Raija Ilmarinen
Hans G. Wenzel
Institute of Occupational Health at the University of Dortmund,
Dortmund, Federal Republic of Germany

A great many publications have dealt with heat-stress reactions of growing children (e.g., Bar-Or, Dotan, Inbar, Rothstein, & Zonder, 1980; Danks, Webb, & Allen, 1962; Drinkwater & Horvath, 1979; Drinkwater, Kupprat, Denton, Christ, & Horvath, 1977; Haymes, Buskirk, Hodgson, Lundegren, & Nicholas, 1974; Haymes, McCormick, & Buskirk, 1975; Mackinnon, 1920; Shoenfeld, Udassin, Shapiro, Ohri, & Sohar, 1978; Wiebers, 1954). However, only a few longitudinal studies (on physical fitness) have reported on the tolerance of children toward heat over a long period of time (Ilmarinen & Rutenfranz, 1980; Ilmarinen, Rutenfranz, & Achenbach, 1979; Kobayashi et al., 1978; Lange Andersen, Seliger, Rutenfranz, & Berndt, 1974; Lange Andersen, Seliger, Rutenfranz, & Messel 1974; Lange Andersen, Seliger, Rutenfranz, & Mocellin, 1974; Lange Andersen, Seliger, Rutenfranz, & Nesset, 1980; Lange Andersen, Seliger, Rutenfranz, Skrobak-Kaczynski, 1976; Rutenfranz, Lange Andersen, Seliger, Klimmer, Berndt, & Ruppel, 1981; Rutenfranz, Lange Andersen, Seliger, Klimmer, Ilmarinen, Ruppel, & Kylian, 1981; Rutenfranz, Lange Andersen, Seliger, & Masironi, 1982; Rutenfranz, Seliger, Lange Andersen, Ilmarinen, Berndt, & Knauth, 1977; Rutenfranz & Singer, 1980). Only a few working groups in Israel (e.g., Bar-Or, 1981; Inbar, Bar-Or, Dotan, & Gutin, 1981) have investigated possible changes in heat tolerance with age in groups of growing children over shorter periods of time.

Therefore, it seemed appropriate to perform a longitudinal study with a small group of children over several years in the moderate climate of Germany. Three questions were asked: (a) Is there an age- or fitness-related change in the body temperature, heart rate, or sweat loss during heat stress in the growing child? (b) Is there an increasing heat tolerance in the sense of a "cross-adaptation" caused by an increased physical fitness with increasing age? (c) Are there sex-specific differences in the heat tolerance of growing boys and girls?

METHODS

The subjects were 4 children, 3 boys and 1 girl. Subject TS was in the upper range of height and body mass (P_{90}), Subject AW was in the lower range (P_{10}), and Subject MW the middle (P_{50}) for children of their age group. Subject AK, a girl, was also in the P_{50} range; her reactions, however, can be regarded to be of alluding character only. The series was started with the subjects at about their 10th year of age.

The investigation was performed in a climatic chamber (Wenzel, Piekarski, Kampmann, Andorf, & Schulz, 1980; Piekarski, 1985). The tests were carried out singularly in order to avoid acclimation effects. Air humidity was kept below 10 mbars, the ambient temperatures ranged between 25 °C and 55 °C, and the wind velocity was set at 0.3 m/s. Two different physical activities were observed: sitting posture and walking at 4 km/h on a treadmill at 0° elevation. The youths wore shorts, socks, and tennis shoes. After an initial 30-min period of rest in bed, the subjects entered the climatic chamber. The exposure time of 3 hr was divided into periods of 30 min, separated by 3-min intervals in which the sweat loss was measured. Body temperature was monitored continuously with a Yellow Springs semiconductor rectal probe, and the heart rate was measured with a 1-channel ECG (Wilson V5). Skin temperature was first measured using thermocouples (ELLAB), and later using YSI Thermistor probes.

In the data evaluation, the means of the 4th half-hour period were chosen for heart rate, body temperature, and skin temperature. These means were assumed to be representative because all of the subjects, even under the most stressful ambient conditions, had stayed in the test chamber for at least 2 hr. The mean values of the periods between the 2nd and the last period served as references for the sweat loss, because in general sweating did not start before the 2nd half-hour period. Oxygen uptake during the walking tests was judged from measurements in every 2nd period. Moreover, measurements of basal metabolism were performed with all children during the entire test series.

RESULTS

For the subjects who performed the longest period of time in the series, heart rates and rectal temperatures showed a decreasing tendency with age, whereas the sweat rate increased. Figure 1 gives an example. This

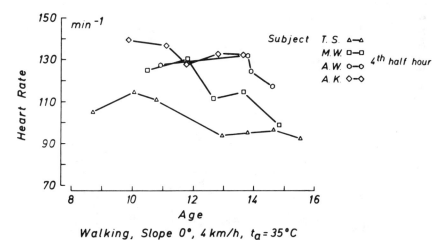

Walking, Slope 0°, 4 km/h, $t_a = 35°C$

Figure 1 Heart rate—means of the 4th half period of heat exposure—versus age at 35 °C ambient temperature.

observation first led to the conclusion that thermal tolerance of children might increasingly develop with growing age and physical fitness. This conclusion would agree with the findings of other investigators (Wagner, Robinson, Tzankoff, & Marino, 1972; Drinkwater & Horvath, 1979).

In the following analysis of the tendencies of heart rate, rectal temperature, and sweat rate, Subject TS can be regarded as representative of the entire group. The slopes of the rectal temperature means in the tests in the sitting posture between 30 °C and 55 °C ambient temperatures showed, in general, a slightly decreasing tendency with age, which did not continue beyond an age of about 13 years (see Figure 2). A temporary inversion of their negative slopes occurred between the 10th and 11th years of age. At the same time, a considerable increase in growing height was observed, after which puberty began. The slopes of the rectal-temperature means during walking between 25 °C and 50 °C ambient temperatures also showed, in general, a negative trend. The tendencies for changes in rectal temperature, which were present before the beginning of puberty, were not evident during walking. Only the 25 °C curve resembled the tendencies in sitting posture. The decreasing trend found with the rectal temperatures can be also observed with increasing age in the range of heart rates, both in sitting and walking activities (see Figure 3). However, sweat rates tended to increase with age in sitting as well as in walking activities.

Oxygen uptake during walking showed an increase with age, whereas practically no difference in oxygen uptake with the changes in thermal conditions was observed. The increasing oxygen uptake with age might be regarded as a measure of the growing of the juvenile organism, which suggests it should be compared with the increase in maximum oxygen uptake. Regarding the specific maximum oxygen uptake, that is, maximum oxygen uptake per kilogram of body weight, an increasing trend could not be identified clearly. Total basal metabolism increases indicated

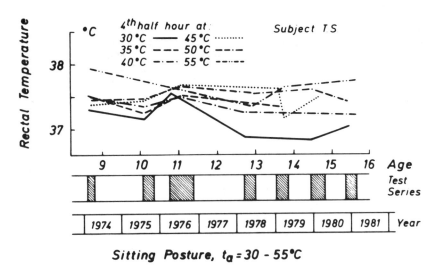

Figure 2   Rectal temperature—means of the 4th half-hour period of heat exposure—versus age at different ambient temperatures at sitting posture.

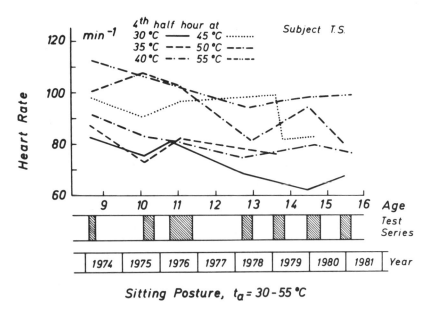

Figure 3   Heart rates—means of the 4th half-hour period of heat exposure—versus age at different ambient temperatures at sitting posture.

the growth of the organisms while the basal metabolism per kilogram of body weight remained constant.

The development of age, the values of heart rate, rectal temperature, and skin temperature at rest with increasing age showed a significantly decreasing ($p < .01$) trend for all three values (see Figure 4). This tendency of values at rest to decrease with age suggested that the increases of heart rates and rectal temperatures over the values at rest should be related to age. This led to the result that the negative trend of heart rates and rectal temperatures with age was no longer existent, if the values at rest were considered (see Figure 5, Tables 1 & 2).

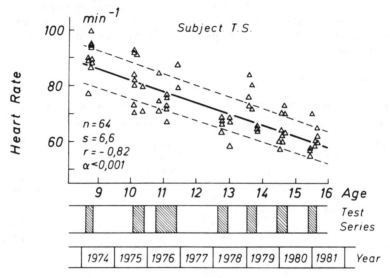

Figure 4 Negative trend of heart rate at rest with age.

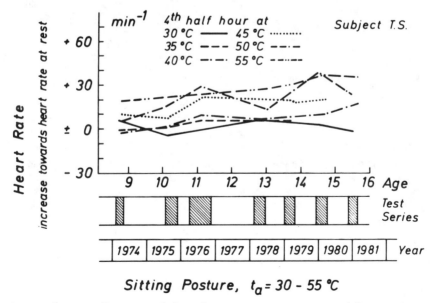

Figure 5 Increase of heart rate relative to heart rate versus age at rest at different ambient temperatures.

Additional attention should be given to a peculiarity in the girl's reactions. Although no qualitative difference in her physiological reactions from those of the boys was seen at first, this changed considerably during puberty. Just temperatures of no more than 25 °C to 40 °C at low physical activity were tolerated more than 3 hr. In cases of aborting the tests, sudden attacks of vertigo, drowsiness, or collapse during the initial test periods were observed without any signs of thermal imbalance manifested. These attacks were only accompanied by a higher readiness for orthostatic irregularity. The progress of puberty reduced the frequency of these phenomena.

Table 1 Mean Annual Changes of the Means of the 4th Half-Hour Period

Subject	Age (yr)			Heart rate (min^{-1}/a)	Rectal temperature (°C/a)	Skin temperature (°C/a)
AK	10.0 to 14.9	Sitting	$\bar{x}$	−2.61	−0.08	−0.22
			±SD	6.7	0.19	0.34
			p	ns	ns	ns
		Walking	$\bar{x}$	−1.56	−0.01	—
			±SD	6.1	0.14	—
			p	ns	ns	—
TS	11.0 to 15.8	Sitting	$\bar{x}$	−3.29	−0.07	−0.36
			±SD	7.27	0.19	0.40
			p	0.05	ns	<0.01
		Walking	$\bar{x}$	−3.39	−0.07	−0.27
			±SD	7.46	0.21	0.38
			p	ns	ns	<0.05
MW	10.4 to 15.6	Sitting	$\bar{x}$	−2.24	−0.10	−0.18
			±SD	6.16	0.19	0.64
			p	ns	ns	ns
		Walking	$\bar{x}$	−4.51	−0.08	−0.22
			±SD	8.88	0.08	0.43
			p	ns	<0.02	ns
AW	11.0 to 14.5	Sitting	$\bar{x}$	−1.99	−0.06	−0.27
			±SD	13.62	0.21	0.55
			p	ns	ns	ns
		Walking	$\bar{x}$	−5.80	−0.07	−0.21
			±SD	10.47	0.18	0.69
			p	ns	ns	ns

Table 2 Mean Annual Changes of the Difference Between the Mean Value of the 4th Half-Hour Period and the Value at Rest

Subject	Age (yr)			Heart rate (min⁻¹/a)	Rectal temperature (°C/a)	Skin temperature (°C/a)
AK	10.0 to 14.9	Sitting	$\bar{x}$	+4.04	+0.09	+0.34
			±SD	12.69	0.20	0.97
			p	ns	ns	ns
		Walking	$\bar{x}$	+1.60	+0.12	+0.34
			±SD	9.03	0.23	0.67
			p	ns	ns	ns
TS	11.0 to 15.8	Sitting	$\bar{x}$	+3.06	+0.10	+0.06
			±SD	7.21	0.19	0.45
			p	ns	ns	ns
		Walking	$\bar{x}$	+1.96	−0.11	−0.08
			±SD	12.62	0.29	0.41
			p	ns	ns	ns
MW	10.4 to 15.6	Sitting	$\bar{x}$	+2.16	+0.05	+0.19
			±SD	11.61	0.28	2.11
			p	ns	ns	ns
		Walking	$\bar{x}$	−3.95	+0.11	+0.15
			±SD	9.54	0.46	1.13
			p	ns	ns	ns
AW	11.0 to 14.5	Sitting	$\bar{x}$	+3.61	−0.02	+0.79
			±SD	12.32	0.35	1.33
			p	ns	ns	ns
		Walking	$\bar{x}$	+1.89	−0.09	+0.95
			±SD	12.04	0.16	0.80
			p	ns	ns	<0.002

DISCUSSION

These first results of this longitudinal study indicate the variety of thermal reactions of a group of children in the growing ages between 10 to 16 years for two activity levels (sitting and walking) in a temperature range between 25 °C and 55 °C. All of the subjects showed a good tolerance toward thermal stress, which was reduced temporarily during the onset of puberty in the case of the girl. In her case, a series of test abortions was necessary due to a reduced stability of peripheral circulation rather than thermal overload (c.f. Drinkwater et al., 1977). A comparable setback of thermal tolerance was not observed in the boys during their period of puberty. In general, thermal tolerance seemed to increase with age, because a decreasing trend of the strain reactions under constant thermal load seemed to exist over the years. At the same time, however, a decreasing trend of practically equivalent amount for the values at rest was found. Considering the difference between both of the observed trends, no decrease of the thermal strain could be demonstrated. The initial assumption of a possible cross-adaptation protecting the growing young organism from thermal stress by simultaneously increasing physical fitness could not be verified.

CONCLUSIONS

The following concluding statements can be made as a result of this investigation:

- Reactions of body temperatures, heart rates, and sweating abilities of the growing child do not allow unequivocal conclusions toward increases of heat tolerance due to age. On the one hand, body temperature and heart rate suggested a negative trend with age; on the other hand, the increase of heart rate and body temperature under heat stress over the values at rest showed no trend because of decreasing values at rest.
- A cross-adaptation that was at first assumed could not be shown.
- The reactions of the girl still leave the question of possible differences in the thermal tolerance of young pubertal girls unanswered, especially whether a temporarily increased lability of circulation exists during puberty that led to frequent aborting of tests.

REFERENCES

Bar-Or, O. (1981). *Climate and the exercising child—A review*. Wingate, Israel: Wingate Institute, Dept. of Research and Sports Medicine; Hamilton, Ont.: McMaster University, Medical Centre.

Bar-Or, O., Dotan, R., Inbar, O., Rothstein, A., & Zonder, H. (1980). Voluntary hypohydration in 10- to 12-year-old boys. *Journal of Applied Physiology*, **48**, 104-108.

Danks, D.M., Webb, D.W., & Allen, J. (1962). Heat illness in infants and young children. *British Medical Journal*, **1**, 287-292.

Drinkwater, B.L., & Horvath, S.M. (1979). Heat tolerance and aging. *Medicine and Science in Sports*, **11**, 49-55.

Drinkwater, B.L., Kupprat, I.C., Denton, J.E., Christ, J.L., & Horvath, S.M. (1977). Response of prepubertal girls and college women to work in the heat. *Journal of Applied Physiology*, **43**, 1046-1053.

Haymes, E.M., Buskirk, E.R., Hodgson, J.L., Lundegren, H.M., & Nicholas, W.C. (1974). Heat tolerance of exercising lean and heavy prepubertal girls. *Journal of Applied Physiology*, **36**, 566-571.

Haymes, E.M., McCormick, R.J., & Buskirk, E.R. (1975). Heat tolerance of exercising lean and obese prepubertal boys. *Journal of Applied Physiology*, **39**, 457-461.

Ilmarinen, J., & Rutenfranz, J. (1980). Longitudinal studies of the changes in habitual physical activity of schoolchildren and working adolescents. In K. Berg & B.O. Eriksson (Eds.), *Children and exercise IX* (pp. 149-159) (International Series on Sports Sciences, Vol. 10). Baltimore: University Park Press.

Ilmarinen, J., Rutenfranz, J., & Achenbach, M. (1979). Some problems of assessing the maximal aerobic power and the daily physical activity of school children in longitudinal and intervention studies. In T. Tammivuori (Ed.), *L'évaluation dans le développement de l'enseignement de l'éducation physique*, publication 64 (pp. 165-176). Helsinki: The Finnish Society for Research in Sport and Physical Education.

Inbar, O., Bar-Or, O., Dotan, R., & Gutin, B. (1981). Conditioning versus exercise in heat as methods for acclimatizing 8- to 10-yr-old boys to dry heat. *Journal of Applied Physiology*, **50**, 406-411.

Kobayashi, K., Kitamura, K., Miura, M., Sodeyama, H., Murase, Y., Miyashita, M., & Matsui, H. (1978). Aerobic power as related to body growth and training in Japanese boys: A longitudinal study. *Journal of Applied Physiology*, **44**, 666-672.

Lange Andersen, K., Seliger, V., Rutenfranz, J., & Berndt, I. (1974). Physical performance capacity of children in Norway. 2. Heart rate and oxygen pulse in submaximal and maximal exercises—Population parameters in a rural community. *European Journal of Applied Physiology*, **33**, 197-206.

Lange Andersen, K., Seliger, V., Rutenfranz, J., & Messel, S. (1974). Physical performance capacity of children in Norway. 3. Respiratory responses to graded exercise loadings—Population parameters in a rural community. *European Journal of Applied Physiology*, **33**, 265-274.

Lange Andersen, K., Seliger, V., Rutenfranz, J., & Mocellin, R. (1974). Physical performance capacity of children in Norway. 1. Population parameters in a rural inland community with regard to maximal aerobic power. *European Journal of Applied Physiology*, **33**, 177-195.

Lange Andersen, K., Seliger, V., Rutenfranz, J., & Nesset, T. (1980). Physical performance capacity of children in Norway. 5. The influence of social isolation on the rate of growth in body size and composition and on the achievement in lung function and maximal aerobic power of children in a rural community. *European Journal of Applied Physiology*, **45**, 155-166.

Lange Andersen, K., Seliger, V., Rutenfranz, J., & Skrobak-Kaczynski, J. (1976). Physical performance capacity of children in Norway. 4. The rate of growth in maximal aerobic power and the influence of improved physical education of children in a rural community—Population parameters in a rural community. *European Journal of Applied Physiology*, **35**, 49-58.

Mackinnon, M. (1920). European children in the tropical highlands. *Lancet*, **199**, 944-945.

Piekarski, C. (1985). *Zur arbeitsmedizinischen Bewertung der Beanspruchung des arbeitenden Menschen unter Hitzebelastung*. Dortmund: Bellmann-Verlag.

Rutenfranz, J., Lange Andersen, K., Seliger, V., Klimmer, F., Berndt, I., & Ruppel, M. (1981). Maximum aerobic power and body composition during the puberty growth period: Similarities and differences between children of two European countries. *European Journal of Pediatrics*, **136**, 123-133.

Rutenfranz, J., Lange Andersen, K., Seliger, V., Klimmer, F., Ilmarinen, J., Ruppel, M., & Kylian, H. (1981). Exercise ventilation during the growth spurt period: Comparison between two European countries. *European Journal of Pediatrics*, **136**, 135-142.

Rutenfranz, J., Lange Andersen, K., Seliger, V., & Masironi, R. (1982). Health standards in terms of exercise fitness of school children in urban and rural areas in various European countries. *Annals of Clinical Research*, **14** (Suppl. 34), 33-36.

Rutenfranz, J., Seliger, V., Lange Andersen, K., Ilmarinen, J., Berndt, I., & Knauth, P. (1977). Differences in maximal aerobic power related to the daily physical activity in childhood. In G. Borg (Ed.), *Physical work and effort* (pp. 279-288). Oxford: Pergamon Press.

Rutenfranz, J., & Singer, R. (1980). The influence of sport activity on the development of physical performance capacities of 15- to 17-year-old boys. In K. Berg & B.O. Eriksson (Eds.), *Children and exercise IX* (pp. 160-165) (International Series on Sport Sciences, Vol. 10). Baltimore: University Park Press.

Shoenfeld, Y., Udassin, R., Shapiro, Y., Ohri, Y., & Sohar, E. (1978). Age and sex difference in response to short exposure to extreme dry heat. *Journal of Applied Physiology*, **44**, 1-4.

Wagner, J.A., Robinson, S., Tzankoff, S.P., & Marino, R.P. (1972). Heat tolerance and acclimatization to work in the heat in relation to age. *Journal of Applied Physiology*, **33**, 616-622.

Wenzel, H.G., Piekarski, C., Kampmann, B., Andorf, P., & Schulz, P. (1980). Klimasimulation industrieller Arbeitsplätze im Laboratorium. *Verhandlungen der Deutschen Gesellschaft für Arbeitsmedizin*, **20**, 577-579.

Wiebers, J.E. (1954). Hand blood flows in young and old adults during standardized thermal exposures. *Dissertation Abstracts*, **14**, 1444-1445.